SHERIDAN

SHERIDAN

the Inevitable

BY Richard O'Connor

MAPS BY WILSON R. SPRINGER

SMITHMARK

This edition published in 1995 by SMITHMARK Publishers Inc.,
16 East 32nd Street, New York, NY 10016

SMITHMARK books are available for bulk purchase for sales
promotion and premium use. For details write or call the
manager of special sales, SMITHMARK Publishers Inc.,
16 East 32nd Street, New York, NY 10016; (212) 532-6600.

This edition published by special arrangement with
W.S. Konecky Associates, Inc., 156 5th Avenue, New York, NY 10010.

ISBN: 0-8317-2440-4

Printed in the United States of America

10 9 8 7 6 5 4 3 2 1

ACKNOWLEDGMENTS

THE AUTHOR gratefully acknowledges the following permission to reprint material in this volume:

From *Sheridan* by Joseph Hergesheimer, The Houghton Mifflin Company, Boston, 1931, reprinted by permission of the publisher.

From *Under the Old Flag* by James H. Wilson, copyright, 1912, D. Appleton & Company, reprinted by permission of the publisher.

From *Some Memories of a Soldier* by Hugh L. Scott, copyright, 1928, The Century Company, reprinted by permission of the publisher.

From *Battles and Leaders of the Civil War*, edited by Robert Underwood Johnson and Clarence Clough Buel, The Century Company, reprinted by permission of the publisher.

From *Rustics in Rebellion* by George Alfred Townsend, The University of North Carolina Press, Chapel Hill, 1950, reprinted by permission of the publisher.

From *The Diary of George Templeton Strong*, edited by Allan Nevins and Milton Halsey Thomas, copyright, 1952, The Macmillan Company, reprinted by permission of the publisher.

From *Ulysses S. Grant, Politician* by William B. Hesseltine, Dodd, Mead & Company, 1935, reprinted by permission of the author.

From *The Great Rascal* by Jay Monaghan, Little, Brown & Company, 1952, reprinted by permission of the publisher.

From *The Wild Seventies* by Denis Tilden Lynch, copyright, 1941, D. Appleton-Century Co., Inc., reprinted by permission of the publisher.

From *A Volunteer's Adventures* by John W. De Forest, Yale University Press, New Haven, 1946, reprinted by permission of the publisher.

From *General George Crook: His Autobiography*, edited by Martin F. Schmitt, copyright 1946 by the University of Oklahoma Press. Reprinted by kind permission of the publisher.

From *Autobiography of Seventy Years* by George F. Hoar, Charles Scribner's Sons, 1903, reprinted by permission of the publisher.

From *History of the United States* by James F. Rhodes, The Macmillan Company, 1920, reprinted by permission of the estate of Daniel P. Rhodes.

From *Memoirs of a Volunteer* by John Beatty, W. W. Norton & Company, Inc., 1946, reprinted by permission of the publisher.

CONTENTS

LIST OF MAPS

SHERIDAN

I

THE BELLS OF SOMERSET

UNLIKE most soldiers, Phil Sheridan had become a legend long before his death. It was pleasant to become so glorified and celebrated well in advance of the funeral orations, the idolatrous biographies and the more measured opinion of posterity. But in Sheridan's case the result was that the legend overwhelmed the truth about the man and his accomplishments. The reality of such figures as Grant and Sherman has been quite adequately preserved; Sheridan, however, lives most vividly as the model for Gutzon Borglum's famous statue and the heroic verse of T. Buchanan Read.

Splendid as they are, the statue and the poem tell only one side of the story. They portray what his contemporaries most devoutly believed about Sheridan—that he was "the embodiment of impulse," as General Grant said, that he was a daredevil, a hell-for-leather cavalryman whose military assets lay chiefly in his personality rather than his brain.

It was hardly avoidable that Sheridan the truly great and peculiarly American general, the prototype of Pershing and Patton, Bradley and Eisenhower, should be overshadowed by Sheridan the hero. Sheridan had an undeniable talent for bravura—calculated bravura in the frontier style rather than the Napoleonic posturing of McClellan, the gasconading of Joe Hooker, the Creole flourishes of Beauregard or the King Arthurian aura of Robert E. Lee. So many images of Sheridan were indelible in the public imagination. Sheridan in his first major battle, frightening off a greatly superior Confederate force by an audacious attack on the enemy rear with only 90 Union cavalrymen. Sheridan the "paladin of Perryville,"

13

holding the ridge when Union divisions to the right and left lost heart, withdrawing through the Round Forest with his division and crippling the terrific Confederate attack on his wing at Stone's River. Sheridan the bulletheaded division commander swigging brandy out of a flask in the captured rifle pits at the foot of Missionary Ridge, drinking a toast to the Confederate artillerymen on the heights and losing his temper when they replied with a round of solid shot. Sheridan riding down on the great Jeb Stuart at Yellow Tavern and leaving the Confederate cavalry and its idolized leader mortally wounded. Sheridan on his big black charger Rienzi riding through a broken army to turn the tide at Cedar Creek. Sheridan devastating the Shenandoah Valley so thoroughly that, as he expressed it with typical pungency, a crow flying across it would have to carry his own rations. Sheridan jumping Rienzi over the breastworks at Five Forks. Sheridan harrying Lee to surrender at Appomattox. Sheridan bluffing Napoleon III and his expeditionary force out of Mexico without armed intervention by United States troops. Sheridan leading the Twenty-Years War against the Indians of the Great Plains. And more, as will be seen.

The military hero as embodied by men like McClellan or MacArthur makes many Americans feel vaguely uneasy or inclined to undermine his pedestal. Phil Sheridan, however, exuded a heroic spirit that owed nothing to Roman, Grecian or later European models. He waved his plug hat rather than his sword to urge his men into battle. His uniforms would have nauseated the tailor who outfitted George B. McClellan and Joe Hooker. His pronouncements to the troops were more likely to be firecracker strings of profanities or sardonic wisecracks than the orotund prose most generals addressed to their soldiers. He was in the tradition of Mad Anthony Wayne, Zachary Taylor and his boyhood hero, Old Tippecanoe Harrison.

Impulsive, inspiring, electrifying as he was in combat, there were solider and more durable qualities in his character that carried him to a commanding eminence among American military leaders.

There was about him a simplicity which, unless carried to extremes, is always valuable in a soldier. He never knew a moment's indecision, even in battle, even when things were going wrong. If it seemed that disaster was about to overtake him, he took immediate measures to avoid it and applied so much faith and determination to his counteraction that it usually prevailed. Part of battle is bluff, deception; Sheridan was sometimes briefly deceived, but he was never bluffed. He never lost control of a battle for more than a moment. If the enemy moved contrary to his hopes or expectations—as at Winchester, Cedar Creek, Dinwiddie Court House, Five Forks—he always managed to adapt himself to changed circumstances and take the proper remedy, for he never conceived of combat as something static, something preordained for victory or defeat. He not only had the will to win, he could never conceive of himself as losing. There was an inevitable progression in his life from childhood to the grave; hesitancy never clogged his footsteps. It was "Onward and Upward"—to borrow a Horatio Alger title—all the way.

Although he was born in poorer circumstances than any other Union general who attained great renown, he never knew the setbacks and confusions that assailed Grant (mostly from his drinking and maladjustment to the rest of humanity), Sherman (whose unstable nervous system led to his removal early in the Civil War and a widespread belief that he was insane), Thomas (the Virginian who loved his state but hated slavery and the idea that the Union should be disintegrated to save that institution) or McClellan (whose posturing concealed a deep-seated doubt of himself and his capacities). No, Sheridan never doubted himself, his capacities or his beliefs. He had no reason to doubt them. From a rocky career at West Point to the post of commanding general of the army he proceeded with never a backward look until his last, brief, fatal illness.

Naturally an optimist, he lacked any trace of morbidity. One of his oldest friends observed that Sheridan "saw more dead men than any man living at that time, but with all this he would, if possible, avoid the sight of one." When General Grant was dying of cancer people wondered why Sheridan did not join the procession of old friends and comrades to Mount McGregor; he explained, "It is unnecessary for me to use words to express my attachment to General Grant and his family. I have not gone to see him, as I could only bring additional distress to them, and I want to remember him as I knew him in good health."[1] Every great soldier is something of an actor, and there was a noticeable split between Sheridan's public and private behavior. A war correspondent noted that Sheridan was "at times almost a recluse," yet "carried on the battle-field the forked lightnings" so that "his brigades swarmed forward under his lead like the mighty nimbus of a storm. . . . Sheridan was more than magnetic. He was electric."[2] No other general in those days of personal leadership ever inspired his men as Sheridan did. All through his career there was evidence of his philosophy that, if he trusted his reputation to the private soldier, he would never be let down.

Part of the Sheridan legend was a belief that he was a callous, blustering fellow with little humanity in his heart. It was, of course, difficult for people to forget his devastation of the Shenandoah, his destruction of the Indians' powers of resistance and his rule of the conquered states of Louisiana and Texas. They thought this unfeeling militarist was epitomized by his remark to a young colonel who had been unduly hesitant to attack with his regiment: "Go in, sir, and get some of your men killed." Long after the war Sheridan told a boyhood friend how he felt about burning out the Shenandoah Valley: "I am sure there is more mercy in destroying supplies than in killing their young men, which a continuance of the war would entail. If I had a barn full of wheat and a son, I would much sooner lose the barn and wheat than my son. . . . The question was, must we destroy their supplies or kill their young men? We chose the former."[3]

Sheridan's approach was entirely pragmatic; he was always honest with himself and usually compassionate in his attitude toward his fellow humans as long as he believed they were dealing honestly with him.

When late in life he bought a farm near his boyhood home he asked an old friend to act as his agent in managing the property. The friend protested that he wasn't hardheaded enough for such work and quoted Shakespeare, "When the poor cry or complain, I pity." And Sheridan replied, "When the poor cry, I want you to pity." He was too honest to succumb to the general corruption that followed the Civil War and caught up so many of his contemporaries and comrades. A. T. Stewart, the New York department store owner, offered him $25,000 a year just so "the public would know he was attached to the store." Sheridan replied that he hadn't worked in a dry goods store since boyhood and couldn't see that his services would be worth that much; he declined "rather unceremoniously."

Sheridan faced life squarely. He never deluded himself that war was something invented to glorify the name of Sheridan. When necessary, he could invoke the old hurrah spirit of a Custer or Stuart and go in at the head of his troopers, but he knew there was more to generalship than flying at the enemy with naked saber. He never forgot that a good general is first of all a good quartermaster, that a soldier who brings an empty stomach and a half-empty bandoleer to the battlefield isn't going to be very efficient. To him, the last of the great horse cavalrymen, the cavalry was a striking arm, not a throwback to the days of chivalry. The horse was a means of bringing a soldier to a battle, but not necessarily into battle. If aimed fire from the Federal army's new repeating rifles and carbines was more effective, then, in his opinion, only a fool would employ sabers and pistols from the unstable platform of a horse's back.

The American Army owes an everlasting debt to Sheridan, not only for the achievements which compelled Grant to say, "I rank him with Napoleon, Frederick, and the great commanders of history," but for his influence on military thinking in the United States. Sheridan's free-wheeling offensives of the Civil War helped to provide the model for the armored thrusts of World War II. His belief that the offensive, invested with all the power and determination possible, is more economic of lives and more effective strategically than more cautious tactics is the animating factor of modern American military thinking. The Sheridan legend maintained that he knew so much success because of his dash, his luck and his talent for quick improvisation. But generals usually deserve their luck. And the ability to scrap a battle plan when necessary, with the coequal capacity for devising a better one, is one of the greatest ingredients of generalship.

During the long period when the United States was not engaged

in foreign wars and the army was in danger of stagnation he urged
and insisted that its officers should not cease to prepare themselves
to defend the nation. He oversaw the establishment of what has
evolved into the Command and General Staff School at Leavenworth.

Finally it can be said that he was one Civil War general who
seems so "modern" that he would not be out of place now, far
removed from those days of stately maneuver, of muskets with an
effective range of 100 yards, of generals who could carry their
offices in their saddlebags. It takes no great exercise of imagination
to visualize little Phil Sheridan as an officer of the United States
Army today; he would reorientate himself, one feels, in a few
weeks. It is much more difficult to imagine Robert E. Lee jumping
out of a transport plane at the head of a parachute division, Sherman's angry face popping out of a tank, Jeb Stuart without braid
or fancy feathers leading a heavy bomber strike from an Okinawa
airfield, or a beardless George H. Thomas peering down from an
L-5 observation plane over an infantry division on maneuvers.

Virtually the only mystery of Phil Sheridan's life concerns the
location of his birth. He was born on March 6, 1831, to John and
Mary Sheridan, the third of their six children . . . but where? His
parents were married in County Cavan, Ireland, and lived and
worked as tenant farmers on the estate of Cherrymount. All that
is known of their forebears is that John claimed descent from the
Irish kings. In 1830 John's uncle, Thomas Gainor of Albany, New
York, persuaded John and Mary to sell their leasehold and invest
the money in passage to America.[4] They landed at Boston and
proceeded to Albany, where John Sheridan soon found that Uncle
Thomas' picture of the opportunities to be found there bordered
on the Micawberish. He moved his family to Somerset, Ohio, and
found employment in the great road-building activity west of the
Alleghenies. Many Catholics, particularly Irishmen, settled along
the Cumberland Road and its tributary turnpikes and canals as
transportation improved and the wilderness yielded to settlement
and civilization.

Somewhere along the way Philip Henry was born to the Sheridans. It may have been in County Cavan just before they migrated; several Roman Catholic priests of the Dominican Order maintained that parish records there supported this claim.[5] (Supposedly Sheridan later concealed his non-American birth because of Presidential aspirations; this, at least, was the view of a boyhood friend.[6]) Various early biographers listed his birthplace as "on the high seas," Boston, Albany and Somerset. The authoritative *Biographical Register of the Officers and Graduates of the United States Military Academy*—and even the government—accepted Albany as his birthplace. Sheridan himself was an uncertain witness. On army documents, acceptances of promotions which required that he name his birthplace, he often gave Somerset, sometimes Albany, sometimes Massachusetts, as the place were he first drew breath.[7] But no record of his birth can be found in Albany, Boston or Somerset. It was the first and last uncertainty of his life—and is a mystery to this day.

Certainly Somerset was his home from infancy. His father managed to support the family, never with any luxury, never without food on the table, by laboring on the roads and canals and subsequently on the railroads pushing their way westward. Since his father was home only on occasion, Phil, his three brothers and two sisters were raised under the firm supervision of their mother, "whose excellent common sense and clear discernment in every way fitted her for such maternal duties."[8] Her neighbors, who believed Phil inherited his best qualities from her, characterized his mother as "clear-headed, resourceful, honest and industrious." She had a strong sense of justice and once wanted to have a neighbor arrested because he struck his stepson repeatedly over the head; only when she reflected on how his wife would be affected did she desist.[9] John Sheridan, a quiet man, sober and hard-working, made much less impression on the community, even after his son became famous.

Boyhood in Somerset, obscure as it may have seemed, brought Phil Sheridan into select company. In the last century Ohio must have had something extraordinary in its soil and climate to nourish aspirants to political or military leadership. Among the Ohioans who reached the White House were Hayes, Garfield, Grant, Benjamin Harrison, McKinley and Taft. A majority of the Union commanders prominent during the Civil War were Ohio-born— Grant, Sherman, McPherson, Rosecrans, Buell, Custer and others. Not that Ohio was particularly kind to its own! General Sherman noted in a letter home while on his March to the Sea, "It is strange that to Ohio sons, Grant, Sheridan, and Sherman, the state has given the cold shoulder, so that none of them claims it as their home, though the state of their nativity."[10]

Somerset was a fine place for a lively, curious and energetic boy. In Sheridan's boyhood it grew rapidly from a dusty village to a town of 1,200 population, although when the Sheridans arrived there was a local joke that, if a single family moved away, Somerset's existence would be threatened. It was among the first settlements resulting from the great tide of migration into the Ohio River valley after the American Revolution, and the construction of the Cumberland Road brought new waves of settlers.[11] The town was built on a high ridge dividing the waters of the Hocking and Muskingum rivers. A quiet place, its daily life was governed by the chiming of two bell towers. The bell in the steeple of the Catholic church rang at 6:00 A.M., which the townspeople regarded as the respectable rising hour. The curfew bell rang in the courthouse tower at 9:00 P.M., bedtime for all but the roisterers in the taverns. Only "during a political campaign, a war or rumor of war" was there any excitement.

One of Sheridan's lifelong friends described Somerset as "a queer old town" where "prejudice yet lurks against much jewelry and 'plug' hats." He remembered that "we had our share of fighting and gambling, with some stealing and not a few drunkards, but for the thief, the swindler and the fraud there was no mercy." A sardonic old lawyer who had lost a case there, however, persuaded a committee that the motto it wanted inscribed over the courthouse door was, "Let Justice be done, if the heavens should fall." The town government did not discover for more than a year the difference between this motto and the Latin motto usually translated, "Let justice be done even though the heavens fall."

The only other nineteenth-century celebrity to come from

Somerset, besides Sheridan, was Januarius Aloysius MacGahan, who became a famous European correspondent for New York newspapers. His articles on Turkish brutality to the Bulgars were credited with starting the Turko-Russian War and resulting in the liberation of Bulgaria.[12]

The first home of the Sheridans was a slab-sided frame house with only three rooms, far from elegant but accounted fairly comfortable for the times, with a fine view of the Hocking Valley. A half-mile away through a large orchard was the St. Mary's Female Academy, established a year before the Sheridans' arrival. All boys living in the western or Hocking side of town were known as the Pig Foots; all those living on the eastern or Muskingum side were the Turkey Foots. Sheridan and his brothers were automatically Pig Foots and enlisted in the bitter childhood wars that were carried on through the generations between the two sections of the town, an unrelenting geographical feud fought with sticks and stones and boyish curses.

From all the available evidence, Phil Sheridan distinguished himself as a boy warrior in Somerset. One early biographer who interviewed townspeople concluded that "when Sheridan left Somerset to go to West Point he could whip any boy there." Sheridan's closest Somerset friend, Captain Henry Greiner, affirmed that Phil was anything but a bully, however, and "his sympathies when a boy were always with the weak, the underdog." From the time he was able to raise his fists Sheridan was ready, often eager, to use them. His temper was highly inflammable whenever anyone tried to take advantage of his small size. The world well knows the fighting quality of undersized Irishmen. Sheridan came out of his trundle bed with fists swinging and did not drop them to his sides until he learned years later that an uncontrollable temper is a disastrous handicap past boyhood years.

It was just as well that fighting came naturally to young Phil; otherwise his schoolmates would probably have ridiculed him unmercifully. He was not only small but decidedly an ugly duckling. His head was endowed with a "posterior bump" which would have delighted any touring phrenologist; it was so pronounced that a cap would not stay on his head. His eyes were long and narrow, so he looked at first glance like a Mongolian lad unaccountably cast up on the shores of the Hocking River. One longtime friend described him thus: "He had arched, heavy eyebrows, from underneath which large, piercing black eyes looked out at you. One could tell from his eyes in a moment whether he was fiercely angry or only indignant; whether he was serious, sad, or humorous, without noticing another feature of his face. I never saw eyes which showed so many shades of feeling as those of Phil Sheridan." Phil's eyes, though not actually black, appeared so when he was excited or angry. Added to these features were long arms and short legs which inspired any boy willing to risk an immediate fist fight to remark on his resemblance to a monkey.

Phil was the most successful of Mary Sheridan's sons, undoubtedly the one who most resembled her own sturdy character, but he was certainly not spoiled and he was not her favorite. After the war she lived in a "Steamboat Gothic" home built for her by Phil, but visitors who asked about her celebrated soldier son were tartly reminded that Mrs. Sheridan's two other sons had served in the Union armies also; and, though John had fought as a private in the Civil War, she regarded him as the brightest in the family. Both parents were as concerned over John's career as a private— and Mike's as a lieutenant on his older brother's staff—as over the fame won by Phil. The elder John Sheridan explained that they worried over his namesake because "he always did love to take things easy in this world" and "we were more pleased to hear that John had done his duty as a private than to hear of all the promotions and praise that Phil had received."[13] It was a level-headed family, with less than its share of vainglory.

Henry Greiner's earliest memory of Phil Sheridan was a Fourth of July when Phil was six or seven years old. It was a suitably pious recollection of the boy destined to become one of the saviors of the Union. The Fourth of July in those days was outranked as a holiday only by Christmas, especially among small boys. At dawn a brass cannon on Reading Hill would start booming out salutes, rousing the boys of Somerset to the noisiest and therefore happiest day of the year.

The townspeople and the farm families from many miles around gathered for an afternoon of oratory in the calliope style which has not altogether disappeared today, although time has muted its brassier tones. Even the patriotic orators were overshadowed by a genuine and certified veteran of the Revolutionary War, an ancient named Dusenbury who lived in the near-by settlement of Grease-town. Every Fourth of July he decked himself out in a suit of homespun linen and, seated in a split-bottom chair, was borne to the scene of the celebration in a wagon. He was so feeble that he had to be carried from the wagon to the platform, but respectful cheers always greeted him. "I never saw Phil's brown eyes open so wide or gaze with such interest as they did on this old Revolutionary relic," Greiner recalled. Phil asked his friend why old Dusenbury was treated with such reverence, and after Greiner explained about the old soldier Phil followed him the rest of the day, feasting his eyes on the senescent veteran.[14]

Otherwise, there was little enough of reverence and more than a little of the Katzenjammer in Phil's boyhood. He joined the other boys in teasing and tormenting an old Negro tramp named Billy Jones who performed odd jobs around the town. "Old Billy Jones, a bag of bones," the boys would sing, capering down the street after him. Billy always wore a castoff army uniform and liked to pretend that he was the veteran of some mysterious war which existed only in his imagination.

Once when Billy Jones turned on his young tormentors and managed to catch young Phil the boy took shrewd advantage of the old man's military pretensions. Billy raised his cane to thrash the boy, but stayed his arm when Phil cried out, "Captain Jones! Let me go, Major! If you will I'll go right back to school and not call you any more names, Colonel!" Overwhelmed by this flattery, Billy loosened his hold on Phil, and the boy scampered away.[15]

That was probably one of the few moments in his boyhood when he thought of school as a refuge. He had a healthy horror of schooling and an intense disrespect for his teachers. The first was a Mr. McNanly, "one of those itinerant dominies of the early frontier" whose method of maintaining discipline was to whip the whole

class if unable to detect a culprit when an offense had been committed.[16] The schoolmasters of the last century were a hard lot,
and they had to be to control row upon row of truculent, muscular
country lads who resented being subjected to any measure of education. But they could not have gloried in their calling, for, according to Henry Greiner, the masters invariably spent their days
off in solitary drinking bouts. From Saturday morning to Sunday
night they were roaring drunk, and on Monday mornings they
faced their classes in a choleric temper. "Their strongest recommendation was that they could whip the boys into submission,"
Greiner said.[17] Sheridan and Greiner usually played hookey
Monday mornings.

The way of the truant, however, was not all idyllic looting of the
orchards along High street, fishing in shaded pools and burying
one's face in the cool waters of Finck's springs in the wild-plum
grove. In the country school system of the day it was customary
for the schoolmaster to take part of his pay in boarding out with
the families of his pupils in rotation.

McNanly particularly liked to tuck his legs under the Sheridan
table, for he had known the Sheridan family in Ireland. First in
the order of business was a determination by the teacher and Mrs.
Sheridan just how often in the past weeks Phil had played the truant and how many times he had been sick at home. The boy's
health was woefully excellent, and "many a time a comparison of
notes proved that I had been in the woods with two playfellows,
named Binckly and Greiner, when the master thought I was home,
ill, and my mother, that I was at school, deeply immersed in
study."[18]

Phil was undoubtedly one of the chief contributing factors in
McNanly's decision to seek his fortune in the howling wilderness
west of the Mississippi, preferring to deal with Indians rather than
schoolboy barbarians. One day Phil fought during recess with a
boy much larger than himself and managed to inflict a bloody nose
and other damage on his opponent. On catching sight of the victim
McNanly reached for his stoutest hickory stick and ran out into
the schoolyard. Phil was sitting on the fence, blowing on his bruised
knuckles. He saw the schoolmaster coming toward him and im-

mediately took to his heels with the teacher in hot pursuit. The
closest sanctuary was the shop of Sam Cassell, the tinsmith.

Old Sam, who at the age of seventy still climbed the courthouse
steeple to repair the brass globe on the spire, was his closest friend
among the adults of Somerset. He had fashioned a tin sword for
the boy, Phil's first weapon, which he brandished in drilling a squad
of his schoolmates; and the boy and the old tinsmith had formed the
sort of alliance, warm and understanding as anything in life, possible between two persons as close in spirit as they were separated
in years.

Cassell immediately hid his small friend under a huge copper pot
brought to his shop for repair. McNanly roared in, demanding that
the culprit be turned over for summary punishment. Cassell pointed
out the rear door, and the schoolmaster resumed his search. Phil
hurried back to the school and was sitting at his desk, smiling
blandly, when his winded preceptor returned. McNanly was so
flabbergasted that he decided not to pursue the matter.

A Mr. Thorne succeeded the Irishman, but the boys of Somerset
were soon disappointed in their hopes of gentler treatment. He
proved to be as heavy-handed a disciplinarian and as hardy a week-
end drinker as his predecessor. Thorne, an imperious Virginian
who may well have initiated Sheridan's lifelong distaste for Southern gentlemen, provided the boy with "a smattering of geography
and history" and some acquaintance with the "mysteries of Pike's
arithmetic and Bullion's English grammar." The arithmetic book
was the same that Abraham Lincoln had studied 20 years earlier.
Thorne kept his lads equally well acquainted with the swish of a
hickory stick descending on their unscholarly backs.[19]

A rather Spartan rule at home and frequently harsh treatment at
school failed to break or even bend young Phil's spirit. Henry
Greiner recalled that at the age of eight or nine Phil Sheridan could
not be overawed, even by visiting dignitaries trailing martial glory.
During the political campaign of 1840 Martin Van Buren was named
by the Democrats for re-election to the Presidency. His Vice-Presi-
dent, the famous Colonel Richard M. Johnson, was renominated
also. It was the year of the tumultuous "coonskin and cider" versus
"silk hat and champagne" issue, resplendent with torchlight parades,

log cabins carried as shrines and cries of "Tippecanoe and Tyler too"—a giddy affair even for American politics, but taken very emotionally by the electorate.

Colonel Johnson, "hero of the battle of the Thames" and slayer of the great Indian chief Tecumseh, appeared in Somerset to take the stump for his ticket. Every boy in the town looked forward to seeing, hearing and possibly even shaking hands with the heroic colonel. Little Phil, with his tin sword and schoolboy battalion, was already stirred by anything even faintly martial—the beat of a drum, the sight of an old veteran limping down the street. And here was a very martial occasion. But the Sheridan family was of the Whig persuasion, and a Democrat was something akin to the devil and all his works; politics was no piddling matter then, even for a frontier boy of nine.

When the colonel appeared at Finch's tavern Phil Sheridan simply could not stay away; hero worship was stronger than political loyalty for the moment. Caught in the Democratic mob, young Phil was pushed forward and jokingly ordered to shake hands with Tecumseh's slayer. What a dilemma! Any other boy in town would have jumped at the honor and refused to wash his right hand for a week. Almost in tears, Phil put his hands behind his back, turned and tried to flee.

Johnson stopped him and asked why he would not shake hands. Phil blurted out, "Because I'm a Whig!"

"Oh, that makes no difference," the colonel assured him.

"Yes, sir, it does. It isn't right. I want to get out of here!"

"Let this little Whig out," Johnson ordered with a laugh. "We can't force or coax him to shake hands with a Democrat."

Next day Phil was still resentful at having been made a laughingstock. He told his friend Henry Greiner, "I would rather have been whipped than laughed at by a room full of Democrats."[20]

Later that year Phil was able to regain a measure of self-esteem when an authentic Whig hero came to town and spoke under the great oak near the Sheridan home. He was William Henry Harrison, "Old Tippecanoe" himself, and he became President of the United States.[21]

Phil's quick wit and mischievous instincts embroiled a couple of the most vociferous Democrats in that section of the state. One was

John Palmer, a Somerset attorney who had an "immense mouth" and employed it in political oratory on every possible occasion. Phil and the other boys called him "Catfish" and then took to their heels with Palmer in pursuit and brandishing his cane.

Once a fisherman whose Democratic tendencies were equally pronounced came to town with a wagonload of catfish. He had difficulty in disposing of them. Phil immediately directed him to the office of "Catfish" Palmer. In a moment or two there was a terrific commotion in the law office, and the fisherman came downstairs with a bruised jaw and a puzzled look on his face.

"What the hell is the matter with that feller up there?" the fisherman demanded. "He must be crazy or drunk, for as soon as I asked him to buy catfish, he up and hit me on the nose. So I goes into him, and he's got a lickin' that he won't forget soon. . . . I'll learn him to hit a feller when he's tryin' to sell fish!"[22]

There were many things besides politics to occupy a boy's time in Somerset. Phil loved horses and found it was a constant temptation to ride the half-broken stage horses. The only time his father ever whipped Phil was when he caught him riding one of these wild, bucking horses out of harness.[23] And there were the attractions of the main street—the taverns, the cigar maker's, the rope factory, the linen importer's, the ax maker's, the cobbler's shop of Christian Greiner, father of his friend Henry, which was also the consulate of the German states for that section of the country—and above all the brawling in the courthouse square.

Teamsters driving the big Conestoga wagons over the Alleghenies and the Cumberland Road would stop at Finch's tavern for refreshment; it was hard and thirst-making work, driving a six-horse team, and Finch's generously provided a tumblerful of whisky or peach brandy for three cents. Drinking led to profane arguments, and arguments led to wild battles in the square. Little Phil learned much about fighting and swearing from the robust fellows who tumbled in the dust outside the taverns.

There were moments of less vulgar excitement, too, such as the day that General Santa Anna passed through while in involuntary exile from Mexico. Less notorious personages, too—Thomas Hart Benton, Henry Clay and John Crittenden—came through the town in all their political splendor.

Phil and his friends gathered also at an old tobacco barn near the Sheridan home and gave combined vaudeville and circus shows for the amusement of anyone who would pay a penny for admission. Phil usually appeared on the program as a trapeze performer, but once he was persuaded to do a wild-animal turn. He was shoved into a cage with a dog and a large tomcat after being presented to the audience as "Herr Dresbach," the noted Prussian animal tamer. Hostilities broke out almost immediately, and "Herr Dresbach," in a most unprofessional panic, howled for the door to be opened. The cage was unbarred, and boy, cat and dog erupted in that order. Phil was badly scratched but not entirely disillusioned. In later life he would often tell people that he "had been in show business" before turning to soldiering.[24]

At the age of fourteen, whatever his inclinations toward show business, driving Conestoga wagons (the ambition of most Somerset boys) or becoming a soldier, Phil went to work at the least venturesome of jobs, clerking in a general store. His father had experienced some success at obtaining subcontracting jobs on various roads and canals under construction in southern Ohio, but there were younger brothers and sisters to educate, clothe and feed, so it was deemed only fair that Phil quit school and go to work. He complied willingly, for school had always been irksome. Except for his quick temper when anyone trifled with his feelings, he left the harum-scarum ways of his mischievous boyhood behind, and townspeople often remarked that he was the politest clerk in the local stores. For a salary of two dollars a month he served a year's apprenticeship in John Talbot's store, then accepted an offer of twice as much to take charge of the bookkeeping at Finck & Dittoe's dry-goods store—"no small work for one of my years," he remarked with understandable pride later, "considering that in those days the entire business of country stores in the West was conducted on the credit system."[25] This bookkeeping experience, much removed as it may seem from the clash of arms, greatly benefited his military career, for it was his work on the accounts of General Frémont early in the Civil War that attracted the approval of the man who was to become briefly the general in chief and later chief of staff of the wartime army.

His commendable progress in the commercial world of Somerset did not distract him from his dream of becoming a soldier. One of the more illustrious figures of his boyhood was a tall, redheaded youth named William Tecumseh Sherman, a cadet at West Point, who lived in near-by Lancaster and often came to Somerset. The girl he was soon to marry, Ellen Ewing, attended St. Mary's Female Academy on the hill. Henry Greiner remembered that he and young Phil once interrupted a game of hopscotch outside the home of Martin Scott, where Sherman and Miss Ewing often met, as Sherman "leaned against the door talking earnestly to his sweetheart."[26]

Phil's half-formed military ambitions were reinforced by the Mexican War. Too young to join the Keokuk Rifles drilling in the courthouse square, he nevertheless became an authority on the progress of the campaigns in the north of Mexico and the operations against Mexico City—in which such future associates and adversaries as Robert E. Lee, U. S. Grant, George H. Thomas, Braxton Bragg, A. P. Hill, James Longstreet and many others were participating, mostly as junior officers in command of volunteer companies and batteries. At Finck & Dittoe's he was accepted as the arbiter of the military "discussions and disputes" that arose around the potbellied stove.

Soon all his hopes were centered on obtaining an appointment as West Point cadet from his congressional district. It developed that this was not so remote a possibility as it seemed. The original appointee from his district, Phil learned, had failed to pass the examination. "When I learned that by this occurrence a vacancy existed, I wrote to our representative in Congress, the Hon. Thomas Ritchie, and asked him for the appointment. . . . He responded promptly by enclosing my warrant for the class of 1848; so, notwithstanding the many romances that have been published about the matter, to Mr. Ritchie, and to him alone, is due all the credit. . . ."[27]

The appointment came easily enough, but there were other issues to be settled. One was his father's objections to Phil's education in an institution predominantly Episcopalian; the other was the scantiness of the boy's education, which cast doubt on whether he could be tutored into passing the examinations.

Inordinately solemn and tremulous, Phil was brought before

Fathers Dominic Young and Joshua Young for a conference on the advisability of a military career. His father accompanied him to the inquiry before the two Dominicans, who had supervised his religious instruction, and explained to them that Phil was determined to attend West Point. John Sheridan posed the question that had been troubling the household: might not his son run the risk of losing his faith in such a secular school? The talk was long and somber. Father Joshua finally announced his opinion that Phil should give up the appointment and not risk his faith.

Knowing his son's heart was set on the appointment, John Sheridan, a simple and devout man who had never before questioned a priest's wisdom, cried out despairingly, "But what shall I do with the boy?" '

Father Joshua replied with measured solemnity, "Rather than send him to West Point, take him out into the back yard, behind the chicken coop, and cut his throat."

Hugh Ewing, brother-in-law of General Sherman and the authority for this episode, said Phil's father "thought this mode of disposing of Phil too drastic and, milder counsel prevailing, sent him to West Point."[28] Still, the matter must have aroused something of a storm in the Sheridan home, and probably little enough of "milder counsel." Sheridan made no mention of the clerical and parental objections to West Point, a reticence which may indicate the appointment was a painful subject long after it had lost its significance to all but his family.

Once he had won over his parents and possibly even the clergy to accepting the appointment, Sheridan doggedly set about preparing himself for the West Point examinations. Even at sixteen he had learned how to concentrate on a distasteful task, whether it was learning to keep books, tame wild horses or be polite to housewives arguing about their grocery bills. This trait was to have more influence on his future success than more flamboyant characteristics which appealed to the romantic-minded public. Somerset's new schoolmaster, William Clark, agreed to help Phil prepare himself. Actually, for all the boy's fears, the examination in those days was not much more than a literacy test, and many cadets came from schools even less advanced than Somerset's. Early in the summer of

1848 he journeyed to the military academy, stopping in Albany to visit his relatives. And on July 1, entrance requirements satisfied, he was admitted to the corps of cadets.

For all his eagerness to become a West Pointer, Phil did not find the military academy all he had dreamed it would be. He resented hazing—it was a far more strenuous pastime in that period—and believed it a "senseless custom."[29] His feeling for the underdog, as noted by Henry Greiner, was too strong to permit him to view the mistreatment of plebes by older and stronger cadets with equanimity, although he "escaped excessive persecution" himself. To a boy accustomed to the democracy and friendliness of a small town, West Point was grim and authoritarian. Smoking, card playing, even visiting from room to room were all forbidden on pain of demerits. The food served in the mess hall, which was Spartan to say the most, could not be supplemented by outside purchases or packages from home. Nor could money be received from any outside source, except illicitly; in theory, all cadets were equally impoverished, no matter how prosperous their families. The only relief from drill, study and discipline was an excursion to Benny Haven's tavern at Buttermilk Falls, to which generations of cadets fled for the solace of a decent meal and a few warming toddies, and of which they sang in a hundred barrack rooms in after years:

> Come, fill your glasses, fellows, and stand up in a row,
> To singing sentimentally we're going for to go;
> In the Army there's sobriety, promotion's very slow,
> So we'll sing our reminiscences of Benny Haven's, oh!

West Point was never a particularly happy memory for Phil Sheridan. Not only did he find his studies a constant struggle and the discipline a continuing affront, but he was almost a misfit in other ways. Undeniably he was not the finest physical specimen ever crammed into the "monkey suit" then worn by cadets: stiff single-breasted gray coat with tails, gray trousers with a black stripe at the sides, white gloves, a high-crowned black hat with an eight-inch black plume and a leather cockade. Phil was simply not constructed for such a uniform. He was barely five feet five inches

tall, long in the arms, short in the legs, with a combative jaw, tradi-
tionally Irish long upper lip and a raw-beef complexion. With his
Tartarlike eyes he must have looked more like one of Ghengis
Khan's horsemen than a soldier of the American Republic. All this
in contrast to the elegant youths from Boston and New York and
Philadelphia and the insolently graceful cadets from the Southern
states. They started their careers at least looking like officers, regardless of the mental or spiritual qualities they brought to their
profession. Sheridan had the constant handicap of looking like a
private in the rear rank.

But the ugly duckling managed to survive the homesickness, the
iron disclipline, the crushing round of study and drill in his plebe
year. To his sister Mary he wrote on January 13, 1849, a letter
that told much about himself—more than he intended, perhaps.
With its uncertain spelling and grammar intact, the letter was as
follows:

In mathematics my standing is 40. [There were 65 members in
Sheridan's class.] In ethics I was so unfortunate to miss two questions and it throughed me 16 files, but I can soon gain my former
standing. . . . I now stand 52 in ethics as you will see from report
of War Department when it comes.

You may think my standing not very good, but out of the 40
that stand above me in Math., 15 are graduates of other colleges
and 30 of them can speak the French language. Then you see what
I have had to contend with. I am well enough satisfied myself and
I think I have done very well. . . .

We had a very interesting time here in New York receiving the
colors taken in the Mexican War. But I suppose you have read an
account of it in the papers before this time. Tell Mrs. D—— that
I am sorry I was not at home, that I would like to have been at the
wedding. I am very sorry about the death of Aunt Mary. I suppose that Uncle Philip will return to Somerset. I hope the girls
will—not—fag out in making that rag carpet for Father Dominic. . . .

Give my regards, esteem, love etc., to those girls you mentioned
in your letter namely: Misses Hewet, Fink, Costigan and Elder.

I want you, Dear Sister, to write often, you never write but in
answer to my letters. I am always anxious to hear from home. Pat
I think never intends to write to me. Tell him if he cannot write

a letter to make some strait marks and send them. I shall be expecting that letter from Johny and Mike before long. Tell Jack to brighten up his ideas and not keep me in suspense. I shall be expecting a pretty present from you and Mother when McKever comes here on his way to Albany.

I have grown about 2 inches during the last 6 months and look a good deal paler than when I left home. Dear Sis, you must always treat Lou as a brother. I like him better than anybody else in the world. You mustn't show my letters to any person. I don't take any pains in writing them, consequently I do not want them seen. Give my love to Sister Ianna and all inquiring friends. . . .[30]

Nostalgia for Somerset and its lack of social barriers was all the keener in contrast with the rigid caste system at the military academy. Sheridan, a Northerner and a Roman Catholic, was at the opposite end of the social scale from the high-caste Southerner of Episcopalian upbringing—particularly a Virginian, who was the Brahmin of Brahmins. The Southerner, reared in the tradition of Sir Walter Scott's novels and believing himself born with the habit of command, thought himself superior to all other members of the cadet corps. Hadn't most of the nation's Presidents, statesmen and political leaders been Southerners? Hadn't most of its great military leaders come from the South? And wasn't War Department patronage controlled mainly by Southerners?

The military academy was dominated professionally as well as socially by Southerners. Before Sheridan was graduated in 1853 three of the leading members of its faculty were Virginians. The superintendent was Robert E. Lee, with Robert S. Garnett as commandant. George H. Thomas was instructor in cavalry and artillery tactics. Another member of the faculty who was to become famous during the Civil War was Fitz John Porter, a Northerner.[31] His preceptors at West Point undoubtedly would have found it hard to believe that Sheridan, far from the most promising of cadets, would have so fateful a bearing on their lives and careers. It was little Sheridan who stood squarely across Lee's line of retreat in April 1865 and persuaded the Confederate leader that continuing the war was hopeless. With Thomas, Sheridan would stand to the death at Stone's River; he would bring his shattered division to bolster the "Rock of Chickamauga" the night of the retreat from the Valley of the Chickamauga; and at Missionary Ridge Sheridan would lead Thomas' assault divisions of the Army of the Cumberland to the victorious crest. Along with his fellows, Sheridan might slip off to Benny Haven's on a dark night and be a hapless collector of demerits, but this was no mark of disrespect for Lee, Thomas and the other officers. These men were heroes as well as disciplinarians of the cadet corps. Colonel Lee's exploits in the Mexican War as a staff officer under Lieutenant General Winfield Scott were an army legend, and Major Thomas, twice brevetted for bravery, had commanded a section in Braxton Bragg's battery at Monterey and Buena Vista ("A little more grape, Captain Bragg!").

Besides being a Northerner and a Catholic, Phil Sheridan had the additional social handicap of being an Irishman. In the years when he was attending the military academy the position of the Irish in America had deterioriated to the point where signs reading "No dogs or Irishmen" were posted, and not in jest. The Irish had filled the ranks of Washington's army and of American forces in subsequent wars and had shown themselves to be good citizens— if sometimes a little less predictable than their neighbors. The famine of 1848-1849 had caused millions to leave Ireland, most of them for the United States. Native Americans became so alarmed by the thought that Irish immigrants might unsettle the political balance and even turn the United States into a Papal colony that they organized to persecute Irish-Americans and deny them their rights and privileges. Such organizations as the Know-Nothings and the American Protective Association succeeded in arousing an enduring bitterness and suspicion against the Irish. Although hundreds of thousands of Irish fought in the Civil War, only a very few— the most prominent being Sheridan in the Federal army, Patrick Cleburne in the Confederate—became general officers.

It was little wonder that Sheridan felt ill at ease and rebellious through most of his cadet years and annually faced expulsion for demerits—many of them for fighting, others for inadequate scholarship. He did find one ally in his struggle to stay at West Point. His roommate, Henry W. Slocum, future Union corps commander at Chancellorsville, Gettysburg, Missionary Ridge and during the Atlanta campaign, had had a sound education before entering the military academy. To Sheridan's lasting gratitude, he was willing to share this knowledge. Sheridan later wrote:

After taps—that is, when by the regulations of the Academy all the lights were supposed to be extinguished, and everybody in bed— Slocum and I would hang a blanket over the one window of our room and continue our studies—he guiding me around scores of stumbling-blocks in Algebra and elucidating many knotty points in other branches of the course with which I was unfamiliar. On account of this association I went up before the Board . . . with less uneasiness than otherwise would have been the case, and passed the examination fairly well. When it was over, a self-confidence in my capacity was established that had not existed hitherto, and at each succeeding examination I gained a little in order of merit till my furlough summer came round—that is, when I was half through the four-year course.[32]

In his second year at West Point, Sheridan thus managed to survive the shaking-out process which disposed of so many of his classmates lacking in the physical and mental stamina required of an apprentice officer, and established himself as at least a mediocre student. He had already impressed the tactical instructors as quick to learn the intricacies of cavalry, infantry and artillery maneuver. On his first furlough in the summer of 1850 he was accompanied to Somerset by two classmates, Nugent and George Crook. Crook was to command a cavalry division in the Civil War, some of the time under Sheridan in the Shenandoah, and become a famous Indian fighter. A cross-grained, independent young man, he was none too popular with his classmates, which may have established a bond of sympathy between him and Sheridan.

At the halfway mark it seemed Sheridan would pass the remainder of his cadethood in comparative ease and assurance, but his hair-trigger temper got him into serious trouble. In September 1851 occurred the episode that almost ended his military career before it had fairly begun. Late one afternoon Sheridan's company formed on the parade ground under the sharp eye and caustic tongue of Cadet Sergeant William R. Terrill, a Virginian with an imperious manner. The manner was anathema to Sheridan and his Ohio-bred outrage over anything faintly aristocratic; the man himself was symbolic of all the slights and snubs he had received.[33]

According to Sheridan's later account, his temper was aroused when Terrill gave him an order "in what I considered an improper tone" to "dress in a certain direction, although I believed I was accurately dressed." Sheridan became so enraged during the ensuing argument that he lunged at the cadet sergeant with lowered bayonet, but "my better judgment recalled me before actual contact could take place."[34] In that split second Sheridan, in restraining himself, changed the course of his life: he never again lost his temper to any dangerous degree. But he was in serious trouble: he had committed a breach of military conduct of nearly disastrous proportions; an enlisted man who lunged at an officer with his bayonet could expect a court-martial and a sentence of many years at hard labor. Terrill, of course, was required to place Sheridan on report for the incident.

By then Sheridan was convinced that Terrill was his personal enemy, but he had sense enough not to challenge him when armed with a dangerous weapon. The next time they met, in front of the barracks, Sheridan's fists started swinging. Terrill coolly took the measure of his smaller assailant and was in the process of thoroughly beating Sheridan when an officer on the West Point staff came along, stopped the fight and ordered both assailants to submit letters of explanation.

Sheridan was obviously the guilty party. The only question in the minds of the authorities was whether to expel him forthwith, which was their first thought, or suspend him for a year. Perhaps one of the higher officers understood how a whole chain of maddening episodes had impelled Sheridan to react so violently to Terrill's order. Anyway, the final decision was to suspend him for one year and set him back in the class of 1853.

Sheridan was anything but grateful for the leniency. "At the time I thought, of course, my suspension a very unfair punishment, that my conduct was justifiable and the authorities of the Academy all wrong, but riper experience has led me to a different conclusion, and as I look back . . . I am convinced that it was hardly as much as I deserved for such an outrageous breach of discipline."[35] But that repentant view came from the Philip H. Sheridan who was commanding general of the United States Army, not the young cadet from Perry County, Ohio, whose Celtic temper flared up at even the suggestion of an insult.

That autumn, "much crestfallen," Phil returned to Somerset and faced the curiosity of the townspeople. The long months before he was allowed to return to West Point were spent on the book-keeper's stool at Finck & Dittoe's dry-goods store.[36] His final year of education at West Point began in August 1852. Although he had learned his lesson about public brawling, he still fought in various secluded places, and his spirit was high and unchastened. The sight of Sheridan being hauled back to the barracks on a shutter was a fairly frequent spectacle. Baiting him was apparently one of the leading sports of the day at West Point, and with his gamecock temperament he took up every challenge almost before it was offered. But he did not commit any more offenses so serious as assaulting a cadet officer in public. In his graduating class of 1853 he was thirty-fourth among 52 in scholastic standing. At graduation time he was within five demerits of expulsion, his many fist fights having come to the attention of the Academic Board.[37] It was an Old Army legend that Sheridan had actually gone over the limit for demerits and was allowed to graduate because the authorities believed his aggressive nature, unseemly in a spit-and-polish cadet corps, would find more suitable employment on the frontier.

The class of 1853 was well represented in the higher echelons of command in the Civil War. Including Sheridan, the class produced four future army commanders. John Bell Hood became a full general in the Confederate Army and led the Army of Tennessee at Atlanta, Franklin and Nashville; his valor was the equal of Sheri-lan's. James B. McPherson, who led his class in scholarship, and John M. Schofield also became Federal army commanders, and Schofield later succeeded Sheridan as commanding general of the United States Army. Another classmate, Joshua Sill, was killed in action at Stone's River while leading a Union division. Among those who went over to the Confederacy, besides Hood, were John

R. Chambliss, Lucius Rich and Reuben Ross, all of them killed before they could gain any great distinction.[38] Of all his classmates only Hood came close to attaining the fame of Phil Sheridan, and he ranked even lower in scholastic standing, forty-fourth in the class—a comment of sorts on the value of scholastic brilliance to the line officer.

Sheridan and his classmates received their commissions as brevet second lieutenants in July 1853. Neither Sheridan nor Hood made any secret of his joy at leaving theory and pedantry behind forever. The engineers, the cavalry and the artillery, in that order, took their choice of the cadets at the top of the class, and the infantry took what was left. With little surprise Sheridan learned that he had been passed over by all arms of the service except the "Queen of Battles" and that he was assigned to the 1st Infantry at Fort Duncan, Texas. It suited him perfectly, for he wanted to see action, and serving with the elite engineers corps—dredging harbors or building fortifications—would have been only drudgery for him.

Phil left for Somerset immediately, determined to enjoy one last Fourth of July at home. If he thought the town girls would be swept off their feet by his new uniform, he was quickly disappointed. Despite a later reputation for gallantry, he had always been ill at ease among girls. "At our little parties when it came his turn to kiss the girls," Henry Greiner said, "it would always be with a blush and hesitancy."[39] He could not even find a girl to drive out to Lydy's Rocks, "a wild romantic glen," to celebrate the Fourth of July with him.

Fortunately Greiner had just returned to Somerset after joining in the California gold rush of 1849 and suffering the penniless fate of all but the luckiest prospectors. Greiner found him a young lady for the carriage ride to Lydy's Rocks, and "the next day I saw him with his new girl, happy and lively."[40] The young lieutenant was fortunate in being able to enjoy his brief leave in his home town and to depart for Texas with pleasant memories. It would be eight years before he saw Somerset again, and then only briefly, for this home-coming would occur months after the siege guns roared across the waters in the harbor of Charleston, South Carolina.

2

EIGHT YEARS A SHAVETAIL

PHIL SHERIDAN was the kind of officer who would never know great success or considerable advancement in a peacetime army. He possessed none of the social graces which in somnolent garrisons would ingratiate him with a commanding officer—and he had no wife to do for him what he couldn't do for himself. Even in the middle of the last century, in the rude forts and shabby quarters which looked out on hundreds of miles of wilderness where only barbaric tribesmen could wander in safety, the officers of the United States Army tried to preserve a semblance of civilized life. To these outposts, especially if they were accompanied by wives and families, they brought as much of Boston or Philadelphia or New Orleans or Charleston as would not wither, rot or look exceedingly outlandish in such remote circumstances.

Garrison soldiering would never find Sheridan at his best; he did not have the hearty fund of small talk, the taste for gossip and banter, the instinct for the amenities that helped to pass the time in the tight circle of duty. Such an officer, thrown on himself, the bottle or roistering company in the nearest town, if any, usually became an outcast or an eccentric. The young Sheridan had inner resources which enabled him to avoid both of these fates; he was interested in his duties, in the life around him, hunting, studying the land and its creatures and finally the Indians whom he was charged with helping to subdue. But he did not make friends easily, particularly with those superior in rank—he was too proud to curry favor or even be suspected of it—and he did not have the typical young lieutenant's puppyish charm with which to win over a superior's wife or other female relatives.

Many of his fellow officers, of course, were Southerners, and he avoided them whenever possible. At West Point he had formed a flaming resentment of the seigneurial manners of the Southern-born cadets, which seemed to him native arrogance, and their suspect ability to turn an elegant compliment.

In so-called "breeding" Sheridan found himself at a disadvantage. Born of Irish immigrants and reared in a border village, he had only disdain for polite society. He had no cozy family income on which to extend himself, attract a wife, entertain his fellow officers. In fact, if Horatio Alger had ever sought a military man as model for one of his chronicles of nineteenth-century success, Phil Sheridan would have served perfectly.

His elegant comrades, on the other hand, must have found intensely irritating his utter lack of comprehension of his "inferiority," his unblinking insistence on his rights as an equal human being, his refusal to be overawed, his thick-skinned confidence that he was as good as the next man!

His appearance was also against him: the most skillful tailor in New York could do little for his long arms and short legs, his bullet-shaped head, his non-ramrodlike posture. He looked more like a tough little sergeant than an officer and a gentleman—and in a peacetime army an officer is often judged, promoted or held back partly on the basis of his appearance and manners.

Still, men usually respected Sheridan on second or third glance. A contemporary wrote that Sheridan "suggested a low comedy man who had walked off the stage all made up for a funny part," but a closer look at his face and "its stern, composed lines were enough to make one forget his grotesque figure and careless dress."

It was early in 1854 when Sheridan joined the forces which, almost from the day of the establishment of a Regular Army, had been fighting to subdue the Indians. His first post, Fort Duncan, was opposite the Mexican town of Piedras Negras on the Rio Grande. He made the long and circuitous journey from Newport Barracks, Kentucky, down the Ohio and Mississippi rivers to New Orleans, across the Gulf of Mexico by schooner and steamer to

Corpus Christi, then overland with an army wagon train to Laredo and finally to Fort Duncan. A "blue Norther" came up as the train made its way across the Texas plains. The freezing wind and rain blurred the land into a Tartar steppe, and it was not much more prepossessing when the storm had passed—vast stretches of sterile gray grass, vistas of dun-colored mountains and mesas, cactus and thorny brush everywhere, the Rio Grande itself "more like a river of sand than a watercourse." Across the river in Mexican territory Piedras Negras and its adobe battlements seemed to offer few of the lively pleasures of a Latin town as imagined by a Northerner with little experience in travel.

Practically from the start of his tour of duty at Fort Duncan, Lieutenant Sheridan found himself in disfavor with the commanding officer of the 1st Infantry, Lieutenant Colonel Thompson Morris. They detested each other on sight. Colonel Morris, however, could make his displeasure felt, while Sheridan, as a brevet lieutenant, could only hold his tongue and suffer in silence. Sheridan's company commander, Captain Eugene E. McLean, and his wife were understanding and tolerant of his unpolished manner, but most of the regimental officers regarded him as a dead loss at the mess table.[1] He even made an enemy of the resident beef contractor by bringing in such supplies of turkeys, geese, antelope and deer that a joint of beef was scorned as iron rations.

It was the McLeans' kindness, Sheridan indicated later, that made the fort on the Rio Grande endurable. Captain McLean administered Company D with a combination of justice and tolerance that made Sheridan regard him as a model in dealing with subordinates. Mrs. McLean charmed him out of his black moods after a bad session with Colonel Morris, coaxed him out of the defensive shell he had built around himself and encouraged him to meet people halfway.

But he found his greatest pleasures in solitude, hunting, studying the customs of the people across the border and, unlikely as it seems, becoming an amateur ornithologist. It may be difficult to visualize the aggressive Sheridan engaged in bird watching, but he said later that his imagination was aroused by the "great number of bright-colored birds that made their winter homes along the

Rio Grande." His lack of popularity among the officers at Fort Duncan made him seek out an enlisted man named Frankman, whom he oddly characterized as "a fine sportsman and a butcher by trade," as his hunting companion. The association of an officer and an enlisted man has always been the great taboo of the military all over the world, so Sheridan was deliberately courting disfavor.

His popularity in the officers' mess was anything but revived by his foresight in building himself winter quarters much superior to those of his fellow officers, who contented themselves with living in tents as they did in summertime. With painstaking effort he built a solid hut of wood and tarpaulin, thatched with prairie grass, and noted rather smugly that he was "more comfortably off than many of the officers."[2] Few vegetables, except those provided by the sutler at prohibitive cost, were available that winter. One of his chief duties was to take Company D out about 40 miles and cut wagonloads of maguey plants from which pulque was brewed and rationed out to the troops as an antiscorbutic. The juice was pressed out, bottled and allowed to ferment until it "became worse in odor than sulphurated hydrogen." It was Sheridan's duty also to ration out the pulque at roll call every morning and see that the men of Company D drank it. "I always began the duty by drinking a cup of the repulsive stuff myself," he said. He had learned a lesson about troop leadership from Captain McLean, and that was to do oneself what was demanded of the men—and do it first. Concern for the welfare of the troops is a characteristic expected of all officers. Sheridan stood out as a line officer because he not only possessed that characteristic but made it his first principle. From Company D, 1st Infantry, to command of all the nation's land forces, he looked out for the welfare of the troops. "Trust your reputation to the private soldier and he will never let your military fame suffer" was later his own advice to young officers.

Opportunities to show leadership in combat were very scarce at Fort Duncan. The post was too strongly held for any mass attacks by the border tribes—the Comanche, the Lipon and the Apache. There were only hit-and-run raids, such as the incident in the winter of 1854-1855 when a hostile band swooped down on the fort and killed a drummer boy. Lieutenant Sheridan joined the pursuit, which ended when the raiders darted across the Rio Grande and took legal sanctuary in Mexico. His only knowledge of the Indians and their ways came in the course of routine patrols and scouting missions, which taught him only that they were "bloodthirsty savages." It was no concern of Sheridan and his brother officers that the tribes had suffered the domination of the Spanish, then the Americans, and might be prejudiced against both types of conquest. Such thoughts would have been unsoldierly, and Sheridan's unconventionality never led him to that extreme.[3]

Even his forays across the Rio Grande among the Mexican maidens, formal and respectable as they undoubtedly were, could not be considered unmilitary, although they probably did not meet with the favor of the ladies of Fort Duncan, who usually had unmarried sisters or cousins visiting them in hope of attracting a husband. The gala nights across the border were the brightest memories of his first tour of duty. Under auspices of the Mexican commandant at Piedras Negras, dances were held frequently during the winter; the host provided the dance floor and girls drummed up among "the élite of Piedras Negras," while the American officers brought over the music and the refreshments. The "greatest decorum" was maintained at the dances, Sheridan recalled. The spectacle of American officers and the señoritas waltzing over the dirt floor of the Mexican commandant's quarters—the Americans, after all, provided the music—was so incongruous it remained in Sheridan's memory long afterward. He had not learned to dance himself, but was delighted to watch the others, shyly lingering in the shadows of the long room. That Sheridan remembered the Mexicans with gratitude for their "graceful manners and their humility before the Cross" was to have important consequences in the liberation of Mexico a score of years later.[4]

That winter Sheridan was promoted from apprentice to journeyman status in the Indian-fighting army. He was elevated, if only slightly, from brevet second lieutenant to second lieutenant and was transferred from the 1st to the 4th Infantry and from Texas to the Pacific Northwest. First, however, he was ordered to report at Bedloe's Island[5] in New York Harbor and take charge of 300 recruits waiting for transportation to their regiments on the West Coast. They were an unruly lot, needing not only discipline but an officer who would show some concern for their welfare. Sheridan provided both the firm hand and the attention to their need of adequate food, clothing and shelter, bringing order to a battalion on the verge of mutiny.

By boat Lieutenant Sheridan and the replacements traveled to Colon and, after an overland journey to Panama City, continued by Pacific steamer to Benicia Barracks, the Army's main depot north of San Francisco. Although Benicia was the headquarters of his new regiment, Sheridan was allowed to linger there just long enough to gather an impression of the low state of morale. Because of the gold hunters still feverishly active, prices were so high that army officers were forced to take up side lines to support themselves. His West Point friends, Lieutenants George Crook and John B. Hood, who had preceded him to service with the 4th Infantry, planted wheat crops on leased land as a profitable and necessary supplement to their army pay.[6] Excessive drinking was another condition of service on the Pacific frontier. George Crook had been shocked shortly after his arrival at Benicia Barracks when one of the senior officers of the regiment, Major Albert S. Miller, died of alcoholism. Major Day, Miller's West Point classmate, commanded the funeral escort. He assembled the post's officers in the room where his old friend's body lay and, to Crook's avowed "horror," announced, "Well, fellows, Old Miller is dead and he can't drink, so let us all take a drink."[7] Not long before, a Captain U. S. Grant had left the service and gone home in disgrace because he could not control his drinking.

Sheridan was ordered to catch up with the Williamson expedition, with which Hood and Crook were serving on escort and quartermaster duty, respectively. Sheridan was to replace Hood in command of 40 dragoons, Hood having been transferred to service with the elite 2nd Cavalry in Texas.[8] The expedition, led by Lieutenant R. S. Williamson, a topographical engineer, was making surveys to determine the practicability of building a railroad to connect the Sacramento Valley with the Columbia River region—

a project given great impetus by the discovery of gold in Oregon Territory.

The territorial governor had entered into a treaty with the Walla Walla and Umatilla Indians for 20,000 square miles of land larded with gold deposits. Without waiting for the treaty to be ratified by the Federal government the prospectors poured into the country and began gouging ore out of the streams and gullies. The Columbia River tribes naturally became hostile: they had not yet been paid for the ceded land, and the mining operations were ruining their rivers, killing the fish on which they largely depended for food.

Lieutenant Sheridan soon learned that it was hostile country indeed. He proceeded from Benicia Barracks to Fort Reading, where the commanding officer suggested that he wait until an adequate escort was available to accompany him on the trail of the surveying party. Eager to take over his command—those 40 dragoons meant more to him than a whole army corps later—he disregarded the garrison commander's advice and insisted on setting out at once, although only a corporal and two troopers could be spared to go with him.

Some of his enthusiasm evaporated when he found the country to be "wild and uninhabited" and "infested by the Pit River Indians, known to be hostile to white people." By traveling fast and light he hoped to catch up with the Williamson expedition in a few days, as he and his escort were mounted and the surveying party was on foot. Hastening northward over the badlands of the Lava Beds, they soon found they were following a double trail: a band of Pit River Indians was following the Williamson party. Sheridan's worries were further increased when they came across a soldier who had fallen ill and been left behind by the Williamson expedition to die or crawl back to Fort Reading. Sheridan, showing his usual concern for the man in the ranks—and more humanity than the leaders of the expedition who had left the soldier to the mercies of the wilderness and the Indians—detached one of his escort to stay with the stricken dragoon. With the other two he pushed on. In Hat Creek Valley Sheridan and his companions managed to circle the band of 30 Indians on Williamson's trail and reach the expedition without firing a shot. "Probably the only thing that saved us," Sheridan believed, "was [the Indians'] ignorance of our being in their rear."[9]

Later Sheridan held a reunion with George Crook, who was off on another surveying mission while Sheridan commanded the dragoons escorting Williamson's main column. Sheridan followed the trail of his old friend's party and, unexpected and unannounced, dropped in on Crook just before dusk. "We had a grand time together," Crook wrote in his diary after Sheridan left to rejoin Williamson.[10]

In October 1855 the expedition arrived in Portland without having had any serious trouble with the Indians.

But there was trouble in the making. Later that month the Yakima Indian War broke out when the Yakima killed their agent and repulsed a punitive expedition sent against them, causing a number of casualties and capturing two mountain howitzers. Sheridan and his dragoons were ordered to join a second expeditionary force under command of Major Gabriel Rains of the 4th Infantry; it was composed of Regular Army troops from that military district and a regiment of Oregon mounted volunteers.

Under unhappy auspices the force set out on October 30. There was bickering over whether Major Rains, Regular or no, had the authority over the leader of the Oregon Volunteers, who was a militia colonel. Moreover, the Regulars were hardly convinced that Rains was fit to command them: he was given to blustering, and "there was a general belief in his incompetency" among both professional and amateur soldiers, according to Sheridan. The fact that he was a South Carolinian did not endear him to Sheridan.

Actually Rains had little taste for Indian fighting, was something of a visionary in military science and was obsessed with the idea that new forms of explosives—booby traps and land mines, as we now know them, "land torpedoes" or "subterra shells," as he called them—would assume a dominating role in warfare of the future. He had experimented with the use of booby traps in 1840 while fighting the Seminole and must have given even those wily swamp warriors a new respect for the floundering Federal forces. It would be a half-dozen years before Major Rains was allowed to put his theories into practice, and then, as usual with such innovations, he would be denounced and scorned.[11]

On the second day of the advance toward the Yakima Valley, Sheridan and his dragoons caught up with a small band of Yakima, sent them flying and seized most of their winter food supply—dried salmon, huckleberries and roots packed in sacks woven from grass. A few days later there was a more serious alarm. While commanding the advance guard of Major Rains's column in the lower Yakima Valley, Sheridan approached the lair of the rebellious tribesmen. He and his troopers became separated from the main body and were alarmed when clouds of alkali dust indicated that the Indians had cut them off. "There seemed no alternative left us," Sheridan said, "but to get back to our friends by charging through these Indians." Sabers raised, the dragoons charged with desperate fury until "we discovered that we were driving into Rains's camp a squadron of . . . Oregon volunteers that we had mistaken for Indians." The incident resulted in a "hearty laugh" all around, but it probably did nothing to ease the strained relations between Regulars and volunteers.[12]

Throughout the frontier days there was much bitterness between Regular Army troops and volunteers. The Regulars believed the volunteers were a pack of cowards and blowhards; the volunteers resented the Regulars' snobbish professionalism, their mysterious pride in their miserable vocation and, above all, their habit of "living off the country" or plain chicken stealing. It could not be said that all Regular officers were models of soldierly deportment. George Crook, for instance, recorded with disgust the conduct of Henry Judah, captain in the 4th Infantry, an 1843 West Point graduate. On returning from an expedition after Indian raiders Captain Judah was "so drunk that he had to be lifted from his horse"; his rear guard also had acquired whisky and "were all drunk and scattered for at least ten miles back," and the next day Judah was "sick all day with delirium tremens." On another occasion the same officer put himself on sick report and ordered Crook and an-

other lieutenant to charge the crest of a slope swarming with Indians. He rescinded the order only after his subordinates threatened
to prefer charges against him.[13]

Almost as tragicomic was a captain of Oregon volunteers who
was a sober version of Captain Judah. This Captain Bowie would
wave his sword and bawl out to his sneering horsemen, "Tenshun
the company!" and be answered with shouts of "Go to hell!" and
"Hold it, Cap, until I go to the rear." Of his company Crook commented that "a motlier crew has never been seen since old Falstaff's
time." His description of Captain Bowie mounting his horse is a
minor masterpiece: "Attempting to mount, his foot slipped out of
the stirrup and his chin struck the pommel of the saddle and his
corporosity shook like a bag of jelly."[14]

Experience with such Falstaffian types on the frontier made Regular Army officers exceedingly skeptical about the volunteers who
swelled the Union armies during the Civil War. Eventually, however, the bitterness of the conflict brought out the best in the volunteers—in most cases—and the professionals were so thinned out that
quarreling about Regular Army "trade-unionism" was confined to
the higher levels of command where political generals and West
Pointers inevitably clashed.

The Yakima Valley campaign turned into a bitter but unbloody
farce. As Rains's column advanced up the valley one day it encountered a large band of belligerent Yakima. The Indians, with
the sort of luring tactics used whenever they encountered the
United States Army, succeeded in provoking a pursuit. Sheridan's
force crossed the Yakima River after them, and the moment it attempted to negotiate the steep bank on the other side the Indians
began their attack. Sheridan and his men dismounted, fired one
heavy volley at the attackers. The Yakima prudently retired to a
high ridge at their rear, made insulting gestures and attempted to
provoke a foolhardy attack up the steep slope. They wore war
paint and bonnets; "a scene of picturesque barbarism, fascinating
but repulsive," Sheridan recorded.[15]

For several days the column engaged in a futile pursuit of the
Yakima. Sheridan and most of his fellow officers were disgusted
with what they termed "extreme caution" on the part of their com-

mander. Finally, however, Major Rains allowed Sheridan and his dragoons to proceed up a canyon leading to the Indians' rear while the main force launched a frontal attack in the hope of trapping them. But the wary Yakima eluded both forces.

Over high snowbound passes shrieking with the first winter winds, the expedition returned to its base in a mood for recriminations. They came soon enough. Captain E. O. C. Ord, 3rd Artillery, preferred charges of incompetence against Major Rains. The infantryman retaliated by accusing Ord of having purloined a pair of shoes belonging to a mission priest. Young Sheridan viewed the bickering of his superior with appropriate distaste and welcomed orders to take his dragoons to Fort Vancouver for the winter.[16]

On the threshold of spring 1856 a much bloodier war broke out east of the Cascade Mountains. A confederation of the tribes of that area was formed, having been encouraged by the failure of the two expeditions sent out against the Yakima the previous autumn. The Walla Walla, Spokane, Umatilla and Nez Percés went on the warpath in Oregon and Washington and simultaneously attacked white settlements from Vancouver to The Dalles, killing men, women and children and capturing the strategic portages at the Lower Cascades of the Columbia River. They also threatened the blockhouse at the Middle Cascades—where many settlers had fled for refuge—by appearing in force and almost surrounding it.

Sheridan's dragoons and other companies of the 4th Infantry were transported by river boats from Vancouver to The Dalles, which was to be the army's base for the campaign against the warring confederation. From The Dalles, on March 27, 1856, Sheridan, his dragoons and one small cannon—hitherto used for firing salutes—were dispatched on the steamboat *Belle* to the Middle Cascades with orders to relieve the virtual state of siege. His first independent command, his first real chance to distinguish himself where it counted—in combat—thus came to Sheridan shortly after his twenty-fifth birthday. A supporting column was to proceed toward the besieged blockhouse by land, but until it joined Sheridan's command the young second lieutenant was in charge of operations.[17]

Sheridan disembarked his force at the Lower Cascades, keeping a Hudson's Bay bateau for possible amphibious maneuvers, and sent the steamboat back to Vancouver to gather volunteers for reinforcement. In the aggressive manner which characterized him from young lieutenant to lieutenant general, he pushed forward without waiting for support. The Indians, he found, were between him and the blockhouse and were too numerous to be attacked with any great hope of success. So he decided to move his command to the opposite side of the Cascades in the bateau, which held twenty men. The movement was accomplished with ease just below Bradfort's Island.

Then came a hitch in his plan. It was found that the bateau could not be moved along the south shore of the river, the rapids being too difficult to negotiate. He asked for ten volunteers to help him haul the boat to the island and work it along the shore where the waters were shallower and calmer. All his men volunteered at once. Some of them had resented his replacement of Hood, who then and until his last tragic campaign in Tennessee was as popular with the ranks as Sheridan, but they had come to respect him and realize that he was the sort of officer who sees his men fed and sheltered before he looks after his own needs. Sheridan took his choice of volunteers, while the balance of his command proceeded along the south shore of the river to a point closer to the blockhouse.

On Bradfort's Island, while working the bateau through the eddying waters, Sheridan and his men came upon a camp of old squaws who had been left there for safety while the braves participated in horse races across the river. Without undue chivalry Sheridan pressed the squaws into service on his hauling ropes; they "worked well under compulsion and manifested no disposition to strike for higher wages," he reported with heavy irony. With the squaws' help he brought the bateau into position to transport his entire force to the beleaguered blockhouse. While the Yakima and their allies were still betting on the races he was joined by Lieutenant Colonel Edward J. Steptoe's supporting column, and the remainder of the 4th Infantry, under Colonel Wright, was not far behind.

In short order Sheridan pushed forward a skirmish line supported by his howitzer, and rounded up the Cascade tribe which lived in the vicinity and was accused of having perpetrated many outrages against the local settlers. The other tribes were dispersed, and the blockhouse was relieved by other elements of the 4th Infantry. Meanwhile, Sheridan held a drumhead court for the Cascade tribe. He found 13 of the braves with muskets which had been fired recently—as he determined by testing the barrels with his finger tip and finding traces of burned powder in their muzzles. It was not the sort of criminology which would be acceptable to a modern court, but it was deemed more than fair in dealing with discontented Indians. Nine of the 13 thus convicted were sentenced and hanged a few days later on orders of Colonel Wright, and the other four were imprisoned.[18]

More than a year later a general order signed by General-in-Chief Winfield Scott commended the senior officers of the 4th Infantry for breaking up the tribal confederation east of the Cascade Mountains. One line in the order read: "Second Lieutenant Philip H. Sheridan, 4th Infantry, is specially mentioned for his gallantry."[19] It was the first of a lifetime of honors.

The years from then until the outbreak of the Civil War passed in comparative peace and order for Phil Sheridan. He had gained the respect of the officers of his regiment, and his personality had apparently become more congenial. In April 1856 he and his dragoons were assigned to duty at the Grande Ronde reservation in Yamhill County, Oregon. His mission was to induce the Indians to abandon their nomadic life and barbaric customs and settle down to farming and other peaceful pursuits. Rather touchingly eager to succeed as a missionary, he studied the Chinook language and was soon able to speak it. But he found an obstinate element among the Chinook, the Rogue River band, which was bitterly determined to continue its ancient ways. The customs attending illness and death particularly repelled Sheridan, the military missionary. If a member of the band fell ill, the witch doctor who "cured" him walked off with all his patient's property, but if the patient died, his family was justified in killing the doctor. At the climax of their funerals the Indians often destroyed their household utensils, tepees and clothing and killed their horses on the grave of the departed tribesman, believing they should undergo "the deepest privation in the property sense" while mourning for their dead.

Sheridan's stern measures to end these barbaric customs incited the Rogue River band to rebellion. It was put down with sterner measures, ending with sixteen male tribesmen being fastened with balls and chain and "made to work at the post until their rebellious spirit was broken." This treatment was justified by the results, Sheridan believed. "When I saw them, fifteen years later, transformed into industrious and substantial farmers, with neat houses, fine cattle, wagons and horses, carrying their grain, eggs, and butter to market and bringing home flour, coffee, sugar, and calico in return, I found abundant confirmation of my early opinion that the most effectual measures for lifting them from a state of barbarism would be a practical supervision at the outset, coupled with a firm control and mild discipline."[20] Whatever the salubrious effects of ball-and-chain discipline on the Chinook, Sheridan was to find a half-dozen years later that the Plains Indians were unwilling to submit to the same sort of "practical supervision." His experience on the Grande Ronde reservation was not particularly helpful in dealing with the Sioux and the Cheyenne and their greater powers of resistance, their greater determination not to give up the freedom of a nomadic life.

News that the North and South had gone to war hardly came as a surprise to Sheridan, for the eventuality had been discussed in army circles for years. Even before the shelling of Fort Sumter, Sheridan was alert for any trickery on the part of Southern-sympathizing officers. He took command of the Yamhill army post and would not relinquish it when Captain James J. Archer, a Marylander, arrived to take over, because "I had been notified that he intended to go South and his conduct was such after reaching the post that I would not turn over the command to him for fear he might commit some rebellious act."[21] Sheridan's suspicions were well founded, for Archer soon departed for the Confederate Army and took command of a regiment in the Texas Brigade led by Sheridan's classmate John B. Hood.[22]

News from the fighting fronts reached Oregon in greatly exaggerated and alarming versions. Most of the time Sheridan and his fellow officers were in "the depths of ignorance as to the true condition of affairs." The first reports of the battle of Bull Run stated that 40,000 men on each side were killed and wounded. As the Federal military establishment expanded in succeeding months Sheridan was promoted to captain and anxiously awaited orders to proceed east on active service. It was a hope deferred until September 1861. Meanwhile, he prided himself that "my patriotism was untainted by politics" and that his unalloyed devotion to the Union had not been "disturbed by any discussion of the questions out of which the war grew." To him the "preservation of the Union" was the sole issue, and the vital question of slavery did not concern him.[23] In his single-minded concern for the Union he was joined by most of his compatriots, for emancipation in 1861 was something that aroused the sympathies of only the Abolitionists.

It was a lighthearted Captain Philip H. Sheridan who, in obedience to orders from the War Department, set out for duty at the St. Louis headquarters of the Union armies of the West—set out, in fact, on his journey to greatness.

3

DESK CAPTAIN TO CAVALRY COLONEL

OF ALL the military men who rose from obscurity in the Civil War, none traveled so far and so fast, with the handicap of a rather late start, as Phil Sheridan. Luck is conceded to be an ingredient in successful generalship as in any other professional career, but Sheridan was considered the luckiest of all the Civil War commanders, mostly because he rose to the first rank in his early thirties while men of equal accomplishment—Grant, Sherman, Thomas, Lee and Jackson—were all considerably older. His contemporaries reasoned luck *must* have been responsible, plus the patronage of Grant, Sherman, Halleck and other seniors who liked or respected him.

Sheridan himself did not agree with this view. He wrote, "It has been said that I was 'lucky' in the success that attended me. . . . I believe there was no general officer in the service who was subjected to harder tests. I was not only changed from one arm of the service to another, but was constantly being changed from one line of operations to another, each involving new geographical and topographical study, the necessity of overcoming the local prejudices of soldiers of different armies, and the old and bitter prejudices between infantry and cavalry."[1] The record of his first year in the armies of the West supported this contention, for he was shifted rapidly from staff officer to quartermaster to cavalry commander to command of an infantry division in less than twelve months.

He came east from the Oregon frontier with little apparent hope of performing great deeds and winning high honors. Just before leaving Oregon he had written a friend in Ohio, "Who knows?

Perhaps I may have a chance to earn a major's commission."[2] There was good reason, aside from modesty, for him to doubt that he would rise to high command. He was thirty years old, an infantry captain of only a few months' standing, and had no friends in Congress or the War Department or even in the top commands of the Union Army. Grant, Sherman and Thomas—all of whom were immediately given colonel's eagles and regimental commands with the outbreak of war—already had started their climb to greatness. Sherman had commanded an army in Kentucky, Grant had won the battles of Donelson and Shiloh, Thomas had gained a victory at Mill Springs and was rising in favor by the time Sheridan was fairly established as an energetic staff officer, an expert at requisitioning fodder, at sending wagon trains forward and keeping his accounts straight—a military bookkeeper, in essence.

Eager to catch up with classmates already colonels, Sheridan hurried east to his new post. Technically he was a captain in the 13th Infantry, a new regiment created by President Lincoln in the swift expansion of the Regular Army and nominally commanded by William T. Sherman, who actually led a division in Grant's Army of the Tennessee. Sheridan's orders, however, were to report at the St. Louis headquarters of General Henry W. Halleck, commanding general of the Armies of the Tennessee, the Ohio and the Mississippi, far from the camps of the 13th Infantry. When he arrived in New York City after the steamer journey from California he paused there only long enough to "replenish a most meagre wardrobe."[3] En route to St. Louis he stopped in Somerset for his first visit with his family in almost a decade—and stayed only 20 hours. Neighbors crowded into the Sheridan home to talk with the professional soldier about how the war was going—it was going badly then, with the memory of First Bull Run still vivid—and whether the North would ever be able to put down Secession and restore the Union. A neighboring farmer, Henry Zortman, asked Captain Sheridan if it was not possible that the Confederacy, with the assistance of a sympathetic Europe, might now destroy the Federal government. Sheridan replied simply and firmly, "This government is too great and good to be destroyed."[4]

Not all Union officers were so unshaken in their faith in ultimate victory. In the Eastern theater prospects were brighter with Major General George B. McClellan reorganizing and revitalizing the Army of the Potomac. But the important border states of Kentucky and Missouri—which Lincoln rightly believed must be kept in the Union—were being endangered not only by the Confederate Army of the Tennessee under General Albert Sidney Johnston but also by a struggle for supreme Northern authority between Major Generals Don Carlos Buell and Henry W. Halleck. Halleck soon won out. Johnston was threatening to advance in Kentucky, or so Buell believed, with resultant danger to the Ohio River line and its booming cities. Meanwhile, Sterling Price was gathering forces in southern Missouri and northern Arkansas for an offensive aimed at the recapture of St. Louis. Perhaps the most hopeful aspects of the Western situation were that the Union armies were becoming stronger daily at a rate which could not be matched by the Confederacy, and growing fleets of gunboats were bringing the vital rivers under Union control.

The man to whom Sheridan reported in St. Louis, General Halleck—"Old Brains," as he was known in the Old Army—has been vigorously denounced by most historians, but he rendered one service to the Union for which he has not been properly credited: he gave Sheridan his chance to prove himself. Halleck was a middle-aged man with owlish eyes, a prissy and hesitant manner and a habit of rubbing his elbows when perplexed that greatly annoyed his associates. Although yearning for authority, he shied away from responsibility in tight spots. The intellect which enabled him to write and translate a number of military textbooks failed to propel him to aggressive action when it became necessary; the pedant almost always triumphed over the soldier in him.

On arrival at St. Louis Sheridan found himself in command of a desk rather than a company of infantry. Halleck needed an officer familiar with Regular Army procedure to deal with the confused accounts left by his flamboyant predecessor, Major General John C. Frémont. There were millions of dollars in outstanding claims against army headquarters, not all of them legitimate, for Frémont had dispensed Federal war contracts with a lavish hand.

Sheridan was appointed president of a board auditing Frémont's expenditures and passing on claims against the army.

For almost two months Sheridan and his board struggled with Frémont's eccentric accounting. He kept his patience in trying circumstances, although it might be expected that a man of his active disposition would resent such dreary chores. To him the duty was "not distasteful" because he had just finished dealing with similar paper work at the Yamhill garrison and, after all, he had been a competent bookkeeper before he ever wore the uniform.[5] He performed his tasks so well that General Halleck marked him down as a most promising officer.

On December 27, 1861, he was transferred to the staff of Major General Samuel R. Curtis, commanding the Army of the Southwest, which was preparing to drive the Confederates out of southern Missouri and come to grips with Sterling Price once and for all. First appointed chief commissary of the army, Captain Sheridan did not hesitate to point out to General Halleck that he ought to be made chief quartermaster as well. He argued that the Army of the Southwest would have to live off the country as much as possible while it moved southward. It would be better if one man controlled the transport of rations as well as their collection and distribution. General Halleck finally yielded to his arguments, and Sheridan proceeded to General Curtis' headquarters at Rolla, the army's railhead.

A fellow staff officer thought Sheridan a "modest quiet little man," but "nobody could deny the vitalizing energy and masterly force of his presence when he had occasion to exert himself. Enlisted men on the staff at headquarters remember him kindly. Not a clerk or orderly but treasures some act of kindness done by Captain Sheridan." His years on the frontier, away from feminine society for the most part, made him "bashful, especially in the presence of the gentler sex." His fellow officer recalled that, while engaged in forwarding supplies from Rolla, Sheridan became attracted to a young lady of Springfield but was too shy to show her any personal attentions. He detailed "a gay young clerk named Eddy" to take her riding, using a carriage and horses furnished by himself. "Courting by proxy seemed to please him as much as if it had been done by himself," his colleague observed. "We never learned the result of the arrangement but we think it most probable that Eddy carried off the prize."[6]

Sheridan found the logistical situation of the newly reorganized army in an unholy mess and his new subordinates an amazing collection of double-dealers, boodlers, intriguers and grafters. He plunged into the job of straightening out the supply system with little regard for the conspiracies around Curtis' headquarters. The distribution of wagons among the various regiments, he found, was awkward and inequitable. Some regiments had 40 to 50 wagons in their trains, others only three or four. Amid the howls of choleric colonels and outraged brigadiers he quickly arranged a more sensible distribution. Colonel G. M. Dodge of the 4th Iowa Infantry "greatly sustained me with General Curtis," he remembered with gratitude; it was the beginning of a long friendship, for Dodge became a great builder of Western railroads while Sheridan's cavalry fought off the Indians for his construction gangs.[7]

Sheridan's name was first mentioned in Civil War dispatches when Curtis reported to Halleck on the difficulty of supplying his army with "the country . . . a . . . wilderness, every road a defile" and warned that "supply arrangements must be extensive." Sheridan, Curtis added, "will be able to report more accurately his power to supply in the course of today."[8] Sixteen days later a new problem had arisen when the Pacific Railroad reported itself in financial difficulty and feared its unpaid employees would go on strike. Halleck telegraphed field headquarters at Rolla that he was forwarding $10,000 to Sheridan—"all we can rake and scrape together"—to meet the railroad pay roll.[9] But labor trouble was one of Sheridan's lesser problems.

When the army advanced against Price and his Confederates, shortly before Grant's Army of the Tennessee was transported down the Tennessee River to Pittsburg Landing in a parallel movement, Sheridan performed his duties with a vigor seldom exhibited by quartermasters so early in the war. Most of his assistants and associates were businessmen, bankers, merchants—and not a few grifters with a keen sense of opportunity. They looked on with awe and dismay as the young Regular Army captain set about keeping the men supplied under adverse conditions—poor communications, rough country, inhabitants reluctant to give up their produce. Curtis moved on Lebanon, then Springfield, with Sheridan collecting cattle and grain in the countryside and keeping them flowing to the marching regiments. General Curtis, who had no great appreciation for Sheridan's accomplishments and tended, in fact, to depreciate them, had an obsession about salt. He believed that the Confederacy would collapse for lack of it, and ordered Sheridan to be very quick about seizing all available salt when the army moved into Springfield. Price evacuated the city without a fight, and Sheridan ironically noted that "about all he left behind was salt."[10]

While Curtis pushed on after Price, Sheridan was left in Springfield to sweat over the army's logistics. A corps of mechanics, millwrights and millers was recruited from the ranks and employed in operating the abandoned gristmills in the vicinity. Other detachments confiscated cattle and kept them moving to the front in vast herds. The army lacked for nothing essential. And on March 6, 1862, it ended its campaign with a decisive victory at Pea Ridge, Arkansas. A good share of the credit belonged to Sheridan for keeping it rolling, well supplied, through a country unsympathetic to the Union and lean in farm produce.

His service with the Army of the Southwest was drawing to its acrimonious end, but he managed to render one more service to his rather ungrateful commander. General Curtis' leading subordinate, General Franz Sigel, a notably inefficient officer, was determined to make off with the major share of the credit for Pea Ridge. Sheridan already had formed a poor opinion of Sigel, who refused to furnish work details from his command and so led Colonel Dodge to turn over the entire 4th Iowa to Sheridan to run the mills and gather forage.

Sheridan was in charge of the military telegraph at Springfield when the dispatches about the victory at Pea Ridge began to come in. Sigel's arrived by special messenger to be relayed north by telegraph before Curtis'. They claimed, of course, all the credit. But, according to Colonel Dodge, Sheridan "was soldier enough to know it was General Curtis who had fought this battle and won it, so he held up Sigel's dispatches until dispatches came from Curtis. Sheridan then sent Curtis' dispatches out first, manifesting soldierly qualities after the treatment he had received."[11]

This rather gratuitous loyalty to Curtis did not protect Sheridan from the intrigues fomenting against him at army headquarters.

The situation reached a crisis when Sheridan discovered that some of his officers were, literally, horse thieves. In their excursions to requisition supplies they stole horses from the farmers and then sold them to the army. Sheridan immediately declared the horses captured property, had them branded "US" and refused to pay out any more money. The assistant quartermaster set up a clamor that reached Curtis' ears. The general ordered Captain Sheridan to pay the claims, and Sheridan answered with a blunt refusal and a request to be relieved of his duties.

Long after the war Sheridan, a good hater, still burned with resentment over his treatment in the Army of the Southwest. The leading member of the anti-Sheridan clique had been an unsuccessful banker from Iowa. Sheridan, through all the momentous events of his postwar life, watched the Iowan's career with keen interest. He was not much surprised when his old enemy, after assuming the presidency of a Chicago bank that subsequently failed, became a United States Treasury clerk and finally was sentenced to a Federal penitentiary for embezzlement.[12]

Sheridan returned to St. Louis to find Halleck immersed in the details of moving Major General John Pope's Army of the Mississippi down that river, the Army of the Tennessee out of its bridgehead at Pittsburg Landing and Buell's Army of the Ohio from Nashville to join General Grant on the Tennessee. Thus preoccupied, Halleck had little time to find suitable employment for his semiprotégé; the best he could do was to send Captain Sheridan on a horse-buying mission to Wisconsin.

In Chicago, on his way back to St. Louis, Sheridan heard the news from Shiloh Meeting House. The first dispatches indicated that Grant and the Army of the Tennessee had won an overwhelming victory. Then rumors of a terrible reverse rolled up like thunderclaps from the battlefield—Albert Sidney Johnston had struck

Grant before Buell and the Army of the Ohio could join him. Grant's divisions, improperly disposed and with virtually no field fortifications, had been caved in, and thousands of men had fled to hide under the mustard-colored bluffs at Pittsburg Landing.

Sheridan hastened to St. Louis, hoping for a combat assignment. By the time he reached army headquarters more of the truth of Shiloh had become known. Grant had indeed been driven back and many of his regiments had become demoralized, but he had held onto the Landing until the end of the day, April 6, when Buell's advance guard arrived to reinforce him. Albert Sidney Johnston had been killed, and his successor, P. G. T. Beauregard, slowly withdrew when he saw there was no longer a chance of annihilating Grant.

Convinced that Grant had failed him, Halleck had hurried to Pittsburg Landing, bemoaning the 10,000 Union casualties (about equal to the Confederacy's) and intimating that Grant had botched his assignment by not intrenching in the presence of an active enemy. Halleck himself took command of the combined advance on Beauregard's base at Corinth and swung three armies, under Pope, Buell and Thomas, into elephantine progress southward. Thomas had replaced Grant as commander of the Army of the Tennessee. Grant, once observed weeping in his tent, had been relegated to the whipping-boy post of Halleck's second-in-command. Meanwhile, Sheridan persuaded Halleck's rear-echelon staff at St. Louis that he should be sent to the front. But his struggle for field duty was not over yet. Halleck, who could think of him only as an able staff officer, assigned him to supervise the corduroying of swamp roads and keep the railroad and wagon trains rolling down to the armies.

But Sheridan had acquired influential allies in his campaign to get away from morning returns, requisition papers and bills of lading. General William T. Sherman, whom Sheridan had admired as a West Pointer calling on his sweetheart in Somerset, recommended that he be given command of one of the Ohio volunteer regiments. In those days it was still up to the governor of each state to appoint such officers. The governor of Ohio turned down Sherman's suggestion. Then General Gordon Granger, a boisterous man with a piratical black beard, whose unbuttoned manner hardly suggested his West Point background, took up Sheridan's case with the governor of Michigan. He requested that his junior be given command of the 2nd Michigan Cavalry, now vacant because of Granger's promotion to brigadier. A young captain of the same regiment with considerable political influence—Russell A. Alger, Secretary of War during the Spanish-American War—added his recommendation to Granger's, and Michigan yielded where Ohio would not. Sheridan jumped from Regular Army captain to volunteer colonel overnight. But there was a last-minute catch: General Halleck, hating to lose a good staff officer and bearing in mind the Regular Army's current reluctance to give up any more of its own to the volunteer regiments, hesitated to ask for War Department approval of the transfer. On May 27, 1862, Sheridan showed General Halleck an order from Governor Blair of Michigan which formally gave him command of the 2nd Michigan Cavalry, and Halleck then threw up his hands, released Sheridan on his own responsibility and wished him well.[13]

Sheridan wanted action, and he found it in large helpings. In the next 35 days he would lead his regiment in a half-dozen skirmishes, several reconnaissances in force and one full-scale battle.

The very night of his appointment to regimental command his troops were going into action as part of a cavalry brigade commanded by Colonel Washington L. Elliott. They had been ordered to conduct a raid south of the Confederate base at Corinth and strike at Beauregard's rail connections, particularly Booneville, Mississippi, 22 miles to the south. Booneville was on the Mobile & Ohio Railroad, the main supply line for the enemy army.

Sheridan hastened to his regiment's headquarters at Farmington, arriving at 8:00 P.M. to find the column already forming under its field officers. With only a small haversack containing coffee, sugar, bacon and hardtack to sustain him on the march, he rode to its head and assumed command. The circuitous route took the brigade on a swing east of Corinth through Iuka and against only scattered resistance, quickly dispelled. Sheridan's regiment and the 2nd Iowa Cavalry occupied Booneville May 29, burned 26 railroad cars and destroyed stretches of track by tearing up rails, building fires of wooden ties under them and twisting them into fantastic and use-less shapes.

While engaged in breaking up the railroad south of town his regiment was attacked by Confederate cavalry squadrons, but man-aged to drive them off easily. Trains from Corinth began piling up at Booneville with significant cargo—wounded and convalescent soldiers from Beauregard's forces, plus the personal baggage of one of his chief lieutenants, Lieutenant General Leonidas Polk. These were unmistakable signs that Beauregard was evacuating Corinth, which indeed was occupied the next day by the Union armies with-out Halleck's once coming to grips with his elusive enemy. Later, in his report to division headquarters, Colonel Sheridan told of cap-turing 500 Confederates retreating along the railroad tracks, but "I turned them loose after breaking up their guns, as we could not be burdened with them in our rapid return to . . . camp."[14]

The cavalry brigade rejoined the Union forces at Corinth after having covered 180 miles in four days, to find that the Confederate base had been emptied of troops, supplies, civilian population and rolling stock. The only interruption to Beauregard's masterly with-drawal had been the raid on Booneville the very day he was pulling out.

Ten days after the occupation of Corinth, Colonel Sheridan led a strong reconnaissance on the heels of the retreating enemy. From Baldwin, Mississippi, on June 9 he reported that Beauregard was heading for Tupelo and applying the scorched-earth policy as he went. The devastated country between Baldwin and Guntown, five miles to the south, showed him how Southern chivalry could crack under the strain of necessity. "The enemy drive away and carry off everything for miles around; many families, even those the wealthiest, are destitute and starving. . . . The cavalry passed many fine houses . . . where the women and children were crying for food. . . ."[15]

On his return to camp two days later Sheridan found himself a brigade commander—just two weeks after he had been appointed colonel of the 2nd Michigan Cavalry. He was not yet a brigadier, but his friends and admirers were working on that, citing his ex-cellent work in leading the regiment on almost daily forays, his ability to ferret out information from hostile residents and evasive prisoners, and his own cool observations in the shock of skirmishing with the enemy cavalry. Colonel Elliott was promoted to brigadier and appointed chief of staff of the Army of the Mississippi. Sheridan's brigade consisted of the 2nd Michigan and the 2nd Iowa Cavalry.[16] In the next few weeks he labored to bring it to a higher degree of combat efficiency, seeing to it that his troops received better food and clothing, healthier campsites and tighter discipline to "allay former irritation." He formulated his credo for the field officer:

Men who march, scout, and fight, and suffer all the hardships that fall to the lot of soldiers in the field, in order to do vigorous work must have the best bodily sustenance, and every comfort that can be provided. I knew from practical experience on the frontier that my efforts in this direction would not only be appreciated, but requited by personal affection and gratitude; and, further, that such exertions would bring the best results to me. Whenever my authority would permit I saved my command from needless sacrifices and unnecessary toil; therefore, when hard or daring work was to be done I expected the heartiest response, and always got it. Soldiers are averse to seeing their comrades killed without compensating results, and none realize more quickly than they the blundering that often takes place on the field of battle. They want some tangible indemnity for the loss of life, and as victory is an offset the value of which is manifest, it not only makes them content to shed their blood, but also furnishes evidence of capacity in those who command them. My regiment had lost very few men since coming under my command, but it seemed, in the eyes of all who belonged to it, that casualties to the enemy and some slight successes for us had repaid every sacrifice, and in consequence I had gained not only their confidence as soldiers, but also their esteem and love as men, and to a degree far beyond what I then realized.[17]

The proof of his methods was soon forthcoming.

Late in June the brigade was ordered to garrison Booneville, well in advance of the main Federal lines, to facilitate its mission as a strong outpost and penetrate deeply into Confederate territory to obtain information on Beauregard's intentions. Remembering the lesson of Shiloh, where Grant had been in a similarly exposed position but had done far too little to protect himself, Colonel Sheridan immediately started in to learn the terrain around Booneville thoroughly. He drew accurate maps of the vicinity for himself and his regimental commanders. He took every precaution against being caught off guard by the enemy, sending out strong patrols constantly and establishing around his camp and the town a picket line whose alertness he guaranteed by incessant tours of inspection. "In such a region," he noted, "there were many chances of our being surprised, especially by an enemy who knew the country well, and whose ranks were filled with local guides."[18]

High recompense—and a whole Confederate cavalry division—were on their way to repay Sheridan for his diligent cultivation of the faith of his troops and his care in preparing against surprise.

It was early morning, July 1, 1862.

On two roads converging near Booneville, Confederate General James R. Chalmers and 5,000 to 6,000 troopers[19] were on the march from the southwest to wipe out Sheridan's annoying outpost.

To defend Booneville Sheridan had exactly 827 men in his two regiments.

The first clash took place three and a half miles from Booneville, where his pickets began firing on Chalmers' advance guard.[20] They fell back slowly, fighting dismounted, delaying the enemy as much as possible with a series of skirmishes before reaching Sheridan's thinned-out defense lines. Most Federal cavalry commanders of that time would have used their horses—either to mount a glorious and utterly stupid charge or, more likely in the adverse circumstances, to ride away as rapidly as possible—but Sheridan was resolved to meet Chalmers dismounted. The heavily wooded terrain gave Sheridan considerable advantage on the defense; his flanks were covered by swampland, channeling the Confederates' attack to a narrow front and nullifying some of their numerical edge. Even more important, most of his troopers were armed with Colt revolving rifles and pistols. Each could fire six rounds rapidly— which gave every man 12 shots before reloading. The enemy knew neither the size of his command nor the fact that it was so well armed. Numerically Sheridan faced odds of 5,000-plus to 827, but 827 men with that sort of fire power were not badly outmatched.[21]

Suddenly Captain Archibald P. Campbell's 2nd Michigan was attacked over an open field by a heavy skirmish line of Confederates. Well posted in a thicket, with many of the troopers in rifle pits or behind breastworks, the regiment held its fire until the range was only 25 yards, then opened up with a terrific volley. The frontal attack failed, but Chalmers kept assaulting the position with everything he had. Often, Sheridan reported, his men used bayonets to repel the enemy.

By noon the Rebel pressure all along his front—and the fact that Chalmers had started a flanking movement toward Sheridan's camp on the north side of Booneville—impelled the Union commander to take desperate measures before he was overwhelmed. His knowledge of every feature of the terrain, of every woodland trail, again came to his rescue. His last and best hope, he believed, was to send a mounted force against Chalmers' rear which would create a diversion and attack simultaneously with the rest of his troops. Dividing his command in that critical hour was bold, if not reckless, but there was no alternative except a rapid retreat—and that was unthinkable. So he directed Captain Alger—the same man who had sponsored him for regimental command with the governor of Michigan—to take a battalion—four saber companies but amounting to only 90 men—ride around the Confederates along a forest trail connecting with the Blackland Road and strike hard in Chalmers' rear. Alger's mounted force was to create as much noise and confusion as possible so that the 2nd Iowa and 2nd Michigan might time their attacks to coincide, with the Iowans hitting Chalmers' left flank and the Michigan regiment charging straight ahead. He instructed Alger in no circumstances to deploy the battalion but to "charge *in column* right through whatever you come upon, and report to me in front of Booneville, if at all possible for you to get there."[22]

Meanwhile, it would be up to the rest of the brigade to hold out until Alger drove through his attack. Despite the incessant onsets of a courageous and wildly yelling enemy, the morale of the troops was excellent. Dr. William Brownell, the assistant surgeon of the 2nd Michigan, testified later that "every man seemed to know his strength and to take pride in using it to the fullest extent. When a charge was made by the enemy, instead of taking to their horses, which were kept under cover a few rods to the rear, they emptied their rifles of six shots at long range, then drew their revolvers, and before they had given them six more the enemy never failed to turn to the rear in confusion."[23] While waiting for the signal to launch the counterattack Colonel Sheridan saw his chance to hearten the men further. A train of forage came up from Corinth, and he ordered it to approach the Booneville station with its whistle blowing for all it was worth. His own troops, hoping for the best, believed reinforcements had arrived from the Union infantry division stationed at Rienzi; the enemy, fearing the worst, believed the same thing.

Still, it was a nerve-racking hour for the Union commander. "All along our attenuated line the fighting was now sharp," he said, "and the enemy's firing indicated such numerical strength that fear of disaster to Alger increased my anxiety terribly as the time set for his cheering arrived and no sound of it was heard."[24]

Although Sheridan failed to hear the noise of Alger's attack over the roar of the battle he ordered the remainder of his forces forward in an all-out attack, reserves included. Fortunately Alger's battalion struck the Confederate rear at almost exactly the same time, shooting up headquarters and creating a panic among the troops. The Southerners believed they had been surrounded by superior forces and, with one impulse, made off for the road to Blackland. General Chalmers was convinced by the fire power confronting him at the outset that he was facing at least a Federal division. The Confederate retreat became a panic as the Northerners hit front, rear and left flank. Chalmers was forced to abandon his dead and wounded, much greater in number than the 90-odd casualties suffered by the Union brigade.

In two hours that afternoon, according to the telegraphic dispatches sent by Sheridan to Rienzi, his mood lifted from alarm to elation and his calculations from a stand-or-die defense to pursuit of the enemy. At three o'clock he telegraphed General Asboth: "I have been holding a large force of the enemy—prisoners say ten regiments—all day, and am considerably cut up. I want Mizner's two battalions and artillery and infantry supports. . . . I am holding my camp."[25] And at five o'clock he wired: "I will not want any infantry supports; I have whipped the enemy today . . . it will be well to let me have a battery of artillery. I might then be able to follow up the enemy."[26] Sheridan ordered a pursuit toward Blackland, but did not feel strong enough to attack on ground of Chalmers' choosing.

The wires between the various headquarters—division to army to army group to War Department, Washington—were soon clattering with praise of Sheridan. The day after the battle of Booneville Major General William S. Rosecrans, who had replaced Pope in command of the Army of the Mississippi when that victim of vainglory went east to deal with Lee and Jackson, telegraphed General Halleck, "Sheridan ought to be made a brigadier. He would not be a stampeding general."[27] Simultaneously Rosecrans issued General Order No. 81, with instructions that it be read to every unit of the army, praising the "coolness, determination and fearless gallantry" of Colonel Sheridan, his officers and men at Booneville.[28] On July 5 General Granger added his praise, singling out for mention "the excellent management of the troops by Colonel Sheridan."[29]

Somewhat resentfully Sheridan found himself ordered to retire to the main Federal line and post his brigade around the town of Rienzi, the division's headquarters. He had one good reason for remembering Rienzi with gratitude. It was there that Colonel Campbell of the 2nd Michigan presented him with a big black gelding which the donor regarded as vicious and unmanageable. He was a three-year-old, "jet black, excepting three white feet, sixteen hands high, and strongly built, with great powers of endurance. He was so active that he could cover with ease five miles an hour at his natural walking gait."[30] Sheridan named him "Rienzi"—and he became one of the most celebrated of war horses, endowed with almost as much fame as his master in Thomas Buchanan Read's poem "Sheridan's Ride."

What irritated Sheridan most about the retrograde move to

Rienzi was that it subjected him to his division commander's "interference," a not uncommon complaint among rising and ambitious young officers eager for independent command. He often "wished the distance between our camps was greater," because General Granger had an "uncontrollable propensity to interfere with and direct the minor matters relating to the command. . . . Ill-judged meddling in this respect often led to differences between us." Sheridan complained that he not only had to yield repeatedly to Granger's judgment but "many a time [I] had to play peace-maker—smoothing down ruffled feelings, that I knew had been excited by Granger's freaky and spasmodic efforts to correct personally some trifling fault that ought to have been left to a regimental or company commander to remedy." But Sheridan, who remained his personal friend until death, did not hesitate to admit that Granger was "so full of generous impulses and good motives as to far outbalance his short-comings."[31] However irksome he found his superior, he could not forget that it was Granger's recommendation that helped him to transfer from staff to line—and besides the association was not destined to last very long.

July 30, 1862, was a fateful day for Sheridan's military career. That day a petition was signed by General Rosecrans and four of his leading subordinates, Generals Gordon Granger, C. C. Sullivan, W. L. Elliott and A. Asboth, and telegraphed from army headquarters to General Halleck, now installed as general-in-chief at Washington. It read:

BRIGADIERS SCARCE. GOOD ONES SCARCER. . . . UNDERSIGNED RESPECTFULLY BEG THAT YOU WILL OBTAIN THE PROMOTION OF SHERIDAN. HE IS WORTH HIS WEIGHT IN GOLD.

Halleck was too busy with the gruesome details of Second Bull Run to give attention to a request from his Western command, even one that gratified him so much—there would be time later for bestowing a young colonel's first star.

The same day occurred an event of much greater importance in the long run. Sheridan had just returned from a long scouting expedition on the track of the Confederate army, now commanded by Braxton Bragg, who was restive and preparing for new efforts to drive out the invaders from the North. It was to General U. S. Grant, recently restored to command of the Army of the Tennessee, that Sheridan brought his information. As Grant briefly noted, "On the 30th I learned from Colonel P. H. Sheridan, who had been far to the south, that Bragg in person was at Rome, Georgia, with his troops moving by rail to Chattanooga and his wagon train marching overland to join him at Rome."[32]

It was the first indication of Bragg's coming invasion of Kentucky. More important, it was Grant's first and entirely favorable impression of the soldier he was to raise to the highest commands and eventually rate above all others in the Civil War on both sides of the battle lines.

4

THE JEALOUS GENERALS

ALL the hopes of the spring of 1862 that the Southern Confederacy could be defeated and broken up by campaigns in Virginia, with Richmond the target, and in the West, with Nashville, Memphis, the fortified islands in the Mississippi and control of the Tennessee and Cumberland rivers deep into Confederate territory firmly in hand—all those fine hopes and careful plans had withered by the end of summer. Wasted opportunities, vain sacrifices, useless bloodshed—they were the rewards, and the North was sick with war-weariness. East and west, the Union's generals had won battles and lost campaigns. Their soldiers died as willingly as men will ever die, but the generals could not see beyond the edges of their tactical maps. Meanwhile, a struggle for power was going on: Radical Republicans striving to make a puppet of President Lincoln, generals scheming for the supreme command, war governors clamoring for a larger share of authority, war contractors scrambling for profits.

In the Eastern theater General McClellan had maneuvered the Army of the Potomac up the Virginia Peninsula to the gates of Richmond, settled down slowly to regroup after being forced to retreat to the James, then had most of his army hastily reorganized under John Pope and thrown into the calamity of Second Bull Run. As summer waned Lee prepared to invade the North through Maryland. Pope was sacked, and McClellan was reinstated as commander of the Eastern army.

The situation west of the Alleghenies was equally discouraging. Halleck had missed the opportunity offered by hard-won victories at Forts Donelson and Henry, at Mill Springs and Shiloh. With the

Confederates retreating after each defeat he failed to pursue, bring them to battle quickly and destroy the army successively commanded by Johnston, Beauregard and Bragg. Instead, his three armies virtually tunneled their way to Corinth, then allowed the enemy army to withdraw almost unmolested to another base at Tupelo. In his new position in Washington as general in chief he committed more and bigger blunders. Buell's Army of the Ohio was ordered to move on Chattanooga and Knoxville, not swiftly and forcefully to snatch victory before the Confederates could organize a defense, but slowly and deliberately, repairing the Memphis & Charleston Railroad as it proceeded. Grant's Army of the Tennessee was flung out in garrisons and rail-guard details.

Bragg made the most of his chance to strike while the Union armies of the West were aimlessly scattered. Moving north with 35,000 men, he formed one prong of the offensive while General E. Kirby Smith's 12,000 troops advanced on a parallel route from Knoxville through the Cumberland Gap. In central Kentucky they were to join forces for operations against Louisville and, if all went well, against Cincinnati, across the Ohio River.

Thus, early in September the Union high command was confronted with a crisis on two fronts. Lee was on the march for Pennsylvania barns bursting with the harvest—a march and countermarch that were to culminate in the Battle of Antietam. While the reinstated McClellan moved to parry this Eastern thrust General Buell began gathering up his scattered divisions and racing northward to interpose his army between the enemy and Louisville. All over the Western theater troops were being collected and sent to the threatened city; there was considerable danger, considering his head start, that Bragg might win the foot race against Buell. Citizens drilled in the streets of Cincinnati; alarm was turning into panic in southern Indiana and Ohio. On September 6 Sheridan was notified that he should conduct five regiments to Louisville: the 2nd Michigan Cavalry from his own brigade, plus four of infantry: the 2nd and 15th Missouri, the 36th and 44th Illinois.

At Corinth he paused to arrange for their transportation and became involved in a seriocomic little drama with General Grant.

Colonel Sheridan was stalking up and down the platform and

sidings at the Corinth railroad station that hot, dusty September afternoon. Loading trains with horses, troops, artillery and enough supplies to see them through their journey is always an arduous task. Tempers flare, horses suddenly become balky, men turn surly and unco-operative; even inanimate objects seem to assume an obstreperous personality of their own. Sheridan prodded his subordinates to hurry the process along; Louisville might even now be within reaching distance of the Confederate columns, with their curious ability to move over the country like phantom hordes. There was glory to be won to the north; none in this sad and conquered part of northern Mississippi. To the north there was the imminence of action; here there was garrison soldiering, with an occasional long, exhausting, not particularly fruitful reconnaissance. Sheridan was impatient to be on his way, and his temper crackled around the balky regiments like a blue spark of electricity leaping from pole to pole.

In that vexing hour General Grant, mild and rather diffident as always, rode up to the station and wistfully watched some of his best regiments being transferred out of his theater. Grant was "much hurt at the inconsiderate way in which his command was being depleted," Sheridan observed.

And in the midst of those milling troops and horses Grant's jaundiced eye beheld Colonel Sheridan. "What's this, Sheridan?" he asked in amazement. "Are you going to Kentucky, too?"

"Yes, General," Sheridan replied curtly. "I've been ordered to take these regiments to General Buell."

General Grant was plainly annoyed by Sheridan's attitude. The young cavalryman, Grant felt, should have shown some sign of reluctance to leave the forces headquartered at Corinth. Hadn't Grant praised his work? Hadn't he singled out Sheridan as one of the best of the younger officers? He had regarded Sheridan almost as his protégé, his discovery. Now it seemed Sheridan was just another curt, ungrateful young man intent only on increasing his fame—and undoubtedly his rank.

"I had not expected to see you go, Sheridan," his senior remarked. "There will be active campaigning here soon, and I'd have much use to make of your ability."

Sheridan turned to him impatiently. "I'll be more useful in Kentucky, sir. That's where the fighting is going to be. Naturally I want to be there. And besides, that's how my orders read."

Sheridan had hopes of being given a division at Louisville, and the thought that this scrubby little Grant—still under a cloud because of the way his army had been taken by surprise at Shiloh—might snatch away the opportunity by countermanding his orders made him speak as sharply as was advisable in the presence of a superior.

Even with the passage of the years that scene at Corinth between two men destined to rise to greatness together still rankled. "I felt a little nettled at his desire to get away and did not detain him" was Grant's stiff reference to it long after.[1] And Sheridan admitted, "I did not wish him to retain me, which he might have done, and I impressed him with my conviction, somewhat emphatically, I fear."[2]

Sheridan and his five regiments arrived at Louisville on September 13 to find the city in the midst of panicky preparations for the first glimpse of the lean, long-striding legions of General Bragg. Rumors of how Bragg was outwitting, outmarching and outfighting Buell on the roads up from the Tennessee border contributed to the atmosphere of alarm. Southern sympathizers began to smirk. Families of the Northern persuasion departed for Indianapolis, Chicago—anywhere across the Ohio.

At dusk on the afternoon of Shiloh the Army of the Ohio's leading divisions had marched off the boats with such imposing confidence that soldiers of the battered Army of the Tennessee cried, "Here come the Regulars!" That confidence was gone now. Perhaps part of it had evaporated because of what Colonel John Beatty, an observant Ohioan, called Buell's "dancing master policy," which the sardonic colonel expressed as, "By your leave, sir, we will have a fight; that is, if you are sufficiently fortified; no hurry; take your own time."[3] The Army of the Ohio had yet to fight a pitched battle involving more than a division. If the city of Louisville was beginning to doubt that it was capable of warding off Bragg, the army also was wondering whether it had been organized only to march and lay railroad tracks and countermarch and look pretty on parade.

Like all the Civil War armies, it was harassed by politics—only a little more so, being closer to the governors who had raised its regiments, particularly the domineering Governor Oliver P. Morton of Indiana. This sort of apron-string influence was soon to have tragic consequences.

Many of the army's senior officers were morning-glory types who made splendid impressions at recruiting rallies, parades and reviews long before they heard a shot fired in earnest. They were the sort that were commissioned at the outbreak of the war through political influence or their own persuasive personalities or impressive European military backgrounds; the sort that abounded in all the armies until the rigors and tests of combat shook them out like clinkers from a grate.

Buell, like his good friend McClellan, proved a better organizer and administrator than a battle captain. Perhaps he had more substance than that "dancing master" epithet would indicate, but there was too much of the office general about him, too much of the "red-tapist," as War Correspondent William F. G. Shanks of the New York *Herald* characterized him. Shanks gave another insight into Buell's character, perhaps, when he reported that the general was overconscious of his small size and liked to show guests how strong he was by lifting his 140-pound wife, holding her at arm's length, then hoisting her to a perch on the mantelpiece. Still, history must credit him with imparting a discipline and a technical efficiency to the army—such as in infantry tactics and the skillful employment of artillery—that were rarely found in the Western forces until the end of the war.

Buell's leading subordinates included some very colorful and curious characters. There was the eccentric Brigadier General Albin Francisco Schoepf, a flamboyant Hungarian who had served in the Austrian army as an officer, then in the Hungarian rebel forces in the uprising of 1848. Another brigadier, the Russian-born John B. Turchin, had been in the Czar's army when it suppressed that same rebellion and then in the Crimean War. Just before

Bragg chased the army north Turchin was charged with permitting his brigade to steal $100,000 worth of watches, plate and jewelry while garrisoning northern Alabama; a court-martial absolved him of personal blame, and he was later allowed to return to active service. And there was Brigadier O. M. Mitchel, who somehow made the remarkable transition from astronomer to general—and not the worst of the assortment by any means.

The corps commanders were an odd lot, too. Major General Alexander McDowell McCook, I Corps, a thirty-one-year-old West Pointer, was described by Shanks as "an overgrown schoolboy"; he was allowed to function disastrously through three major battles in his rollicking way before he was removed to less responsible duties. Major General Thomas L. Crittenden, II Corps, was dignified enough and well liked by his troops, but Shanks compared his talents to those of a "country lawyer," and he had little to recommend him except fanatical devotion to the Union—all the more fanatical, perhaps, because his brother was Major General George B. Crittenden of the Confederate Army.

C. C. Gilbert, commanding III Corps, was certainly the most inexplicable of the lot—an infantry captain who in the space of a few weeks managed to talk himself into command of a corps. While Buell was bringing his troops up from the south, General Wright, at Cincinnati, was in charge of the department embracing both that city and Louisville. He issued a general order appointing "Captain C. C. Gilbert, 1st Infantry, United States Army, a major general of volunteers and commander of the Army of Kentucky." The Army of Kentucky was the short-lived combination of forces being sent from all over the West to Louisville for its defense. Gilbert held that ephemeral command only a few days before General William Nelson took charge. Although he had already been appointed a major general, Gilbert was then given the rank of brigadier general of volunteers by President Lincoln, subject to confirmation by Congress—and that was only the beginning of the confusion caused by Gilbert and his grandiose ambitions. He was cordially detested by his fellow officers. Correspondent Shanks described him as a "martinet of the worst sort."

Shortly after his arrival at Louisville Sheridan was informed by

General Nelson that his appointment as brigadier general had been confirmed, dating from July 1, 1862, the date of the battle of Booneville. He rushed out immediately, he admitted later, to find the pair of stars for his shoulder straps. And he lost no time in requesting that his command match his rank. On September 25 General Buell reached Louisville with the first of his footsore infantry divisions, the rest being brought north under General Thomas, his second-in-command. Sheridan had already made the acquaintance of General Gilbert and knew he was going to demand a corps. He hurried to Colonel James B. Fry, Buell's chief of staff, and declared that he had superior claim to higher rank by virtue of the date of his commission and his service in the field. "While not questioning Buell's good intentions nor his pure motives, [I] insisted that my rights in the matter be recognized."[4] It may be seen that false modesty was never one of Sheridan's vices. But Buell, in announcing the reorganization of the army on September 29, appointed Gilbert to command of the III Corps, and Sheridan was ordered to serve under him as commander of the newly formed Eleventh Division.

Brigadier Sheridan could not be entirely disappointed with his progress; it was less than a year since he had arrived from the Far West as an infantry captain, and already he was commanding three brigades and two batteries of light field artillery. Included in his command were the 35th Brigade, made up of the 44th Illinois, the 73rd Illinois, and the 2nd and 15th Missouri; the 36th Brigade, consisting of the 85th, 86th and 125th Illinois and the 52nd Ohio; the 37th Brigade, comprising the 36th and 88th Illinois, the 21st Michigan and the 24th Wisconsin; Battery I, 2nd Illinois Artillery, and Battery G, 1st Missouri Artillery.

The army was already in a state of shock from its series of reverses, but another blow was struck at its morale the evening of September 29, just after Buell announced his plans for reorganization. Two of its leading generals and Governor Morton of Indiana involved themselves in a melodrama more appropriate to a frontier saloon than to the high councils of an army approaching battle.

The principals, besides Governor Morton, were Major General Nelson and Brigadier General Jefferson C. Davis. Nelson, who had the nickname "Bull" and lived up to it with his 300 solid pounds, his roaring voice and his frequent rages, had been a Navy lieutenant before the war. Then, being a Kentuckian and a strong Unionist, he transferred to the volunteer forces being formed underground by direction of President Lincoln. He drilled the first companies of what became the Army of the Ohio and led the first division to reach Shiloh and go into the line beside Grant's troops. General Davis, who was regarded as a slightly satanic fellow, possibly because of his name (he was no relation to the Confederate President), had fought as a noncommissioned officer in the Mexican War, stayed in the Regular Army and been commissioned from the ranks. He was a lieutenant with the forces at Fort Sumter when it was bombarded, and later had risen rapidly to divisional command because of the patronage of Governor Morton.

The situation was this: Governor Morton, a fiery and fanatic believer in the Union cause, had dispatched a number of untried Indiana regiments to Kentucky as soon as Bragg's invasion was under way. Several of these, under Nelson's command, had been smashed at Richmond when they were driven in by Kirby Smith's advancing columns, and at Munfordville two weeks later four Indiana regiments had been trapped in the Union fort and captured en masse. So Morton came to Louisville to demand of Buell better handling of the regiments for which he was answerable to the people of his state. With him he brought Davis, who had recently been sent north with an official rebuke from General Nelson.

To meet these two angry gentlemen General Buell selected the worst possible emissary—General Nelson. The three men, stiff-legged and bristling, sat down and snarled at one another across a table in a private dining room of the Galt House. As the scene was reconstructed later by Colonel Fry, Buell's chief of staff, Davis flicked a card in Nelson's face; Nelson called Davis an "insolent puppy" and slapped him, then stalked majestically out of the room. Davis borrowed a pistol, pursued Nelson into the corridor, called out his name and fired point-blank. Nelson's huge frame went crashing down, and a moment later he said to the proprietor of the Galt House, "Send for a clergyman; I want to be baptized. I have been basely murdered."[5] A short time later he died.

That night his troops rioted in the streets of Louisville, demanding vengeance for their general. By Buell's orders General Davis was placed in arrest. "Nothing but the law of violence could, under any circumstances, justify the manner of the killing for the alleged provocation," Buell said.[6] Despite his recommendation that Davis be tried by a military court for murder, the charges were eventually dropped—the restraining hand of Governor Morton may be discerned there—and Davis was restored to duty as a division commander in the army. Civil charges against him also evaporated in the passage of time.[7]

Almost simultaneously another shock hit the army's leadership. A War Department courier brought an order directing General George H. Thomas to supersede Buell at once. While the courier was on his way the order was countermanded, but Thomas turned down the promotion without knowing it had been canceled. Even though Buell was retained in command, it shook the confidence of his generals, and Buell's faith in himself, to know he had almost been removed.

Meanwhile, Bragg and Smith had brought their invading columns together at Frankfort. Strangely they dawdled there over the feckless business of installing a Confederate "governor" of Kentucky and thereby lost the opportunity of advancing on Louisville before Buell had drawn his army together. Smith had thrown Cincinnati into a panic by appearing on the southern bank of the Ohio, but he withdrew to unit with Bragg. Already the Confederate leaders were experiencing disappointment: Kentuckians were generally reluctant to contribute their produce and horses to the Southern army and were even less eager to take up the 20,000 rifles Bragg had brought along for the expected recruits. The two generals decided to pull out before Buell could cut off their retreat.

This was exactly what Buell had decided to do. He sent the Army of the Ohio marching in three columns toward Perryville, and they arrived in that vicinity the evening of October 7. Near by, along the heights bordering the Chaplin River, four Confederate divisions already were ranged with the mission of holding the roads open for the balance of their army. Neither side wished to bring on a general engagement. General Buell repeatedly cautioned his corps commanders against risking a battle. He believed that he was confronted by the entire Confederate army, and that ground more favorable for engaging it could be found elsewhere. The Confederates, entertaining their own misapprehension, thought they were facing the Union advance guard but still refrained from taking the offensive because their mission was solely concerned with keeping the path southward open.

The necessity of obtaining water for the men and horses of both sides actually brought the opposing forces to the point of contact. "During the night it was ascertained that there were some pools of water in the bed of Doctor's Fork . . . of which the enemy's rear-guard held possession," Buell explained.[8] He ordered Sheridan's Eleventh Division to attack at "day dawn" and obtain control of Doctor's Creek, a tributary of Chaplin River, for the Union army.

That night Sheridan wandered among the camps of the army, wearied by its long forced march from Louisville. At one of the campfires he came across an old enemy, William R. Terrill, former cadet sergeant at West Point, now—despite his Virginia birth—a brigadier general in the Union Army. They stared at each other across the fire for a moment, then mutually declared the old grievance forgotten. Before parting they shook hands again and wished each other well.[9] Later that night Colonel Charles Denby of the 42nd Indiana overheard the conversation of General Terrill, General James Jackson and Colonel Webster as they sat around the dying embers—a somber moment with two armies stirring restlessly under the autumn moonlight. The three men talked of their chances of being hit the next day, or whenever the battle was fought. They agreed that it was unlikely, considering the thousands of men involved and the proportionately small number of casualties to be expected. The next day all three were killed.[10] Afterward Sheridan always congratulated himself on having instinctively reached for Terrill's hand and made up their old and adolescent quarrel.

At daylight Sheridan sent Colonel Daniel McCook, his brigade and a battery of artillery across Doctor's Creek, which was "done very handsomely after a sharp skirmish. . . ."[11] Sheridan went forward with the assault brigade. It was well that he was a troop leader who believed in leading his men rather than directing them from a position in the rear, for after crossing the creek he found "we could not hold the ground unless we carried and occupied a range of hills, called Chaplin Heights"[12] a few miles northwest of Perryville. The effect of this attack was to draw considerable attention from the Confederates, who were worried by the prospect of being driven away from the roads they needed to make good their retreat.

The alarm at III Corps headquarters was as great as among the Confederate generals. While Sheridan quickly and energetically studded Chaplin Heights with rifle pits and sighted his artillery to hold them, General Gilbert sent message after message to caution his division commander against bringing on a general engagement contrary to General Buell's orders. Both Gilbert and Buell, as was later testified, stayed in the rear areas and had little idea of what was developing on their front. (Buell was incapacitated by illness; Gilbert, perhaps, by his congenital incompetence.) Sheridan "replied to each message that I was not bringing on an engagement, but that the enemy evidently intended to do so, and that I believed I should shortly be attacked."[13]

Two hours after Sheridan carried Chaplin Heights by assault the Confederates counterattacked in considerable force to drive Sheridan's division back across Doctor's Creek. He ordered Colonel Laiboldt's brigade and Hescock's battery forward to thwart the counterstroke, and they succeeded after a "stubborn contest." The next enemy thrust was directed at McCook's Corps, which was posted on Sheridan's left, Gilbert's Corps being the army's center, Crittenden's its right flank. Three enemy divisions hit McCook, and it was obvious in a matter of minutes that he would not be able to hold his position and that the Confederates would then attempt to roll up the Union line.[14]

Sheridan, in the forefront of the battle, dashing from regiment to regiment, placing his batteries in the exact position he desired, directed an enfilading fire from Hescock's battery which caught the Confederate skirmish lines in the flank and left the gray-clad infantrymen sprawled in death or injury on the thicketed slopes. "The enemy attacked me fiercely, advancing with great determina-

tion almost to my very line . . . notwithstanding a heavy fire of
canister from both of my batteries." Only Sheridan's grim defense
of Chaplin Heights prevented the four enemy divisions from smashing the Union army. Crittenden's Corps never fired a shot while
the other two corps were desperately engaged.[15]

Five assaults swept up against Sheridan and his intrenched infantry, but he held the position and saved the army.

By four o'clock that afternoon the battle had ended with about
5,000 casualties on each side and the Confederates slowly withdrawing to the south. Despite the bitterness of the fighting for
Chaplin Heights, the Eleventh Division had suffered only 350 casualties, 44 killed, 292 wounded, 14 missing.[16] The next day Sheridan pressed forward cautiously and reported to II Corps headquarters: "I have possession of the ridge occupied by the enemy. They
have moved off, citizens say, on three roads, one of them toward
Danville, the others southeast. . . ."[17] He was still adept at gathering information.

Whatever Sheridan's opinion of his immediate superior, General
Gilbert had only praise for his division commander. "He held the
key of our position with tenacity and used the point to its utmost
advantage. I commend him to notice as an officer of much gallantry and of high professional ability." The soldiers of the Eleventh Division were more succinct. They boasted of Sheridan as a
"fighting general" who "cared more for victory than he did for
bullets."[18]

The Army of the Ohio settled down for a period of recrimina-
tion, courts-martial and courts of inquiry. From the commanding
general on down, officers were called up to explain their actions or
lack of action. Behind all this was the unstated question: why did
four enemy divisions almost overwhelm the whole Union army?
It was Correspondent Shanks's opinion that jealousy among the
higher officers was largely responsible: McCook was too jealous of
Gilbert to ask for reinforcements when he was virtually overcome,
and Gilbert "looked upon his [McCook's] defeat with positive
pleasure." Colonel John Beatty was even blunter when he wrote
in his diary, "May it not be true that this butchery of men has re-

sulted from the petty jealousies existing between the commanders of different army corps and divisions?"[19]

The testimony before Buell's court of inquiry—he was acquitted of any wrongdoing but was subsequently relieved of his command—had moments of insight into the mood and character of some leading figures.

There was, for instance, the testimony of Brigadier General R. B. Mitchell, commanding the Ninth Division, which was on Sheridan's right during the battle of Perryville. "I never saw anything of General Gilbert from the time the fight commenced till 3 o'clock the next morning," he said. Members of Gilbert's staff would give him an order, but "when I talked to General Gilbert he denied authorizing such an order." He quoted Gilbert as saying to him, "You may think it strange that I was not in the front, but I remained in the rear for the purpose of supporting you." And General Mitchell bitterly concluded, "I had lost all confidence in General Gilbert. I did not know whether he was captain or general. I only knew him from the fact that he wore two stars."[20]

Phil Sheridan, who kept his own counsel and envied no man, became known in the newspapers as "the paladin of Perryville." To be thus recognized by the journalists was the first mark of military fame. He was accorded also the dubious honor of being reported by the newspapers as killed in action, but he "was pleased to notice, when the papers reached us a few days later, that the error had been corrected before my obituary could be written."[21]

Sheridan had time to think over two indelible lessons of Perryville—a commander should be close enough to the front to grasp the situation immediately and act quickly; and vigorous attacks by an enemy may actually be concealing inferiority.

5

DEATH IN THE ROUND FOREST

AFTER less than a year's service in the armies of the West, Brigadier General Philip Sheridan was regarded in the autumn of 1862 as one of the most promising of the Union's division commanders as well as the youngest. His appearance was not imposing: five feet five inches of height, rather short legs and disproportionately long arms, almost Mongolian eyes. He had his hair clipped short—in that day of flowing locks and romantic manes—because it had a tendency to curl and he had an aversion to curly hair. Often his uniforms looked as though they had been slept in, and often they had. Occasionally he smoked cigars, but he preferred a little curved meerschaum, yellow with seasoning, which he had smoked since his cadet days. He was brusque toward senior officers and more democratic than most West Pointers toward subordinates, or so the volunteers observed with approval. Clearly his promise was implicit in his combat record rather than in any ability to play the courtier or cut a dashing figure.

More important than uniformed elegance or polished manners, however, were the confidence of his superiors and the respect of his officers and troops. Sheridan really worked at his job, constantly roaming through the camps of his regiments, poking into quartermasters' accounts (in bitter remembrance of the Pea Ridge campaign), inspecting the sanitary facilities and company kitchens, questioning his men about their rations in such a democratic fashion that they sometimes offered him a chew of tobacco. He was always noting the topography of the countryside as they moved through it, orienting himself every night before he felt easy enough to settle down in his tent.

His greatest concern was with matters of intelligence. At that time, of course, there was no such service attached to the army; knowledge of the enemy, his strength, movements and intentions came from the army's own scouts and from the unreliable reports of countrypeople who claimed to be Union sympathizers but who might have been carefully coached in their revelations by the other side. So Sheridan went searching around as his own G-2. "No man ever had such a faculty of finding things out as Sheridan," General Grant subsequently said of him. "He was always the best informed man in the command as to the enemy."

Sheridan was also highly interested in any prisoner captured by his division. One Confederate remarked after an exhaustive interview with the brigadier, "That there man, he'll talk the eyes right out of your head."

A fire-eater in battle, he was a quiet, almost reticent man in camp. Only when he sat at a campfire with old friends of his service in the Northwest did he become animated and even a little boisterous. Often in recalling some incident they would lapse into Chinook, mystifying companions who had not served in Oregon.

An Illinois private, Henry A. Castle, remembered General Sheridan as one of the few on whose shoulders the silver stars of rank rested lightly. Shortly after his regiment joined the army Castle's colonel ordered him to find the divisional quartermaster and draw the daily ration of fresh beef. Castle rode off to a row of tents pitched in an orchard and found only one man in sight, "a careless but keen-looking little man, about thirty years old, with his pants tucked in his boots, no coat on, a black hat canted on one side of his head and a cigar projecting upwards at an acute angle from his lips." The young private asked the man, who was "sitting on a stump, enjoying the sunset breezes," where the quartermaster's tent was located.

Castle recalled that "my horse nearly ran into him and as he drew back on his feet he said, pleasantly, 'Who the hell are you, anyway?'"

"Oh, I'm a high private of respectable parentage like yourself," Castle replied.

"What do you want?"

"The quartermaster."

"Yes, but what do you want of him?"

Castle explained his mission, and his new acquaintance "proceeded to give me minute instructions." Aware at last that he might have mistaken the other's rank, Castle was about to adopt a more respectful attitude when an officer approached and addressed the little man as "General." Castle then learned that he had been interviewing the commander of his division, and Sheridan "turned to me with a quizzical smile and said he wanted it understood that he was never too busy to give any information he possessed." Castle's regiment, the 73rd Illinois, was known as "the Preachers' Regiment." Its colonel, lieutenant colonel, one major, six captains and several lieutenants were all Methodist ministers. Prayers were said at company roll call every morning and evening, but the prevalent piety did not prevent the regiment from rendering excellent service in battle.[1]

After the battle of Perryville, General Buell had engaged in a pursuit of the retreating Confederates which the War Department considered so dilatory that there was little hope he would develop into an aggressive field general. Just after the Army of the Ohio bogged down at Bowling Green its commander was removed. This was Buell's farewell to active service, although Sheridan believed that his organizing and administrative abilities could have been used to advantage in some other capacity. His successor was Major General William S. Rosecrans, whose command was redesignated the Army of the Cumberland. Under this banner it became one of the Union's three principal armies. General Thomas took command of the center, replacing Gilbert; Crittenden was assigned to the left wing, McCook to the right.[2]

Sheridan's command also underwent reorganization and was designated the Third Division of McCook's wing. McCook's brigade was replaced by Colonel George W. Roberts' from the Nashville garrison, and one of Sheridan's classmates of '53, Joshua W. Sill, took command of the brigade relinquished by Colonel Nicholas Greusel. Sill, whose "modesty and courage" were highly regarded by Sheridan, had requested the transfer. The army as a whole looked favorably on the reorganization, Sheridan said, "for the campaign from Louisville on was looked upon generally as a lamentable failure." Buell's detractors pointed out that "Bragg's retreat . . . so jeopardized the Confederate army, that had a skillful and energetic advance . . . been made, . . . the enemy could have been destroyed before he could quit the State of Kentucky."[3]

The new commanding general came to the army under auspices both favorable and unfavorable. Rosecrans had commanded the Army of the Mississippi briefly after Pope went east and had won the battle of Corinth, October 3-4, 1862. His failure to pursue and destroy the enemy after that battle, however, had earned him the enduring contempt of General Grant. He had an Old Army reputation for brains, but—like another military intellectual, General Halleck—tended to become panicky in the midst of battle. Old Regulars called him "that wily Dutchman," and he had a definite inclination toward playing politics, military and civil. Nor was he immune to the glory fever which infected so many Civil War commanders. Shortly after his arrival at army headquarters he made war correspondents and visiting editors exceedingly welcome and persuaded them to echo his sentiments. His first chief of staff, Colonel Milo Hascall, noted disdainfully that Rosecrans brought along "jobbing presses and other means of reaching the public." Unlike General Buell, who had offered such scant hospitality to Governor Morton of Indiana, Rosecrans warmly welcomed junketing politicians and visiting state officials. "His head seemed to have been completely turned," Hascall said.

There were other unfavorable aspects to Rosecrans' assumption of command. Many of his subordinates believed the post should have gone to Buell's second-in-command, General Thomas, the stanch, slow-moving but sure-footed Virginian who had searched his conscience and sorrowfully turned his back on the claims of his native state. But when President Lincoln, Secretary of War Stanton and General in Chief Halleck discussed the matter of Buell's successor it was pointed out that Thomas had refused the command—the tender of which had been withdrawn, actually, before word of his refusal came—just before the battle of Perryville. With Halleck and Lincoln favoring Rosecrans, Thomas' only advocate at the council was Stanton, who bitterly prophesied, "Well, you have made your choice of idiots! Now you can await the news of a terrible disaster."

With the blessings—in fact, the urgings—of the War Department and the Administration, the Army of the Cumberland left its winter quarters at Nashville and moved in the direction of General Bragg's forces, which were coiled around Murfreesboro in the loop of Stone's River. The chill rainy December of Middle Tennessee did not provide ideal conditions for an offensive campaign, but the Union needed a victory: the Army of the Potomac had almost smashed itself to pieces against Lee's fortifications at Fredericksburg earlier that month, and Great Britain and France again were wondering whether it was not time to recognize and openly support the Southern Confederacy.

On the day after Christmas 1862 the Army of the Cumberland began its long miserable march on Murfreesboro. Meanwhile, the Confederates were snug and unsuspecting in their comfortable winter quarters. Shortly before Christmas, in an atmosphere resembling that of the British officers and their ladies dancing on the eve of Waterloo, the great cavalry raider General John H. Morgan married one of the belles of Murfreesboro. General Bragg was among the wedding guests, and General Polk, the peacetime Episcopal bishop of Louisiana, officiated at the ceremony. That evening Morgan rode off with his men on a raid into Kentucky. "The young officers of our army were all bent on fun and gayety," recalled Colonel David Urquhart, Bragg's chief of staff. "Invitations were out for a ball on the day after Christmas."[4]

On December 30 Rosecrans aligned his divisions along the narrow, winding Stone's River several miles east of Murfreesboro, near where the Nashville Turnpike and the Nashville & Chattanooga railroad bisected it. The western or right bank had been fortified by the Confederates, and Rosecrans assumed that the enemy would stay on the defensive. He deployed his army with Crittenden's divisions on the left, Thomas' in the center, McCook's on the right. His plan was to throw Crittenden's divisions across the river, which was fordable, and attack with all possible energy on the enemy's right. This was to be followed by an assault and a wheel to the right by Thomas and McCook. The sardonic Colonel Hascall commented that Rosecrans' plans "might have worked well enough perhaps—if the enemy had waited for us."

The battle of Stone's River developed on the pattern of First Bull Run, with the opposing commanders deciding on exactly the same tactics (they had, after all, gone to school together and learned the same lessons in Florida and Mexico). Sheridan's later summation was:

From the movements of the enemy at daylight next morning, it was plainly indicated that Bragg had planned to swing his left on our right by an exactly similar manoeuvre, get possession of the railroad and the Nashville pike, and if possible cut us off from our base at Nashville. The conceptions in the minds of the two generals were almost identical; but Bragg took the initiative, beginning his movement about an hour earlier than the time set by Rosecrans, which gained him an immense advantage in execution in the earlier stages of the action.[5]

The right wing of the army had a difficult mission to perform, but, as at Perryville, General McCook was brimming with confidence. Rosecrans asked anxiously if he was sure he could hold his ground for three hours after dawn the next day, December 31, when Crittenden's attack would be well under way and enemy pressure would be removed from Thomas and McCook. McCook was bumptiously positive that he could, although his three divisions—with R. M. Johnson's on the right, Jeff C. Davis' in the center (Davis being out on bail in the General Nelson murder case) and Sheridan's on the left—were spread out over half the Union line. Crittenden had four divisions in his attacking wing, while Thomas also had four in the center.

On the eve of the battle General Johnson, on the far right of the army, extended the line still farther by building a series of campfires a mile long to his right. This attempt at camouflage—excellent for the purpose of concealing the strength of an attacker but dangerous when hiding the frailties of a defender—had only disastrous effects. It persuaded the Confederates to strengthen their own attacking wing and completely skirt the Union line to strike it right and rear where it was most vulnerable.

Sheridan was up and around most of the night of December 30-31, inspecting his brigades, conferring with his chief subordinates and frequently staring intently across the dark valley where the enemy stirred and rustled in the cedar brakes throughout the night. At 2:00 A.M., he later reported, the Confederates showed "great activity" opposite Sill's brigade on the right of his division's sector, only 300 to 400 yards away, so he ordered two regiments from the reserve to reinforce Sill.[6] The men needed their sleep, but Sheridan's intuition—not the least of his military qualities—told him that Rosecrans' cozy plan might be upset and that the Federal right wing would be the logical place to turn the tables.

At 4:00 A.M., long before the chill winter dawn, his division "was assembled under arms and the cannoneers at their pieces."[7] Unfortunately Davis and Johnson did not take the same precautions and were still asleep in their tents. Henry Castle, now a sergeant in the 73rd Illinois, said that "Sheridan came along the line, on foot and unattended. . . . He called for the major, ordered him to arouse his men quietly, have them breakfast and form in line of battle at once. He personally visited each of his twelve regiments and saw that his orders were executed. An hour after daylight the expected attack came on Johnson's division a half mile to our right and found it unprepared. Many of the officers were asleep or at breakfast . . . the division commander was at his tent, half a mile to the rear. . . ."[8]

There was a long, tense wait. Then as a gray light filtered through the trees heavy firing broke out on the Third Division's right and grew louder and closer. The Confederate assault columns under Lieutenant General William J. Hardee, Bragg's best commander, swung wide around the spurious line of campfires and struck Johnson a shattering blow. In less than an hour his division was routed and Davis' was hammered front, rear and around the flanks, disintegrating almost as quickly as Johnson's.

At 7:15 the agonizing wait ended for Sheridan and his men and new, more volatile agonies began. Sheridan stayed with Sill just behind the lines of his infantry and watched the first gray skirmishers flitting through the thickets across a cotton field on their

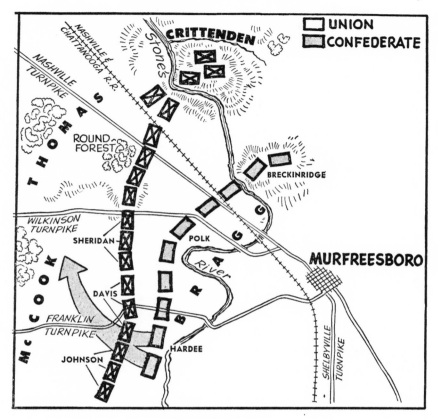

STONE'S RIVER

front. Suddenly Hardee's assault division, Cheatham's, which had tested Sheridan at Perryville and reeled back in defeat, came on[9] with a rush, a howl of triumph and a flutter of red battle flags. Sill's infantry stood their ground with the determination of men who had been all through this before—the shock and terror of the first moments of battle, the first sight of the enemy, the first bullets ripping through branches overhead.

As the masses of enemy infantry appeared in the cotton field Sheridan's three batteries opened on them with "terrible effect"—18 guns pouring an enfilading fire on them as fast as the cannon could be swabbed, loaded and aimed. Sill's infantry held their fire until the enemy came within 50 yards, and the death-dealing shock of that first volley was overwhelming. "The destruction to the enemy's column, which was closed in mass, being several regiments in depth, was terrible," Sheridan said. The Confederates broke and ran for cover.[10] But the repulse of the Rebels had cost the Union heavily, not the least of the losses being the death of General Sill, Sheridan's friend and classmate. With his last breath he ordered his brigade to charge and pursue the enemy.[11] Panicky survivors of Davis' and Johnson's divisions fled through Sheridan's lines, but his men stood firm. Sheridan ordered Sill's brigade and Schaeffer's withdrawn to a new line at right angle to his original position. Meanwhile, Roberts' brigade delivered a counterstroke to allow time for this movement to take place, then fell back to the new line.

Back at army headquarters Rosecrans and his staff refused to believe the heavy firing on the right indicated anything so unthinkable as a break-through. But a rush of fugitives, carrying the news faster than any courier, convinced him that Bragg had indeed struck the first blow. A short time later an adjutant brought word that two divisions had been shattered on the right.

Orders were dispatched to Sheridan to hold the line formed by the Wilkinson Pike and give General Thomas time to swing his divisions around to keep possession of the Nashville Pike and the Nashville & Chattanooga Railroad. Otherwise there was grave danger that the rest of the Federal army would be driven into a loop of Stone's River, surrounded and destroyed. The only hope in the situation depended on Sheridan's gaining time for the Union line to be bent back—"refused," in the language of Civil War dispatches—to face Hardee's attack on its right flank.

At the "bloody angle" Sheridan, endeavoring to carry out Rosecrans' order, was attacked with the full fury of an enemy who saw overwhelming victory within easy grasp. It was "one of the bitterest and most sanguinary contests of the day," he reported. At the edge of the Round Forest Sheridan's brigades made a stand that was equaled a few times but never surpassed, even at Chickamauga,

Cold Harbor or the Peach Orchard at Gettysburg, during four years of war.

A young war correspondent who witnessed that holding action wrote, "The history of the combat of those dark cedars will never be known. No man could see even the whole of his regiment, and no one will ever be able to tell who they were that fought the bravest, or they who proved recreant to their trust. It was left to Sheridan to stay the successful onset of the foe. Never did a man labor more faithfully than he to perform this task."[12]

Three times Cheatham's division swept on against the Union lines, grappled among the cedars for a moment, then receded to re-form for another attack. Opposing artillery dueled at "not over 200 yards," and "there was no sign of faltering with the men, the only cry being for more ammunition," Sheridan said. Colonel Roberts was killed there, the second of his brigade commanders to fall. Private George Daggett recorded that:

A few of the more venturesome Rebels reached a rail fence less than twenty yards from the muzzles of our muskets, but none ever returned. Others paused at a distance of seventy-five to a hundred yards, delivered their fire and dropped to the ground to load and fire again. Others came up in their rear, but no human endurance could withstand the murderous fire poured into them from our well-protected line, reinforced now on the right and left by other troops who had rallied to our assistance. . . . For at least a half an hour this bloody angle at the edge of the cedars was held, and it could have been held indefinitely but for the fact that, the crumbling remnants of the defeated divisions on our right having fallen back into the cedar forest, we were likewise compelled to retreat. . . .[13]

All but two regiments of Schaeffer's brigade had now run out of ammunition. The corps' ammunition train had disappeared in the first assaults of the morning, and it was feared that the Confederates had captured it. Actually it was in the process of being saved by the heroic work of a young ordnance officer, Captain Gates P. Thruston. His men cut a road through the cedars and reached the Nashville Pike just in time to avoid capture and bring the ammunition around to the new Union line at the moment it was most needed.[14]

Sheridan knew his men had to be pulled back or wiped out within a matter of minutes, so he ordered Schaeffer's two regiments into a counterattack that drove Cheatham back and gave the division time to complete an almost successful withdrawal. Eight guns had to be abandoned, but the rest were hauled over the rough floor of the Round Forest. In the execution of the last orders he received from Sheridan, Colonel Schaeffer was killed, the third brigade commander to die within three hours.

Private Castle told how quickly the officers fell—or were promoted—that bloody morning:

I saw a Rebel battery come up. I started promptly for the center of the regiment to notify the major, but heard that he had just been carried off wounded. I then ran to the right to find the adjutant, and learned that he, too, had retired for the same reason. I assumed the responsibility of marching the company double-quick out of the defile, trusting the rest to follow, which they did with alacrity, as just then the shells came shrieking through the straight and narrow gorge with a venom that would have left few unscathed in five minutes more. I then notified the four remaining captains that they were without a commander. Being of equal rank, they sent me to the brigade commander, sitting on his horse 200 yards to the rear, with a request to settle the matter of procedure. I started toward him, but before I had made half the distance he, the last of our brigade commanders, was shot before my eyes and fell to the ground a corpse.[15]

Little wonder that many years later one of General Rosecrans' old staff officers wrote that "since the annihilation of the 'Old Guard' at Waterloo, there has probably not been an instance of so great a slaughter in so short a time as during this repulse of the Rebel left at Murfreesboro."

That retreat through the Round Forest toward the railroad embankment, where Thomas' divisions and the remnants of others were waiting now to bear the full weight of the enemy onset, was conducted with complete order and discipline. Although Sheridan's division had lost one third of its effectives, it was still a fighting force, still ready to face the enemy. With only their naked bayonets they counterattacked when necessary to keep the Confederates off their flanks and rear as they withdrew.[16] Artillerymen hauled their guns through the forest by hand. Walking wounded struggled to keep up with their companies. But all too often a man, crudely bandaged or without any medical treatment at all, would drop by the way, with his comrades promising to send the stretcher-bearers after him as soon as the Southerners had been driven off, or come after him themselves that night. Many seriously wounded were carried off to the main Union lines. It was a ghastly procession of powder-stained, exhausted, bloody-bandaged men; youth made weary and sick in a few hours of killing and maiming in the dark forest.

Yet there was no respite even though they had saved the Army of the Cumberland that morning and suffered losses great enough to ruin the morale of most divisions. The moment they emerged from the Round Forest, at eleven o'clock, General Rosecrans galloped up to Sheridan and ordered him to replenish his cartridge boxes, march one regiment at a time to the rear, then join Thomas' divisions of the center in waiting for the Confederates' new onslaught.[17]

Sheridan's depleted brigades stood on the new defense line behind the railroad embankment, beside the divisions of Palmer and Negley and one brigade of Wood's. Along the line rode General Rosecrans, his reddish face alight with excitement, and General Thomas, "calm, inflexible, from whose gaze skulkers shrank abashed."[18] They complimented Sheridan on his stand of that morning—and forthwith gave him orders to send Colonel Roberts' brigade in a counterattack against Confederate forces endangering the Union army's communications along the Nashville Turnpike. "The brigade," Sheridan said in his report, "having but three or four rounds of ammunition, cheerfully went into action. . . ." It not only drove off the enemy along the road but recaptured two of its guns lost in the Round Forest retreat.[19]

All that afternoon Sheridan's remaining troops stayed behind the embankment and helped Thomas' fresher divisions beat back the relentless but unsuccessful attempts of the Confederates to break through and trap the Union army.

Finally dusk and rain fell, and the fighting died down to sporadic fire fights in the sodden forests. Both armies were badly mauled, glad to lay down their arms while darkness covered them. All through the night thousands of wounded men in blue and gray, lost in the forests and thickets, called out for a stretcher, for water, for death.

New Year's Eve at army headquarters was a despondent affair. Rosecrans, with his predilection for councils of war, especially when things were going badly, had called all his corps and divisional commanders into conference. He asked them individually and collectively for their advice. Should the army stand and continue the fight or retreat to Nashville?

To two of those present it was obvious that Thomas' fire power and the undiminished spirit of his divisions and that of Sheridan had taken the hardest blows Bragg was capable of inflicting and had destroyed most of the enemy's offensive potential. But the others were pessimistic. Division after division reported heavy losses—but none heavier than Sheridan's. The usually ebullient General McCook stared at the floor with hardly a word to say. The high-tempered General Wood, who that morning had jovially remarked to General Crittenden, "Good-by, General, we'll all meet at the hatter's, as one coon said to another when the dogs were after them"—even Wood was nervous and apprehensive.[20]

General Rosecrans asked Eben Swift, medical director of the Army of the Cumberland, whether there was "transportation sufficient to carry off the wounded." Swift replied that his wagons could remove the seriously wounded; the others would have to walk.

Rosecrans' next question was directed at General Stanley, commanding the army's cavalry units: "Is your command in shape to cover a retreat?" Stanley said he believed it could.

"It was a weird firelit scene," Adjutant John L. Yaryan recalled. "These men looked as if each had been a gunner all day and had taken special pains to get himself smoked and powder-grimed. Battered as to hats, tousled as to hair, torn as to clothes and depressed as to spirits, if there was a cheerful-expressioned face present I did not see it." General Thomas alone, he said, looked "determined and perfectly self-possessed. It was a tonic to look at the man."

Reiteration of the word "retreat" suddenly roused Thomas from his silence. Some witnesses said he had been dozing until that word jabbed him into wakefulness. General Rosecrans asked him for his opinion. Deliberate as always, Thomas waited a moment before replying; only the steady drumming of rain on the clapboard roof could be heard.

Then he "rose slowly to his feet, buttoned his greatcoat from bottom to top, faced his comrades and stood there, a statue of courage chiseled out of the black marble of midnight, by the firelight. 'Gentlemen,' Thomas said, 'I know of no better place to die than right here.' "

Sheridan, who had been listening to his colleagues' despairing comments with barely repressed annoyance, jumped to his feet. He ranged himself beside the massive Thomas, somewhat like a terrier leaping to the defense of a St. Bernard, and declared, "I request for my division the honor of leading the attack tomorrow!"

The determination of Thomas and Sheridan swayed Rosecrans in favor of standing and fighting, and he told his commanders, "If you are not attacked by six o'clock this morning, you will open the fight promptly, posted as you are, and move on to Murfreesboro. Clear the field yet tonight of all wounded and see to it that your ammunition is well up; we will whip this fight tomorrow."[21]

The next day, however, both exhausted armies remained on the defensive, with occasional reconnaissances in force probing at each other's positions. On Sheridan's front the enemy attacked in brigade strength, and heavy skirmishing developed, during which Sheridan's men captured 86 Confederates.[22] But that midnight council of December 31-January 1 had resulted in a more effective plan of defeating Bragg than crashing forward on all sectors. Throughout January 1 Rosecrans and Thomas were shifting all available artillery and the less battered of their infantry across Stone's River and combining them with Crittenden's left wing. Fifty-eight guns were massed on high ground dominating the terrain between the river and Murfreesboro. Then, on January 2, the crushing counterstroke was launched with the Union cavalry reaching out to sever Bragg's communications to the south. Bragg quickly evacuated the town and left the grisly field to Rosecrans.

It was a sorry sort of victory, with about 10,000 casualties on each side. "And we," wrote General Crittenden, "although we were the victors, virtually went into hospital for six months before we could march after them again. . . . Yet it was a triumph. It showed that in the long run the big purse and the big battalions—both on our side—must win; and it proved that there were no better soldiers than ours."[23] More important, from the political and diplomatic viewpoint, were the boost this victory gave to morale in the North and its value as United States propaganda abroad, especially in England and France. Several times President Lincoln told of his intense gratitude for that victory—out of proportion as far as its purely military importance was concerned—and plainly kept Rosecrans in command, long after the Presidential patience was frazzled, in remembrance of that dark December day in the cedar forests.

Even more than Booneville and Perryville, the battle of Stone's River was an indication to the Union high command of Sheridan's military qualities. His division had suffered 1,633 casualties out of a prebattle strength of 4,164, including 237 killed, 989 wounded, 407 missing.[24] But it had not disintegrated under that terrible infliction, and it needed only replacements to bring it up to its previous high standard.

In the course of the three-day battle there had been four critical moments, and in two of these Sheridan had been a decisive factor. They were: (1) The last stand in the Round Forest, which saved the bulk of the Union army from destruction before a defense line could be firmly established. This sacrificial effort was performed almost entirely by the Third Division. (2) Thomas' defense of the secondary line protecting the Nashville Pike and the railroad. (3) The quick action of General McCook's ordnance officer, Captain Thruston, in saving the corps' ammunition train from capture. (4) The council of war at which Sheridan and Thomas successfully argued against withdrawal.

After the war General Grant, whose subsequent habit it was to praise General Sheridan a little too highly perhaps while being too constant in disparaging General Thomas, gave this opinion of Sheridan's conduct at Stone's River: "It was from all I can hear about it a wonderful bit of fighting. It showed what a great general can do even in a subordinate command; for I believe Sheridan in that battle saved Rosecrans' army."[25] With the addition of Thomas' name it would have been a just verdict on Stone's River.

6

INTO THE VALLEY

AFTER the battle of Stone's River the Army of the Cumberland settled down in its camps around Murfreesboro. There was a long lull in its fighting which extended from January to the end of June 1863, except for scattered engagements with the enemy cavalry along the lines of communication.

In the East the Army of the Potomac prepared for its spring campaign, which was to end in the defeat of General Hooker at Chancellorsville. To the West the Army of the Tennessee laboriously advanced, fought, fell back and advanced again on the approaches to the Mississippi River fortress of Vicksburg, which did not surrender until early in July. Kentucky and the portions of Tennessee technically under Federal occupation suffered greatly from the incursions of the Confederate cavalry raiders, Generals Morgan and Forrest. These raids became so irksome, so potentially dangerous to the morale of the border states that Lincoln even proposed the organization of a counterraiding force but was overruled by his generals.

During this sylvan interlude Sheridan managed to keep his troops occupied with training maneuvers, extended reconnaissance missions and foraging expeditions in brigade strength against the possibility of interception by the very active enemy cavalry. The most memorable event of the six inactive months, perhaps, was the unmasking—to put it delicately—of a couple of "men" who had been on duty around Third Division headquarters for almost a year.

The two soldiers, one serving as a trooper in the cavalry company assigned to escort duty and the other a teamster in the quartermaster's department, had been sent on a foraging mission which ended abruptly when the pair acquired a supply of applejack. In the ensuing revelry they fell into Stone's River and had to be rescued. Over their soggy protests their clothing was removed, and it was discovered that the swaggering troopers were, in biological fact, females. In a spirit not altogether lacking in levity General Sheridan ordered an inquiry into how the "Amazons," as he called them, had managed to enlist. He learned that they were dispossessed East Tennesseans who had fled to Louisville early in 1862. The city was flooded with refugees from the loyal section of Tennessee around Knoxville, and they were unable to find means of support. They managed to pass themselves off as men with both the recruiting sergeant and the examining surgeon during the hectic weeks when Bragg was advancing on Louisville. Sheridan promptly discharged them and sent them back to Louisville, but he often wondered how they managed to adjust themselves to civilian, and female, society.[1]

The only fair-sized action during that period was a probing advance toward Franklin, Tennessee, where Confederate General Earl Van Dorn was making a nuisance of himself. Sheridan set out with his division and a cavalry brigade, tricked the enemy into attacking him and captured 50 prisoners and a number of wagons. Van Dorn eluded further contact, and Sheridan returned to Murfreesboro with his wagon train loaded with requisitioned fodder. In April he was notified of his promotion to major general, U. S. Volunteers, principally for his services at the battle of Stone's River.

Even as it enjoyed the flowering springtime of Middle Tennessee the army was uneasy with rumor and conjecture. The higher officers, of course, knew that Rosecrans was being prodded into an offensive campaign by the War Department. An advance on Chattanooga, Washington believed, would halt the enemy raids in Kentucky and Tennessee, relieve some of the pressure at Grant's rear as he moved closer to Vicksburg and strike at a vital center of Confederate resistance.

Chattanooga was indeed a prize. It was the center of a network of railroads from the east, south and west; it was the logical springboard for any offensive aimed at Atlanta; and it would be the starting point of any movement to liberate East Tennessee and break in the rear door to Virginia. In Confederate hands it had served as the main base for Bragg's army and the invasion of Kentucky and Tennessee.

It would not be easy to take. Between Murfreesboro and Chattanooga lay the great Cumberland plateau, with its rough terrain, vast pine barrens and crisscrossing ravines and rivers. And there were Bragg and his hard-fighting divisions, strongly entrenched in the Duck River valley, ready to take every advantage of the topography.

In urging the movement toward Chattanooga the War Department was quite considerate of Rosecrans' sensitive nature. Extremely concerned about a new vacancy among the six major generalcies in the Regular Army, he demanded that his commission be antedated to make him senior among the Western generals and therefore eligible for the promotion. To this rather arrogant request the President replied most tactfully, "The world will not forget that you fought the battle of Stone's River, and it will never care a fig whether you rank General Grant or he ranks you."

That might have mollified Rosecrans if General in Chief Halleck, as tactless as Lincoln was tactful, had not made an unprecedented proposal. To the rival generals, Grant and Rosecrans, he suggested that the promotion go to the one who first won an important victory, virtually proposing a gigantic foot race to Chattanooga and Vicksburg. Grant kept silent, although this grab-bag settlement of the vacancy probably annoyed him greatly. Rosecrans, however, lowered his standing with Halleck by writing a bitter protest against "auctioneering of honors." Later Rosecrans complained to the President that he felt, because of a letter from Halleck, that Lincoln was "dissatisfied" with him. Again Lincoln, with the infinite patience he accorded even his most temperamental generals, supplied a soft answer: "I can never forget whilst I remember anything that about the end of last year . . . you gave us a hard-earned victory, which, had there been a defeat instead, the nation could scarcely have lived through."

All this affected the subsequent fortunes of the Army of the

Cumberland, for it governed the atmosphere in which the generals of that army fought the great battles around Chattanooga. It contributed to the nervous, moody climate at headquarters and naturally influenced the attitude of the higher officers. Among these men confidence had been waning ever since the council of war the night of December 31 at Stone's River when most of them had been willing to admit defeat. There was a question in many minds whether Rosecrans fully deserved the glory which he flaunted in bargaining with Washington. His quality of indecision—which amounted almost to a shirking of responsibility—was again in evidence when he circularized his division and corps commanders with a set of questions relative to the army's future movements. These were the questions he posed:

From the fullest information in your possession, do you think the enemy in front of us has been so materially weakened, by detachments to Johnston [in Mississippi then, threatening Grant's rear] or elsewhere, that this army could advance on him at this time with strong reasonable chances of fighting a great and successful battle?

Do you think an advance of our army at present likely to prevent additional reinforcements being sent against General Grant by the enemy in our front?

Do you think an immediate or early advance of our army advisable?

Sheridan and most of the other generals agreed that such an advance was not advisable, predicting that Bragg would withdraw to the Tennessee River and citing the difficulty of pursuing him over such rugged country. To the enemy, possessing superior knowledge of the terrain, mountain passes, ravines, rivers and valleys offered countless opportunities for ambush. (Even a modern general with all his tracked vehicles, trucks and bulldozers would find the country around Chattanooga a serious problem.) Later Sheridan gave an additional reason for opposing an immediate movement on Chattanooga: "While General Grant was operating against Vicksburg, it was better to hold Bragg in Middle Tennes-

see than to push him so far back into Georgia that interior means
of communication would give the Confederate Government the
opportunity of quickly joining a part of his force to that of General Johnston in Mississippi."[2]

Despite all the pessimism at Rosecrans' headquarters and among
his subordinate generals the campaign against Chattanooga was
finally undertaken. Sheridan's prediction that Bragg would fall
back south of the Tennessee was quickly confirmed. Still, Rosecrans conducted a masterly and almost bloodless campaign—one of
the finest examples of maneuver, feint and thrust in the Civil War—
and forced Bragg to retreat without once allowing him the opportunity of launching an effective counterstroke.

Sheridan's Third Division was part of the offensive wing assigned
to force Bragg to withdraw through constant flanking maneuvers.[3]
The Union army demonstrated against the Confederate center at
Shelbyville, then struck heavily at the right, anchored at Tullahoma. Sheridan moved out of his camps around Murfreesboro on
June 24. His first objective, the enemy-held pass at Hoover's Gap,
was attained June 27 after a march impeded by the drenching
spring rains. Bragg chose not to defend the pass and even withdrew from Tullahoma without offering battle. Sheridan's division
occupied the town on July 1 and found only a few prisoners and
three pieces of heavy artillery as the prize. An arabesque of maneuver by all three Union corps and the reserve divisions under
General Gordon Granger, Sheridan's old benefactor, resulted in
Bragg's final withdrawal to the defenses of Chattanooga. The Confederates began digging in around that city on July 3 while the
great victories of Gettysburg and Vicksburg were being won by
Federal arms to the east and south.

Rosecrans sent Thomas and McCook sweeping far to the south
to seize the passes in the long rocky spine of Lookout Mountain
and pushed Crittenden's corps to Harrison, which guarded the
northern crossings of the Tennessee. From the north Crittenden's
artillery began bombarding Chattanooga just enough to arouse apprehension.

Bragg, facing a prolonged and possibly disastrous siege, was in
danger of being cut off from his bases at Dalton, Resaca and At-

lanta, and further alarm was created in his mind as Thomas' advance guard poked its way through the mountains to Stevens Gap. McCook's corps, meanwhile, was swinging even farther south and operating around Alpine and Valley Head. Sheridan's division, occupying the mountain village of Alpine, was on the extreme right of the army. By early September Bragg had drawn up new plans for containing Rosecrans' southward thrust. He had evacuated Chattanooga and retreated on his bases.

Sheridan handled his division with distinction in the Tullahoma campaign. After the Confederates had crossed the Tennessee with the bulk of their forces he was sent forward in support of Stanley's cavalry to try to capture the great bridge at Bridgeport intact. He dashed ahead so energetically that he "outstripped the cavalry" and captured the Confederate rear guard (but not before the latter had largely succeeded in wrecking the bridge). The enemy prisoners insisted that Sheridan's division must be the cavalry because it had moved so swiftly.[4]

Despite his major general's stars and braid, Phil Sheridan had not entirely lost the impetuosity and hot temper that had marked his boyhood and caused his suspension from West Point. One summer day while his troops were engaged in rebuilding the spans at Bridgeport he asked General Thomas to accompany him from Deckerd, Tennessee, then the XIV Corps' headquarters, to inspect his engineering feats. They were accompanied by William F. G. Shanks, the war correspondent. At one of the way stations their train halted for a long time. Concerned about wasting General Thomas' time, Sheridan asked the conductor, "a great, burly six-footer," what was holding them up. The conductor made a "gruff" and noncommittal reply and slouched off. Still the train did not move. Some time later Sheridan stopped the conductor as he passed along the aisle and again demanded why they were delayed. This time the conductor growled that he took orders only from the military superintendent of the railroad. Sheridan raised himself to his full five and a half feet and, "without giving him time to finish the insulting reply, struck him two or three rapid blows, kicked him from the cars and into the hands of a guard, and then ordered the train forward, acting as conductor on the down and return trip." When the train started moving Sheridan returned to his seat next to General Thomas and resumed their conversation as if nothing had happened. Thomas, of course, was always the imperturbable Virginian: he gave no sign of having noticed the violent scene only a few feet away.

On another occasion, Shanks recalled, Sheridan observed a newspaper vender "in some imposition on the soldiers" at a railroad station. "Without waiting for an explanation" the general seized him by the neck and "thumped his head against the car, although he had to stand on tiptoe to do it."[5] Needless to say, such forthright measures delighted his soldiers, who compared him with older and more dignified officers to their detriment.

After ten days of hard marching over the mountains and through gaps so deep they were "never reached by sunlight" Sheridan and the Third Division encamped at Alpine, but their rest was brief indeed. Whatever the optimism at Chattanooga headquarters, the front-line divisions were uneasy about the lack of resistance, not at all convinced, as Rosecrans was, that the enemy was in full retreat. By September 10 Rosecrans' forces were covering a front of 50 miles from Crittenden on the left to McCook on the right, from Lee and Gordon's Mill to Alpine. Communication among the three Union corps was most uncertain; they would be unable to support one another if attacked in turn by Bragg and his aggressive army. Several generals of the Army of the Cumberland were becoming aware of the danger that Bragg might be luring them into a trap instead of conducting a retreat.

Washington, too, was growing uneasy about the possibility of a gigantic ambush. Lincoln and Stanton dispatched Assistant Secretary of War Charles A. Dana—formerly one of Horace Greeley's bright young editors, he had recently observed the operations at Vicksburg—to find out just what Rosecrans was thinking and doing. As late as September 12 Rosecrans was still confident that Bragg was not luring but retreating, and at the first interview with Dana he occupied most of the time ranting at the War Department for withholding supplies and reinforcements. Dana left immediately for the front to determine for himself if Rosecrans' optimism extended to the lower and more active echelons.[6]

Two days before Dana and Rosecrans conferred, Sheridan was convinced that the latter had misread the enemy's intentions and capabilities. That night an old friend appeared at divisional headquarters—General George Crook, who was now commanding the Second Cavalry Division and had been scouting extensively. They went into "private conference for hours." Crook wrote in his diary that "after seeing the almost impregnable position the enemy had evacuated, I was convinced they did it to draw us across the river, and so reported to General Rosecrans. But he said he had information that the enemy was preparing to retreat, but my opinions were not changed all the same."[7] The next day Sheridan, talking with a war correspondent, pointed out dust clouds in the direction of Lafayette, Georgia. When the newspaperman asked, "Is our cavalry over there?" Sheridan said, "Our cavalry can't get there!"[8] His corps commander, General McCook, usually the most expansive optimist in the army, agreed that something sinister was happening across the ridges.

General Sheridan decided to send his chief scout, James Card, across the lines for more definite information on the enemy's dispositions and intentions. Card, an East Tennessean, had already rendered valuable service dating back to November 1862, when he had appeared at Third Division headquarters and volunteered for scouting duty. A small, wiry and active man with considerable native intelligence, he had peddled books all over Tennessee and Georgia, had preached in the little mountain churches and even practiced as an unlicensed physician where no professional medical men were available. He knew the countryside and its people as well as any outlander could.

Card, however, located a fervent Unionist living on Sand Mountain who agreed to undertake the mission, provided the army would buy his livestock and enable him to go west immediately, since he feared retribution from his bushwhacking neighbors. Sheridan agreed to the terms. The spy's experiences were harrowing; he was arrested by the Confederates, managed to escape and passed through the enemy lines by concealing his movements with an imitation of the wild hogs' grunts and squeals. The mountaineer reached General Rosecrans' headquarters with the information,

Sheridan said, that "Bragg intended to fight and that he expected to be reinforced by Longstreet."[9]

By that time Thomas, commanding the center, also had come to the realization that "nothing but stupendous blunders on the part of Bragg can save our army from total defeat," as he told his staff.[10] His own chief scout learned that large numbers of prisoners whom Grant had paroled at Vicksburg were present in Bragg's army.[11] One of Thomas' divisions had been hit hard as it ventured out of Dug Gap and was forced to retreat to McLemore's Cove.

The realization that in a few days the army had passed from victory to the edge of disaster was spreading like a cholera epidemic. A Union captain who had ventured across the lines in Confederate uniform returned with further testimony that Bragg had now achieved superiority in numbers and was ready to strike back. From Mississippi a corps placed under the command of Lieutenant General D. H. Hill, formerly one of Lee's able subordinates, had arrived 15,000 strong. Almost an equal number was being rushed west from the Army of Northern Virginia—Longstreet's Corps in which John B. Hood led one division and Lafayette McLaws another, all veterans of Antietam, Bull Run, Chancellorsville, Gettysburg. Bragg would take the field in a few days with an army numbering about 70,000 to Rosecrans' 60,000.

After listening to almost frantic appeals from his field commanders for concentration of the army General Rosecrans, finally convinced that Bragg was preparing a counterstroke of terrific potentiality, quickly changed his mind about continuing the "pursuit." Orders were dispatched to McCook and Thomas to begin moving north hurriedly and link up with Crittenden, then in the vicinity of Lee and Gordon's Mill. The concentration point would be the valley of Chickamauga Creek, a heavily wooded and thicketed region with only a few clearings under cultivation. In that valley, commanded by the towering Missionary Ridge, the first Confederate cavalry patrols were probing up the back-country roads and feeling for the Union left flank.

Actually things weren't going too well at Bragg's headquarters, either. The Confederate commander was at odds with Polk and other field generals, he was worried about the Federals' ability to

"pop out" of the mountain wall at him (as he told D. H. Hill), his
attack on Thomas at Dug Gap had not been pushed with the vigor
it demanded for a real success. It was also apparent that he did
not have the full confidence of his troops after the defeats and
withdrawals of the past two years. As General Hill said, "The one
thing that a soldier never fails to understand is victory."[12] Finally,
he was depressed because General Polk had attacked Crittenden so
slowly and feebly that the Union force had escaped virtually undamaged. His plan to smash the Union army apart before it could
be concentrated was rapidly disintegrating.

But Bragg's disappointment over the failure to defeat Rosecrans
in detail, traceable partly to his reluctance to invest all available
forces in the project until Longstreet's divisions arrived by railroad
on their circuitous journey from Virginia, was nothing compared
to the alarm and confusion at Union headquarters. Rosecrans was
close to panic over the exposed condition of Thomas' and—even
more so—McCook's corps.

McCook's XX Corps began its movement toward the Valley of
the Chickamauga on September 13 with Sheridan's hurried march
out of Broomtown Valley. In an unusually prudent mood McCook
had kept his corps train on the summit of Lookout Mountain, so
the withdrawal was considerably less difficult than it might have
been. It was still not easy, especially for Sheridan's division, which
had the most ground to cover; the divisional artillery and supply
wagons had to be hauled over the steeper passes by the troops. On
September 16 Sheridan's division arrived in McLemore's Cove to
join the general movement northward. Sheridan recorded his great
relief at accomplishing the juncture with the XIV Corps without
interference from the enemy.[13] There was much more hard marching ahead of the Third Division as McCook and Sheridan hurried
their corps to connect with Crittenden's and establish a firm hold
on the roads leading through the gaps in Missionary Ridge to Chattanooga.

Sheridan remained at McLemore's Cove all of September 17 to
act as rear guard. Although there was not even a skirmish with
the mysteriously inactive enemy, it was a most responsible post, an
indication of McCook's and Thomas' esteem for his nerve and

ability. Uppermost in the minds of all the senior officers and of many of their men was the nightmarish possibility that they might suddenly be ambushed in the maze of mountain walls and passes by vastly superior Confederate forces. Every bugle call, every rustling sound in the night, every dust cloud over the horizon caused a collective chill of apprehension.

On September 18 Sheridan's division was shifted northward to Pond Spring, and on the nineteenth to Crawfish Springs, where it again took up the anchoring position to protect the army's right and rear.[14]

General Rosecrans was able to bring his troops into line quickly and effectively, partly because the Chattanooga-Lafayette Turnpike ran through the Valley of the Chickamauga parallel to the creek. This swift movement forestalled Bragg's plan to cross the creek, flank Rosecrans, seize the turnpike and drive on to block the passes leading to Chattanooga. The danger of Bragg's suddenly attacking the Union army as it moved across his front was always present, of course, with the probability that the Federals would then be hurled against Missionary Ridge and annihilated. Instead of seizing this opportunity, however, Bragg busied himself with grouping and regrouping his forces. Finally he placed most of his own Army of Tennessee, including Forrest's cavalry, on the right under Polk. The Confederate left wing was placed in command of General Longstreet, some of whose brigades were still en route from Virginia as the first skirmishes developed. Sheridan thus found himself opposing Longstreet, Hood and their veterans of the Eastern campaigns.

Meanwhile, Rosecrans moved Thomas' XIV Corps, the largest and most dependable in the army, past Crittenden to form the Federal left. Crittenden's XXI Corps took over the center, with McCook's still on the right. Granger's reserve corps, consisting of only three brigades, was posted at Rossville to hold the pass there in case Bragg's flanking operations succeeded beyond the estimates of Rosecrans and his staff. The Army of the Cumberland kept shifting left, like a shield held up to cover the vital lines of retreat, and fighting off the enemy's persistent probing. Sheridan joined the "sidewise" movement, taking position at Lee and Gordon's

Mill, scattering a few squadrons of Confederate cavalry and then driving an enemy infantry force away from the ford across Chickamauga Creek. On the Federal left, meanwhile, Thomas repulsed a disconnected series of attacks aimed at turning his flank. From the northward movement of dust clouds behind Pigeon Mountain to the east, it was obvious that Bragg was continuing to pump reinforcements into his right wing.

With the crescendo of battle rising ominously, Sheridan was not heavily engaged on September 19, although he came to the support of Davis' division, also of the XX Corps, and Wood's division of the XXI Corps who "were being hard-pressed and their troops nearly exhausted." Colonel Bradley's brigade drove back an enemy thrust across the Lafayette Turnpike, an assault in which Bradley was seriously wounded. The casualty rate among Sheridan's brigade commanders was abnormally high; it was the belief at Third Division headquarters that a commander should give the order "Follow me" rather than "Forward, men!" At 11:00 P.M. his division was directed to move again, this time to cover the Widow Glenn's house—a landmark of the subsequent battle, since it served as army headquarters.[15]

That night there was another of those nervous midnight councils of war to which Rosecrans was addicted. Instead of stiffening the resolve of his field commanders he apparently required encouragement from them. To his corps and division commanders he appeared close to breaking down.[16] The worry of the preceding six days had deprived him of all but a few hours' sleep since the army began its withdrawal and concentration, and the shock of having a triumphant pursuit turned into a swift retreat was another contributing factor.

General Thomas, himself often sleepless for the past two weeks, kept falling into a doze during the conference. "Every time Rosecrans spoke to him he always said the same thing," Dana observed, " 'I would strengthen the left,' and then he would be asleep again, sitting up in his chair. General Rosecrans, to the proposition to strengthen the left, made always the same reply, 'Where are we going to take it from?' "[17]

From all accounts the atmosphere at that council in army headquarters at the Widow Glenn's house was thick with gloom. Rose-crans was close to panic, and the stolid Thomas, hitherto the moral and mental anchor of the army, seemed to have almost ceased to function. Around midnight coffee was served and General Mc-Cook, whose high spirits could rarely be repressed for long, sang "The Hebrew Maiden." Why McCook felt called on to vocalize at this desperately serious moment, with two great armies stirring within a mile of each other on the eve of the bloodiest battle ever fought on the American continent, and how he came to select that curious melody, was unfortunately lost to history.

Sheridan's reaction to this strange assemblage of the brains of the Army of the Cumberland also was not recorded, but it can be divined. He heartily deplored eccentricity, especially in such circumstances. The spectacle of an unstrung commander begging for advice from his subordinates and of his direct superior braying at the moon must have exercised considerable influence on his controversial actions of the following day.

Next morning the army awoke in its rifle pits and behind its breastworks in a fog so thick that each man was isolated from the sight and sound of all but his nearest comrades, an eerie muffled world where the opposing forces could only move blindly and grapple in sporadic little fire fights until visibility improved. Once the fog lifted, Polk finally opened the great battle of Chickamauga by attacking the Federal left under Thomas with a fury that steadily increased. Meanwhile, in the heavy screen of woods and thickets opposite the Union right and center Bragg was concentrating a heavy assault column from Longstreet's left wing and preparing to change the direction of his offensive since Thomas' Corps, stoutly reinforced during the night, proved unmovable.

Still, the pressure from Polk caused Thomas and Rosecrans to decide on further reinforcement of the former. At 10:30 A.M. Rosecrans sent word to McCook: "The general commanding directs you to send two brigades of General Sheridan's division to support General Thomas, and send the third brigade as soon as the lines can be drawn sufficiently. March them rapidly as you can without exhausting the men." A half hour later Sheridan was ordered to send his remaining brigade, Laiboldt's, to cover ground

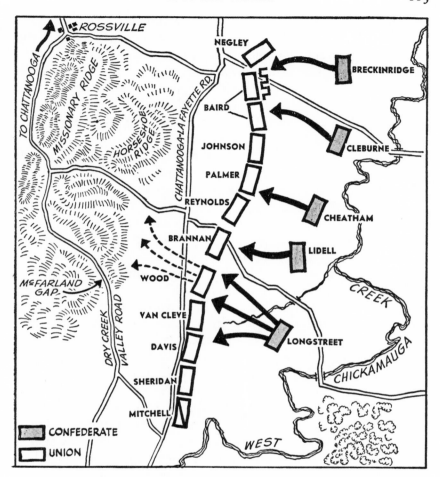

THE OPPOSING FORCES AT CHICKAMAUGA

formerly occupied by Negley's division, but before it got into this position "the ground was occupied by Carlin's brigade of Davis' division."[18] This was just one of the instances of bad staff work that day; a worse was to follow shortly. Laiboldt took position on a ridge at the rear to cover Davis' flank.

While Sheridan's brigades were pulling out of line as part of the general transfer from the Federal right and center of divisions and brigades assigned to support Thomas, a terrible blunder opened the Union army to a crushing blow. Through faulty staff work and Rosecrans' apparent ignorance of the placement of his own forces, Wood's division was ordered out of the battle line. It left a sizable gap opposite where Longstreet's spearhead was ready for the plunge, with Hood's Texas Brigade and other crack assault units, the hardest fighters in the Confederacy, waiting for the signal to advance.

The Confederate attack came on like a hurricane. "I had just abandoned position and was moving at the double-quick," Sheridan reported, "when the enemy made a furious assault with overwhelming numbers on Davis' front, and, coming up through the unoccupied space between Davis and myself, even covering the front of the position I had just abandoned." General McCook ordered Sheridan to send Laiboldt into a counterattack, but the brigade was unable to fire because Davis' fleeing troops were caught between it and the onrushing enemy. Lytle's and Bradley's brigades, recalled from their march to the left, were hurled into another counterattack "under a terrible fire of musketry from the enemy." The overwhelmed brigades fell back 300 yards to the Lafayette road, recoiled and "drove the enemy back with terrible slaughter," said Sheridan, regaining the ridge formerly held by Laiboldt's brigade and capturing prisoners and colors from the 24th Alabama.[19]

Counterattacking against Longstreet's hard-driving spearhead cost the Third Division heavily in officers, men and equipment. Among those who fell in the hopeless attempt to close the widening gap was Brigadier Lytle, a brave and energetic officer whose avocation was writing poetry. In a few minutes the division lost almost as many men as fell during the daylong fighting at Stone's River. The Federal right and center had disintegrated, except for the brigades already absorbed by Thomas' defense of the left below Horseshoe Ridge, and 30,000 Confederates were yowling with triumph in the rear of the Union army. The attack swept over Rosecrans' headquarters and sent the commanding general, two of his corps commanders, McCook and Crittenden, and Assistant Secretary of War Dana, along with thousands of terrified and completely demoralized troops, fleeing up the Dry Creek Valley road toward McFarland's Gap. This sole escape route was soon littered with hundreds of abandoned supply and baggage wagons, smashed gun carriages, millions of dollars' worth of food, munitions and equipment.

Sheridan pulled his command together as best he could. The 73rd Illinois Infantry, the "Preachers' Regiment," which was part of Laiboldt's brigade, had driven so far ahead that it was stranded and other regiments had to be hurled into the bloody confusion to rescue it before the remnants of the Third Division could withdraw.[20] The division fell back onto a ridge which overlooked the whole scene of the rout, the agonized confusion, the trampled field where thousands of men in blue and gray lay dead and dying.

Another withdrawal was made in the direction of the lower slopes of Missionary Ridge. Subsequently in his official report Sheridan gave this account of his movements: "I here learned positively what I had before partially seen, that the divisions still farther on my left had been driven, and that I was completely cut off. I then determined to connect myself with the troops of General Thomas by moving on the arc of a circle until I struck the Dry Creek Valley road, by which I hoped to form the junction. . . . On reaching the Dry Creek Valley road I found that the enemy had moved parallel to me and had also arrived at the road, thus preventing my joining General Thomas by that route." On the way, Sheridan said, he gathered up sixteen pieces of artillery, 46 caissons, one whole battery of field guns, all formerly attached to other divisions and all in "wild confusion." He rode to his left with members of his staff, endeavoring to find an opening through which he might join whatever Union forces were still resisting the enemy, but apparently Thomas was almost surrounded. The only fairly certain way of reaching him would be through Rossville, where Granger's reserve corps had been posted specifically to keep that route open regardless of all hazards. So, Sheridan's report goes, "I then determined to move quickly on Rossville and form a junction with him on his left flank via the Lafayette road. This was successfully accomplished about 5:30 P.M."[21]

Had it not been for the intense recriminations that welled up in the aftermath of Chickamauga, the account of Sheridan's participation in the battle might virtually end there. But because of the long controversies which impinged unjustly on his reputation it will be necessary to examine the closing phases of his action in greater detail than is justified by their intrinsic importance.

While Sheridan was slowly retreating, reorganizing his shattered brigades and gathering up fugitives from other divisions, Thomas and his heavily reinforced corps were still valiantly fighting on the left, although the break-through on their right had come as a great shock. The XIV Corps and its supporting divisions withdrew to the Horseshoe Ridge and, backed up by all the available artillery, put up one of the greatest defensive fights of the war. At the same time Rosecrans, McCook, Crittenden and Dana were galloping for Chattanooga, unaware that Thomas was still resisting. As soon as he reached his headquarters Rosecrans began wiring Union garrisons northward to the Ohio River to prepare for Bragg's coming at any moment. McCook and Crittenden hovered around their chief instead of returning to the field. Dana telegraphed Washington in a state of extreme alarm: "My report today is of deplorable importance. Chickamauga is as fatal a name in our history as Bull Run."[22] There was more panic in the rear than at the front, where men were dying by the hundreds on the slopes of Horseshoe Ridge.

At Rossville, General Granger, commanding the reserve corps, "a rude, rough and tough soldier" as War Correspondent Shanks characterized him, was erupting with impatience. "Why the —— does Rosecrans keep me here?" he demanded of his chief of staff, Colonel J. S. Fullerton, before he learned that Rosecrans had fled to Chattanooga. "Don't you see Bragg is piling his whole army on Thomas? I am going to his assistance." Granger marched his three brigades to Horseshoe Ridge despite warnings from his staff that he had been ordered to stay at Rossville and hold the gap, that he had not received any countermanding orders to justify moving. He allowed himself to be guided instead by the Napoleonic adage, by which so many Civil War generals lived and fought, "March to the sound of the guns"—not always the wisest of homilies. Almost at the moment Granger's brigades arrived on the embattled ridge Thomas asked if they could be thrown into a counterattack on the right. Granger replied, "Yes. My men are fresh. . . . They are raw troops, and they don't know any better than to charge up there."[23]

There was very little corresponding spirit animating Phil Sheridan as he marched his division in the direction of Rossville. Anger, disgust and a sense of outrage that hundreds of his troops had fallen in futile counterattacks against overwhelming forces dominated him at the moment. He had been caught so far off balance and had suffered such heavy losses without recompense that he could only seethe inwardly at the bungling of his superiors. General Rosecrans, on his way through Rossville to Chattanooga, sent to ask Sheridan to confer with him "if practicable." Sheridan ignored the suggestion, later explaining, "Affairs were too critical to admit of my going to him at once. . . . It is to be regretted that he did not wait till I could join him, for the delay would have permitted him to see that matters were not in quite such bad shape as he supposed."[24] (That evening Rosecrans was treated even more brusquely by General Granger, who rode back to Chattanooga to learn the commanding general's plans. Rosecrans began writing out an elaborate order. Granger blurted, "Oh, that's all nonsense, General! Send Thomas an order to retire. He knows what he's about as well as you do."[25]) In Sheridan's opinion, "the battle . . . was fought under the most disadvantageous circumstances, without time being given to form line of battle, without supports, and contending against four or five divisions."[26] He had fought against long odds at Booneville, Perryville and Stone's River, but never so futilely as at Chickamauga. The mood of his surviving troops was even less sanguine than their commander's. When an officer on the staff of the XX Corps asked soldiers for information they replied, "We'll talk to you, my son, when we get to the Ohio River."

"General Phil was furious . . . he was *swearing* mad, and no wonder," according to the recollection of Gates P. Thruston, now McCook's chief of staff. He was the young captain who had saved the corps' ammunition train at Stone's River. He added, "The devoted Lytle and the truest and bravest had fallen in vain resistance around him. . . . [Sheridan] had lost faith. . . ." Colonel Thruston believed that Sheridan's "splendid fighting qualities and his fine soldiers had not had half a chance."[27] When Thruston arrived at

McFarland's Gap, where the Dry Valley road crosses Missionary Ridge, he found Sheridan in conference with General Davis, who also had only half of his division intact; General Negley, who had become separated from his broken command; and Colonel Arthur C. Ducat, inspector-general of the Army of the Cumberland. With them was Colonel Parkhurst and the 9th Michigan Infantry, the XIV Corps' provost guard, which was gathering up stragglers on General Crittenden's orders. Colonel Parkhurst contributed to the pessimism of the council by remarking that Crittenden had ordered him to fall back on Chattanooga with his regiment and all its refugees. General Negley, who had taken command of almost 1,000 stragglers from various other divisions, opposed any withdrawal until, at least, General Thomas had been consulted.

Colonel Thruston apparently arrived at a critical point in the conference, which was trying to decide whether to attempt a break-through to Thomas, retreat to Chattanooga or take a middle course and fall back only as far as Rossville. The young colonel volunteered to ride to Thomas, if possible, and find out what the senior general on the field thought should be done. Meanwhile, according to Colonel Ducat's report, it was decided that Sheridan would continue toward Rossville, Davis would "remain where he was and cover the retreat of the trains, & etc., and General Negley should march to Rossville, as a support to either."[28] At his subsequent court of inquiry General Negley affirmed that this was indeed the decision reached by his fellow division commanders and himself, as well as by Rosecrans' only representative on the scene, Inspector-General Ducat.

Although Thomas and his corps were almost surrounded by the Confederates and were under constant attack around their horseshoe-shaped perimeter, Colonel Thruston managed to reach him. Thruston said that Thomas "directed me to bring them [Sheridan and Davis] up on his right at once . . . or support the right by active operations if circumstances seemed to demand it." Thruston indicated that this was an oral order, although General Turchin, who was anything but friendly toward Sheridan, declared it was embodied in a written message. If so, the message cannot be located in the official records, nor have its contents ever been directly quoted. All the evidence indicates it was an oral order hastily given by General Thomas during the crisis of his great defensive battle.

Thruston rode back to Sheridan and Davis, who "had drifted down the road to Rossville and had already entered the defile at McFarland's Gap, halfway between the field and Rossville." On receiving Thomas' message, Thruston reported, Davis immediately ordered a "right-about . . . and marched briskly to the front," but "Sheridan was still without faith. He may have thought there was danger at Rossville, or that his troops had not regained their fighting spirit. He insisted on going to Rossville."[29] As it turned out, Davis' "right-about" was futile—and Sheridan's would have been equally so—for his troops did not arrive in time to join the fight at Horseshoe Ridge. Thomas had already received orders from Rosecrans to disengage and fall back on Rossville.

Instead of reinforcing Thomas' right, therefore, Sheridan marched as swiftly as possible to Rossville, then along the Lafayette Turnpike to join Thomas' left. This was the only route he knew to be open, since Granger and his reserve corps had used it to march on Horseshoe Ridge. It was one thing for a staff officer to ride across country and reach Thomas; it was another for a division, its wagons and artillery—which needed a fairly good road—to accomplish the same mission. According to General Negley's testimony at his court of inquiry, even this march was undertaken with difficulty, for it was harassed along the Lafayette road by Forrest and his hard-striking cavalry. The junction with Thomas' left was made at 5:30 P.M. near the Cloud Church, about three miles from Rossville. Considering that it was necessary to halt briefly in Rossville to distribute ammunition and other supplies sent on from Chattanooga by Rosecrans, the reinforcement of Thomas' left had been accomplished in good time. There was some dispute later about the time of Sheridan's arrival at Cloud Church, but Rosecrans' chief of staff, General Garfield, telegraphed army headquarters at 8:40 P.M. from Rossville that "Sheridan gathered 1500 of his division and reached a point three miles south of here at sunset." Colonel Silas Miller, now commanding Lytle's brigade, reported the new defensive position was taken "about dusk."

That evening it was obvious that, while the Army of the Cum-

berland had suffered a defeat in being driven from the field, the
Confederates had little to celebrate. They had suffered 20,000
casualties to the Union army's 16,000. It was the sort of Pyrrhic
victory that the Confederacy of 1863 could ill afford.[30] But this
was of little comfort to the Union commanders on the evening of
September 20. At a crossroads outside Rossville, Sheridan met
General Thomas, who had just earned the eternal sobriquet of
"The Rock of Chickamauga" by his stand at Horseshoe Ridge but
who was anything but impressed by the glory of it all. Sheridan
recorded that "Old Pap" was weary and depressed. Thomas and
Sheridan shared the brandy remaining in Thomas' flask and sat on
a rail fence, watching the decimated army march past in the Indian
summer's dusk. Even at midnight the army was "simply a mob,"
according to General Beatty. "There appears to be neither organization nor discipline. The various commands are mixed up in
what appears to be inextricable confusion. Were a division of the
enemy to pounce down upon us between this and morning, I fear
the Army of the Cumberland would be blotted out."[31] There was,
of course, one element of order and discipline unknown to General
Beatty—Sheridan's division blocking the Rossville Gap and assuring
the army of a safe withdrawal to the defenses of Chattanooga the
next day. Had Bragg launched a night attack, as some of his generals urged, it would have crumbled, in all probability, against
Sheridan's division, once again capable of offering a stern resistance.

Long after the battle there arose a superficial controversy over
Sheridan's conduct in the closing phases of the action. No responsible military authority, professional or pedantic, has asserted that
his course was anything but reasonable, correct and, especially from
hindsight, the best of tactics. Morally it took more courage than
dashing his remaining troops, if they could be led into such a
situation, against the Confederates in Thomas' rear. But some of
Thomas' partisans, after his death, sought to glorify Thomas at
the expense of Sheridan and hint that the latter barely escaped a
court of inquiry along with Rosecrans, McCook, Crittenden, Negley and Van Cleve. The "controversy" over Sheridan's conduct
actually arose out of the postwar "battle of the memoirs" rather
than the battle of Chickamauga. Nothing of record can be found

to indicate anyone critized Sheridan at the time. Colonel Thruston's inferential criticism was published long afterward, as was the more virulent biography of General Thomas written by Donn Piatt and Henry V. Boynton, in which one chapter was headed "Sheridan Deserts the Field."[32]

In the most impartial and painstaking study of the battle, a volume which took years of investigation and was written by a participant, Archibald Gracie concluded that "General Sheridan owes no apology for his conduct or for any order that he delivered that day. On the other hand, when we consider the extraordinary movement made by his division, from the extreme right wing of the army to the extreme left, after receiving the terrible punishment in the morning, we cannot but consider the performance a remarkable one, which, so far as I can learn, has not its counterpart in any other great battle. General Sheridan marched his troops into the battle, as he supposed, at the most important point where his men might render the most service and have the opportunity of redeeming their noontime discomfiture."[33]

Official approval of Sheridan's conduct was no less enthusiastic. He was praised in the reports of his two immediate superiors, McCook and Rosecrans, and even more conclusive sanction came from General in Chief Halleck's report to the Secretary of War on November 15, 1863: "After gallant but fruitless efforts against this rebel torrent, he was compelled to give way, but afterward rallied a considerable portion of his force, and by a circuitous route, joined General Thomas."[34]

General Sheridan's military record requires no defense, especially since its principal critics regarding Chickamauga were the biographers of another general whose fame certainly was not enhanced by their defamation of Sheridan, and a young staff officer whose opinions were not only impetuous but later, in a measure, recanted. Gracie quoted a letter from Colonel Thruston in which that officer admitted his view of the battle was from a narrow angle and based on less than a sufficiency of the facts. There were two unofficial criticisms: that Sheridan "deserted the field," as Piatt and Boynton claimed, and that he did not hurry to Thomas' assistance. The *Official Records* and other primary sources show conclusively that

Sheridan's actions were not only correct but, in the judgment of a professional and competent soldier, inevitable.

In summation, Sheridan, it was agreed even by his critics, could not have returned immediately to the front where Thomas was holding out. His division was broken, dispirited, disorganized. He would have had to march far to the left, in any case, to bring his division through the Confederate lines. The question was, how far to the left? Staff officers could find paths leading to Horseshoe Ridge, but a division needed a road. The only safe road led through Rossville; furthermore, it was necessary to march through Rossville to receive ammunition for empty cartridge boxes. Since Granger had marched to Horseshoe Ridge without orders, leaving the vital gap unprotected, it was also necessary for a strong force to hold that escape route open. The presence of Forrest's cavalry on Sheridan's flanks as he marched to Cloud Church showed that the route through Rossville needed protection. Furthermore, Sheridan had received no *written* order to plunge through the Confederates ringing Thomas' rear and reinforce his right. An oral order delivered by an excited young staff officer and issued by the general commanding another corps was not likely to impress a Regular Army officer unduly; Thomas, after all, knew as little of Sheridan's condition as Sheridan knew of Thomas'. This was substantiated by the fact that Davis, in obeying the order, did not reach Thomas in time to participate in the defense of Horseshoe Ridge. Sheridan's brave and sensible course resulted in the Union army's left resting securely against night attacks and being able to withdraw the next day without disastrous interference from the enemy.

The melancholy glory of Chickamauga was Thomas'. The shame —perhaps more than he deserved—was Rosecrans'. The sober afterthought that a general must see beyond the momentary aspects of battle, the death and agony, the conflicting impressions and mind-numbing events, and look to the result, can only credit General Sheridan with being, for once, an unsung hero.

7

THE RANKS TAKE COMMAND

TWO days after the battle of Chickamauga the Army of the Cumberland was fairly secure behind the defenses of Chattanooga. The army dug in for a siege and all its consequent hardships. The enemy, meanwhile, ringed the surrounding high ground and brought up his heavy artillery for a constant bombardment; his lines were moved closer to the Federal army's earthworks, rifle pits and hastily constructed forts. Semi-starvation—"half rations of hard bread and beef dried on the hoof," as they described it with desperate jocularity—became the regimen of the crippled and surrounded Cumberlanders. The siege was all but leakproof: only a bad mountain road leading from Chattanooga to the depot at Bridgeport was still open. It passed through the Sequatchie Valley and over Walden's Ridge, difficult in the summertime and often impassable during the winter rains.

Even less reassuring than the prospects of a long and grim siege, at least to the higher officers, was the mental state of General Rosecrans. The watchful Dana described it thus:

In the midst of all his difficulties General Rosecrans dawdled over trifles in a manner which scarcely can be imagined. Precious time was lost because our dazed and muzzy commander could not perceive the catastrophe that was close upon us, nor fix his mind on the means of preventing it. Our animals were starving, the men had starvation before them, and the enemy was bound soon to make desperate efforts to dislodge us. Yet the commanding general devoted that part of the time which was not employed in pleasant gossip to the composition of a long report, to prove that the government was to blame for his failure on September 20.[1]

Changes in the army's composition and command came soon after it settled down to the state of siege. Because of the losses incurred at Chickamauga, and because McCook and Crittenden had been relieved and ordered north, the XX and XXI Corps were combined into the IV Corps, with General Gordon Granger given command as a reward for his decisive action in marching from Rossville to Horseshoe Ridge. General Thomas remained in command of the XIV Corps, although Dana recommended that he replace Rosecrans as commanding general; "he had more the character of George Washington than any other man I ever knew." Dana felt that since Rosecrans "fled to Chattanooga ahead of his men . . . he could not clear himself either in his own eyes or in those of the army."[2]

Sheridan's division, redesignated the Second, first took up a position "under the shadow of Lookout Mountain" near the old ironworks. The enemy batteries on the mountain were busy, but "fortunately no casualties resulted from this plunging fire, though . . . at first our nerves were often upset by the whirring of twenty-pounder shells dropped inconsiderately into our camp at untimely hours of the night." Sheridan's headquarters were established in the home of William Crutchfield, a strong Union sympathizer who, according to local legend, had once engaged in a fist fight with Jefferson Davis over the prospect of Secession.

As usual, Sheridan set out to learn the countryside, including a thorough knowledge of its "roads, by-paths and farm-houses," with Mr. Crutchfield acting as his instructor. The division had suffered a total of 1,366 casualties at Chickamauga—including 151 killed, 939 wounded, and 276 missing—but it was soon reinforced far above its previous maximum strength. There were now 25 regiments and six batteries of field artillery in the division, with the three brigades commanded by Colonel Francis T. Sherman, Brigadier General George D. Wagner and Colonel Charles G. Harker; many of the regiments, however, were much below normal strength.[3] And with the coming of the chill autumn rains they faced considerable hardship since winter uniforms and camp equipment had been left in Murfreesboro.

The rains also reduced severely the amount of food and fodder brought to Chattanooga, with wagon trains taking longer to make the journey and their draft mules dying by the hundreds. The Confederate cavalry under Joe Wheeler made countless raids on the trains, swooping down out of coves and valleys which offered perfect facilities for ambush. With only a trickle of hardtack and bully beef coming from the quartermaster's depots in Chattanooga, General Sheridan decided to try local remedies; he was always expert at seeing that his own troops were properly fed and sheltered. A stray unit of the 2nd Kentucky Cavalry was attached to his headquarters, and he sent that intrepid squadron along with Chief Scout James Card to the Sequatchie Valley as a sort of mobile commissariat. Under Sheridan's instructions the company "hid itself away in a deep cove in the upper end of the valley, and by keeping very quiet and paying for everything it took from the people" was able to send large quantities of corn for the horses and mules and food for the men in a few days. The Kentuckians became so accomplished as commissaries, in fact, that Sheridan was soon sharing the eggs, turkeys, chickens and ducks with less fortunate divisions in the line. Sheridan took great pride in the fact that "Wheeler's cavalry never discovered my detached company." It was one of the rare instances in warfare where a line division was better nourished than the rear-area quartermasters, clerks, orderlies and other noncombat soldiers. The scheme of draining supplies out of the Sequatchie Valley prospered so magnificently that the Second Division even had a small herd of beef cattle built up when it came time to move out.[4]

In other ways, too, the front-line troops had it easier during the two months of siege than those confined to the muddy streets and tin-roofed shacks of Chattanooga several miles in the rear of the outer defenses. The pickets on both sides were becoming friendly and rarely fired at each other any more, a sensible arrangement in the circumstances and one that frequently and unofficially obtained during inactive stretches of "the brothers' war."

Colonel Moxley Sorrell, Longstreet's chief of staff, told how a Federal band came down to the riverbank one afternoon and began playing Northern patriotic airs. "Now give us some of ours!" the Southern pickets called across the river. The Northern bandsmen obliged with "Dixie," "My Maryland" and "The Bonnie Blue Flag." There was loud applause from the Confederate audience, and then the band played "Home, Sweet Home." Said Sorrell, "On both sides of the river there were joyous shouts, and soon many wet eyes could be found among those hardy warriors under the two flags."

It was still possible to be killed or wounded, of course, but the chances were apparently slight enough not to be taken very seriously. A story went the rounds of the 18th Ohio of how, while Confederate batteries on the point of Lookout Mountain were shelling the Federal positions below, a solid shot entered the opening of a pup tent near which two infantrymen were standing. It passed through the tent and buried itself in the ground. One soldier turned to the other and said, "There, you damn fool, you see what you get by leaving your door open?"[5]

The close proximity of the opposing forces produced an eerie feeling in Colonel John Beatty, who confided to his diary:

> The two armies are lying face to face. The Federal and Confederate sentinels walk their beats within sight of each other. The quarters of the rebel generals may be seen from our camps with the naked eye. The tents of their troops dot the hillsides. Tonight we see their signal lights off to the right on the summit of Lookout Mountain and off to the left on the knobs of Missionary Ridge. Their long lines of campfires almost encircle us. But the campfires of the Army of the Cumberland are burning also. . . .

The camps of Sheridan's division were enlivened by the appearance of a distinguished actor, James E. Murdock, who stayed at Sheridan's headquarters when he came down to recover the body of his son, a casualty of Chickamauga. For weeks Murdock toured the campfires and improvised theaters (built of scrap lumber and canvas) of the division and entertained his son's comrades with recitations.

During this time, while the Army of the Cumberland waited for reinforcements and the opening of a supply line, desertions became a serious problem. At the beginning of the siege three men of

Sheridan's Second Division deserted and made their way north. They were arrested and returned to face a court-martial, which sentenced them to be shot. Sheridan paraded the whole division to witness the execution. "It was the saddest spectacle I ever witnessed," he explained, "but there could be no evasion, no mitigation of the full letter of the law; its timely enforcement was but justice to the brave spirits who had yet to fight the rebellion to the end."[6]

Yet the siege of Chattanooga did not rival in suffering the only similar operation of the Civil War, the siege of Vicksburg. The Union armies were trapped in and about the little city for almost exactly two months, but there was at least that uncertain route to Bridgeport, and the famous "Cracker Line" was opened exactly 39 days after the battle of Chickamauga ended. Thousands of men fell ill of scurvy and other diseases caused by nutritional deficiencies, but there was no serious epidemic and no downright starvation.

Almost from the day the Army of the Cumberland retreated behind the city's defenses Washington began to plan and initiate operations to raise the siege. The army was to be reinforced from both the eastern and western forces. First, two corps of the Army of the Potomac—XI Corps under Major General O. O. Howard, XII Corps under Major General Henry W. Slocum (the roommate who had helped Sheridan with mathematics at West Point)— were to be shipped by rail to Bridgeport under Major General Joseph Hooker, who had commanded the Eastern army during the Chancellorsville campaign that spring. This force, numbering about 12,000, was then to break its way into Chattanooga through Lookout Valley. Second, Grant's Army of the Tennessee was to be concentrated at Vicksburg and brought north by steamers and the railroads to join in relieving the siege.

The new and growing importance of the telegraph and the railroad to warfare was never so apparent during the war as in the measures taken to reinforce the Army of the Cumberland. Wire communications allowed Secretary of War Stanton and General Grant to discuss these moves at long distance with almost the facility of today's Joint Chiefs of Staff conferring in the Pentagon with a theater commander over the teletype machines. "Occasionally, at night, [Stanton] would order the wires between the War Department and my headquarters to be connected, and we would hold a conversation for an hour or two," General Grant said. And the growing network of railroads allowed transportation of Hooker's corps to the railhead at Bridgeport in less than two weeks.[7]

A plan to open a shorter route to Bridgeport via the river—what became known as the "Cracker Line," in honor of the crackers, or hardtack, which were one of the staples of the army's diet—was already being drawn up. Its capable architect was the army's chief engineer, General W. F. Smith—"Baldy" Smith, the center of several Civil War controversies involving George B. McClellan, Ben Butler and U. S. Grant.[8] Hooker and his divisions were to ram their way through Lookout Valley while an amphibious force of two brigades and pontoon boats from the Army of the Cumberland cut across the huge loop of the Tennessee River and joined Hooker in the vicinity of Brown's Ferry.

Meanwhile, the Administration had decided that the man to command these vast, complicated movements was General Grant. Having successfully besieged Vicksburg, he was now expected to perform a reverse miracle at Chattanooga. He was ordered to meet Secretary of War Stanton at Louisville, and on October 16 was formally assigned to the task. The War Department gave him the alternative of retaining Rosecrans in command or replacing him with Thomas. The evening of the day he decided, with little hesitation, to give Thomas the command, Dana wired Stanton from Chattanooga that, "unless prevented," Rosecrans would retreat. An exchange of telegrams between Grant and Thomas, with all the terseness characteristic of these two men who "could be silent in seven languages," assured Stanton before he returned to Washington that such a possibility would not be considered by the new setup. "Hold Chattanooga at all costs," telegraphed Grant to Thomas. "We will hold the town until we starve," Thomas replied.[9]

On October 20 General Thomas gave his approval to Smith's plan for the operation to unite his army with Hooker's corps. Three days later General Grant, "wet, dirty and well," as Dana reported to Stanton, arrived in the beleaguered city and told Thomas to go ahead with the plan. Grant was greatly relieved to find that the sentiment in favor of a retreat existed only in Rosecrans' mind— if there—for Grant believed that abandonment of the city would result in annihilation of the army "either by capture or demoralization." He had met the departing Rosecrans at Stevenson, Alabama, and credited him with making "some excellent suggestions. . . . My only wonder was that he had not carried them out."[10]

Within a week after Grant's arrival the prospects brightened immeasurably. Hooker and the Cumberlanders effected a juncture at Brown's Ferry after the former fought one of the few night battles of the war in Lookout Valley and beat back Longstreet's attempts to block his advance. Meanwhile, the Confederate high command was doing its best to co-operate, unwittingly, in assisting the Union. President Jefferson Davis arrived at Bragg's headquarters and, noting that Longstreet and Bragg were at swords' points, decided Longstreet should take his corps of 20,000 and march to Knoxville to badger the Federal garrison under General Burnside. As Grant sardonically expressed his gratitude, "On several occasions during the war he [Davis] came to the relief of the Union army by means of his *superior military genius*." (Italics are Grant's.)

In a general realignment of the army Sheridan's division was shifted to a sector of the line parallel to Missionary Ridge, roughly between Forts Negley and Wood. Hooker's two small corps were assigned to the right flank in Lookout Valley. When the Army of the Tennessee arrived from its long trek across the midriff of Tennessee it was to take position on the left of the Army of the Cumberland, which formed the center of what would now be called an army group.

While all these preparations were going forward with the impetus demanded by General Grant, the War Department almost disrupted his careful planning by growing alarmed over Burnside's situation at Knoxville. Burnside had 25,000 troops to cope with Longstreet's 20,000, but Knoxville had always been a highly sensitive point in President Lincoln's military thinking. It was the cen ter of a strongly pro-Union population. From the beginning of the war Lincoln was determined to liberate East Tennessee and keep it liberated. So the War Department harassed Grant daily with telegrams suggesting that he push forward an attack on Bragg— well-intrenched as he was—to bring about Longstreet's recall to Chattanooga. There was little military justification for this pro- posed feint, which would involve Thomas' IV Corps, including Sheridan's division, in an attack on Missionary Ridge. General Thomas flatly told Grant that the diversion could not be under- taken, and the proposal was dropped. But Burnside's rather silly alarms and appeals had come close to committing the largest part of the Union forces to a reckless maneuver which could only result in strengthening Bragg or, at best, weakening the Army of the Cumberland before the crucial battle was fought. It was obvious to the field officers that Missionary Ridge could be stormed with hope of success only if the operation was preceded by attacks else- where on the Confederate battle line.[11]

On November 15 Sherman arrived in Chattanooga, well in ad- vance of his army, to confer with Grant and Thomas. For the second time during the war the four most celebrated generals of the Union were associated in a campaign. The first time, of course, had been at Corinth, when Sheridan was only a staff captain. Even now, as a division commander, he did not participate in the high- level conferences. But the muralistic aspects of the battle for Chat- tanooga, occurring in a great natural amphitheater which was the delight of heroic-style painters for years after the war, were en- hanced by the very successful collaboration of Grant, Sherman, Thomas and Sheridan, as well as the showy presence of "Fighting Joe" Hooker. A week after Sherman arrived his vanguard was streaming into Chattanooga and moving in considerable secrecy to its position on the Cumberlanders' left.

Essentially Grant's battle plan called for Hooker to demonstrate against the Confederate forces on Lookout Mountain; Sherman's column was to pass behind the positions of the Army of the Cum- berland and carry the northern extremity of Missionary Ridge, with the center under Thomas co-operating with Sherman. Both Hooker and Sherman were reinforced from the Army of the Cum- berland, leaving it with only the four divisions of IV Corps under Granger to demonstrate against Missionary Ridge and support Sherman's attack. The four divisions of the IV Corps were Sheridan's, Wood's, Baird's and Johnson's. It was obvious to the Cumberlanders, who were suffering from a sort of collective inferiority complex after Chickamauga, that Grant was entrusting Sherman and his Army of the Tennessee with the heavy-duty role. It was this feeling in the ranks as well as in the councils of its leaders that was primarily responsible for the privates and noncoms and company officers fighting their own battle of Missionary Ridge without much consideration for Grant's carefully conceived plan to have Sherman carry off the victory.

The co-ordinated assaults were ordered for November 24. But on the night of the twenty-second a Confederate sentinel deserted and was brought before General Sheridan for questioning. The deserter said that "Bragg's baggage was being reduced and that he was about to fall back." Grant wanted Bragg pinned down rather than fleeing southward through the passes toward Atlanta, so he immediately ordered a probing attack for the next morning, November 23, at eleven o'clock.[12]

The objective of the attack was Orchard Knob, which lay in front of Missionary Ridge and had been occupied by the Confederates as a sort of outpost. Wood's division was to make the assault with Sheridan's division supporting it on the right flank to prevent the enemy from countering in that direction. Wood's men marched toward the objective with all the calm and precision of a divisional review. The Confederates, in fact, sat on their breastworks and watched what they thought was a very pretty parade until the shots started flying. They were easily driven off, and the Union division took possession of Orchard Knob while Sheridan's troops settled down on a low ridge to the right. On orders from General Thomas, Sheridan covered his front with a strong line of rifle pits and brought up two batteries of Regular artillery which had been borrowed from the XI Corps.[13]

Next day the great double envelopment which developed into the battle of Missionary Ridge was put into motion. Grant, Thomas, Granger, Dana and other high officers used Orchard Knob as a sort of reviewing stand from which to watch operations on the right and left. Sherman sent his long assault lines forward at the northern end of Missionary Ridge. The attack was only partly successful, but it drew Confederate strength away from Lookout Mountain, and Joe Hooker's divisions went charging up the northern face of that steep bastion. Their comrades watching in the valley below cheered an impressive omen: the Stars and Stripes raised on the summit of Lookout above the layers of clouds. Then a heavy fog bank closed down on the mountain, and the battle was lost to view. There was heavy cannonading, and Sheridan sent a staff officer spurring off to Hooker with an offer of assistance. Sheridan soon was advised that the alarm was more acoustical than actual. What he heard was "only a part of a little rear-guard fight, two sections of artillery making all the noise, the reverberations from point to point in the adjacent mountains echoing and re-echoing till it seemed that at least fifty guns were engaged."[14]

On November 25 dawned the day of decision. Hooker, with Palmer's division of the Army of the Cumberland reinforcing his two small corps, drove across Chattanooga Valley in an attempt to get in the enemy's rear while Sherman attacked the Rebels' right flank with characteristic energy and purpose. A soldier who participated in the action told how Sherman's forces hammered at a railroad tunnel which cut a notch in Missionary Ridge and was strongly held by the Confederates. "Instantly whole divisions of Sherman's and Bragg's troops commenced slaughtering one another for the possession of single hills and spurs. At times the battle in front of Sherman was a hand-to-hand encounter. My own brigade was so close that the Rebels even threw stones down on us." At two o'clock that afternoon the order to "fix bayonets" was given, and an attack began all along Sherman's line. "We had to charge over the open, and the storm of shot and shell became terrific. . . . We could see the enemy working his guns, while in plain view other batteries galloped up, unlimbered and let loose at us. Behind us our own batteries—forty cannon—were firing at the enemy over our heads."

Four times Sherman was repulsed among the hillocks and arroyos on the north end of Missionary Ridge, while on the Union right Hooker's advance was delayed by the necessity of bridging the swollen Chickamauga Creek. Until midafternoon the IV Corps of the Army of the Cumberland was comparatively inactive, waiting for the signal to demonstrate against the towering center of the ridge and relieve some of the pressure against Sherman.

Ever since the last gun of the battle was fired there has been controversy over the disposition of Bragg's army during the hours before the climactic Union assaults. It seems obvious that Bragg reinforced his right to oppose Sherman, but Confederate sources have always stubbornly denied this. After a lengthy study of the battle General James H. Wilson of Grant's staff concluded that Bragg had not weakened his left and center to strengthen his right. Eyewitness testimony indicates the opposite: many in the Federal ranks from general to private caught sight of Confederate troops moving to the northern sector of Missionary Ridge, and only thus could Bragg have held back the determined attacks by Sherman's divisions.

At 3:00 P.M. General Sherman decided the time had come for the Army of the Cumberland to assume its share of the burden. He told a staff officer, "Go signal Grant. The orders were that I should get as many as possible in front of me and God knows there are now enough. They've been reinforcing all day."

Grant, Thomas and Granger received Sherman's message at field headquarters on Orchard Knob. Both Grant and Thomas were surrounded by their staffs, like stately planets with revolving satellites, each group a little cool, a little jealous. Like the men in the ranks, Grant's officers felt a bit superior because they had been summoned to rescue the Army of the Cumberland, and Thomas' officers naturally resented this attitude, within the bounds of military etiquette. This feeling was reflected in the four divisions of the IV Corps, where it was noted that for the first time quartermasters, cooks, clerks and other service troops had armed themselves and joined the assault formations. Vengeance for Chickamauga was uppermost in their minds that day; as the men of the 6th Indiana put it, "We were crazy to charge."

Nowhere, his officers said, was the enthusiasm for a charge against the masked artillery and the rifle-studded pits and trenches of Missionary Ridge stronger than in Sheridan's Second Division. Its only activity so far had been to drive in the Confederate pickets on its front and so allow Sheridan to "prolong my line of battle on that of General Wood's."[15]

The firing of six signal guns, it had been arranged, was to send Sheridan's and Wood's divisions forward with Baird's and Johnson's closely following in support. The troops would need all their enthusiasm, for the crest of the ridge rose 400 feet, and its broken, crumbling face, Bragg had declared, gave the defense such an advantage that "a single cordon of skirmishers could hold it against the whole Federal army." Before the skirmish lines and assault columns even reached the first line of rifle pits at the base of the ridge the Second Division had to traverse from 400 to 900 yards of open ground swept by enemy fire. Opposite the center of the division, on top of the ridge, was the Thurman house where Bragg had established his headquarters.[16]

At 3:40 P.M. the six signal guns roared out their message, and a charge unique among all "hopeless charges" from Balaclava to Omdurman was under way.

The infantry stepped out as briskly and erectly as if forming for a parade, then increased its pace to the double-quick under the deadly salute of 60 Confederate field guns and a crackling fury of musketry all along the front. Like a blue surf washing against the bottom of the ridge the Union infantry swept into and over the lower line of enemy rifle pits. "Without awaiting further orders or stopping to re-form," Grant noted with surprise as he and Thomas watched the operation through their field glasses, "our troops went to the second line of works, over that and on for the crest."

General Grant turned to Thomas and Granger and demanded to know who had ordered them to proceed after capturing the first enemy line; the IV Corps had been clearly informed that its demonstration would involve only the lower rifle pits. Both insisted they had not, and the exuberant Granger added, "When those fellows get started all hell can't stop them." According to Colonel Fullerton, Grant, seeing his battle plan going to pieces because the common soldiers had taken it into their own hands, could only grumble that it would be all right if it turned out well—otherwise somebody would be made to suffer.

Sheridan was as surprised as his superiors when the men in the ranks, by a simultaneous and collective impulse, paused only momentarily in the first line of pits and then started up the ridge, howling and capering like dervishes. Until the troops themselves went on in their own inspired initiative Sheridan had had no thought of taking the crest of the ridge, for he had watched the enemy's center being reinforced from the abandoned positions opposite Hooker. "He [Bragg] marched regiments from the right, waving their blue battle flags," Sheridan said in his official report. Actually it occurred to Sheridan just before launching the attack that a question might arise over how far to advance; he sent back a staff officer to Granger with the query, but the signal guns sounded before a reply could be received. Soon after his men took the enemy's outer line "with a mass of glistening bayonets which was irresistible," Captain Avery of Granger's staff came up with the corps commander's permission to take the ridge if possible.

Just before that, however, another courier had reached General Wagner of the Second Brigade with an admonition that "it was General Granger's order not to go beyond the works at the foot of the ridge." Although part of his command was already beyond that line, Wagner ordered it back; withdrawing under heavy fire, it suffered unnecessary casualties. Wagner then sent an aide to Sheridan, "asking permission to carry the heights, as I saw we must do that or we could not remain in the works, the enemy having complete control of them with his artillery." Even before hearing from Sheridan, Wagner on his own initiative brought up the 15th Indiana and the 97th Ohio from reserve and sent them charging up the ridge.[17]

The Second Brigade was the only one to receive orders from Granger to halt at the first line of Confederate works, and its temporary and unavoidable lagging behind opened a dangerous gap between it and Colonel Harker's Third Brigade in the center, and Colonel Sherman's First Brigade on the right. Harker reported that Wagner's delay left him "entirely without support and partially exposed to cross-fire."[18] Sheridan ordered him to advance as soon as his troops had caught their breath.

Because of the understandable confusion at army headquarters—

with the troops wrenching control of the battle out of their superiors' hands and exceeding orders—Sheridan's division was momentarily imperiled. If the enemy had been able to mount a counterattack on Sheridan's left between Wagner and Harker, his division might have been badly damaged. But he knew this was a moment to be seized and exploited. Having received Granger's permission to use his own discretion and "believing the attack had assumed a new phase, and that I could carry the ridge," he decided that "I could not order those officers and men who were so gallantly ascending the hill, step by step, to return."[19]

Indeed, the wisest thing was to give the division its head. The charge of the troops to the crest was their own idea; how he was to use it was a new indication of his ability to wring every advantage out of an unexpected situation and show himself at variance with the many generals who are as unhinged by unexpected success as by sudden adversity.

General Sheridan, standing in the captured trenches at the bottom of the ridge, turned to Captain Avery and borrowed the silver flask carried by the staff officer, threw back his head and swallowed an outsize drink of brandy. "Here's to you!" he shouted to a group of Confederate officers watching from the Thurman house. Near by was the famous "Churchbell Battery" whose guns, the Lady Buckner, the Lady Breckinridge, the Lady Bragg, etc., had been cast from bells contributed by the churches of Atlanta. A Southern officer ordered two of the guns depressed and a volley given the little gamecock toasting them from below. A moment later the shells kicked up dirt all around Sheridan. He yelled back, "That is ungenerous; I shall take those guns for that!"[20]

Men of the various regiments under Sheridan and Wood raced one another for the privilege of reaching the crest first. "Our men drove the troops in the lower line of rifle pits so rapidly, and followed them so closely, that Rebel and Union troops went over the first line of works almost at the same time," Grant observed. "Many Rebels were captured and sent to the rear under the fire of their own friends higher up the hill. Those that were not captured retreated and were pursued. The retreating hordes being between friends and pursuers caused the enemy to fire high to avoid killing their own men." Enemy gunners, unable to depress their cannon sufficiently, lighted the fuses of shells and rolled them down the slope at the advancing Federals. But the men of Wood and Sheridan charged into and over the second line of works with hardly a pause to club down or bayonet a few resisting Southerners or send them to the rear as prisoners. "Chickamauga!" screamed the attacking Northerners as if the word itself was a talisman.

The men clambered up the rocky surface of the ridge in wildgoose formation, with the V's pointed toward the enemy works and guns surmounting the ridge. Color-bearers were picked off by Southern sharpshooters, but their flags were snatched up before they could fall, and the charge went on without a flicker of hesitation. Desperate Confederates even rolled boulders down on the advancing blue line when shot and shell seemed to have little or no effect. Sheridan, on horseback, followed Harker's and Sherman's brigades and waved on Wagner's to join the assault on the crest. And soon the log parapet of the Confederate works crowning the ridge was swarming with the battle-mad Federals.

In the valley below, on Orchard Knob, the commanding generals were awestruck at the all but impossible victory achieved by their men. Dana wired Secretary of War Stanton that evening: "The storming of the ridge by our troops was one of the greatest miracles in military history. No man who climbs the ascent by any of the roads that wind along its face can believe that 18,000 men were moved up its broken and crumbling face unless it was his fortune to witness the deed. It seems as awful as a visible interposition of God."[21]

Bragg's headquarters was carried so swiftly that the Confederate commander escaped capture by seconds and the adjutant generals of two division commanders, Bate and Breckinridge, were taken prisoner along with many other enemy staff officers. The "Churchbell Battery" fell into the pious hands of the 73rd Illinois, the "Preachers' Regiment," or so its historians claimed. Sheridan, as excited as any of his capering young privates, straddled one of the captured cannon and crowed with triumph. "You'll all be courtmartialed for this," his rival, General Wood, shouted at his soldiers . . . and guffawed. General Granger, his black beard bristling with excitement, came spurring up the ridge a few minutes later. Soldiers of the 36th Illinois yelled at him, "What do you think of this, General?" And Granger growled with mock anger, "I think you disobeyed orders, you damned rascals!"

The Confederate line was smashed now. Grant had expected to flank it with Sherman's army on the left, with Hooker enveloping it on the right. Instead, Thomas' forces had broken through its center and sent it into a panic-stricken retreat, the first such wholesale rout in the Western theater. As one of the two spearheads which had accomplished this near miracle Sheridan's division had suffered heavily. Out of a prebattle strength of about 6,000, its commander reported, 130 were killed, 1,213 were wounded and three were missing in action, a total of 1,346, approximating the losses of Stone's River and Chickamauga.[22]

General Bragg tried desperately to rally his fleeing divisions for a stand, pleading, "Here's your commander," and receiving the reply, "Here's your jackass," from his men. Sheridan watched a fugitive column in the valley below, wagon train, guns and caissons tangled in fearful confusion, and decided on pursuit.[23] Merely defeating the enemy was never enough for Sheridan; he always aimed at annihilation and accepted grudgingly anything less.

While the other Union generals congratulated and raised their flasks to one another, Sheridan pushed his division down the eastern face of the ridge on the heels of the enemy. He sent Harker and Wagner forward against the Confederate rear guard, with Sherman's brigade in reserve. The two brigades were deployed along the sides of the road leading to Chickamauga Station. Wagner snatched up nine pieces of Confederate artillery in his advance. One mile from the crest of Missionary Ridge Sheridan ran into strong resistance—a "high formidable ridge" spiked with eight guns and considerable infantry commanding the road along which his brigades were advancing. Dusk had fallen, and a night battle was the riskiest of operations, but Sheridan was determined to drive ahead. The troops rested while he brought up the 26th Ohio and the 15th Indiana from the reserve. At midnight the ridge was stormed by the two fresh regiments followed by Wagner and

Harker. Although without artillery support, they carried the position with a rush and broke the Confederate rear guard, captured many prisoners and drove the rest across Chickamauga Creek. The enemy's artillery, much ammunition and stacks of small arms remained behind for the Federals to seize.[24]

In his report of this midnight engagement Sheridan became almost lyrical, especially for a hard-bitten soldier whose official papers were usually written in a colorless if taut and precise style. "When the head of the column reached the summit of the hill, the moon rose from behind, and a medallion view of the column was disclosed as it crossed the moon's disk and attacked the enemy . . . who fled. This was a gallant little fight."[25]

General Sheridan wanted to drive on after the enemy, hoping to destroy a large part of Bragg's army, but he could not enlist the enthusiasm of General Granger, who "told me finally to push on . . . and if I encountered the enemy he would order troops to my support." At two o'clock on the morning of the twenty-sixth, while most of the forces under Grant were claiming their well-earned slumber, Sheridan was still active and scheming to obtain support for his pursuit. He found Chickamauga Creek fordable, but "feared to go farther without assistance." Later he admitted without much embarrassment, "I caused two regiments to simulate an engagement by opening fire, hoping that this would alarm Granger and oblige him to respond with troops, but my scheme failed. General Granger afterward told me that he had heard the volleys, but suspected their purpose, knowing that they were not occasioned by a fight, since they were too regular in their delivery."[26] Although his ruse failed, Sheridan believed that if his pursuit had been properly supported, the Confederate retreat would have been "incalculably" endangered, "for the force that had confronted Sherman did not pass Chickamauga Station in their retreat until after daylight on the morning of the 26th."

While the enemy was making good his withdrawal Sheridan and other generals of the combined armies indulged in recriminations. Hooker asserted that after Missionary Ridge had been seized Grant, disappointed by the way his plans had been disrupted by the Cumberlanders' victorious charge, exclaimed, "Damn the battle! I had nothing to do with it."

Sheridan's complaint concerned the guns captured near Bragg's headquarters on the ridge. Begging "pardon for this unpleasant digression," he declared in his official report that "eleven of these guns were gleaned from the battlefield and appropriated while I was pushing the enemy on to Chickamauga Station." The culprit, he indicated, was General Hazen, who commanded a brigade in Wood's division. His officers and men were also quarreling with Wood's division over which unit had reached the summit first. From all the evidence, they finished in practically a dead heat. But the controversy was still going strong more than 20 years after when the two generals sat down to write their autobiographies.

General Hazen devoted 57 pages to claiming that his brigade won the palm and that it captured the 11 guns which Sheridan asserted had been "appropriated." The night after the battle, Hazen wrote, Sheridan came to his headquarters and "insisted rather imperiously upon an unquestioning giving up of the guns." Hazen refused.[27]

Sheridan's book acidly replied that "at the time the occurrence took place, I made the charge in a plain official report, which was accepted as correct by the corps and army commanders, from General Granger up to General Grant. General Hazen took no notice of this report then, though well aware of its existence. Nearly a quarter of a century later, however, he endeavored to justify his retention of the guns by trying to show that his brigade was the first to reach the crest of Missionary Ridge, and that he was therefore entitled to them. This claim of being the first to mount the ridge is made by other brigades than Hazen's, with equal if not greater force, so the absurdity of his deduction is apparent."[28]

Less apparent to General Sheridan was the fact that, if all the artillery claimed by his brigade and regimental commanders had actually been captured, the enemy armies would hardly have been able to raise a battery for the balance of the war. The controversy over the captured cannon was always good for a few fist fights at reunions of the Army of the Cumberland until the veterans of Wood's and Sheridan's divisions were too old for saloon combat.

Well, there was glory enough for all in the victory. The siege of Chattanooga had been raised, and Chickamauga had been avenged.

A vainglorious postscript to the Chattanooga campaign may be noted: President Lincoln and his advisers were again alarmed over the safety of Knoxville, which was still under siege by Longstreet. Only four days after the storming of Missionary Ridge the IV Corps was marching to relieve Burnside, for Lincoln believed that the Union's secure possession of Knoxville would destroy the Confederacy like "an animal with a thorn in its vitals." General Sherman and his divisions were sent in a separate column to co-operate with the IV Corps in driving Longstreet off, although Sherman protested to Grant: "Recollect that East Tennessee is my horror. That any military man should send a force into East Tennessee puzzles me. Burnside is there and must be relieved, but when relieved I want to get out and he should come out too. . . . Cumberland Gap should be held simply as an outpost of Kentucky."[29]

Knoxville was even more of a "horror" to Sheridan and the men of his division, who had naturally been looking forward to going into winter quarters. The troops needed winter clothing and camp equipment, all of which had been left behind in Murfreesboro the previous spring, and all Sheridan could procure before their departure was "a few overcoats and a small supply of India-rubber ponchos"; most of the men were expected to march and fight in the chill, rain-swept mountains of East Tennessee with only their worn and ragged summer uniforms.[30]

The forced march by Granger and Sherman had almost a farcical ending. On December 5, when they reached Marysville, fifteen miles west of Knoxville, they learned that Longstreet had assaulted the fortifications of the city, had been easily repelled and had retreated eastward to the mountains, evidently planning to return to Lee's army. The commanders rode on to Knoxville and found Burnside's troops well-fed and clothed; the "rescue" expedition had been an unnecessary hardship on exhausted survivors of the battle of Missionary Ridge. To the disgusted generals their dinner at Burnside's mess seemed almost epicurean.

Sherman and his forces returned to Chattanooga and settled in winter camps in the vicinity, while the IV Corps was given the mission of helping Burnside to hold East Tennessee until spring. Sherman rejected Grant's proposal that he pursue Longstreet over the Blue Ridge mountains into North Carolina, saying, "A stern chase is a long one."[31]

The IV and XXIII Corps (the latter composing Burnside's Army of the Ohio) were dispatched to Strawberry Plains, 18 miles from Knoxville, in pursuit of Longstreet, who had settled down for a month of bridge building at Blain's Crossroads. Six hundred of Sheridan's men were so poorly shod they had to be left behind until a wagon train from Chattanooga arrived to outfit the division. Sleet and snow fell in the mountains and the suffering of the soldiers increased. ". . . While in bivouac their only shelter was the ponchos with which they had been provided before leaving Chattanooga; there was not a tent in the command. Hence great suffering resulted," Sheridan wrote. And when the wagon train finally reached Knoxville it was seized by the headquarters officers there, and the winter clothing Sheridan had been expecting was distributed "pro rata to the different organizations of the entire army."[32]

Meanwhile, the high command in the city indulged itself in various comedies which were little appreciated by the men shivering in mountain camps. During the Christmas jollification at headquarters General Granger, in an uproarious holiday mood, sent General Grant a facetious telegram evidently parodying General Thomas' message from besieged Chattanooga a few months earlier. "We are in Knoxville and will hold it until hell freezes over," Granger assured his superior. General Foster, Burnside's second-in-command, wrote "tight" at the end of the message to "indicate that Granger was under the influence of liquor and that the message should not go." The operator, failing to understand Foster's postscript, sent the message with "tight" at the end. General Grant was "both puzzled and indignant" and was "convinced that Granger was a trifler and unworthy of high command," according to General James H. Wilson of his staff. At Missionary Ridge Granger had annoyed Grant by personally firing a field gun instead of concerning himself more intimately with the IV Corps and had had to be instructed by Grant to go to his troops. This freakish juvenile streak appeared in Granger at the least appropriate times. He "occasionally fell into fits of indolence and wasted hours," General Wilson said. He would probably have been accorded the opportunity which was soon given General Sheridan if he had not fallen out of favor with Grant. Wilson characterized him as "brave, brilliant and aggressive, a bolt of steel in action," with "as much courage and more brains than Sheridan." As it was, he was to disappear before long in a series of lesser commands, although he was a national hero for his quick march to Thomas' assistance at Chickamauga.[33]*

On December 27, in fact, General Grant had telegraphed General Foster: "If you find it necessary for the efficiency of his command relieve him [Granger] from duty . . . and place Sheridan in command of his corps."[34] The Christmas telegram only intensified Grant's determination to place Sheridan over Granger.

Meanwhile, an elaborate game of buck passing was being played by Sheridan's superiors, who could see little glory in fighting the mountain snows and an elusive enemy and were wholeheartedly concerned with leaves of absence until more clement weather arrived. The army moved from Strawberry Plains to Dandridge after bridging the Holston River. Command of the operation was juggled like a hot stove lid. Burnside was superseded by Foster. Foster complained of a recurrence of Mexican War wounds and handed the command to the Army of the Ohio's chief of staff, General Parke. Parke turned it over to Granger. And Granger, deciding it was necessary for him to stay at Strawberry Plains for a few days to "hurry up supplies," passed the baton to Sheridan.

General Hazen grumbled that the army was being led by "a divisional commander, and four removes from the proper commander. There was no end of talk and fun about this shifting of command." Another brigadier, Willich, who had served his apprenticeship in the Prussian army and had a natural feeling for punctilio, observed that "the plan ought to have been carried out

---

* From *Under the Old Flag* by James H. Wilson (copyright, 1912, D. Appleton and Company). This and other passages from the same book used by permission of Appleton-Century-Crofts, Inc.

to its utmost limit, when we should have had the anomalous spectacle of an army in the field in the command of a corporal."[35] The reason for Willich's annoyance, according to Sheridan, was that his brigade had been placed "beyond the shelter of the timber" by the temporary commanding general.

It looked momentarily as if Sheridan might be called on to direct the army in a pitched battle, as General Sturgis' cavalry units were driven in and required a brigade of infantry to cover their withdrawal.[36] Having no wish to assume responsibility without an increase in authority, Sheridan sent word to Granger that he had better hasten to the front. By the time Granger arrived it was known that Longstreet had merely been making a demonstration to conceal the fact that he was finally withdrawing to Virginia and reunion with Lee's Army of Northern Virginia. General Granger called a council of his subordinates and was in such a "petulant'" mood that he ordered General Hazen's arrest because Hazen had demanded that his superior's "tone and manner be corrected." Hazen was released from arrest the following night, but the mood of the army was still one of disgruntlement from its commander down to its rear-ranking privates.[37]

"A series of blunders" was Sheridan's laconic comment on the operations in East Tennessee after the departure of Sherman for Chattanooga. The Second Division was ordered into winter quarters at Loudon, and its health and spirits were soon restored by suitable clothing, decent quarters and an assured food supply. General Sheridan took his first leave of absence since 1853 and went North for several weeks.

Shortly after his return to division headquarters at Loudon, on March 23, 1864, he received a telegram from General Grant in Washington. Grant had been appointed general in chief of the Union armies on March 12. The telegram read:

LIEUTENANT-GENERAL GRANT DIRECTS THAT MAJOR GENERAL SHERIDAN IMMEDIATELY REPAIR TO WASHINGTON AND REPORT TO THE ADJUTANT-GENERAL OF THE ARMY.

8

CAVALRY IN THE WILDERNESS

ON HIS way to Washington, General Sheridan stopped at the headquarters of the Army of the Cumberland in Chattanooga. There he learned from General Thomas that he was to be appointed Chief of Cavalry, Army of the Potomac, commanding three full cavalry divisions. It was a big if not overwhelming promotion. He knew he was in line for a corps command, but he was surprised that it was with the Army of the Potomac, since he had never served in the East, indeed had never been over the ground where the Eastern armies were grappling.

Both sentiment and wisdom governed his choice of staff officers to accompany him eastward. Captain James W. Forsyth, 18th Infantry, was an old friend, and, having served in the Peninsula and Antietam campaigns under McClellan, he knew the ground over which the armies were fighting and was acquainted with the personalities of many of the Army of the Potomac's commanders. This last special knowledge is often as important to a rising officer as an understanding of the enemy. As aides-de-camp Sheridan brought along his brother Michael and Lieutenant T. W. C. Moore. Mike, a lieutenant, was detailed to take charge of the horses, while Captain Forsyth and Lieutenant Moore went ahead with the general. Both Forsyth and Mike Sheridan stayed with Phil, in one capacity or another, until his death. Sheridan had a strong clan feeling, not only toward his family but toward the men who served with him—"loyalty up and down," as the modern army phrase has it.

Fellow passengers on the train that bore him and his two companions to Washington would have found it hard to believe they were traveling with a man of destiny. Hard service in the mountains had worn down his body that winter, and his uniform hung on his frame like castoff clothes on a scarecrow. He puffed on his yellowed little meerschaum, breezily chaffing and arguing. Without taking a close look at the insignia, the passengers might have mistaken Sheridan for a hard-bitten sergeant going home on furlough and being allowed to take liberties with the two more elegant officers in his company. It would have been difficult for strangers to visualize him mounted on Rienzi, clouded in battle smoke, carrying the "forked lightnings" (as one newspaper correspondent observed) which so electrified his troops. Sheridan put away his forked lightnings, his air of command, when they were not needed. Let the glory hounds swagger around as they pleased! Captain Forsyth observed that Sheridan was so impressive in the saddle because he "sat tall," so that with his long torso he gave the appearance of possessing a magnificent physique.

At the age of thirty-three he was being given command of the Federal Army's largest cavalry force, but he found little joy in the prospect. As his train carried him east he brooded over the fact he was leaving the free-and-easy Western armies for the starchy Army of the Potomac, with its record of consistent failure in the field against Lee. After the Eastern army had driven Lee back from the heights around Gettysburg it had failed to pursue him vigorously and, during the autumn of 1863, had sparred indecisively with him in the Mine Run campaign. The opposing armies had faced each other across the Rapidan and seesawed back and forth between that Wilderness river and Bull Run, with little advantage to either side. Then they had settled down for the winter.

He felt depressed over leaving the Second Division, almost half of whose regiments had served with him since the fall of 1862. When he left his troops at Loudon they had gathered on a hillside overlooking the depot and cheered him. "They had never given me any trouble," he reflected, "nor done anything that could bring aught but honor to themselves. I had confidence in them, and I believe they had in me. They were ever steady, whether in victory or in misfortune, and as I tried always to be with them, to put them into the hottest fire if good could be gained, or save them from unnecessary loss, . . . they amply repaid all my care and anxiety."[1] In the Eastern army he would have to win confidence all over again. Furthermore, he had hoped to get an infantry corps in the spring offensive against Atlanta. Sherman was the kind of commander he could understand, while George Gordon Meade of the Army of the Potomac was a frosty formalist with the rigidity and caution often inculcated by the Corps of Engineers.

Nor was there any comfort in dwelling on the record of the Army of the Potomac's cavalry, whose road-bound regiments had twice allowed Jeb Stuart and his horsemen to ride around them and who had never managed to defeat the Southern cavaliers in a pitched battle. Some good men had gone down trying to make that cavalry corps effective, Stoneman and Pleasanton particularly, in the Chancellorsville and Gettysburg campaigns. Young Grimes Davis had been one of the most promising of its leaders, but had been killed in action, a Mississippian fighting for the North. John Buford, who had been working gradually to revise the inept doctrine on the use of cavalry in the East, had died that December of complications resulting from his wounds.[2]

The Army of the Potomac's cavalry corps had been used mainly for picketing, occasional patrols and guarding the wagon trains— more like the feelers of a blind insect than a vital striking arm. Too many cavalry officers dreamed of saber-swinging charges in the style of Murat and of the much-publicized six hundred of Balaclava. It would be difficult to persuade them to share Sheridan's view—that a cavalryman was "only an infantryman with four detachable legs," that mounted men with repeating revolvers and carbines could bring heavy fire power swiftly to a critical point without necessarily charging forward on horseback as the inevitable climax.

Undoubtedly reform would meet with the sort of opposition from old-line officers that only traditionalists can summon up when shibboleths are being destroyed.

Not the least troubling prospect was the danger of becoming involved in the barracudalike political maneuvering which many army officers held responsible for the disposal of General McClellan and other military leaders. Even Grant, as general in chief, it was feared, would not be protected against military and civilian politicians who were relentless in tearing down a man who failed to conform to their beliefs. General Sherman, for instance, believed that "Grant would not stand the intrigues of the politicians a week," and sent his friend the famous letter warning: "You are now Washington's legitimate successor. . . . For God's sake and your country's sake, come out of Washington!"

Sheridan was somewhat puzzled, too, by his selection for the command, since he had so few friends at court. He did not realize how much he had impressed both Grant and Halleck. Halleck was now chief of staff of the Union armies, presiding over the administrative detail in Washington while Grant took the field with the Army of the Potomac.[3] At the military conferences of the winter of 1863-1864 it was generally agreed that General Alfred Pleasanton must be replaced. The foremost of his three division commanders, Judson Kilpatrick, was a flamboyant battle leader but had a bad habit of driving his division so hard it would arrive at the scene of action with horses winded and incapable of further service. He was known as "Kill-cavalry." D. McM. Gregg was adjudged too unstable for increased responsibility, although a dashing field commander. Wesley Merritt was too young and too junior in rank and experience. General Grant first suggested General William B. Franklin, whose son-in-law had commanded the 1st Infantry in Texas when Sheridan served with the regiment. But War Department generals closer to the Eastern campaigns recalled that Franklin had failed to throw in 50,000 men of his "grand division" during Burnside's attack at Fredericksburg, and they pointed out that he was too old for a command requiring agility and a measure of daring.

"How would Sheridan do?" murmured General Halleck.

"The very man!" said General Grant. And so the matter was decided.

Halleck gratefully remembered Sheridan's precision in staff duties which would have driven a less determined man to drink and distraction. Grant admired Sheridan's ability to ferret out information about the enemy, as demonstrated during the Corinth campaign; his stubborn stands at Perryville and Stone's River; his cool generalship at Booneville; and his relentless pursuit of Bragg at Missionary Ridge when the other Union generals were well content with breaking the enemy's line. "To Sheridan's prompt movement," Grant said, "the Army of the Cumberland and the nation are indebted for the bulk of the capture of prisoners, artillery, and small-arms that day. Except for his prompt pursuit, so much in this way would not have been accomplished."[4]

War Correspondent Shanks, pondering that virtually the only time Grant and Halleck ever agreed wholeheartedly on anything was the appointment of Sheridan, commented, "To have equally pleased Halleck, the theoretical, and Grant, the practical soldier—Halleck, the wily and polite lawyer, and Grant, the simple-minded, straightforward soldier—Halleck, who attempted to rise by arts, and Grant, who trusted solely to action for promotion, required very great qualities in a mind as young as Sheridan's."[5]

It was well that Sheridan held the confidence of those on the highest army level, for Lincoln, Stanton and many of the desk wallahs at the War Department found him a rather depressing choice to attempt success where such a swashbuckling series of predecessors had failed. Sheridan checked into Willard's Hotel on the morning of April 4, 1864, with his two aides. The hotel was crowded with officers of the Army of the Potomac returning for the spring campaign after leaves in their home towns. Sheridan was chilled by the realization that he did not recognize a single face among the swarming magnificoes; and no one singled him out as the young savior from the West. When Grant arrived in Washington he had been greeted with the same sort of incredulity; people found it hard to believe that generals coming to take over high commands could be so small, quiet and modest as Grant and Sheridan. For the capital was accustomed to the pomp of McClellan, Burnside, Hooker, Hancock, Sickles, Frémont, Pope and others who made the very atmosphere tremble with their passing.

Sheridan had grown an imperial as well as a mustache to give an appearance of added years and dignity, but it was not altogether successful. Red-faced and "coarse-featured," as he was described by at least one elegant staff officer, Sheridan was a soldier's general who belonged in the field and was ill at ease during War Department councils, White House balls, receptions and stately dinner parties. Whatever dash he possessed as a conversationalist was better suited to a campfire than a drawing room. To Colonel Horace Porter of Grant's staff he appeared "worn down almost to a shadow by hard work and exposure in the field . . . , anything but formidable as a candidate for a cavalry leader."[6] Sheridan himself said his weight had dropped to 115 pounds after the rigors of the siege of Chattanooga and the winter campaign in the mountains of East Tennessee.

General Halleck received him courteously and took him to see Secretary of War Stanton, who was evidently a little disappointed. Stanton kept "eying me closely and searchingly" throughout the interview, Sheridan said, "endeavoring to form some estimate of one about whom he knew absolutely nothing." He was thoroughly chilled by the war minister's manner. "If I had ever possessed any self-assertion in manner or speech, it certainly vanished in the presence of the imperious Secretary, whose name at the time was the synonym of all that was cold and formal."

On first acquaintance Sheridan and Lincoln, to whom the general was escorted by Halleck immediately after the cold immersion offered by Stanton, were not greatly taken with each other. Lincoln was almost a foot taller than his new cavalry leader and evidently expected someone more physically impressive, but he took Sheridan's hand in both of his and spoke to him "very cordially." The President "hoped I would fulfill the expectations of General Grant . . . , adding that thus far the cavalry of the Army of the Potomac had not done all it might have done," Sheridan recalled. The President quoted a well-worn jest, first uttered by General Hooker according to most historians: "Who ever saw a dead cavalryman?" General Sheridan stiffened with initial resentment, but "I parted from the President convinced that he did not believe all that the query implied."[7]

When asked for a description of General Sheridan, the President was not particularly flattering. "I will tell you just what kind of chap he is. He is one of those long-armed fellows with short legs that can scratch his shins without having to stoop over." It was not too long before the President realized that, while Sheridan may have looked like a starveling, he had the spirit and determination which more magnificent specimens had only pretended to have. When a War Department officer remarked to General Grant, "The officer you brought on from the West is rather a little fellow to handle your cavalry," Grant replied, "You will find him big enough for the purpose before we get through with him."[8]

The day after his round of duty calls Sheridan left Washington with little regret, accompanying General Grant to the headquarters of the Army of the Potomac at Culpeper Court House, Virginia. En route the new general in chief told Sheridan of his plan to follow that army in its campaign against Lee and the Army of Northern Virginia, while also exercising authority over the rest of the 1,200-mile battle line that extended from the Atlantic Ocean to the Rio Grande—a command that included 21 army corps of 533,000 officers and men present and fit for duty. In one month all those armies of the Union were to be in motion against the enemy, so that, for the first time since the war began, he would be under attack from all quarters and unable to use his interior lines to advantage. While Meade struck at Lee in the direction of Richmond, Sherman was to drive on Atlanta with three combined armies, Butler was to move up the James, Sigel up the Shenandoah Valley, Averell in West Virginia, Banks up the Red River toward Texas. Thus eight armies were to take the field with the objective of crushing the Confederacy finally.

That evening of April 5 Sheridan arrived at the headquarters of the cavalry corps near Brandy Station and formally assumed command. The next few days were spent in sizing up his leading officers, deciding to retain most of the staff left by General Pleasanton, inspecting his command and finding that the men were in excellent condition but their mounts were deplorable. He was favorably impressed with the three division commanders. Brigadier General Alfred T. A. Torbert was a newcomer, having commanded an infantry brigade until Grant promoted him to head the First Cavalry Division, with its three brigades under Generals Custer and Merritt and Colonel Thomas C. Devin. The Second Division was led by Brigadier General Gregg, a holdover from the Pleasanton regime, with two brigades under Brigadier Henry E. Davies, Jr., and Colonel J. Irvin Gregg. The Third Division was handed over to Brigadier General James H. Wilson, a staff officer under Grant since the Vicksburg campaign; now in his mid-twenties, he had graduated from West Point in 1860, the class ahead of Custer's.

A few days after his arrival at Brandy Station Sheridan reviewed his corps, totaling about 12,000 in the three divisions and the 12 batteries of horse artillery. General Meade and two of his corps commanders, "Uncle John" Sedgwick and Winfield Scott Hancock, attended the review. General Sedgwick explained that as an old dragoon he had come to offer moral support "because of the traditional prejudices the cavalrymen were supposed to hold against being commanded by an infantry officer." The jovial Sedgwick made it clear that he was only joking.

A long thorough look at the state of his horses convinced Sheridan that there was very little else to joke about. They were "thin and worn down" by the necessity of doing picket duty for the whole army, covering a distance of almost sixty miles around its camps, and also providing escort service every time a column of infantry moved down a back-country road or a wagon train rolled into the rear areas. The enemy, instead of wasting the strength of his mounted forces, kept them massed and in the rear, "so that in the spring he could bring them out in good condition for the impending campaign." Sheridan decided to remedy this situation at once.

The cavalry review had hardly ended before he braced Meade on the subject, conscious of the difficulty he faced in convincing such a traditionalist that mounted forces, like infantry, must be concentrated to be effective. The ideas he presented are summarized most expertly in a report on the cavalry-corps operations in the Wilderness written and forwarded on May 13, 1866, two years after they had taken place and he had had the time to consider his experiences as coolly and dispassionately as possible for a man of his temperament:

After carefully studying the topography of the country from the Rapidan to Richmond, which is of a thickly wooded character, its numerous and almost parallel streams nearly all uniting, forming the York river, I took up the idea that our cavalry ought to fight the enemy's cavalry, and our infantry the enemy's infantry. I was strengthened in this impression still more by the consciousness of a want of appreciation on the part of infantry commanders as to the power of a large and well-managed body of horse, but as it was difficult to overcome the established custom of wasting cavalry for the protection of trains, and for the establishment of cordons around a sleeping infantry force, we had to bide our time.[9]

The "biding of time" was a great strain on Sheridan and actually did not continue very long after the campaign in the Wilderness began. It was the beginning, doubtless, of the misunderstanding and ill feeling that existed between Sheridan and Meade from that time forward. Sheridan recorded that his proposal for concentration of the cavalry "seemed to stagger General Meade not a little." Meade's concept of a cavalry commander was as "an adjunct at army headquarters—a sort of chief of cavalry" rather than the leader of an integrated fighting force. "General Meade deemed cavalry fit for little more than guard and picket duty, and wanted to know what would protect the transportation trains and artillery reserve, cover the front of moving infantry columns, and secure his flanks from intrusion, if my policy were pursued." Meade, of course, had not been at Booneville—that perfect, small-scale model of how cavalry could be used offensively—and probably knew little or nothing of the operation. And he put little faith in Sheridan's assurance that "with a mass of ten thousand mounted men . . . I could make it so lively for the enemy's cavalry that . . . the flanks and rear of the Army of the Potomac would require little or no defense. . . . Moving columns of infantry should take care of their own fronts."[10] Sheridan's proposals, he conceded, had one beneficial result: Meade relieved the cavalry of most of its picketing duties after Sheridan convinced him that the horses would be incapable of sustained effort unless rested before the spring campaign opened.[11]

In the few weeks that remained before the concerted offensive was to begin Sheridan argued his point with Grant as well as Meade, whipped his command into the best possible shape and pounded his opinions on cavalry tactics at Torbert, Gregg and Wilson and their brigade and regimental officers. As usual, he drilled himself night and day on the topography of the Wilderness—a nightmare, as will be seen, especially for a man who had never fought there—and the disposition of Lee's army south of the Rapidan. Topography was an obsession with him, and in the tangled, blind, head-on battles that ensued the knowledge he had gained was a great blessing. He persuaded Grant that the cavalry must be concentrated, at least by brigades, and he would have 10,000 troopers in the saddle under his direct supervision when the Army of the Potomac went forward. The balance was detached for various inescapable escort duties. Grant wasn't willing to go all the way with Sheridan's aggressive plans for the cavalry corps, but he was willing to give them a chance. Sheridan's pleas for more horse artillery, however, were firmly turned down by the general in chief.

Even to a general who knew the terrain as well as Robert E. Lee, the Wilderness was a hellish place to fight a campaign involving almost 200,000 men. The roads were few and were more like forest paths than roads. There were not many inhabitants to fight the everlasting battle of encroachment by the scraggy pines, the scrub oaks, the proliferating laurel bush. In low places the streams became sluggish and spread out into dank marshes where human beings could not venture and only the lonely cry of an occasional bird pierced the silence. Over it all flourished the densest tangle of undergrowth on the continent, a dismal snaggle of vine and thorn, with occasional flowerings of dogwood like banners in the desolation. It was the home of insect, reptile and rodent, which were welcome to it. Spring rains turned the clay roads into quagmires, and only the few plank roads were dependable.

Lurking in this maze of thicket, swamp and forest was the great Lee, who already had demonstrated his mastery of its military advantages to the defending forces at the battle of Chancellorsville. With him were the three corps under A. P. Hill, R. S. Ewell and James Longstreet, plus the cavalry under J. E. B. Stuart. His headquarters when the fighting began were at Orange Court House. From there to Fredericksburg he had three roads, roughly parallel—

the Orange Turnpike, the Orange Plank Road and the Catharpin Road—along which he could send his forces to block the path of the Union advance and fall on its flanks at any well-screened point he chose.

Shortly after midnight, May 3-4, General Grant sent the Army of the Potomac across the Rapidan and into the Wilderness. The crossing at Germanna Ford was led by Sheridan's division under Wilson; the crossing at Ely's Ford by Gregg. Torbert was detailed on Meade's orders to remain in the rear and guard the various fords and the wagon trains tumbling across them. The V Corps under Warren, the VI Corps under Sedgwick and, somewhat in the rear, the IX Corps under Burnside crossed at Germanna Ford, while the II Corps under Hancock marched on Chancellorsville across Ely's Ford and swung over to form the Union left, with Sheridan protecting his flank.[12] May 4 was a day for marching and maneuvering—and waiting for Lee to come roaring out of the forest in his usual style. The apprehension on the faces of officers who had already fought against Lee seemed a little on the timorous side to Phil Sheridan; Lee and his slashing saber arm Jeb Stuart were merely another brace of Confederates who must be taught that the Rebellion would be crushed for all their vaunted cavalierism. Indeed, it often appeared during the opening days of the campaign that Sheridan was worried more about Meade's intransigent attitude toward the proper use of cavalry than over anything Jeb Stuart might do.

On May 5 the series of brutal slugging matches which opened the Wilderness campaign indicated that Lee meant to oppose the Union army's advance with all the spirit and skill that had carried the Army of Northern Virginia through three years of war against all odds. Ewell's Corps came down the Orange Turnpike and struck so hard it took both Warren and Sedgwick to contain the thrust. Hill's Corps marched down the Orange Plank Road to find Hancock's II Corps, steadiest in the Union army, confronting it. Longstreet followed Hill along the same road with the intention of working around Hancock's flank while the two big Confederate corps engaged the three Federal corps. The plan called for Longstreet, playing the role assumed by Stonewall Jackson before he was killed in this same country, to batter the bulk of Meade's army from the left and rear before Burnside could bring his corps into action. Meanwhile, an even wider flanking movement was being made down the Catharpin Road to the south—Stuart and his cavalry aiming to cut Meade's communications and capture his transport. Hancock and his II Corps gave ground, rallied, retreated slowly, but held themselves together under the hardest blows of Hill and Longstreet.

In cold type it sounds as neat as a surgical operation, but actually it was a ghastly, confused series of fire fights in forest clearings, of wounded screeching for help as gunfire ignited the thickets. "It was a battle fought where maneuvering was impossible," wrote one survivor, "where the lines of battle were invisible to their commanders, and where the enemy also was invisible." A Union artilleryman called it "bushwhacking on a grand scale" and recalled, "I knew a Wisconsin infantryman who walked right into the Rebel skirmish line. He surrendered, and a Rebel was sent to the rear with him. In two minutes he and his guard walked into our own lines, and that in broad daylight." A veteran Confederate of the 5th Texas was wounded and rescued from the burning brush by Union soldiers, who asked him what he thought of the battle. "Battle be damned! It ain't no battle. It's a worse riot than Chickamauga was. At Chickamauga there was at least a rear. . . . It's all a damned mess. And our two armies ain't nothing but howlin' mobs!"[13]

While all this rioting was going on in the underbrush bordering the Germanna Plank Road, General Sheridan was fretting the hours away. Night orders from Meade's headquarters on May 5 warned him to "protect the trains." That would have meant—in Meade's book—withdrawing his divisions toward Fredericksburg and covering the Rappahannock crossings. At 11:10 P.M. he sent word to army headquarters: ". . . I cannot do anything with the cavalry except to act on the defensive, on account of immense amount of material and wagons here. . . . Had I moved to Hamilton's Crossing early this morning, the enemy would have ruined everything. Why cannot infantry be sent to guard the trains, and let me take the offensive?"[14] There was no answer from Meade to this midnight blasphemy, so Sheridan decided to interpret the orders his own way—and go out to meet Stuart on ground of his own choosing.

With some astonishment Meade received a dispatch from Sheridan at 11:00 A.M., May 6, telling that the "cavalry has been . . . heavily engaged at Todd's Tavern" and every attack was "handsomely repulsed."[15] In the clearing at the junction of the Brock and Catharpin roads, where Stuart was pivoting north to get in the Union rear while Longstreet attacked the Union left, Sheridan met the enemy horse with his own men dismounted and already placed behind log breastworks. The fire power of Gregg's division and two of Torbert's brigades induced Stuart to believe he had encountered Union infantry. He reported that Meade must have extended his line to Todd's Tavern and that repeated assaults failed to brush his opponent aside.

Instead of being delighted with this "handsome repulse," General Meade could only feel concern for his wagon trains. His chief of staff replied on Meade's behalf at 1:00 P.M. that "General Hancock has been heavily pressed, and his left turned. The major-general commanding thinks that you had better draw in your cavalry, so as to secure the protection of the trains. . . ." Misinformed about Hancock's flank, Meade was determined to block any raid in his rear and sacrifice whatever advantage Sheridan had gained at Todd's Tavern, rather than turn Sheridan loose to strike at Stuart as he kept proposing.

Sheridan obeyed the order to draw back, but at least his corps was now concentrated and capable of meeting Stuart on equal terms or better.

It was well that the Union cavalry was finally united, for that night (May 6-7) Stuart, believing Sheridan to be in full retreat after the engagement at Todd's Tavern, was following on its heels like a timber wolf and looking for a chance to strike. With or without the blessings of the army commander, Sheridan finally got the chance to come to grips with Stuart and show him that the Army of the Potomac's cavalry could no longer be handled like so many louts on plow horses.

Unfortunately for Stuart, the brigade he attacked first, as the

Union cavalry withdrew to Piney Branch Church, was Custer's of Torbert's division—four regiments of Michigan troopers long trained in the hell-for-leather tactics of George Armstrong Custer. It was that day, perhaps, that the long golden locks of Brigadier Custer—a native of Ohio, a West Pointer who graduated as the war broke out—first caught the eye of General Sheridan. It was the beginning of an association and comradeship that ended only on the red Sabbath of the Little Big Horn a dozen years hence. After serving as staff officer and idolator of General McClellan, Custer had obtained a cavalry command and by his dash and leadership had risen swiftly to brigadier's rank at the age of twenty-three. His conceit and vainglory were notorious, his sense of proportion was sadly lacking, but Sheridan quickly saw that his reckless courage could be extremely useful in the type of campaign he visualized for the coming months.

When Stuart nipped at his heels Custer spun his brigade around and counterattacked immediately. Prisoners were captured and given the customary questioning by General Sheridan, who elicited the information that a lot more of Stuart's cavalry was in the vicinity. Sheridan immediately ordered Wilson's and Gregg's divisions to turn in their tracks. The fighting whirled back to the clearings around Todd's Tavern and became "exceedingly severe and fluctuating." After it ended, with the Confederate horsemen pursued almost to Spotsylvania Court House, Sheridan reported to army headquarters: "I attacked the rebel cavalry at Todd's Tavern this afternoon and drove them in confusion." A second dispatch at 8:00 P.M. should have shown Meade that his cavalry was being used in a new and much more effective manner; it told of driving on Beech Grove Church, where the brigades led by Merritt, Davies, Irvin Gregg and Devin were dismounted and sent charging over barricades and rifle pits.[16] Hitherto the sketchiest sort of fortification had meant right-about-face for the Union horse.

Sheridan's comparatively small-scale triumphs of May 7 went almost unnoticed, however, as a new battle plan was being drawn up at Grant's headquarters. Grant had decided that butting against the Confederate corps of Longstreet (wounded and now replaced by Lieutenant General R. H. Anderson), Hill and Ewell was liable to end indecisively. Besides, the Union army had suffered thousands of casualties in the battles of position. Maneuver might do it. The Army of the Potomac was to move by its left flank to Spotsylvania Court House and draw Lee out into the open.

A swift movement, carried through, would have accomplished much. The swirling cavalry engagements of May 7 had knocked out Stuart's divisions for at least 24 hours, and the flank of Anderson's corps was hanging in air. Sheridan did move quickly to take advantage of the situation, but Meade again appeared on the scene to muddle the execution of his plan. Wilson's division, approximately 3,000 men equipped with repeating carbines, made a night march and seized Spotsylvania Court House. Sheridan had proposed to follow him up with Gregg's and Torbert's divisions so the place could be held against whatever Lee threw into the game—and, since Spotsylvania was on the sensitive route to Richmond, the counterstroke could be expected to be fast and furious. At 9:00 A.M., May 8, Sheridan received a dispatch from Wilson saying the Third Division had driven the enemy cavalry out of Spotsylvania but was under heavy attack by Confederate infantry, General Lee having reacted with his usual celerity.

Torbert's division should have been at hand to support Wilson, with Gregg not far behind, but Meade had countermanded Sheridan's orders. Meade wanted infantry—Warren's V Corps—in there, because he did not believe dismounted troopers could hold the town. The result was that Wilson was driven out, with Torbert's cavalry and Warren's infantry all tangled up on the road and wagon trains only adding to the confusion. Instead of leading the infantry into Spotsylvania, Torbert's division was well behind it when the masses of men, horses and wagons were sorted out, and then it was too late. A further and sadder result was the battles around the Bloody Angle several days later with some 14,000 Union casualties. Sheridan wrote: "Had Gregg and Merritt [temporarily commanding in place of Torbert, who was ill] been permitted to proceed as they were originally instructed, it is doubtful whether the battles fought at Spotsylvania would have occurred, for these two divisions would have encountered the enemy at the Po River, and so delayed his march as to enable our infantry to reach Spotsylvania first, and thus force Lee to take up a line behind the Po." His three divisions, he added, were rendered "practically ineffective" because of Meade's "disjointed and irregular instructions."[17]

Thus, as was inevitable, Sheridan and Meade came to quarrel shortly before noon of May 8 at Meade's headquarters. It was a collision of high tempers from which neither party fully recovered and which neither was ever to forget or forgive, a scene that was recorded with sorrow and embarrassment by several witnesses. It was inevitable because these two men, both of them proud and high-spirited, were utterly opposed in personality and background. Meade was a Philadelphia aristocrat, Sheridan a backwoods Irishman; Meade the engineer who relied on well-laid plans, Sheridan the cavalryman who placed just as much faith in dash, intuition and taking advantage of opportunities as they suddenly presented themselves in battle; Meade the military intellectual, Sheridan the opportunist (in the best sense of the word); Meade the ill and aging, Sheridan the hale and youthful; Meade the aloof and lonely, Sheridan the personal idol of his officers and troops.

Sheridan stormed into Meade's headquarters to find Meade equally wrathy and blaming Sheridan for the confusion on the road to Spotsylvania. Meade was an honest, honorable and just man. The differences that existed between him and Sheridan were based, not merely on personal antagonism, but on a fundamental disagreement in method and doctrine. As yet he was not convinced that the cavalry could or would perform any better than it had in previous campaigns; nor was he convinced that it could be used in any different manner, as Sheridan kept insisting. No doubt he was irked by Sheridan's independence, his barely subordinate attitude, his readiness to appeal to Grant as supreme arbiter. All these feelings were reflected in the diaries and journals kept by officers at his headquarters. He could not have been pleased by the way Sheridan regarded his cavalry as an almost autonomous arm. But Meade's firm sense of justice and his intellectual balance would never allow personal feelings to intrude on his actions as a commander. In view of their subsequent relations it was ironic that Meade thought Sheridan "quite distinguished" on first appraisal.[18]

In the ensuing argument, from Sheridan's viewpoint, Meade's "peppery temper had got the better of his good judgment, he showing a disposition to be unjust, laying blame here and there for the blunders that had been committed." Among other things Meade accused the cavalry of having impeded the march of the V Corps. Colonel Theodore Lyman of Meade's staff wrote in his journal that Sheridan was equally intemperate, criticizing both Meade's generalship and Warren's lack of initiative in pushing his infantry forward.[19] Colonel Horace Porter of Grant's staff observed that Sheridan's "language was highly spiced and conspicuously italicized with expletives," that "all the Hotspur in his nature was aroused."[20]

Sheridan did not hesitate to point out that Meade had broken up his dispositions, exposed Wilson's division to disaster and kept Gregg unnecessarily idle. He warned his superior that, if the disjointed operations of the cavalry for the past four days were repeated, the corps would be rendered "inefficient and useless." He concluded, as he later recalled, by telling Meade that "I could whip Stuart if he (Meade) would only let me, but since he insisted on giving the cavalry directions without consulting me or even notifying me, he could henceforth command the Cavalry Corps himself— that I would not give it another order."[21]

General Meade immediately repaired to Grant's headquarters to repeat Sheridan's statements, possibly believing the general in chief would rebuke Sheridan for insubordination. Finally he told of Sheridan's boast that he would whip Stuart if turned loose.

If Meade hoped that Sheridan would be relieved—there is nothing on record to show that he did—he was quickly disenchanted. Grant puffed at his cigar, reflecting that Sheridan had always made good his promises in the past. "Did he say that?" murmured the general in chief. "Then let him go and do it."

Grant had come to the realization that unless Sheridan's opinions on the strategic use of cavalry were right the Union army would continue to be humiliated by Stuart and his lighthearted romps in the rear areas.

That day an order went out to Sheridan under the signature of Meade's chief of staff, General A. A. Humphreys:

The major-general commanding directs you to immediately concentrate your available mounted force, and with your ammunition trains and such supply trains as are filled (exclusive of ambulances) proceed against the enemy's cavalry, and when your supplies are exhausted, proceed *via* New Market and Green Bay to Haxall's Landing on the James River, there communicating with General Butler, procuring supplies and return to the army. Your dismounted men will be left with the train here.[22]

The road to Richmond was open.

9

A CHARGE AT YELLOW TAVERN

SHERIDAN'S duel with Stuart lasted exactly one week.

From the day he crossed the Rapidan until his cavalry and Stuart's met at Yellow Tavern, May 4-11, Sheridan defeated the Southern cavalry leader every time they clashed on the muddy roads and fields of northern Virginia. That their final combat took place only a half-dozen miles from Richmond was bitterly symbolic for the South: Sheridan, the utilitarian, the epitome of all that was practical, hardheaded and determined in the North's attitude toward the war, had stolen the thunder of the South's great cavalry raider, Stuart, the plumed knight, the laughing cavalier, the embodiment of its vaunted chivalry. The South placed much more value on its hero-generals, Lee, Jackson and Stuart, than the North on Grant, Sheridan, Sherman, Thomas.

Perhaps there was something of that same symbolism in the way Sheridan and his troopers set out on the raid which would slash at rail communications north and east of Richmond and do as much damage as possible in Lee's rear, terminating at a Union army base on the James River. It was no thundering gallop down Virginia roads, but a careful and calculating jab at the Confederate vitals. Sheridan called in his division commanders, Wilson, Gregg and Merritt (Torbert's illness still keeping him out of action) and explained his plans to them. "We are going out to fight Stuart's cavalry in consequence of a suggestion from me; we will give him a fair, square fight, . . . and in view of my recent representations to General Meade I shall expect nothing but success." He added that they would attempt to ram through all opposition to Haxall's

163

Landing, but would turn back via Gordonsville if the enemy strength was greater than anticipated. "At first the proposition seemed to surprise the division commanders somewhat," Sheridan remarked, "for hitherto even the boldest mounted expeditions had been confined to a hurried ride through the enemy's country, without purpose of fighting more than enough to escape in case of molestation, and here and there to destroy a bridge. Our move would be a challenge to Stuart for a cavalry duel behind Lee's lines, in his own country. . . ."[1]

Most of the night of May 8-9 was taken up with preparations for the raid and concentrating the corps at Aldrich's Station, for the expedition was to jump off early the morning of May 9 before any superior officers or overriding events could prevent its departure. Nine thousand men, seven batteries of horse artillery and an ammunition train were to take part in the raid. The men were to be provided with three days' rations, the horses with only a half-day's fodder; Sheridan was determined to attain as much mobility as possible.

Long before dawn bugles roused the men from their few hours' sleep in the bivouacs around Aldrich's Station. At 6:00 A.M. the column of cavalrymen, four abreast and 13 miles long, moved out along the Telegraph Road leading from Fredericksburg to Richmond. A hundred guidons whipped in the morning breeze. In the vanguard the headquarters flag, red and white with twin stars, rode with Sheridan and his escort. There was the long-stilled symphony of cavalry on the march: creak of saddles, bray of pack mules, beat of hoofs, clatter of metal accouterments, rumble of forage wagons, murmur of sleepy men. The long column proceeded at a walk, something unknown to previous raids, which were conducted at the gallop. Under Kilpatrick, Pleasanton and Stoneman the cavalry always clattered off on several parallel routes and arrived at the scene of action off schedule and with winded horses. Sheridan was determined to put in all his men at once, if necessary, and have them and their mounts in condition to fight. "I preferred this, however, to the combinations arising from separate roads, combinations rarely working as expected . . ." he explained in a subsequent dispatch.[2]

Morale was high. Sheridan's leadership had made itself felt in the ranks of the cavalry corps. General Davies, who led a brigade in Gregg's division, said the troops already had faith in their new commander because "they had observed and appreciated his efforts to relieve them of useless and wearing toil; they even perceived that they were better supplied and cared for than at any previous period," and they valued his "constant and inspiriting presence" when they were under fire.[3] On the way to Yellow Tavern, one of his men said, "We saw him daily, whether we were in the advance, at the rear, or the center of the column, and he would as soon borrow a light from the pipe of an enlisted man as from the cigar of an officer. The common soldier's uniform was good enough for him."

The Ny, Po and Ta rivers—which flowed together to form the Mattapony River to the southeast—were crossed without interference from the enemy cavalry, and "all anxiety as to our passing around Lee's army was removed," Sheridan said. Shortly after crossing the Ta, however, Gordon's Rebel brigade came thundering down on the Union rear guard. It did not perturb Sheridan or halt his march for a moment. He simply detached Davies' brigade to snap back whenever Gordon came too close.

Close to dusk the North Anna River was reached. Merritt's division crossed over while Gregg's and Wilson's remained on the north bank. At Beaver Dam Station across the river Custer's brigade found a rich and varied prize, an assortment of rolling stock belonging to the Virginia Central Railroad. The Union troopers, with the whooping Custer in the lead, swooped down on a train, shooting up the guards, but withheld their fire when they found in some of the cars 378 Union soldiers who had been captured and were on their way to prison camps. By nightfall a mighty bonfire was made out of the depot itself, three large trains, two locomotives, 100 cars, 1,500,000 rations (enough corn meal and pork to feed the Army of Northern Virginia for 20 days) and extremely valuable medical stores, according to Sheridan's dispatch. Merritt's troopers then proceeded to tear up 10 miles of track and telegraph wire below Beaver Dam Station.[4]

The overnight halt at the North Anna only contributed to Stuart's bewilderment. The Rebel leader had a brigade following

Sheridan at a respectful distance, but could not divine his intentions: Sheridan might turn due north and strike at the rear of Lee's army or he might be heading straight for Richmond. Stuart's only feasible move was to ride like the wind around the head of the long Union column and interpose himself in front of Richmond. This, of course, would leave the Virginia Central and the Potomac railroads open to Sheridan's depredations—and they were the north-south lines pumping supplies to Lee's army.

In the bivouac on the North Anna, Sheridan's troopers were pleasantly surprised by the fact that—instead of having to stay on the alert all night in little picketing groups—they were allowed to bed down in one big camp that needed few sentinels. Men and horses could rest themselves before the next day's march. In the morning the men were singing around their breakfast fires.

The next afternoon, May 10, Sheridan reached the South Anna River and leisurely settled down for the night by its lushly pastured banks. He could have pressed on, but his horses must be fed and rested, ready for combat. Meanwhile, the puzzled Stuart concentrated his forces near Beaver Dam Station the same day, then realized he had made a mistake and sent them beating down the roads toward Richmond. As Sheridan remarked, Jeb Stuart was "urging his horses to the death so as to get in between Richmond and our column" while Sheridan was conserving his strength for the inevitable clash. By the evening of May 10, his aptitude for intelligence as acute as ever, Sheridan was aware of Stuart's intentions. "All the information that could be obtained led me to believe that the rebel General Stuart was concentrating his cavalry at Yellow Tavern," he said in his report of the operation.[5] It was all so calm and effortless, this saunter through the green countryside, the leisurely bivouacs beside cool flowing rivers, that many of the troopers found it difficult to believe they were raiding deep in enemy territory.

Next morning the atmosphere changed quickly from the pastoral to the military.

Sheridan's advance guard reported that Stuart had ranged himself at the crossroads settlement of Yellow Tavern, six miles north

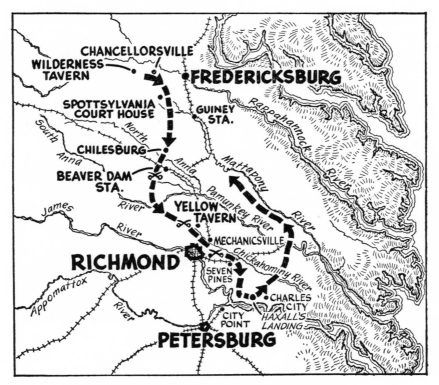

SHERIDAN'S CAMPAIGN AGAINST STUART

of Richmond.[6] A few prisoners were brought in, from whom, with his usual skill at interrogation, Sheridan learned that Stuart was preparing to make a last-ditch stand there, although all his forces had not been concentrated. It was a logical point to hold with all tenacity the junction of the Mountain Road from Louisa and the point where the Telegraph Road from Fredericksburg joined the Brook Turnpike leading directly into Richmond. The Confederate had already planned a trap for Sheridan. If the Union cavalry attacked the city's defenses, Stuart hoped to catch him in the rear while the 4,000 to 5,000 troops available to General Braxton Bragg (now Confederate chief of staff and commanding the

Richmond defenses in the current emergency) attacked Sheridan frontally. In a dispatch to Bragg, Stuart had paid Sheridan and his troopers a higher compliment than any they had received from Grant or Meade: "His force [Sheridan's] is large, and if attack is made on Richmond it will be principally as dismounted cavalry, which fights better than the enemy's infantry."[7]

No time was lost in pressing the attack against Stuart: there was no point in giving the enemy an interval to intrench and bring up reinforcements. Merritt's division moved down the turnpike and drove the Rebels several hundred yards east of the road after an "obstinate contest." Sheridan then brought up Wilson's division and one brigade of Gregg's to form a line of battle alongside Merritt's. A hot enfilading fire descended on the Union battle front from a masked battery. Sheridan, riding down the line of his formations, shouting encouragement and waving his little black hat, hurried the assault forward. Two of Merritt's brigades advanced and swept through the first line, only to be taken in the flank by a howling counterattack urged on by Stuart himself. But Sheridan had foreseen the possibilities of a trap. Custer's brigade, mounted this time, was sent against Stuart's left while Wilson's and Gregg's brigades, dismounted, charged the rest of the Confederate forces.[8]

"Come on, Wolverines!" Custer shouted to his Michigan regiments. They stormed right over the Rebel left, taking three pieces of artillery and sending Stuart's troopers into a quick retreat. The blue cavalry, mounted and dismounted, swarmed all over the Confederate line. For a few minutes there were a dozen semiprivate little battles where a scattering of Rebels stood and fought to the death. In their midst—it was only to be expected of the man who said, "I'd rather die than be whipped"—was Jeb Stuart trying to rally his men, heedless of the Union troopers milling all around him. One of Custer's men, a dead shot with the revolver, aimed, fired and sent a .44-caliber bullet into Stuart's right abdomen.

The great enemy cavalry leader was mortally wounded. His aides carried him off to Richmond to the home of his physician brother-in-law, and there he lay throughout the night of May 11, half delirious, suffering internal hemorrhages and listening to the tocsin sounded by the church bells of Richmond against the invaders only a few miles across the Chickahominy. Shortly after dawn he asked the few friends gathered around his bedside to sing with him "Rock of Ages." At 7:28 A.M. he died with quiet gallantry.[9]

Shortly after Sheridan's forces had swept the enemy cavalry from their front, Confederates under General Gordon attacked them from behind. The attack was not unexpected, and Sheridan had placed the remainder of Gregg's division behind breastworks to protect his rear. Gordon's assault came too late—"combinations rarely work," as Sheridan had pointed out—to effect the outcome of the battle of Yellow Tavern. General Gordon was killed and his brigade driven off before it reached the Union breastworks.

It was late in the afternoon, but Sheridan pressed on, and a Union spearhead easily broke through the outer line of the Richmond defenses near Mechanicsville. Sheridan decided to move on to Fair Oaks, a few miles east of Richmond, having received reports that General Ben Butler and his Army of the James had advanced to a point on the south bank of the James within four miles of the city. If he could manage a quick meeting with Butler's forces—the bells of Richmond were ringing the alarm with a stridency that suggested desperation—it might be possible for them to take the city.[10]

In fact, Sheridan was positive he could take Richmond without Butler's help. In his report to Meade he said, "It is possible that I might have captured the city of Richmond by an assault, but the want of knowledge of your operations and those of General Butler, and the facility with which the enemy could throw in troops, made me abandon the attempt."[11]

General Wilson, who had a tendency to be hypercritical of Sheridan in later years, believed the Confederate capital could have been captured. He wrote: "In his reports, as well as in his less formal explanations, Sheridan always claimed that he did not go into Richmond merely because he had no orders to do so, and this was literally the truth, but from the Confederate reports of the situation it is now certain that the capture of that place would have been easy work for the twelve thousand troopers [actually only 9,000] Sheridan had with him. According to the facts, it was an opportunity in which audacity and a bold stroke might gain a notable success."[12] It was one of the few times Sheridan was accused of lacking audacity.

Many years after the war General Sheridan gave Senator Plumb a more intimate account of his reasons for not storming Richmond, "the greatest temptation of my life. There lay Richmond before us. . . . It would have cost 500 or 600 lives, and I could not have held the place, of course. But . . . I should have been the hero of the hour. I could have gone in and burned and killed right and left. But I had learned this thing—that our men knew what they were about. I had seen them come out of a fight in which only a handful were killed . . . mad clear through, because they knew an opportunity had been missed, or a sacrifice had been needlessly made. . . . They would have followed me, but they would have known as well as I that the sacrifice was for no permanent advantage."[13]

All through the night of May 11-12 Sheridan moved his troops toward the Chickahominy crossing at Meadow Bridge. Near the crossing the middle line of Richmond's defenses bristled with most of the 4,000 irregular troops available to General Bragg and enough artillery to keep the Union corps out of its range until a general assault could be undertaken. Along the route of his night march the enemy had planted torpedoes—land mines they are now called—which killed a number of horses and wounded several men. Sheridan had 25 prisoners brought up to the mined portion of the road, where they were "made to get down on their knees, feel for the wires in the darkness, follow them up and unearth the shells."

In ordering this rather harsh measure he was only following the practice of General McClellan, who had forced prisoners of war to de-activate such torpedoes during his Peninsula campaign of 1862. Apparently the enemy resorted to mining roads only when their capital was threatened. Later Sheridan, informed that a neighboring planter had led the mine-laying expedition, ordered that the shells dug up from the road "be carried and placed in the cellar of his house, arranged to explode if the enemy's column came that way, while he and his family were brought off as prisoners and held till after daylight."[14]

At daylight another engagement with the enemy front and rear began at Meadow Bridge. General Bragg was bringing up three infantry brigades from General P. G. T. Beauregard's forces opposing Butler south of the James at Bermuda Hundred, and the reorganized Confederate cavalry under Fitzhugh Lee was pounding at Sheridan's rear along the Brook Turnpike. Sheridan swung Wilson's and Gregg's divisions around to stand off the enemy infantry, then directed his attention to the bridge. An attempt had been made by the retreating Confederates to burn it, but heavy rains during the night had put out the fire, and the stringpieces and ties were still sound. Sheridan, turning engineer in the emergency, directed his troopers to cover the skeleton woodwork with fence rails. All the time the bridge was under heavy musketry and artillery fire.

It was a rather desperate moment for the corps—caught between two enemy elements of unknown strength, with a partially destroyed bridge blocking one means of escape. Some of Sheridan's officers experienced a moment of panic and suggested that the enemy had them surrounded.

"Surrounded!" the general snorted to Lieutenant Charles Fitzhugh of the 4th United States Artillery. "I could capture Richmond if I wanted to, but I couldn't hold it. Surrounded by a lot of war department clerks! Take it easy."[15]

His excellent Regular artillery poured shrapnel on the enemy forces across the river. Then Sheridan sent Custer charging across the bridge and into the cavalry that had sent over such a galling fire. The defenders fled with little concession to honor. Sheridan ordered the other two brigades of Merritt's divisions across the bridge and into the pursuit, which whirled down the road to Gaines' Mill, site of a great battle in 1862.

Meanwhile, a nondescript force marched out of the defenses of Richmond—not all of them "war department clerks"—and attacked Wilson and Gregg. Wilson was driven back, but the assault had been anticipated and prepared for. Gregg's brigades, hidden in a ravine, opened a heavy fire from repeating carbines and artillery that enfiladed the Confederates and took all the enthusiasm out of their charge. Wilson succeeded in rallying his men and struck the enemy right flank; the casuals quickly departed for the security of their earthworks.

The rest of the day the men spent collecting the wounded, burying the dead and reading newspapers brought out by two small but enterprising boys from Richmond. That evening Wilson and Gregg joined Merritt near Gaines' Mill, and by easy marches the entire corps proceeded to Haxall's Landing on the James. Here they procured supplies from General Butler and sent the Union wounded and the Confederate prisoners north on boats from the fleet in the James. Three days later, on May 17, the cavalry corps started on its journey north to rejoin the Army of the Potomac.[16]

Sheridan was well pleased with his first independent operation, whose most important aspect, he considered, was the thorough defeat of Jeb Stuart. "Since the beginning of the war this general had distinguished himself by his management of the Confederate mounted force. Under him the cavalry of Lee's army had been nurtured, and had acquired such prestige that it thought itself wellnigh invincible. . . . The discomfiture of Stuart at Yellow Tavern had inflicted a blow from which entire recovery was impossible."[17] Sheridan believed that the effect of Stuart's death on Rebel morale, civilian and military, was also close to disastrous. The Confederacy had always been supremely proud of its cavalry, of the belief that only the Southern chivalry could be victorious in that knightly arm of the service. And this was a legend now destroyed forever.

IO

ACTION AT TREVILIAN

AS COMMANDER of the Army of the Potomac's cavalry corps with a group of youthful, hard-driving, headstrong and ambitious men leading his divisions and brigades, General Sheridan must often have been reminded of the stagecoach drivers of his native Somerset handling their teams of half-wild horses. It took a firm hand to keep proud and volatile young commanders all pulling in the same direction. But there was no doubt of the respect they showed and felt for Sheridan. However much they might kick up their heels at one another, none of them was foolhardy enough to display anything but deference to their superior. Sheridan was modest and soft-spoken, anything but a martinet, although demanding the best performance of every officer in camp and in battle. They had noted, however, that he did not hesitate to stand up to Meade when he thought him wrong, and how in battle his narrow eyes took on a reddish "glow" that was almost frightening.

As the corps returned to Meade's army Sheridan was able to sum up his impressions of his young generals in combat. Torbert had been ill almost since the army crossed the Rapidan, but he appeared a solid and hard-working division commander if not a brilliant one or a born cavalryman. Merritt, who had taken his place, was first-rate, a man of high promise. Custer had been magnificent leading the charges at Beaver Dam Station, at Yellow Tavern and over Meadow Bridge. Gregg, soon to leave the service, possessed "a high order of capacity and sound judgment" and showed "firmness and coolness" as commander of the Second Division.[1]

One of Gregg's brigadiers, Henry E. Davies, Jr., was neither a

173

West Pointer nor a hot-blooded bravo like most of his high-ranking comrades, but he had gained Sheridan's approval and respect
by his rear-guard action during the advance to Yellow Tavern.
Davies was a quiet and unassuming New Yorker, a lawyer in
civilian life.

As for General Wilson, in the postwar years he and Sheridan
tended to be rather critical of each other and of certain phases of
the campaigns they had fought. And during the war, with Wilson
established as a personal favorite of Grant's and Sheridan growing
in the general in chief's professional esteem, there was an under-
current of dislike between them. The Third Division was Wilson's
first field command, quite a jump for a young man hardly out of
West Point when the war began and with only his excellent record
as an engineer officer on Grant's staff to recommend him. Wilson
wrote:

As my services had been confined so far to the staff and to the
War Department, my assignment to the command of a division,
under the circumstances, gave particular offense to my seniors of
the line and led to hard feelings and complications which were not
without influence in the cavalry operations and which did not entirely disappear till I was relieved from duty with the Army of the
Potomac and sent West. . . .[2]

One fellow officer who harbored "hard feelings" toward Wilson
was George Custer. In a series of boastful letters to his beautiful
young bride from the base at Haxall's Landing he expressed complete contempt for Wilson's generalship, declaring that Wilson had
"proved himself an imbecile" and "almost ruined the corps by his
blunders."[3] Actually Custer's envy was a sort of accolade to those
he regarded as his rivals, a backhanded and sometimes underhanded
compliment.

Sheridan was not personally enthusiastic about Wilson—there
was too much unstated rivalry between them—but he was well satisfied with the handling of his division on the expedition to the
James. And the shrewd, watchful Grant continued to hold Wilson

in high esteem and marked him down for higher command in the West.

Sheridan could only admire his subordinate's cool and confident conduct during the fighting at Meadow Bridge, when the corps was virtually surrounded. He sent a staff officer to Wilson with an order to "hold your position at all hazards while I arrange to withdraw the corps to the north side of the river." Wilson replied, as his firing lines slowly withdrew under heavy attack, "Our hair is badly entangled in his fingers and our nose firmly inserted in his mouth and we shall, therefore, hold on here till something breaks."[4] All very much in the blithe style of the rejuvenated cavalry of the East.

By the time Sheridan and his divisions rejoined the Army of the Potomac, May 24, at Chesterfield Station, the bloody battles around Spotsylvania Court House had been fought. Union men by the thousands had fallen in front of the "Bloody Angle," in large part because General Meade had not allowed the cavalry corps to occupy the place in strength before it went off on its first expedition. The raid around Richmond, with the cavalry cutting railroad lines and preventing the Confederate high command from reinforcing Lee, had allowed Meade to proceed around the Confederate right flank to the North Anna. Spotsylvania being impossible to take by frontal assault, Grant had decided to force Lee to withdraw again by moving closer to Richmond. The value of Sheridan's raid to this movement was recognized by Grant and Meade. It had resulted in the destruction of "great quantities of provisions and munitions"—"stores that the enemy had accumulated at sub-dépôts from strained resources and by difficult means"—and had occasioned the death of the South's most successful cavalry leader and "the most thorough defeat that had yet befallen" the enemy's mounted forces in Virginia.[5]

Nowhere had the spring campaigns of the Union armies met with notable success. Banks, with 40,000 veteran troops, had already bogged down in his Red River campaign. Of the Shenandoah Valley "advance" Halleck reported to Grant, "Sigel is in full retreat on Strasburg. He will do nothing but run; never did anything else." The Army of the James, under Ben Butler, had seized

City Point and Bermuda Hundred, but Beauregard's boldness and skill prevented the Union army from occupying the vital railroad center of Petersburg, the key to Richmond. The Army of the Potomac had maintained a measure of momentum but only at a terrible cost, including the losses during the first battles of the Wilderness and the two assaults on the Confederate positions at Spotsylvania on May 12 and May 18, before maneuvering around Lee's right. Sherman's army group was meeting stanch resistance on the road to Atlanta.

General Grant made it clear immediately that there would be no rest for the cavalry corps. Reporting at his headquarters, Sheridan was greeted with the jocularity Grant reserved for the few friends and fewer officers in whom he had complete confidence. He turned to Colonel Horace Porter of his staff and said, "Now, Sheridan evidently thinks he has been clear down to the James River, and has been breaking up railroads, and even getting a peep at Richmond; but probably this is all imagination, or else he has been reading something of the kind in the newspapers. I don't suppose he seriously thinks that he made such a march as that in two weeks." Sheridan replied with a gallant attempt at humor, "Well, after what General Grant says, I do begin to feel doubtful as to whether I have been absent at all from the Army of the Potomac."[6] This exchange is quoted, not as an example of the heavy-artillery type of wit common to Grant and Sheridan, but to indicate Grant's growing respect and affection for Sheridan. Sometimes a commanding general's joke is worth a dozen citations.

Grant explained to Sheridan that the cavalry divisions would now be used both to lead the army's advance by its left flank in the direction of Cold Harbor—a road junction between the Pamunkey River and Richmond not far from many battle sites of 1862— and also to divert the enemy's attention. For this dual purpose Wilson's division would operate on the right flank, covering the river crossings for the infantry and probing ahead on reconnaissance. The divisions of Torbert (now returned to duty) and Gregg were to seize and protect the crossings of the Pamunkey, which was formed by the confluence of the North and South Anna rivers near Hanover Court House. Reinforcing Meade for these complicated and hazardous maneuvers in Lee's rear, Grant placed Burnside's IX Corps under his command and ordered W. F. (Baldy) Smith's XVIII Corps to move north from Bermuda Hundred and away from the laggard operations of General Butler.[7]

On May 27 Torbert's and Gregg's divisions, with Sheridan at their head, moved out to lead the VI Corps south of the Pamunkey. The corps had suffered only 425 casualties, including the missing, on the expedition to Haxall's Landing. Its horses were in good condition—better than they had been in the camps north of the Rapidan when Sheridan assumed command. The Confederates contested almost every mile of the advance. There was fighting at every crossroads, every ford where their lighter forces might engage the Union cavalry at an advantage.

The first pitched battle took place at Haw's Shop, where the enemy's dismounted cavalry was posted behind breastworks to hold the road to Cold Harbor. The Confederate cavalry, which had been reinforced by M. C. Butler's brigade from South Carolina, was now organized in three divisions under Hampton, Fitzhugh Lee and W. H. F. Lee.[8] The Second Division under Gregg attacked the breastworks with more vigor than success. Sheridan knew that the position had to be broken—and quickly—if Cold Harbor was not to be another Spotsylvania. This time, at least, he had two divisions instead of one for the job, and the infantry was *following* him in support rather than snarling up the traffic on the narrow woodland roads. He ordered Custer, the rawboned paladin with his velveteen jacket and excess of gold braid, his vain golden curls and his undeniable courage, to lead his Michigan regiments in a charge to break the line. Custer wanted to go in on horseback, but Gregg ordered him to dismount. To give the occasion as much glamour as could be provided in the swampy woods, thick with malaria and late-May humidity, Custer directed his splendid band to play while the troopers went forward in a column of platoons.[9] Gregg and Custer drove through the Confederate positions at dusk and scattered their defenders.

The enemy had put up such stiff resistance that Sheridan reported to Meade he was confronted by infantry. Meade said it was only cavalry, and for once Meade was right. But the Confederate infantry was not far behind. Lee saw that Sheridan's assault at Haw's Shop meant the Federal cavalry intended to seize Cold Harbor at any cost. He began moving troops up from Beauregard's army south of the James to hold a line at or behind that road junction. The Army of Northern Virginia also was moving toward the critical point. The Confederate commander told one of his chief lieutenants, "We must destroy the Federal army before they get to the James River. If they get there it will become a siege and then merely a question of time. We must destroy them!"

Skirmishing all the way, Sheridan followed the Rebel cavalry to within a mile and a half of Cold Harbor. There he found himself confronted by Fitz Lee's cavalry division and a brigade of Hoke's infantry. How much support they had Sheridan did not know, and he moved with unusual trepidation that day of May 31. He sent Torbert's division forward, and, with Merritt and Custer leading the assault, the enemy was driven out of Cold Harbor. Sheridan hurried a message to Meade: "I do not feel able to hold this place, and have directed General Torbert to resume his position of this morning. . . . I do not think it prudent to hold on. . . ."[10]

Meade and Grant thought otherwise and sent an urgent reply— Sheridan was to hold Cold Harbor at all costs. The VI Corps—now commanded by Major General Horatio G. Wright in place of John Sedgwick, who had been killed at Spotsylvania—was coming up by forced marches to support him; the XVIII Corps under Baldy Smith, hero of the Cracker Line operation at Chattanooga, had been transported from Bermuda Hundred up the Chickahominy to White House, from which it would hurry to swing in on Sheridan's flank.

It was an anxious night for Sheridan, who realized that the countryside was alive with enemy infantry marching, as only the Southern foot could march, to hang onto Cold Harbor. At 9:00 A.M. on June 1 he advised Meade that his men had captured prisoners from three different infantry brigades; "I have been very apprehensive, but General Wright is now coming up." The First and Second Divisions had dug in during the night and managed to repulse the attacks of the Confederate infantry until they were relieved at 10:00 A.M. by the VI Corps.

On June 3 the Army of the Potomac underwent the shortest but bloodiest combat experience of its history. No more flanking, Grant had decided. He was determined to batter his way through the Rebel positions at Cold Harbor. On the eve of battle the assaulting forces were seen sewing patches bearing their names, survivors and addresses as they had at Fredericksburg and on other foredoomed occasions. Grant could not be dissuaded from the frontal assault, which was perhaps the most disastrous move of his career. Three Union corps attacked Lee's line early on June 3 and left behind from 6,000 to 7,000 of their number in dead, wounded and captured, with only 1,500 casualties on the Confederate side and not even a dent in the enemy position. A Confederate general wrote that, although he was posted near the center of the line where the "murderous repulse was given," he was "not aware at any time of any serious assault having been given." The attack lasted less than eight minutes. It was one of the costliest brief assaults in modern warfare, rivaling the subsequent Confederate charge at Franklin and the bloody and futile offensives of World War I in the trenches of northern France.

A terrible gloom settled over the Army of the Potomac as bodies festered in no man's land between it and the Army of Northern Virginia. In one month, since crossing the Rapidan, the Union army had suffered 54,000 casualties—more than one third the total of the past three years. The title "Butcher" was conferred on Grant in the North. Never had the Union been sicker of war and death, never more susceptible to suggestions for a negotiated peace, to Copperhead propaganda that the South was invincible and would drain the North white if the war continued. High-ranking generals succumbed to the morbid atmosphere. The haggard General Gouverneur K. Warren, commander of V Corps and hero of Gettysburg, told a member of Meade's staff: "For thirty days now, it has been one funeral procession, past me; and it is too much! Today I saw a man burying a comrade, and, within half an hour, he himself was brought in and buried beside him. The men need some rest. . . ."[12]

General Grant himself was shaken by the ghastly failure. Colonel Porter of his staff heard him say on the evening of June 3, "I regret this assault more than any one I have ever ordered. I regarded it as a stern necessity, and believed that it would bring compensating results; but, as it has proved, no advantages have been gained sufficient to justify the heavy losses suffered."[13]

So another move by the left flank was indicated, and the attempt to annihilate Lee north of Richmond was abandoned. Grant decided to move the Army of the Potomac to the James River, crossing the Chickahominy and the intervening swamps where McClellan had struggled two years before. Sheridan was ordered to set out at once on a second expedition, with Wilson's division left behind to seize the Long Bridge, guard the infantry crossing there and cover the advance through White Oak Swamp. Meanwhile, Sheridan was to draw off the enemy cavalry by proceeding up the Virginia Central Railroad toward Charlottesville and doing as much damage as possible to Lee's communications with the Shenandoah Valley. A force emerging from the valley under Major General David Hunter, which was joined June 8 at Staunton by two cavalry divisions under Generals Crook and Averell from the West Virginia mountains, was ordered to meet Sheridan at Charlottesville and unite with him on the march back to the Army of the Potomac.[14]

The First and Second Divisions, mustering about 6,000 men, were concentrated at Newcastle Ferry and provided with three days' rations for the men—which were supposed to be stretched out over five days—and two days' supply of grain for the horses. On June 7 they were put in motion along the north bank of the North Anna. They were stripped to the essentials. Each man carried his 40 rounds of ammunition on his person and his horse's grain on the pommel of his saddle. The only wagons authorized were for the reserve ammunition, one medical wagon, eight ambulances, and one wagon for each brigade and division headquarters. Enough canvas pontoons for a small bridge also were carried by the column. Sheridan planned to cross the North Anna at Carpenter's Ford and turn south to strike the Virginia Central at Trevilian Station.

On the night of June 10 it appeared that the Rebel cavalry was determined to disrupt this program. The woods were alive with their scouting parties.

A two-day battle began the next morning. Two of Torbert's brigades dismounted and deployed before a line of barricades about three miles from Trevilian Station. Meanwhile, Custer's brigade of the same division slipped around the left along a wood road to destroy the station in the enemy's rear. Instead, Custer swooped on the rear of Wade Hampton's division and captured a large number of wagons, horses and caissons and 350 prisoners.

Custer was gloating over his booty when he found that he had stirred up a hornet's nest. He had gobbled up Hampton's train all right, but in the process was caught between Hampton, who wheeled his division around in a counterattack, and Fitz Lee's division. There was a whirling, scrambling cavalry battle in the underbrush—more of a riot than a formal military engagement. The Confederates not only snatched back their own treasures but captured Custer's headquarters wagon with his papers and Mrs. Custer's rather intimate letters, and his colored servant Eliza (who escaped and rejoined him in a short time), not to mention guns and caissons.

Captain Pennington, commanding one of his batteries, told him the enemy had seized one of his guns and "I think they intend to keep it." "I'll be damned if they do," Custer roared, and organized 30 men to charge and retake the gun. Torbert and Gregg were pressing hard to rescue him from the trap, but Custer was surrounded on three sides, and it looked as though he might be wiped out. When his color-bearer was shot down he ripped his battle flag from its staff and hid it under his gaudy jacket. The touch of melodrama was unnecessary, however, for Torbert broke through late that afternoon and achieved the rescue.[15]

Rather halfheartedly Sheridan ordered the tracks to be torn up a few miles toward Gordonsville. In bivouac that night he thought over the potentialities of the situation. From prisoners and other sources he had learned that General Hunter had failed to carry out Grant's directive. Instead of marching toward Charlottesville for a junction with Sheridan, he was moving through Lexington southward to Lynchburg, where the Orange and Alexandria Railroad met the Virginia & Tennessee.[16] (A week later General Early engaged Hunter at Lynchburg and sent him quickly into retreat.)

The next morning, while Gregg wrecked railroad back toward Louisa Court House, Torbert rode out on a reconnaissance up the Gordonsville Road, ran into Hampton's intrenched troopers with Lee's drawn up on their right flank, and was soon engaged in a bitter battle for possession of the road. Sheridan could not budge the Rebels, even after one of Gregg's brigades came up to join the attack.

That night Sheridan decided to return to the army. His two divisions already had suffered several times as many losses as on the expedition to the James River, Torbert's division having been heavily engaged both June 11 and 12.[17] There was no chance of co-operating with Hunter as Grant had directed, for Hunter was marching away from the assigned meeting place. According to all reports, the enemy cavalry could be quickly supported by its infantry from the Shenandoah Valley and elsewhere. Furthermore, Sheridan's ammunition was running low, and he had to convoy back to comparative safety 400 wounded, 500 prisoners and approximately 2,000 Negroes who had liberated themselves and insisted on following his column.[18]

During the next four days, suffering greatly from lack of food, water and medical attention, this Golgothian procession traveled over the dusty roads to the north bank of the Mattapony. The Negroes, the prisoners and the wounded were sent under escort of two regiments to West Point on the York River, while the rest of the command proceeded to White House Landing on the Pamunkey, a subdepot where supplies were waiting. The plight of the Negro refugees bothered Sheridan long after their weary column shuffled down the road to West Point. "Probably not one of the poor things had the remotest idea, when he set out, as to where he would finally land, but to a man they followed the Yankees in full faith that they would lead to freedom, no matter what road they took."[19] It may have been the memory of that trusting procession that partly accounted for Sheridan's measures as an occupation commander after the war.

At White House Landing Sheridan found unpleasant orders awaiting him from General Meade. He was to destroy the depot there, then convoy an immense train of 900 wagons to the south bank of the James on his return to the Army of the Potomac. It sounded as though Meade still stubbornly clung to his theory of cavalry as a collection of wagon guards. Besides, Sheridan believed, the train "ought never to have been left for the cavalry to escort, after a fatiguing expedition of three weeks." The Confederates, of course, attacked his long and vulnerable column with great vigor, and disaster might have resulted if Gregg had not fought a heroic holding action in the vicinity of Charles City Court House.

Sheridan returned to the army with far from friendly feelings toward Meade. No other general, one of Sheridan's subordinates remarked, "would have dared to show the indifference to his [Meade's] explicit orders that was manifested throughout this juncture by Sheridan." Between the two generals "there was, if not a feeling of positive jealousy and dislike, at least a noticeable lack of that comradeship and sympathy which usually grow out of common dangers and intimate personal acquaintance."[20]

Part of Sheridan's ill temper grew out of concern over his Third Division, which, during his absence, had been dispatched on a raid to break up the Danville and Southside railroads south and west of Petersburg. Wilson had struck as far west as the Staunton River bridge over the Danville road, which he found too heavily guarded to capture and destroy. On his way back he was roughly handled by the Confederate cavalry at Ream's Station on June 28 and lost all 12 guns and his wagon train, as well as many of his troopers. Sheridan and units of the VI Corps were ordered to rescue him, but Wilson found his way to the Union lines by a circuitous route.

Sheridan's feelings toward Meade, which never improved materially, were illustrated by an incident after the reunited cavalry corps went into rest camp at Light House Point early in July. The Richmond *Examiner* of July 2 accused Wilson of stealing church plate, wine and delicacies on his expedition and of being "a highwayman, a wine-bibber and a modern Sardanapalus." General Grant, knowing Wilson was a teetotaler, paid no attention to the journalistic frothing, but Meade sent to Wilson for an explanation. Wilson showed the communication to Sheridan, who growled, "Damn him! Give him hell!"[21] Indeed, at that point, with the Union generals' nerves twanging over Lee's continual frustration of their best-laid plans, it was a wonder that tempers did not explode more often.

Wilson complained to Sheridan of the irascible Warren's conduct while the rest of the cavalry corps was off on the Trevilian raid. Wilson's division was screening Warren's V Corps in its advance over the Chickahominy. At the north bank Wilson paused and sent back to inquire where the pontoon train was keeping itself; a pontoon bridge would have to be thrown across the river near the site of the destroyed Long Bridge. General Warren cursed Wilson's aide and returned him with the message, "Tell General Wilson if he can't lay that bridge to get out of the way with his damned cavalry and I'll lay it."[22]

In its rest camp at Light House Point the cavalry corps refitted and recruited after 50 days of hard and almost constant campaigning. Fifteen hundred horses were sent down from the north to replace those killed in battle and on forced marches from the Rapidan to the James. As the infantry corps of the Army of the Potomac closed in for the siege of Petersburg, that ominous preview of the trench warfare of World War I, the cavalry corps recuperated from its exertions in a score of pitched battles, many of them so obscure and bewildering they were mentioned in dispatches only as fragments of the great battle pattern which composed Grant's "hammering campaign."

General Sheridan's thoughts turned to gentler pursuits during the rest period from July 2 to 26. The wives of many of his officers, including the doe-eyed Mrs. George A. Custer, came down to City Point, Grant's headquarters on the James. One night there was a gala ball on the Presidential boat anchored offshore. A cavalry band played for the dancing on deck, with the siege guns of Petersburg contrapuntal to the gavottes and reels. Mrs. Custer wrote her friends in the North that General Sheridan stepped out to dance dismounted assaults on the enemy. His dancing was "too funny," for the first time with all the assurance and enthusiasm of one of his but she considered the general "so bright," much like General Pleasanton except that "General P. is quieter and has exquisite taste." Sheridan, she added, was such a "jolly" and "agreeable" bachelor that she wished she could take him to her home town of Monroe, Michigan, and marry him off.[23] It was the beginning of a long friendship between the general and Mrs. Custer, whom he considered one of the few officers' wives with a beneficial effect on their husbands' efficiency.

On July 26, with Hancock's II Corps, the cavalry was assigned to another diversionary operation. In a section of the lines around Petersburg the engineers were preparing a surprise for the defenders. A tunnel had been dug under the Confederate sector opposite Burnside's IX Corps, and a gigantic mine of 8,000 pounds of gunpowder was to be exploded under the enemy position. Through this gap two assault brigades were to spearhead an attack by three supporting divisions. It was up to Sheridan and Hancock to cross the James, threaten the Virginia Central Railroad and persuade the enemy that Richmond might be the objective, thus drawing divisions away from the defenses of Petersburg.

Both cavalry and infantry crossed the James safely, but at Bailey's Creek came up against Lee's cavalry and two infantry divisions under General Kershaw. Kershaw drove back the Union cavalry until it reached a ridge, where it dismounted and aligned itself along the crest. The assault of the ridge was torn apart by volleys from the troopers' repeating carbines, and a Union counterattack won the field and what became known as the Battle of Darbytown.

From then until the eve of July 30, when the mine was to be exploded, Sheridan and Hancock[24] occupied themselves with various stratagems to persuade Lee that the bulk of the Union army was crossing over to the North side of the James, further weakening the Petersburg defenses. One night Sheridan marched a division over a bridge muffled with hay and the next day brought it back over with bands playing to heighten the impression that Grant was turning on Richmond. All the vast effort was wasted, however. The mine was exploded almost on schedule, but the ensuing attack was bungled with the carelessness and ineptitude which characterized Burnside's military career.[25] Sheridan remarked bitterly that "all the opportunities opened by our expedition to the north side were irretrievably lost."

Two days later, on August 1, 1864, Sheridan was relieved of duty with the Army of the Potomac and detached for an independent operation that formed the brilliant climax of his life as a soldier.

II

"HE WILL WORRY EARLY TO DEATH"

WHILE Phil Sheridan was refitting his divisions, playing the gallant to colonels' wives and learning how to dance during the month of July 1864, the ghost of Stonewall Jackson was being raised behind the mountain barriers to the west. This ghost assumed the solid, somewhat surly form of Jubal A. Early, lieutenant general of the Confederate Army. As Grant tightened his hold on Lee at Petersburg, the Confederate leader began thinking of 1862 and an almost equally dire emergency which had arisen when McClellan advanced up the Peninsula to within a few miles of Richmond. At that time Lee had turned Jackson loose down the Shenandoah Valley and caused so much consternation that the Union high command weakened McClellan to protect Washington. It might work again, although Jackson was dead and most of his gaunt "foot cavalry" with him.

Early's task force consisted of his own corps, Breckinridge's Division and various cavalry commands, altogether about 20,000 troops. He came swinging down the Valley at a 30-mile-a-day pace, reached Winchester on July 2 and Martinsburg on July 4. The Federal troops opposing his advance were brushed aside with ease. General Hunter, after his defeat at Lynchburg, had fled through the mountains to West Virginia; instead of trying to guard the Valley approaches to Washington and Baltimore, he had preferred to eliminate himself from any of the risks attendant on fighting even a rear-guard action. General Sigel's small and demoralized command at Martinsburg was scattered by a mere demonstration on Early's part. Early then turned east and rampaged through

Maryland, sending Baltimore and Washington into a panic reminiscent of Jacksonian days.

Only a day before his intentions became clear to the Federal government, on July 2, Congress had adopted a resolution asking the President to appoint a day of prayer and humiliation, which was the Radical Republicans' way of covertly striking at Lincoln and his Administration. As the Confederates came closer to the capital Lincoln himself was one of the few leaders to keep his head. In a letter to the mayor's committee of Baltimore he advised, "Let us be vigilant but keep cool. I hope neither Baltimore nor Washington will be sacked. . . ." But the omens were bad.

Early demanded and received $20,000 from Hagerstown and $200,000 from Frederick on threats of burning those Maryland towns. He looted the summer home of the Blair family (Postmaster General Montgomery Blair and his politically powerful father, Francis Preston Blair, Sr.) at Silver Spring and then set it afire. Greater loot was in prospect for him if his campaign proved completely successful—he was under orders from Lee to raid the Federal prison camp at Point Lookout and reclaim 17,000 Confederate soldiers. The primary purpose of the offensive, as Early understood it, was to draw troops from the Union lines around Petersburg. If possible, he was to raid the capital and seize Lincoln, but there was no expectation that he would capture Washington and hold it.

The efforts to withstand Early were necessarily hurried and haphazard. Four separate military departments were involved, in addition to whatever forces Grant could send from Petersburg. At Monocacy a scratch force of 7,000 Union troops under General Lew Wallace, many of them recruits, was hurled at Early on July 9. Wallace's men fought better than could be expected and held up the Confederate advance for a whole day at a time when hours counted. Lincoln suggested that Grant come up from City Point and take charge of the capital's defenses, but the general in chief telegraphed, "It would have a bad effect for me to leave here." The day's delay at Monocacy gave the War Department time to collect thousands of convalescents from the military hospitals, casuals, militia, quartermaster troops, government clerks—anyone

willing to shoulder a musket. They were marched into the fortifications around the city before Early appeared on the outskirts
July 11.

The telegraph wires to the north were cut. Washington that
night was a city in despair. But in the morning there was a vast
improvement in morale. General Wright's VI Corps, dispatched
by Grant from the siege lines around Petersburg, had arrived to
assume the major responsibility.

Knowing that he was confronted by veteran troops, Early made
a few halfhearted stabs at the Union fortifications. Lincoln watched
on the parapet of Fort Stevens, looming as a very tall target until
a soldier was killed only three feet away and he was persuaded to
take cover. On July 13 Early withdrew from the vicinity.

Assistant Secretary of War Dana, who had come up from City
Point to act as observer for Grant (in a significant reversal of his
role at Vicksburg and Chattanooga), was very pessimistic about
the measures taken to ward off another foray against Washington.
He wired Grant: "General Halleck will not give orders except as
he receives them; the President will give none, and until you direct
positively and explicitly what is to be done, everything will go in
the deplorable and fatal way in which it has gone on for the past
week."[1]

General Wright and his two divisions of the VI Corps set out in
a rather fainthearted pursuit of Early but did not interfere with
his crossing of the Potomac. Commenting on one of Wright's dispatches regarding a reconnaissance in search of Early's column,
President Lincoln remarked that Wright acted as though he feared
he "might come across the rebels and catch some." The real trouble lay, not in Wright's courage which was well proved on other
fields, but in the disunity of command, which Early was using to
advantage just as Jackson had two years ago.[2]

Not only did the pursuit of Early fall under the jurisdiction of
four military subdivisions—the Middle Department and the Departments of the Susquehanna, West Virginia and Washington—
but General Wright was technically under the command of the
senior general in the vicinity, Hunter, who had ventured as far as
Harper's Ferry from his panicky flight into the West Virginia

mountains. Other generals commanded the troops in the defenses of Washington and Baltimore. Halleck, the chief of staff, refused to issue orders unless they came through channels from the White House, but this did not inhibit him from operating behind the scenes, scheming for power but avoiding responsibility. And there was always the Secretary of War, the complex and ambitious Edwin M. Stanton, working in ways frequently mysterious. In the crosscurrents of politico-military intrigue more than one good general had gone down in ignominy, and for this reason Grant hesitated to come to Washington and try to correct a situation that promised to continue breeding trouble and failure.

An incident typical of this disunity, at a time (July 18) when the Administration was calling for 500,000 more volunteers, concerned Halleck and his bitterness over being reduced from general in chief to a deskbound chief of staff. Grant sent a staff officer to bring back Wright's divisions after the pursuit of Early had obviously failed. Halleck refused to order them released without written instructions from Grant. The chief of staff also wrote Grant stuffily asserting, "I shall exercise no further discretion in this matter, but shall carry out such orders as you may give."[3]

Grant's proposal to unify the command in what constituted his rear area was to combine the military departments of Susquehanna, West Virginia and Washington and place them under General William B. Franklin, that elderly, capable but hardly vigorous figure whom he had suggested for the cavalry command.[4] Halleck replied that Lincoln, believing Franklin had not obeyed orders at Fredericksburg, could not agree to that appointment.[5] Grant then suggested Meade for the post, explaining that General Rawlins was on his way to Washington and would tell the President of Grant's reasons for preferring the change. The reasons, Rawlins informed Lincoln, were that Meade had lost the confidence of his corps commanders by his explosive temper and that his transfer would not only save face all around but make continued use of his superior qualities as a general.[6]

The President delayed acting on the suggestion, and a few days later word came from the Valley that Early was striking northward again. Lincoln immediately placed Halleck in temporary command of the four departments, explaining that the operations against Early would have to be planned in Washington rather than at City Point as a measure to avoid delays in communications.

Two days after Grant learned that Halleck had been given the post he wanted first for Franklin, then for Meade, he went on a drunk—for the first time since Vicksburg, according to the best calculations of his biographers. General Rawlins wrote his wife on returning to City Point: "I find the General in my absence digressed from his true path. The God in Heaven only knows how long I am to serve my country as the guardian of the habits of him whom it has honored." At least one prominent historian has held that the general's intemperance was caused by anger over Halleck's appointment.[7] In choosing Halleck even temporarily, Lincoln was defying the advice of Horace Greeley in his New York *Tribune* that Halleck, "with that cabbage head of his," should be returned to his "ancestral kraut gardens on the Mohawk."

On July 30 events made it apparent that a more vigorous general than Halleck would be needed to deal with Early and all future threats. The Confederates showed up at Chambersburg, Pennsylvania, and demanded $100,000 in gold or $500,000 in greenbacks on pain of destruction by fire. The money could not be raised, and the 3,000 inhabitants were driven out into the fields while two thirds of the town was burned to the foundations. That same day, 10 miles east of Chambersburg, a Confederate force burned down the ironworks owned by Thad Stevens, one of the most vociferous Abolitionists in Congress. Early said that, if he managed to capture Stevens, he would "hang him on the spot and divide his bones and send them to the various states as curiosities." This was the kind of enemy a Union field commander would have to deal with—and such men as Halleck, Franklin, Meade and Hunter were plainly incapable of carrying out the assignment. In this dilemma it was probably inevitable that Grant should turn his thoughts to the one general who had never let him down—Phil Sheridan.

The day after the Chambersburg raid Grant telegraphed Sheridan that he wanted to see him at City Point. There Sheridan learned that the general in chief, in preparation for a crushing offensive against Petersburg and Richmond, was determined to halt the Confederate attacks on his strategic rear. Grant proposed that General Hunter be left in command of the four military departments combined into the Middle Military Division, a purely administrative function, while Sheridan led the troops in the field. Sheridan was to pursue Early if he retreated up the Shenandoah Valley from his Pennsylvania foray or, if the enemy crossed the Potomac, put himself south of Early and "try to compass his destruction."[8]

President Lincoln approved of Sheridan's appointment to command all Union forces which were to drive the Confederates out of the Valley and seal it off forever as an avenue of aggression. But he wired Grant on August 3:

I have seen your dispatch in which you say, "I want Sheridan put in command of all the troops in the field, with instructions to put himself south of the enemy, and follow him to the death. Wherever the enemy goes, let our troops go also." This, I think, is exactly right as to how our troops should move; but please look over the dispatches you may have received from here, ever since you made that order, and discover, if you can, that there is any idea in the head of anyone here of "putting our army south of the enemy," or of following him to the "death," in any direction. I repeat to you, it will neither be done nor attempted, unless you watch over it every day and hour and force it.[9]

If this is not a clear enough glimpse of the obstructionist tendencies of the War Department, there is the testimony of General Grant: "I knew it was impossible for me to get orders through Washington to Sheridan to make a move, because they would be stopped there, and such orders as Halleck's caution (and that of the Secretary of War) would suggest would be given instead." Grant yielded immediately to President Lincoln's suggestion that he supervise the organization of Sheridan's army; his succinct reply was "I start in two hours for Washington."

Sheridan followed Grant northward, stopped in Washington to confer with Halleck, Stanton and Lincoln on August 4 and 5, then proceeded to Monocacy to receive more detailed instructions on the Valley campaign from Grant. From his four superiors Sheridan learned of several important factors affecting his new command:

(1) There was serious objection to Sheridan as commander of an army on independent operations. "Mr. Lincoln candidly told me that Mr. Stanton had objected to my assignment to General Hunter's command, because he thought me too young, and that he himself had concurred with the Secretary; but now, since General Grant had 'ploughed round' the difficulties of the situation by picking me out to command the 'boys in the field,' he felt satisfied with what had been done, and 'hoped for the best.' Mr. Stanton remained silent during these remarks, never once indicating whether he, too, had become reconciled to my selection or not." Thus Sheridan was in the unenviable position of being nobody's choice for the job, not even his own. Lincoln and Stanton thought him too young; Grant would have liked Franklin or Meade. Sheridan himself was reluctant to leave the Army of the Potomac's cavalry corps for operations in a field which had brought nothing but disgrace and disaster to his predecessors.[10]

(2) The coming election made victory in the Valley a political as well as military necessity, "the authorities at Washington having impressed upon me that the defeat of my army might be followed by the overthrow of the party in power, which event, it was believed, would at least retard the progress of the war, if, indeed, it did not lead to the complete abandonment of all coercive measures."[11]

(3) Sheridan would have administrative as well as field command, General Grant informed him at Monocacy. General Hunter had asked to be relieved, not because he disliked serving under Sheridan, but because he believed he had lost the confidence of his superiors in Washington.

(4) Sheridan was expected to leave "nothing . . . to invite the enemy to return" after defeating the enemy forces in the Valley. "Take all provisions, forage, and stock wanted for the use of your command. Such as cannot be consumed, destroy," read Grant's formal letter of instructions.[12]

With all these responsibilities attached to the command, it was not surprising that Lincoln and Stanton feared Sheridan would prove too young, too inexperienced in political and administrative matters. They should have been cheered by the message General Sherman, then on the approaches to Atlanta, sent to General Grant: "I am glad you have given Sheridan the command of the forces to defend Washington. He will worry Early to death."

On assuming his new command, General Sheridan, as always, sat himself down for a series of geographical and topographical lessons. His instructor was a young lieutenant of engineers, the best available expert on the region. For several days they traced fingers over maps of the Shenandoah Valley in a small and dilapidated hotel at Harper's Ferry where Sheridan established his first headquarters. Lieutenant John R. Meigs knew every wrinkle of the landscape, "even down to the farm-houses."

From the beginning of the war the Shenandoah, the "Valley of Virginia," had been a menace to the Union in several ways. It was a chute down which Confederate armies could roll, almost as if the topographical incline gave them momentum, to Washington and the cities of Pennsylvania and Maryland; it had been the storehouse of the Confederacy, providing the grain and other provender by which it lived even after the Union blockade strangled most of the overseas commerce; and it had been a source of military man power to some degree, although many of its inhabitants were pacifist by religion and inclination, too satisfied with the natural abundance of their land for military adventures. From Harper's Ferry, where the Shenandoah River joins the Potomac, it runs southeast between the Blue Ridge Mountains on the east and the Alleghenies on the west, a wide green trough of the best farmland in America, checkered with fields of grain, ripe with orchards, hazy with burning hickory from smokehouses. Confederate troops transferred there from northeastern Virginia's battlefields recovered their vitality in a few weeks, turning from skeletal fugitives to bounding youth on the ham and hominy, apple pie, juicy beef, buckets of milk and all the other foods they had been lacking for months and even years. For Northern generals it had a grimmer meaning: the reputations of Frémont, Banks, Shields, Sigel, Hunter lay buried there, wherever they had brushed up against Jackson or Early.

The area of the Valley that concerned Sheridan in particular had its northern limit along the Potomac, the southern just south of Staunton on the high ground that separated the waters flowing into the Potomac from those emptying into the James. At Martinsburg to the north the Valley is 60 miles wide; at Winchester, 45 miles; and at Strasburg it narrows down to about 25 miles—the narrow end of the funnel points southeast. Just south of Strasburg the Massanutten Range rises to divide the Shenandoah into two valleys, the one nestling against the Blue Ridges being called the Luray, the western retaining the name Shenandoah. Even in Civil War times there was a good network of metaled roads.

To Sheridan in the autumn of 1864 it looked like anything but a land of milk and honey. It had been burned brown by the summer drought, and it was infested with the men of John Singleton Mosby, that extraordinary leader of irregulars. They were enrolled as members of the 43rd Battalion, Virginia Cavalry, a legalistic maneuver by which the Confederates hoped to avoid having them labeled guerrillas. They hid in the homes of Rebel sympathizers, gathering only on Mosby's command to swoop down on an enemy column or raid a Federal headquarters. Sheridan proposed to treat them as the "ruffians" and "murderers" he believed them to be. He organized a ranger force under Major H. K. Young of the 2nd Rhode Island Infantry to operate as Mosby and his merry men did, appearing and vanishing when necessary. Whenever a masquerade was deemed essential for setting countertraps and counterambushes they wore Confederate uniforms, and their tendency to loot in any uniform won them the Army of the Shenandoah's sobriquet of "Sheridan's Robbers." Even with these nimble counterraiders, Sheridan lost horses, mules, men, munitions and supplies to the frequent and waspish swarming of Mosby's men on wagon trains and storehouses.

General Early's army was even less likely to make the Valley a garden spot for Sheridan and the forces gathering under his command in the vicinity of Harper's Ferry. The Confederate order of battle included Early's own corps, with divisions under Rodes, Ramseur and Gordon; Breckinridge's division, recently arrived from southwestern Virginia; and four brigades of cavalry shortly to be organized in a division under General Lomax. These forces were to be augmented in a few weeks by Anderson's command from the Army of Northern Virginia, which consisted principally of Kershaw's veteran division.

When Sheridan took command of the Army of the Shenandoah it consisted of the VI Corps under Wright, summoned again from the Petersburg lines; one division of the XIX Corps under Emory, which had been on occupation duty in Louisiana and was considered dubious combat material; the VIII Corps under Sheridan's old friend and classmate, George Crook,[13] which was formerly the Army of West Virginia but actually was an undernourished corps; and Torbert's division from the cavalry corps of the Army of the Potomac. In a few weeks Wilson's division was sent along from Petersburg, and, before long, Averell's cavalry from West Virginia. Sheridan chose Torbert as his chief of cavalry, a choice dictated more by seniority than relish, and promoted Wesley Merritt enthusiastically to command of the First Cavalry Division. When Anderson reinforced Early, Grover's infantry division of the XIX Corps also was ordered to join Sheridan.

There was no doubt that Sheridan had considerable numerical superiority over Early (not that numbers had ever before underwritten Federal victory in the Valley). Exactly how much superiority is difficult to determine; numbers and losses in the Civil War, on both sides but particularly the Confederate, can be ascertained accurately in very few instances. Shortly before the battle of Winchester General Early stated that he had 8,500 infantry, 2,900 cavalry and three battalions of artillery—a total of 12,150 soldiers.[14] In his field return of September 10, 1864, Sheridan reported his strength as follows: VI Corps, 12,674 infantry, 648 artillery; XIX Corps, 12,810 infantry, 215 artillery; VIII Corps, 7,140 infantry, 720 artillery; Torbert's cavalry, 6,465; Military District of Harper's Ferry, 4,815, all arms. Not included in this return for the Middle Military Division were the troops in the Washington, Susquehanna and Middle departments, or Averell's 2,500 cavalry on their way from West Virginia. Thus Sheridan reported a total of 45,487 troops shortly before Winchester.[15]

These exact-seeming figures are misleading, however; the ratio of Sheridan's superiority was certainly not 45 to 13. An army advancing into and occupying enemy territory loses strength with every forward step. In a constant process of detachment guards must be posted at every bridge, guides at every crossroads, garrisons for every village and town to maintain civil order, patrols for every foot of railway, guard details at every wagon park and supply dump. Sheridan himself claimed he had only 26,000 troops actually available for combat, but the authoritative Douglas Southall Freeman believes that his field strength, including the additional cavalry, was closer to 40,000. Considering that all his field forces were not available for the firing line, Sheridan's combat strength was probably a little under 40,000.

Except for Wright's VI Corps—with its divisions commanded by George W. Getty, David A. Russell and James B. Ricketts—and the cavalry—Wilson's and Merritt's divisions—which General Sheridan had led against Lee and Stuart, the army consisted mostly of untried units which had served as policemen in occupied territory or, worse yet, in unsuccessful activity across the Alleghenies in West Virginia. Many of Sheridan's subordinates were his seniors in the Regular service. General Emory, for instance, had graduated from West Point in 1831, the year Sheridan was born. General Wright, already a major general and a department commander when Sheridan was a colonel bringing regiments from Mississippi to Kentucky before the battle of Perryville, had recommended Sheridan's promotion to brigadier. Whatever their seniority in years and service, however, Sheridan's corps and division commanders accepted his leadership cheerfully enough; he had Grant's permission to relieve them immediately if they did not.

Even before Wilson's and Grover's divisions joined the army, Sheridan moved up the Valley, pushing the Confederates ahead of him as far as Cedar Creek. But in mid-August Anderson's infantry and a division of cavalry under Fitz Lee reinforced Early, and Grant ordered Sheridan to "act now on the defensive until movements here force them to detach to send this way." He slowly retired to a strong defensive line at Halltown, and, keeping in mind Grant's earlier instructions, as he moved north he destroyed hay and grain, carried off livestock and arrested all the men of Loudoun

County under fifty years and capable of bearing arms. Sheridan agreed that these measures were necessary, and he showed some comprehension of total war when he wrote, "Death is popularly considered the maximum of punishment in war, but it is not; reduction to poverty brings prayers for peace more surely and more quickly than does the destruction of human life. . . ."[16]

Along the Halltown line Sheridan could cover the roads to the north and the strategic point of Harper's Ferry with its Federal arsenal and its memories of past defeats for the Union cause. Both of the Union flanks were protected by rivers, and the Army of the Shenandoah was well dug in, as Early could see for himself as he cautiously approached the Federal dispositions. Already he knew that this was a tougher enemy than had confronted him before. There had been no real test of strength as yet, but at Cedarville, on August 16, there was a sharp little fight indicative of a vitalized army. Fitzhugh Lee's cavalry and a brigade of Kershaw's infantry, both veteran formations, attacked the First Cavalry Division under General Merritt, which was acting as flank guard for the Union withdrawal to Halltown. The Confederates assaulted Gibbs's Union brigade, dismounted, which coolly waited until they came "within short carbine range" and then delivered "a murderous volley"; the Southern casualty list was 500 names long, the Union's 60.[17]

All in all, the advance to Cedar Creek had been profitable, even though its primary purpose—to "occupy Early's line of retreat and force him to fight before reënforcements could reach him"[18]—had not been achieved. Sheridan had learned at first hand the arena where he would grapple with Early and had done much damage as he retreated. To the Northern newspapers, however, not informed that Grant had ordered it, the withdrawal seemed a repetition of previous humiliations in the Valley. Their criticism was to grow much more vitriolic as all of August and most of September passed without a hard blow struck.

One message, Sheridan to Halleck, contained the keynote of those drowsy autumn days: "I have thought it best to be prudent, everything considered." He need not have apologized; warning after warning came from Secretary of War Stanton that every-

thing, including the November election, Union morale, a successful end to the war itself, depended on victory in the Shenandoah.[19]
Defeating Early would be more than a military triumph after years
of disaster; it would help insure Lincoln's election and would thereby guarantee that the war continue until the South was whipped.
The Democrats, who had nominated General George B. McClellan,
were campaigning on an "end the war" rather than a "win the
war" platform.

From mid-August to mid-September the only Union victory was
a psychological one: Sheridan's inert attitude at Halltown convinced Early that his opponent was another of those gasconading
Frémonts, and underestimating an enemy commander is one of the
cardinal sins of the military profession. Early posted one division
on Sheridan's front, marched north to Shepherdstown and sent
Fitzhugh Lee ahead to cross the Potomac. He believed Sheridan
would retreat, like most of his predecessors. If Sheridan attacked
the Confederate division that faced him, Early would take up the
challenge and fight it out there.

Sheridan, always loath to fall in with an opponent's schemes, did
neither. Early found that the South Mountain passes had been
secured by Wilson's cavalry, the Potomac crossings by Averell's
cavalry dismounted and waiting in trenches, and that the third
Federal mounted division under Merritt had cut in behind him
and was wrecking his communications. Sheridan had deployed his
cavalry to deny mobility to the enemy and force him to attack the
intrenched infantry before Halltown, or else give up the venture—
which he did. Early was baffled, but still believed Sheridan to be
an unduly cautious fellow.

Until Grant gave him the word to attack, Sheridan had to endure
the public criticism in the North. He resolved to cut the waiting
period as short as possible. Grant planned to worry Lee with
a diversionary offensive and cause the recall of Anderson's command to Petersburg, making certain that Early would be weakened
enough to be attacked with an assurance of success. It took moral
courage for Sheridan to hold back and act in concert with Grant's
strategy. In notes found among the Sheridan Papers, probably
made in preparation for his memoirs, he wrote, "I could have de-

feated the enemy as he stood, but considering the great investments at stake and the additional loss of life that Kershaw's division would inflict, I felt that it was better to wait . . . than to allow popular pressure to force me to fight with increased risk, and greater loss to our own army."[20]

It was a Quaker girl, loyal to the Union, who let Sheridan know when Anderson's command was recalled by Lee. Through a Negro who crossed the Confederate lines to sell vegetables to the towns-people of Winchester, then Early's headquarters, Sheridan made contact with Miss Rebecca Wright, who taught school there and was known to one of Sheridan's generals as a Union sympathizer.[21] In a tissue-paper note wrapped in tin foil and secreted in the Negro messenger's mouth Sheridan asked Miss Wright to "inform me of the position of Early's forces, the number of divisions in his army, and the strength of any or all of them, and his probable or reported intentions." Sheridan's anxiety over the detachment of Anderson's command was reflected in a flow of dispatches to Chief of Staff Halleck concerning enemy activity. One of them, September 5, informed the War Department that Sheridan had captured prisoners from Kershaw's division and, considering information gleaned from scouts and cavalry reconnaissance, it was apparent that "as yet no rebel troops have gone toward Richmond."[22]

On September 16 came the message from Miss Wright that set the Army of the Shenandoah in motion three days later. It read:

I have no communication whatever with the rebels, but will tell you what I know. The division of General Kershaw, and Cut-shaw's artillery, twelve guns and men, General Anderson commanding, have been sent away, and no more are expected, as they cannot be spared from Richmond. I do not know how the troops are situated, but the force is much smaller than represented. I will take pleasure hereafter in learning all I can of their strength and position. . . .[23]

Almost simultaneously an order arrived from General Grant for Sheridan to meet him at Charlestown the next day. At this conference Sheridan not only told his superior of Anderson's return to Petersburg but laid out an almost bumptiously confident plan for annihilating Early by attacking him at Winchester, then moving around his flanks and cutting off his retreat along the Valley Pike. Sheridan was so enthusiastic that Grant did not have a chance to give his own ideas. "Before starting," Grant later wrote, "I had drawn up a plan of campaign for Sheridan which I had brought with me; but seeing that he was so clear and so positive in his views, and so confident of success, I said nothing about this, and did not take it out of my pocket."[24]

After listening to the flood of words from his volatile junior, Grant gave him a two-word instruction which has become famous in military history as a model of soldierly brevity: "Go in." The rather one-sided conference was ended.

At one o'clock in the morning of September 19 the Army of the Shenandoah moved out for Winchester from its camps around Berryville, to which it had advanced in preparation for the offensive up the valley.

From the Union viewpoint Early's forces were nicely scattered. Only two divisions were posted in front of Winchester: Gordon's was at Bunker Hill, and Rodes's and Breckinridge's at Stephenson's Depot on the Valley Pike north of Winchester.

In planning the expedition to Haxall's Landing that spring during the Wilderness campaign Sheridan had reminded himself again that "combinations rarely work." Now, scheming to bag Early's whole army, he ignored this generally excellent rule. The main obstacles before Winchester, as one approached it from Berryville and the east along a good road, were the deeply banked Opequon Creek and the low plateau before the town. Wilson's Third Cavalry Division was to lead the advance, followed by the infantry, VI Corps and XIX Corps, which were to engage the Confederates at the foot of the plateau and hold them there while the cavalry swerved to the left and worked around their flanks and rear. In the infantry line, VI Corps would form the left, XIX Corps the right. The VIII Corps under Crook was to be held in reserve while this line was being formed, then thrown in to the left of VI Corps to help Wilson's cavalry seize the Valley Turnpike south of town. Meanwhile, General Torbert was to lead his other two cavalry divisions, Merritt's and Averell's, down the Valley Pike from the north and smash into the enemy's left and rear while his center was under attack and his right was being turned.

There was a possible flaw in this neatly worked-out plan: Wilson's cavalry and the three infantry corps would have to move down a single road from Berryville, which ran for three miles through a narrow ravine. A traffic jam would be disastrous.

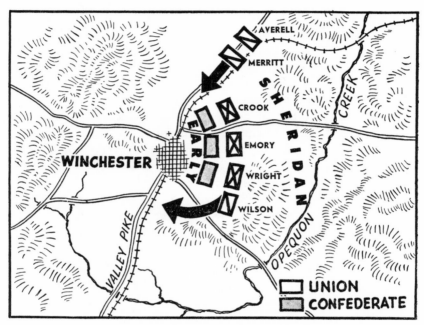

THE BATTLE OF WINCHESTER

The first part of Sheridan's plan was smoothly accomplished. Wilson's division struck the enemy's right and seized a small fort which commanded the Berryville Road where it emerged from the ravine. It was not yet dawn, but Sheridan followed up the cavalry attack and selected the ground where the VI and XIX Corps were to align themselves and keep Early so busy he wouldn't notice that the Union cavalry was behind him. Wright and the VI Corps came up on schedule and went into line under heavy artillery fire.[25] The enemy was thoroughly awake and stirring now, and the morning hours were swiftly passing. What had happened to the XIX Corps, which was to take position on Wright's right flank? Wright's three divisions were hard pressed to hold their ground against the Confederates before them.

Sheridan went back to investigate. To his rage and consternation he found that Wright, sturdy formalist, had brought his whole train behind him—ambulances, supply wagons, baggage wagons, forage wagons, all his rolling stock—and it was jammed together in the narrow defile, blocking the advance of Emory's XIX Corps.

"Get those damned wagons into the ditch," the red-faced and roaring Sheridan ordered the teamsters. Most of Wright's train was pushed off the road, and Grover's division of XIX Corps was allowed to resume its advance.[26]

It was noon, and Sheridan saw that "General Early was not slow to avail himself of the advantages thus offered him, and my chances of striking him in detail were growing less every moment, for Gordon and Rodes were hurrying their divisions from Stephenson's depot. . . ."[27] Emory's divisions were finally guided into line beside Wright's, and Sheridan ordered an advance all along the front. The Union infantry drove forward into heavy woods on their left, sloping cornfields and underbrush in the center, a forested slope behind Red Bud Run on the right. Early, as Sheridan feared, had been granted enough time to build up his line. A heavy artillery fire and musketry drummed down on the waves of Union infantry.

Suddenly Early hurled a counterattack at the point where the VI and XIX Corps were somewhat loosely hinged together. Led by his best field commander, General Rodes, it crashed through one of Wright's brigades. There was nothing to stop the storming column except Battery E, Fifth Maine Light Artillery Regiment. The Maine gunners slung grapeshot into their guns by the hatful and, unsupported by infantry, halted the break-through. With his center caved in, Sheridan later reported, "It was at this juncture that I ordered a brigade of Russell's Division [VI Corps] to wait till the enemy's attacking column presented its flank, then to strike it with vigor." Losses were heavy on both sides. Sheridan managed to wipe out the Confederate salient with Russell's counterattack, and both sides settled down to exchange small-arms fire.[28] The decisive blow would have to come from another direction, and Sheridan waited anxiously for the sound of his cavalry going into action on the right.

General officers had fallen like the autumn leaves in the seesawing struggle at the base of the plateau. Generals Russell and Upton had led the Federal assault against Rodes's division; Russell was killed, Upton wounded. That same day two other Union brigade commanders were wounded, McIntosh and Chapman. On the Confederate side Generals Rodes and Godwin were killed in action.[29]

Enemy pressure on the Union right now obliged Sheridan to change his plans for committing the VIII Corps. He had planned to throw Crook in on the left to follow up Wilson's impending attack on the Confederate right and rear. Crook was waiting in reserve, and he now marched behind the XIX Corps front.[30] In midafternoon he placed his artillery on an eminence which enfiladed the Rebel line and suddenly opened up on it from his masked position. His infantry stormed ahead to turn the enemy left flank.

Just as Early was beginning to worry about this development, the Union cavalry's hammer strokes fell on him left, right and rear with an unnerving precision. "Combinations rarely work"—but this was a rare occasion.

Wilson's cavalry division, which had been making a wide circle around the Confederate right, suddenly appeared in a massed formation. Early believed all the Union cavalry was bearing down on him and threw his own cavalry in that direction. His front, too, was engaged by the Federal infantry all down the line. As Crook and the VIII Corps advanced, the VI and XIX Corps "executed a left half wheel of the line of battle to support him."[31]

The fortunes of war were with Sheridan late that afternoon, despite his earlier difficulties. For suddenly Averell's and Merritt's cavalry divisions came down the Martinsburg Pike on the gallop, having broken up Breckinridge's infantry farther up the line. They drove a confused mass of stragglers into the Confederate infantry. Early changed front to repel the attack on his rear; his left was already turned by Crook. "These attacks were made by the cavalry," General Merritt reported, "without any knowledge of the state of the battle except what was apparent to the eye." The First Cavalry Division scooped up 775 prisoners, seven battle flags and two guns in its whirlwind charge. The shadows of night were lengthening over the battlefield now, and this circumstance alone, Merritt believed, "saved Early's army from capture."[32] Sheridan, too, believed Early would have been annihilated had it not been for the delay in Emory's corps reaching its position. Crook would have gone into action on the left and probably would have reached the Valley Pike to cut off Early's escape.

A captured Union officer provides a graphic picture of the confusion in the Confederate rear when the Union cavalry delivered the decisive stroke against Early's left:

The confusion, disorder, and actual rout produced by the successive charges of Merritt's division would appear incredible did not the writer actually witness them. To the right a battery with guns disabled and caissons shattered was trying to make to the rear, the men and horses impeded by broken regiments of cavalry and infantry; to the left, the dead and wounded, in confused masses, around their field-hospitals—many of the wounded, in great excitement, seeking shelter in Winchester; directly in front, an ambulance, the driver nervously clutching the reins, while six men in great alarm were carrying to it the body of General Rodes.[33]

The Confederate army, whose front had been overextended in trying to cope with Sheridan's superiority in numbers, was sent "whirling through Winchester"—as Sheridan exuberantly reported to the War Department—and up the Valley Pike. The rout was "sad, humiliating, disgusting," said a Rebel officer who "never saw our men in such a panic before." The Shenandoah Valley, so long a hunting preserve for Confederate generals, was no longer a highway of invasion for the Rebellion.

That evening Sheridan and his old friend Crook strode down the main street of Winchester arm in arm. Three young girls danced around them until Crook "reminded that the Valley had hitherto been a race-course—one day in the possession of friends, and the next of enemies—and warned of the dangers they were incurring by such demonstrations." When they finally detached themselves from the young ladies they proceeded to the private school where Rebecca Wright taught. From the Quaker schoolteacher Sheridan learned how she found out Anderson's command had marched away—a convalescent Confederate officer had visited her mother's house and casually given the news.[34]

Sheridan sat down at a desk in Miss Wright's schoolroom to write his dispatches. To Grant at 7:30 P.M. he telegraphed that the conduct of his largely untried troops had been "most superb—they charged and carried every position taken up by the rebels from Opequon creek to Winchester." He reported also that the enemy had left 3,000 wounded in Winchester—a figure based on a very hasty and exaggerated estimate, later scaled down—and that his army had captured five guns, 4,000 small arms, 2,500 prisoners. His own losses were heavy, about 4,000 in killed and wounded; the enemy's slightly less, since they had remained on the defense except for Rodes's counterattack.[35]

Messages of congratulation came singing over the wires from Washington and City Point. Secretary of War Stanton informed him that 100 guns had been fired in honor of the victory, and that he had been promoted to brigadier general in the Regular Army. General Grant said he considered the victory "most opportune in time and effect. . . . It wipes out much of the stain upon our arms by previous disasters in that vicinity."[36] And from President Lincoln came the glad words, "Have just heard of your great victory. God bless you all, officers and men. Strongly inclined to come up and see you."[37]

Laurel was fine, but the enemy was still battleworthy. The Union cavalry followed Early's retreat to Fisher's Hill near Strasburg, where the Massanuttens divide the Valley into two channels. Through the night Sheridan put aside thoughts of the day's triumphs, studied his cavalry reports and his maps and planned the immediate movement of his army. It was no time to allow "Old Jubilee" Early a rest. The army, except for its patrols on the pike toward Strasburg, could sleep tonight, but it would march at dawn for Fisher's Hill.

12

"FORWARD EVERYTHING!"

WHILE the North was reading one of Sheridan's gleeful dispatches over its breakfast tables—"We have just.sent the enemy whirling through Winchester, and are after them tomorrow"—the Army of the Shenandoah was marching on Fisher's Hill.

Early believed himself so impregnable there that he unlimbered his artillery and sent away its teams of horses. His army was seriously depleted by the battle of Winchester, but he had only three or four miles of front to cover between his right flank, resting securely on the Massanutten Mountains and the north fork of the Shenandoah River, and his left stretching toward Little North Mountain with its steep and thickly timbered slopes. His infantry was intrenched on Fisher's Hill, a steep bluff overhanging the south bank of Tumbling Run and overlooking the town of Strasburg from the south.

By the night of September 20 Sheridan had formed his plan of attack. The XIX and VI Corps moved to positions opposite Fisher's Hill. The VIII Corps was kept concealed in the forests for a wide flanking maneuver. Averell's cavalry was pushed around to the right to feel out the location of the Confederate left. The rest of the cavalry, except for Devin's brigade, was sent under General Torbert to make a forced march up the Luray Valley, come out at New Market in Early's rear and cut off his retreat. Again Sheridan aimed, not merely for victory, but for annihilation.

Working around Early's flanks would take time. The Federal attack would have to be delayed until the twenty-second, with the VI and XIX Corps moving closer to Fisher's Hill and doing their best to attract and hold Early's attention. Meanwhile, Crook's VIII Corps marched by a circuitous route through heavy timber on the north bank of Cedar Creek. It was not until the morning of the twenty-second that it began ascending the slope of Little North Mountain, where it was to stay under cover until the time came to assault Early's left and rear.

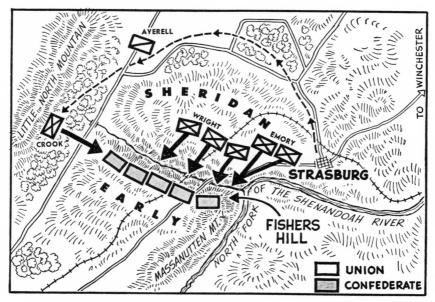

THE BATTLE OF FISHER'S HILL

In later years Crook claimed that the flanking attack from Little North Mountain was his own conception. "Gen. Sheridan's first idea was for me to turn the enemy's right flank, but after discussion saw the folly of such an undertaking, and finally let me go to the right, their left," he wrote.[1] Henry A. DuPont, who devoted a whole book to a study of Sheridan's campaign in the Valley, stated it "was fully understood by everyone at Corps headquarters" that Crook had planned and advocated the movement of his infantry to Little North Mountain.[2] A letter by one of Crook's brigadiers, Rutherford B. Hayes, future President of the United States, supported this contention that Crook proposed the flanking march "against the opinion of other Corps generals." In Hayes's opinion—doubtless somewhat colored by his great admiration for his immediate superior—"General Sheridan is a whole-souled, brave man," but "intellectually he is not Crook's equal, so that . . . General Crook is the brains of this army."[3]

Sheridan simply stated that he "resolved on the night of the 20th to use again a turning-column against his [the enemy's] left, as had been done on the 19th at the Opequon."[4] Whether the suggestion for another flanking march was Crook's, Sheridan's or some staff captain's, the responsibility was Sheridan's. No one but Sheridan was ever the "brains" of his army. He had managed to achieve much at Perryville, Stone's River, Chattanooga, Yellow Tavern, and he was to win great victories after the Valley campaign, without Crook's intellect to assist him. Military plans are rarely the product of the mind of one man, barring Napoleon and his imitators. In the operations against Vicksburg, it was noted, Grant sat silently for hours listening to the theorizing and debating of his subordinate officers and, almost as if by osmosis, absorbed the best features of the discussions and adapted them for his subsequent movements. Crook served as sort of an ex-officio chief of staff to Sheridan in the Valley, but there was never a moment of doubt about who made the command decisions.

The whole battle plan for Fisher's Hill depended on maintaining the secrecy of Crook's movement to Little North Mountain. Daylight transfer of such a large body of troops could be spotted by the enemy's Three Top signal station, so the VIII Corps lay concealed in the forest north of Cedar Creek all of September 21. That night it set out along a back road for Little North Mountain, moving up behind Averell's cavalry. Crook took every precaution against the enemy's catching sight of his marching column. Weapons were wrapped in rags to prevent light from gleaming on them, and Crook even ordered his color-bearers to trail their flags and guidons.[5] On the twenty-second the VIII Corps proceeded through a series of ravines to reach their jump-off position, still undetected by the Confederates. One of these days in hiding, Crook's high-spirited men almost gave the game away by engaging in an impromptu fox hunt. A fox was sighted between the two divisions, and the soldiers "set up such a yell that poor Reynard was paralyzed by fear, lost all his cunning . . . and allowed himself to be captured."[6]

It was close to sundown, September 22, and cook fires were being lighted all along the Confederate line on Fisher's Hill. Early's officers were beginning to congratulate themselves that their position was so strong Sheridan did not dare to assault it. There had been skirmishing and exchanges of artillery fire that day but nothing to show the Federals intended a decisive attack. Far out on the Confederate left came a report that pickets had sighted Union troops moving along the steep slope of Little North Mountain, and a battery in the valley below opened fire on them. Probably the false alarm of nervous recruits.

Suddenly the Rebel left was struck in flank and rear by howling waves of Union infantry. Crook's men came down the mountainside, and even the heavy artillery fire directed on the wooded slopes did not deter them. Early's men were as astounded as if the Yankees had dropped on them from the sky. The West Virginians had developed an eerie battle cry that, according to General Crook, was most unnerving. "You can form no conception of it. It beggars all description. The enemy fired a few shots afterwards, but soon the yell was enough for them."[7]

At the base of Little North Mountain, Ricketts' division of the VI Corps swung in to join the attack. The Confederate left disintegrated, and the two Federal corps proceeded to roll up their line. Sheridan went in with the VI Corps. Men long remembered the picture he made, waving his little black plug hat and spurring his black charger Rienzi into the thick of the assault.

"We're flanked," the Southerners yelled as they ran.

Sheridan cut loose with everything he had "so suddenly as to cause the enemy to break in confusion and flee."[8] "Forward everything! Don't stop! Go on!" he said whenever he was asked for instructions.

Rarely had a Confederate army been broken so quickly. The gunners fled on the heels of the infantry, abandoning 16 guns along the crest of Fisher's Hill although "until that moment they had felt their position so secure that they had even taken the ammunition boxes from the caissons."[9]

"An indescribable panic," Sheridan called it, attributing the rout to the Confederates' fear of being caught in the pocket formed by Tumbling Run (which ran in front of Fisher's Hill) and the north fork of the Shenandoah River.[10] The Southern army fled up the Valley Pike in complete disorder, closely pursued by the Union infantry. Hot-tempered Crook was all over the field, hurrying troops forward. He came across 50 men who busied themselves at hauling captured artillery out of the vacated breastworks, and ordered them to join the pursuit. "I pitched into them for not being at the front . . ." he said. "They replied that they were pulling [the guns] by order of their general, Ricketts." General Ricketts appeared, looking "as though he was stealing sheep," and explained that he wanted to make sure of receiving credit for having captured the guns. It seemed a feckless task for combat troops at that moment, and Crook told Ricketts with considerable asperity that "all able-bodied men were needed at the front."[11]

All three Union infantry corps pounded down the Valley Pike in the darkness. The Confederates set up a road block spiked with two pieces of artillery, but it was quickly brushed aside. The men of the XIX Corps had not seen much action in the general assault at sundown, but they boasted that they marched so fast it was ten o'clock that night before Devin's cavalry brigade was able to "take the road abreast with the XIX."[12] Devin's troopers continued the pursuit until daylight, picking up Confederate stragglers and sending them to the rear as prisoners.

On the Union side it was a comparatively tidy little battle. The Union casualties totaled 528, with only 52 men killed in action, certainly one of the most economical victories of the war. The Confederates admitted to a total casualty list of only 1,235. This may have been somewhat less than accurate, as Early, in common with many generals of all wars, had a tendency to minimize his own losses as well as the effectives in his command. (During Sheridan's entire campaign in the Valley, for instance, the Federal provost marshal certified that 13,000 Confederate prisoners had been turned over to him. This was several hundred more men than Early represented as forming his total effective force at Winchester.[13])

In the North the news of the battle of Fisher's Hill confirmed the impression that Sheridan was making himself the master of the Valley. Hundred-gun salutes were fired at the headquarters of the various field armies. Atlanta had fallen early that month to General Sherman's armies, and this, coupled with Sheridan's victories, convinced the North that Union arms would soon triumph. The South had lost its greatest arsenal in Atlanta and its richest granary in the Shenandoah; the Lincoln Administration's conduct of a war of attrition at last seemed successful, and its continuance was soon to be assured by the electorate.

To Sheridan the battle in itself was much less satisfactory; he had "anticipated results still more pregnant." His cavalry, for once, had let him down. Both Torbert and Averell failed completely in their missions.

Torbert, with Wilson's full division and Merritt lacking only Devin's brigade of his, had been detailed to advance up the Luray Valley, east of the Massanutten range, and place himself across the Valley Pike at New Market. This would have trapped Early between Sheridan's infantry and Torbert's cavalry. Perhaps it was a "circuitous and obstructed march," as General Merritt said,[14] but Torbert had three days in which to cover 40 miles. What really stopped him was a light cavalry force under General Wickham, who had two brigades of the wounded Fitzhugh Lee's division. It was two brigades against four, and Torbert had a half-dozen batteries of horse artillery, mostly Regular Army units, with enough fire power to blast their way through a corps. At Milford, Wickham put up a brave front, and Torbert immediately withdrew, pulling all the way back to Front Royal and wondering what to do next. A sergeant in a New York cavalry regiment gave an explanation of sorts: "At close quarters we can whip them; they have no sabres and generally no revolvers. But at long range we are rather afraid of them; they carry Enfields which shoot farther than our carbines."[15]

Sheridan confessed himself "astonished and chagrined" when he received a dispatch from Torbert on September 23 saying the cavalry had failed to force a passage of the Luray Valley. "Torbert ought to have made a fight," Sheridan believed. ". . . It does not appear that he made any serious effort at all to dislodge the Confederate cavalry."[16]

From General Averell's supineness during the same period it was even more apparent that a shake-up in the cavalry command was necessary.

The pursuit of Early's disorganized forces was left to the infantry, except for Devin's cavalry brigade. On the morning of September 23 the army had reached Woodstock, having accomplished a night march of 15 miles after fighting a battle the previous day. Sheridan ordered Averell to join Devin in leading the pursuit. It was nearly noon before Averell came up. He had spent the night in comfortable bivouac, having politely given the infantry priority on the roads. It was the very thing to arouse Sheridan's Celtic temper, remembering, as he did, how Warren's corps had clogged the cavalry advance on Spotsylvania that spring. "Hot words" passed between the commanding general and Averell, Sheridan reported, and Averell lackadaisically set out to join Devin in front of Mount Jackson. Devin was attacking Early and forcing his withdrawal, but Averell declined to co-operate on the grounds that he had received reports an enemy division was turning his flank. Sheridan shot off a message to Averell that should have rankled any soldier not of the most bovine temperament:

I do not want you to let the enemy bluff you or your command, and I want you to distinctly understand this note. I do not advise rashness, but I do desire resolution and actual fighting, with necessary casualties, before you retire. There must now be no backing or filling by you without a superior force of the enemy actually engaging you.

A short time later Sheridan learned that Averell had disregarded the direct order and had gone into camp near Hawkinsburg. Sheridan immediately relieved him of command, with Colonel William H. Powell named in his place.

General Torbert escaped such drastic treatment, perhaps for sentimental reasons, perhaps because he had not actually disobeyed orders, although the effects of his dilatory conduct were much more serious. If Torbert had moved with the vigor expected of him, he could have cut off Early's army, and active fighting in the Valley would have ended at New Market instead of at Cedar Creek almost a month later, for in his retreat from Fisher's Hill General Early had "scarcely preserved the semblance of even a company organization."[18] The enemy's rear guard was composed mostly of officers, the rest of the army being too demoralized to offer resistance. As far away as Richmond it was apparent that Early would need considerable reinforcements and refitting before he could even attempt a stand against Sheridan. In the Confederate capital, when new guns were being shipped to replace the 16 Early lost at Fisher's Hill, cynical loafers at the railroad station chalked on the cannon, "To General Sheridan, care of General Early."

On September 26 the pursuit ended. Early retired to the vicinity of Port Republic, where he awaited reinforcements of both infantry and cavalry, as well as those derisively inscribed field guns. For the next 10 days Sheridan and his whole army, Torbert and his command having arrived to the jeers of their comrades in the infantry, settled down around Harrisonburg to do as much damage as possible in the upper reaches of the Valley. This section had scarcely felt the weight of a conqueror's heel since hostilities began, but now it suddenly received a full measure of the brutality of war. With a cold and calculating supervisory eye Sheridan burned, blasted, slaughtered, destroyed. It was necessary, it had been so ordered from Washington, it was the act of a soldier obeying his orders. Nevertheless, burning out the Valley of the Shenandoah must have been a haunting memory to Sheridan, for he was not a monster nor a sadist, in spite of his often-quoted pledge to strip the Valley so that even the crows would have to carry their own rations.

Torbert was given another chance to show a more aggressive spirit as chief of cavalry. While Merritt's division diverted Early's attention by a demonstration against Port Republic, Torbert took the rest of the mounted forces to Staunton. Here he destroyed "immense quantities of army stores," blew up the railroad bridge over the west fork of the Shenandoah and, on his return journey, drove off all the cattle he could find, destroyed all the food and forage he couldn't carry off and burned the mills along the way. There was other work of the same nature for the infantry.

General Sheridan's feeling about the people of the vicinity who were suffering these harsh measures was anything but softened when on October 3 Lieutenant Meigs, the young engineer who had acted as his topographical instructor before the Valley campaign began, was murdered by bushwhackers while out on a surveying mission. Without too much investigation Sheridan convinced himself that the slayers either lived in the neighborhood or were sheltered by neighboring residents. He ordered all homes in a five-mile radius to be burned to the ground and appointed General Custer—now in command of the Third Cavalry Division, replacing General Wilson who had just been assigned as chief of cavalry in the west[19]—to carry out the order. Custer could always be counted on for enthusiasm in such tasks, if not too much discretion. After watching Custer's men running from house to house in the village of Dayton, torches in hand, Sheridan called off the house burners and ordered instead that all able-bodied men be seized as prisoners of war.

Three days later Sheridan began his movement back down the Valley. He intended to establish himself at Cedar Creek until it was decided what his army should do next. Suspicion was growing in his mind that he would be ordered to follow Early through the passes of the Blue Ridge Mountains toward Charlottesville and Gordonsville and operate on that line against Richmond. To such a scheme he was heartily opposed. It may have been a matter of higher strategy than an army commander was expected to concern himself about, but Sheridan did not hesitate to state his opinion that the Army of the Shenandoah should scorch the Valley from one end to the other, then entrain on the Baltimore & Ohio via Washington for Petersburg. The other plan, which was finding favor in the War Department, would involve the opening of the Orange & Alexandria Railroad and the detachment of several divisions, perhaps, to drive off guerrillas and keep it running. He would also be forced to leave in the Valley a strong enough force, probably Crook's whole command, to guard the line of the upper Potomac and the Baltimore & Ohio, if the Jackson-Early type of diversionary offensives were not to be expected again. Such detachments, he believed, would leave him "a wholly inadequate number of fighting men to prosecute a campaign against the city of Richmond." While he was approaching Richmond from the west, enough of Lee's army might be switched over to "crush me . . . and after overwhelming me be quickly returned to confront General Meade." The long line of communication necessary to supply such a movement could easily be cut and disrupted, leaving Sheridan stranded in hostile country far from any source of nourishment.

Even General Grant favored the plan of driving Early into eastern Virginia. Telegrams and letters by the score were exchanged between Grant and Sheridan as they debated the next operation of the Army of the Shenandoah. Sheridan stubbornly maintained that the gains of September should not be cast away in October and November, and Grant, under great pressure by the Government and the public, clung with "some tenacity" to the plan for an offensive against Richmond.

Meanwhile, with Grant's permission, Sheridan withdrew toward Strasburg. The cavalry ranged from the western slope of the Blue Ridge to the eastern flange of the Alleghenies, driving off cattle and destroying barns, storehouses, grain and other supplies. The infantry did its bit, too, according to Captain John W. DeForest of General Emory's staff. Between Mount Crawford and Woodstock alone, 2,000 barns and more than 70 mills, bulging with the recent harvest of wheat, corn and hay, were destroyed. The army's passing was marked by column after column of smoke rising in the autumn sky. "The inhabitants were left so stripped of food," Captain DeForest observed, "that I cannot imagine how they escaped starvation." The Valley, Sheridan informed Washington, "will have but little in it for man or beast."[20]

Meanwhile, Early was becoming bolder. Angered by the devastation executed by Sheridan's army, he began nipping at the Union flanks and rear. To reinforce him General Rosser had brought his cavalry command, including the Laurel Brigade, notorious among

Valley residents for its swaggering and boasting. When Rosser first came to the Shenandoah he was proclaimed "savior of the Valley," and his regiments marched in decked with self-bestowed laurel.

Rosser's prickling forays annoyed Sheridan, so he issued an order to General Torbert which became famous in the army: attack Rosser and "either whip the enemy or get whipped yourself."

Next morning Sheridan climbed Round Top Mountain, from which he had a perfect spectator's view of the fight. Near Tom's Brook crossing Custer's division spun around and attacked Rosser's three brigades, while Merritt swung in beside it and charged the Confederate brigades under Lomax. It was an old-time cavalry battle, both sides staying in the saddle most of the time. Charge and countercharge, assault and retreat—the opposing troopers fought it out with both sides resorting to the saber in that open country. Suddenly their flanks gave way, and the Confederates fled as precipitately as if they had seen the folly of war in a flashing instant. They left behind 11 of their 12 guns, all their caissons and wagons and 300 prisoners.

Sheridan, in a jovial mood as he watched Rosser and Lomax turn tail, offered a $50 reward to the trooper who captured their twelfth piece of artillery. (The Confederates managed to make off with it.) The vainglorious Laurel Brigade and its companions fled for 26 miles with the Union cavalry encouraging them most of the way. The battle became known in history as Tom's Brook, but to everyone but the War Department it was dubbed the "Woodstock Races."

This action redeemed the cavalry in Sheridan's and the infantry's eyes. But when a young West Pointer on Torbert's staff heard the remark that "Sheridan can even make the cavalry fight," he replied angrily that "Sheridan had nothing to do with it. Torbert was just about to pitch into the Rebs when Sheridan happened to come along. The fight would have come off just the same if he had kept away and minded his own business."[21] Dismayed by the slack generalship of Torbert and Averell after Fisher's Hill, Sheridan was determined to sting the cavalry into a more aggressive attitude, and the "Woodstock Races" proved the soundness of his "whip or get whipped" psychological gambit.

The next day, October 10, the army crossed to the north side of Cedar Creek and began digging in for an indefinite but hardly peaceful stay. The VI Corps was ordered to march to Ashby's Gap in preparation for the general movement to Petersburg advocated by Sheridan. On October 13, however, Early suddenly appeared in force around Fisher's Hill, and Sheridan ordered Wright to rejoin the army at once.

That same day he received a telegram from Secretary of War Stanton suggesting an immediate conference. Stanton was going to City Point to gather the views of General Grant on future operations, but he wanted to see Sheridan first. To Sheridan it did not seem a propitious time to leave his army with a strengthened and emboldened Early before it, but the Secretary of War could hardly be ignored.

He decided to send the cavalry to raid Charlottesville and break up the railroad in its vicinity. On his return he would decide how to deal with General Early. His opponent had been reinforced with Kershaw's fine infantry division—obviously a storm signal, for Lee could not spare men like Kershaw's for any piddling purpose.

Sheridan had an acute military intuition, close to infallible, and he was a worried man as he accompanied the cavalry to Front Royal, where it would turn south on its raid and he would take the train for Washington. Well might he fret over leaving the Army of the Shenandoah this October 16. Its greatest test—and his—was only three days in the future.

13

A FORTRESS BECOMES A SLAUGHTER PEN

LONG files of cavalry trotted briskly into the mountain town of Front Royal on the afternoon of October 16, 1864. With his escort, powdered by dust and bearing the headquarters flag of the Army of the Shenandoah, General Phil Sheridan galloped on ahead of the blue column winding over the sere and rustling countryside. He was anxious for news of the army he had left behind, digging itself in along Cedar Creek.

A dispatch from army headquarters was waiting for him, and the news was not good. General Wright, commanding the VI Corps but now in charge of the army until Sheridan returned from Washington, sent a message intercepted from the Confederate signal station on Three Top Mountain. It read:

To Lieutenant-General Early:
Be ready to move as soon as my forces join you, and we will crush Sheridan.

It was signed LONGSTREET, the ablest of Lee's surviving lieutenants, who had been wounded in the Wilderness but was reported almost ready to return to duty as a corps commander. Early already had been reinforced by Rosser's cavalry brigade and Kershaw's division. If Longstreet was bringing his corps to the Valley, the Union army was in for a hard fight. Sheridan was inclined to look on it as "a ruse," although he could not see what purpose such a trick would serve except to put the Union army on its guard.[1] In his covering message, General Wright said, "I shall hold on here until the enemy's movements are developed, and shall only fear an attack on my right, which I shall make every preparation for guarding against and resisting." (It was Wright's obsession with his right flank which almost proved disastrous.)

Sheridan called off the cavalry raid on Charlottesville and ordered Torbert to take his three divisions back to Cedar Creek at once. He advised Wright to "look well to your ground and be well prepared. Get up everything that can be spared," and promised to hurry back to the army as soon as possible. He also wired General Halleck to ascertain if any information had come from Grant's headquarters to corroborate the Longstreet-Early message.

With his usual tendency to deprecate Grant and all his works, Halleck replied that evening, "General Grant says that Longstreet brought with him no troops from Richmond, but I have very little confidence in the information collected at his headquarters. If you can leave your command with safety, come to Washington, as I wish to give you the views of the authorities here."

Worried though he was by Early's aggressive activities before his army, Sheridan decided to continue his journey to Washington. The Army of the Shenandoah was not in an ideal position for defensive fighting, and Sheridan knew it, but changing dispositions in the face of an aggressive enemy could also be dangerous. A calculated risk was necessary. It was urgent that the Government be informed of his view that advancing against Richmond from the west, instead of joining Grant in operating against Lee's army at Petersburg, would be risky if not foolhardy. So he would have to take the chance that he could confer with Halleck and Stanton, then hurry back to Cedar Creek before Early was ready to move, if that was what his opponent really intended. Sheridan and his staff even brought their horses on the train with them to Washington so they would be prepared for any eventuality.

Early in the morning of October 17 Sheridan consulted with Stanton and Halleck about the advisability of operating east of the Blue Ridge. Even before the conference began he requested the Secretary of War to have a special train waiting at noon to take him to Martinsburg; from there he and his staff would journey to Winchester and Cedar Creek on horseback.

He argued the case with his usual logic, precision and enthusiasm—perhaps with a little more than his accustomed vehemence since he expected to meet firm opposition. It developed that Stanton and Halleck were not at all in agreement with Grant's plan for the advance up the Valley and over the Blue Ridge to Richmond. Sheridan found that "my views against such a plan were practically agreed to," and the War Department heads decided to send two Engineer Corps colonels with him to determine where a defensive line could be staked out in the Valley which could be held while the bulk of Sheridan's forces were transferred to Petersburg.[2]

Accompanied by the Engineer colonels and his staff, Sheridan hastened to rejoin the army. They detrained along with their mounts that evening in Martinsburg. Early in the morning of the eighteenth the party set out for Winchester, somewhat hampered because one of the Engineers was "enormous," the other a wisp of a man, and both were more accustomed to their War Department chairs than the saddle. It was 4:00 A.M. before they reached Winchester. For his night's lodging Sheridan selected the comfortable house used by Colonel Oliver Edwards as his headquarters.[3] Before retiring he received a courier from the army at Cedar Creek. All was quiet there, he was informed. He went to bed less anxious than he had been for a number of days.

Cedar Creek and vicinity were, in fact, too quiet, as General Merritt of the cavalry noted.

Even as Sheridan was sleeping that night, the Confederates were stirring with preparations for a bloody dawn. Sheridan's scorched-earth policy had rendered the Valley untenable for an army that was forced to live off the country. As Early said in explanation of his attack across Cedar Creek, "I was now compelled to move back for want of provisions and forage, or attack the enemy in his position with the hope of driving him from it; and I determined to attack."[4]

The Federal position against which he intended to move was vulnerable to a whirlwind dawn attack such as General Early had in mind. Said General Merritt:

The approaches from all points of the enemy's stronghold at Fisher's Hill were through wooded ravines in which the growth and undulations concealed the movement of troops, and for this reason and its proximity to Fisher's Hill the pickets protecting its front could not be thrown, without danger of capture, sufficiently far to the front to give ample warning of the advance of the enemy.[5]

On the north bank of Cedar Creek the Union army was aligned with Crook's VIII Corps on the left, behind which were army headquarters, the artillery reserve, the wagon parks and the ammunition dumps; with Emory's XIX Corps in the center, and Wright's VI Corps, the only standard-size corps in the field, on the right.

Early's scheme was simply to throw his best divisions under General John B. Gordon, the ablest of the new corps commanders rising through attrition in the Confederate high command, in a hook around the Union left and rear. Crook's corps was weakest—numerically it was only a division—Emory's was next in size, and Wright's was the largest and most battle-hardened. Early would strike at enemy weakness first. The Federal cavalry was on both flanks, but too far away to intercept any such movement—Merritt and Custer out on the right flank, Powell at Front Royal watching the mountain gap for Confederate reinforcements. With his usual readiness to take large risks Early planned to send four separate columns, marching through darkness over difficult terrain, in a concentric attack on the Union army. "It was about as venturesome an enterprise as the nocturnal escalade of a strong fortress," Captain DeForest commented.[6]

Misconceptions of at least two of the Federal commanders would help this risky enterprise. General Wright, insisting that the only possible enemy approach was against his corps, kept the bulk of the cavalry on his wing. And General Crook seemed to have lost interest in reconnoitering on his own front when Wright failed to provide cavalry pickets to patrol the fords across Cedar Creek. (Sheridan's doctrine, of course, was that the infantry should be responsible for protecting itself, the cavalry kept concentrated for shock action.) Some sort of alarm should certainly have electrified VIII Corps headquarters the night of October 18-19, as Crook tacitly admitted. "During the night my Officer of the Day in making his rounds heard noise outside of my pickets and, thinking it

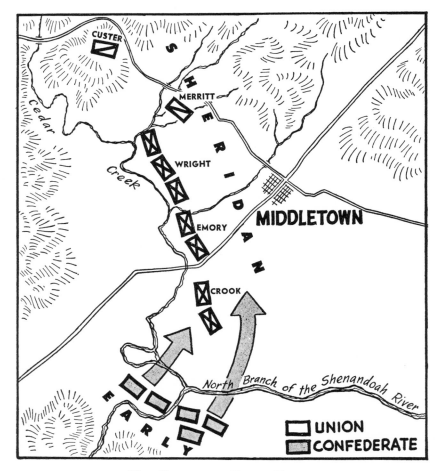

THE BATTLE OF CEDAR CREEK

was our cavalry, went out alone to investigate it. He was captured by the enemy without being able to give the alarm."[7]

Only General Emory, commander of the XIX Corps, seemed to be aware of the Federal left's dangerous weakness and approachability. Crook's position, he believed, was endangered because it did not command the valley in front of it. "The enemy could march 30,000 men through that defile, and we would not know it till they were on our left flank," he said.[8]

While VIII Corps headquarters was calmly accepting the disappearance of its officer of the day early on the morning of October 19, Gordon and his Confederate divisions under Ramseur and Pegram were marching around its position, their arms muffled in rags to prevent the clank and clatter from reaching the Federal army's ears. They started on their march at 3:30 A.M. The previous day General Gordon had climbed Massanutten Mountain and "with powerful field glasses saw every man, horse and gun at his feet, and the soldiery taking things as coolly as if there was not a Rebel closer than Richmond. . . . He must have felt the same fierce joy that Stonewall Jackson did when he saw Hooker's wing at Chancellorsville. . . . The total destruction of Sheridan was inevitable." By false dawn the Confederate army was ready to strike; its initial movements had been carried out with precision—and luck.

Back in Winchester, General Sheridan was awakened at six o'clock. The officer on duty at Colonel Edwards' headquarters reported at his bedside that artillery fire was heard in the direction of Cedar Creek. "Is the fire continuous?" Sheridan asked. "Irregular and fitful, sir," the officer replied. Sheridan decided it was a Union brigade out on reconnaissance and tried to go back to sleep.

Something told him, however, that this was no time to be sleeping. He got up, went downstairs for breakfast and received another report from the picket officer: artillery fire could still be heard from the south. Sheridan concluded not to linger any longer and ordered his staff and escort to saddle up at once. As they rode through town he noticed "many women at the doors and windows of the houses, who kept shaking their skirts at us and who were otherwise markedly insolent in their demeanor." Outside town he observed that the sound of artillery was now an "unceasing roar." "I felt confident that the women along the street had received intelligence from the battlefield by the 'grape-vine telegraph,' and were in raptures over some good news, while I as yet was utterly ignorant of the actual situation." As they trotted along Sheridan and his men became convinced from the mounting crescendo of gunfire that the Union army must be withdrawing. The cavalcade crossed Mill Creek and ascended a low sloping hill.

At the crest the eyes of Sheridan, his staff and escort were confronted by a confirmation of their worst fears, "the appalling spectacle of a panic-stricken army." There were hundreds of walking wounded in a long pathetic file, jostled by other hundreds of hurrying men who bore no trace of injury. Racing baggage wagons, their drivers white with fear, careened through this mass with little or no heed for the wounded. Unhurt fugitives from the battle told Sheridan—with that certainty which all skulkers affect to justify their absence from the firing line—that the battle was lost, the army was routed, disaster had befallen them all. Sheridan disregarded their opinions and sent an order back to Colonel Edwards in Winchester to post his brigade across Mill Creek and stop all fugitives and transport. Then he hastily considered what must be done.

His first impulse was to withdraw the army to the vicinity of Winchester and regroup for a last-ditch stand. His second thought was to reorganize what was left of the army on the ground it now occupied. At that moment his chief commissary rode up with the news that Sheridan's headquarters had been captured and much of the army dispersed. This did not deter him: he took two aides and 20 troopers, detailing the rest of his staff and escort to assist in halting the stragglers and deserters. Then, at the gallop, he began the ride to Cedar Creek.[9]

Out of a foggy dawn the sleeping camps of the Army of the Shenandoah had been struck a paralyzing series of blows. "At the peep of day," as Crook said, his attenuated line was struck by Gordon's Corps. For more than an hour the men of the three Confederate divisions had lain shivering a few hundred yards outside the Federal lines, listening to the tramp of sentries. With that high-pitched "yi, yi, yi" of the Rebel Yell they fell on the tents of the Yankees, shooting, bayoneting, sending hundreds to their death or into blind, panicky flight.

Captain S. E. Howard of the 18th Vermont Infantry, attached to the XIX Corps in the center of the Union line, recalled that he was awakened by "a clap of thunder" at dawn. Moments later fugitives from Crook's corps streamed through Emory's positions, heedless of pleas to stand and fight. The Confederate skirmish line appeared on the heels of Crook's remnants, flushed with their easy victory to the left. The colors of Thomas' brigade were captured, and Captain Howard saw the 8th Vermont, "with one impulse," fling itself "into the boiling cauldron where the fight for the colors was seething and dragged them out. . . . Men fought hand to hand; skulls were crushed with clubbed muskets; bayonets dripped with blood. Men actually clenched and rolled on the ground in the desperate frenzy of the contest for the colors. . . . The men realized they were in a terrible mess and fought like tigers. . . ."[10]

Captain DeForest, serving on General Emory's staff, watched Kershaw's division join Gordon's attack and observed that "no day-break rush of moccasined Shawnees or Wyandots was ever more dextrous and triumphant than this charge of Kershaw's Georgians, Mississippians and South Carolinians."

Emory's divisions, not having suffered the complete surprise which befell Crook's, offered stout resistance, enough to allow Wright's VI Corps to swing around to the left and cover its en-dangered flank. Then the XIX Corps broke and fled, too, with a few exceptional formations retreating in order. Grover's division, in particular, performed well under the terrific pressure, firing and falling back and taking heavy losses with every temporary stand. But, as Captain DeForest said, "Our camp, overlooked as it now was by the enemy, had been changed from a fortress into a slaughter pen. Our men knew this as well as if they were all major generals, and wanted to get out of their trap before they recommenced fighting."

All that were left to make a stand now on the plateau to the north were Wright's divisions and the cavalry and two brigades of Grover's division, XIX Corps. Merritt's and Custer's cavalry divi-sions, which had been preparing breakfast at dawn when the can-nonade on the left began, were in line of battle when the time came to beat back a probing attack by the Confederate cavalry.[11]

The gray tide was washing up against the plateau. General George W. Getty, commanding the Second Division, VI Corps, was about to lead his troops into a counterstroke against the flank of the advancing Confederates when he saw the divisions on both his own flanks break and run. "In this emergency—without sup-ports, without orders—in the open indefensible plain where a few moments would bring the victorious Confederates charging upon his defenseless flanks, and not one ray shone amid the universal

wreck and ruin—Getty, with prompt and cool decision, moved his
troops in line facing by the rear rank, back across the brook to the
foot of the ridge."

Pegram's Confederate Division was soon on their front, charging
ahead with the impetus of their earlier victories. Getty sent his
troops forward in a frontal counterattack that rocked the enemy
back in woeful surprise. The Second Division retired to the crest
of the ridge, and when the Confederates came on again Getty delivered a volley that crackled all along the line, followed by a
countercharge at the crest that routed the attackers.[12] Early hesitated to follow up with an attack on the Federal flank, with Merritt
and Custer waiting for just such an eventuality. The fire went out
of the Confederate assaults, partly, according to most accounts, because the hungry Southerners were more concerned with looting
the Union camps than joining in the battle.[13]

Sheridan's 14-mile ride to the battlefield at Cedar Creek became
the subject of heated controversy almost as soon as the clatter of the
hoofs died down on the flint-hard Valley Pike. It was glorified by
the poem of T. Buchanan Read (which made the general's horse
Rienzi almost as famous as his rider), it was given a muck-raking
by historians of a more skeptical era, it was argued in the newspapers and at veterans' reunions for years afterward. There were
those who said it was only a cautious canter, and there were others
who contended it was the maddest gallop since the headless rider
pursued Ichabod Crane.

According to most eyewitnesses, it was a good hard ride, everything considered. Much of the way Sheridan and his escort were
forced to ride off the road and through the fields, since the pike was
clogged with retreating or fleeing soldiers and transport. He observed that some of the stragglers coolly settled down in the fields
to boil coffee, but when they saw him riding toward the battle they
cheered and began to follow him. A Vermont private wrote his
parents that

the first thing that attracted my attention was the clatter of horses'
feet on the pike, and the most vociferous cheering that I ever heard.

When I looked up I saw General Sheridan coming, followed by his bodyguard. Sheridan was about fifty yards in advance with his hat in his hand, saying as near as I could understand, "Come to the front with me, boys, and we will make this matter all right." It was an awful moment, but I could not help thinking of Jack the Giant Killer. But everybody and everything followed Sheridan. . . .[14]

One of Sheridan's companions on that historic ride, his aide-de-camp Captain Forsyth, also observed that the commander's appearance turned the tide of retreat. "Sheridan, without slowing from the gallop, pointed to the front; men cheered and shouldered arms and started back," he wrote. His chief began emanating the famous magnetism which drew men after him and toward danger. "As he galloped on, his features gradually grew set, as though carved in stone, and the same dull red glint I had seen in his piercing black eyes when the battle was going against us was there now." Sheridan was too preoccupied by military problems to notice it, but the day was better suited for wandering over the russet and gold slopes of the valley than for the harsh business ahead. "On either side we saw, through the Indian summer haze, the distant hills covered with woods and fairly ablaze with foliage; and over all was the deep blue of a cloudless Southern sky, making it a day on which one's blood ran riot and one was glad of life and health," Forsyth said.

Some of the higher officers were not so easily convinced as the privates that the day might be redeemed at Cedar Creek. Along the way an infantry colonel hysterically shouted to the commanding general, "The army is whipped." Sheridan replied, "You are, but the army isn't." Occasionally he paused to address a few words to units in retreat but still organized. "If I had been with you this morning," he said, "this disaster would not have happened. We must face the other way; we will go back and recover our camp." At Newtown the streets were so crowded with a jumble of troops, horses, wagons, caissons, that he had to ride around the village. In his detour he "met a chaplain digging his heels into the sides of his jaded horse, and making for the rear with all possible speed." Sheridan asked him how things were going at the front and received the reply, "Everything is lost; but all will be right when you get there." Sheridan noted that "notwithstanding this expression of confidence in me, the parson at once resumed his breathless pace to the rear."[15] His first direct news of the disaster to the Federal left and center was provided near Newtown by Major William McKinley of General Crook's staff—McKinley, the Ohioan who became President in 1896.

As Sheridan approached the battle line there was a swelling roar of men returning by the thousands to follow the general who had led them to victory at Winchester and Fisher's Hill and a dozen lesser engagements. Rarely in military history has the presence of one man affected so positively the outcome of a battle.

"Here's Phil Sheridan—we're going back!" men shouted to one another, throwing their caps in the air, leaping and dancing in wildest glee.[16] One of Emory's staff officers told Captain DeForest, "I am glad Sheridan has come. He may help us to retrieve our character. I am perfectly ashamed of our defeat this morning. The enemy certainly had not more than eighteen thousand men." DeForest watched Sheridan come riding up on his big black horse, shouting, "About face, boys! We are going back to our camps. We are going to lick them out of their boots."[17]

In his subsequent report to the War Department, Sheridan said he found only Getty's division, VI Corps, and Merritt's and Custer's divisions of the cavalry corps in line and ready to oppose Early. He "suggested" to General Wright that "we would fight on Getty's line." Two other divisions of the VI Corps and the XIX Corps, to the right and rear of that line, were reorganized sufficiently to be brought back into action.[18]

He rode up and down his battered force, ordered that breastworks of logs and rails be thrown up as quickly as possible and repeated over and over in his animated way, "We are going to get a twist on those fellows. We are going to lick them out of their boots."[19] To a XIX Corps staff officer he said almost gaily, "Tell General Emory if they attack him again to go after them, and to follow them up, and to sock it to them, and to give them the devil. We'll have all those camps and cannon back again."[20] General Torbert of the cavalry rode up and blurted out, "My God, I'm glad you've come!"

To the rear, behind Getty, Custer and Merritt, the stragglers were coming back. They were made welcome. Sheridan reported, "None behaved more gallantly or exhibited more courage than those who returned from the rear determined to reoccupy their lost camp."[21] A forest of colors from the stampeded regiments of the VIII Corps appeared at the rear; Crook's men were still disorganized, but they were ready to follow Sheridan back into battle. Twenty-four cannon, their plundered camps and their self-respect must be retrieved before the Army of the Shenandoah would rest that night.

General Sheridan established his new headquarters on a crest behind Getty's line and ordered the XIX Corps and the other two divisions of the VI Corps to fall in beside it, along with Merritt's and Custer's cavalry. He was certain there would be another strong Confederate attack. About 3:00 P.M. the enemy attempted an assault on the XIX Corps sector, but it was easily repulsed. General Emory told his staff, "We might as well whip them tonight; if we don't we shall have to do it tomorrow. Sheridan will get it out of us some time!"[22]

Rallying and reorganizing the Army of the Shenandoah was no quick, hurrah-boys-hurrah process, as poetic descriptions of the battle of Cedar Creek—a favorite of muralists and patriotic litterateurs—would have one believe. Sheridan arrived on the field about 10:30 A.M., according to his own account, and the army was not whipped into shape for the counterattack until shortly before 4:00 P.M.

Part of the delay was caused by alarming reports that Longstreet was indeed marching via Front Royal to join Early as the intercepted signal message had indicated. Sheridan did not want to move until their truth or falsity was definitely established. He ordered Merritt to charge an exposed battery near Middletown and take some prisoners. When they were brought in Sheridan, with his aptitude for wheedling information out of captives, took charge of the interrogation himself. The prisoners said Longstreet was not expected. Further comfort was received in a dispatch from Powell, commanding the cavalry division which was watching the gap at Front Royal: the heavy column of enemy infantry reported moving along the pike from that direction was nonexistent.[23]

It was time to go forward. Emory, Wright, Crook and the men of his shattered corps who had returned to the front, the cavalry under Merritt and Custer—all swept forward in a long blue line. The Confederates, protected by a stone fence and impromptu breastworks, were in a strong position and put up "very determined" resistance, as Sheridan reported. Early saw a chance to smash the counterattack, for "his line of battle overlapped the right of mine, and by turning with this portion of it on the flank of the Nineteenth Corps caused a slight momentary confusion."[24]

Actually the confusion was more than momentary. The XIX Corps was caught in a vicious enfilade and was in danger of buckling under the strain. Its task was to strike hard at the hinge of the enemy flankers, always a difficult operation in the midst of a hotly contested engagement. McMillan's brigade of the XIX Corps found the sensitive spot, however, and hit Gordon's flank "at a double-quick with a scream of delight and triumph."[25] Sheridan sent Custer in with his full division, and the Confederate line began to crack. Before attacking, Custer's troopers "made the air tremble" with cheers for Sheridan as he rode down their line, Private Isaac Gause of the 2nd Ohio Cavalry recorded.[26]

The enemy was driven back against Cedar Creek, and in the confusion of attempting to ford it under heavy musketry and artillery fire the withdrawal began to turn into a rout.[27] Early was beaten; the question was how much damage could be inflicted on him. Two previous defeats had resulted only in his snapping back on this almost disastrous day of October 19. The Shenandoah must be knocked out of the war, once and for all.

Sheridan was all over the field, urging his troops into the pursuit. "Run! Go after them!" he shouted to a group of infantrymen who had fallen behind.

"We can't run—we're all tuckered out," gasped a private.

"If you can't run, then shoot and holler," Sheridan replied. "We've got the goddamnedest twist on them you ever saw!"

From then on the battle of Cedar Creek was a spectacular race up the Valley Pike. Cavalry and infantry vied to see which could take in the most prisoners, battle flags, equipment. "The usually gallant and elastic Southern infantry was so cowed by defeat and stupefied by fatigue that it offered scarcely any resistance to its pursuers," Captain DeForest observed.[28] Early, not even attempting any further resistance, ordered his fleeing army 'way up the pike to New Market. The Confederate lost most of his artillery—25 guns—all his ambulances and ammunition wagons, most of his baggage and forage wagons. "The road from Cedar Creek to Fisher's Hill, a distance of over three miles," Sheridan reported to the War Department, was "literally blockaded by wagons, ambulances, artillery, caissons, etc."[29] Custer's division and Devin's brigade of Merritt's division continued the pursuit from Fisher's Hill after nightfall.

Even in this hour of triumph Sheridan retained his passion for precise information, which would have probably surprised his old instructor of mathematics at West Point and his earlier preceptors. When Captain Forsyth rode up to him to report on the number of artillery pieces captured that afternoon, Sheridan demanded, "How do you *know* that we have that many of the enemy's guns?"

He was satisfied only when Forsyth replied, "I have placed my hand on each and every gun."[30]

The news of Early's final defeat in the Valley, one month after Sheridan began his active campaign, arrived in the North at a politically strategic moment. "Sheridan and Sherman have knocked the bottom out of the Copperheads," Horace Greeley commented.

It had been an expensive victory, culminating a campaign costly in lives and equipment. The losses at Cedar Creek alone had totaled almost 6,000, nearly twice what Early admitted. Throughout the campaign Federal casualties, Sheridan reported, amounted to 16,-952, including 1,938 killed, 11,893 wounded and 3,121 missing.[31] But even this cost in blood and anguish could not be measured against the value of helping to break down Lee's enfeebled army and the defeat of McClellan's peace-at-any-price platform for the November elections.

To his officers it seemed that Sheridan had literally converted defeat into victory by the alchemy of his inspiring presence, his extraordinarily quick grasp of the methods of counterattack and how and when to employ it. "It took less time to drive the enemy from the field than it had for them to take it," General Merritt pointed out. "They seemed to feel the changed conditions in the Union ranks, for their divisions broke one after another and disappeared toward their rear."[32]

President Lincoln, finding no less merit in the victory, wrote Sheridan on October 22:

> With great pleasure I tender to you and your brave army, the thanks of the nation, and my own personal admiration and gratitude, for the month's operations in the Shenandoah Valley; and especially for the splendid work of October 19, 1864.[33]

Delight was, indeed, widespread. The Army of the Potomac fired a hundred shotted guns into besieged Petersburg. Secretary of War Stanton congratulated him on "personal gallantry, military skill, and just confidence in the courage and patriotism of your troops." General Sherman, crowned with the laurel of Atlanta's capture, wrote home about his satisfaction over Sheridan's victories. "Sheridan . . . the poor Irish boy of Perry County, is making his mark. . . . Sheridan is like Grant, a persevering terrier dog and won't be shaken off. He too is honest, modest, plucky and smart enough."[34]

In his report to Washington, General Sheridan could not resist a little crowing. After Cedar Creek "practically all territory north of the James River now belonged to me," he announced. His aim in the Shenandoah campaign, he expatiated, had been to destroy "that which was truly the Confederacy—its armies."[35]

But he had not really lost the modesty which General Sherman claimed for him. Around the campfire shortly after the battle of Cedar Creek, General Crook quoted him as saying, "I'm going to get much more credit for this than I deserve, for, had I been here in the morning the same thing would have taken place, and had I not returned today, the same thing would have taken place."[36] History does not agree with this excess of self-depreciation.

Next to Grant and Sherman, the favorite general of the Administration now was Phil Sheridan. Lincoln's first impression of him as being too scrawny for heavy duty was obliterated by the dispatches from Cedar Creek. Grant wrote to Stanton, "Turning what bade fair to be a disaster into a glorious victory stamps Sheridan what I always thought him, one of the ablest of generals." Lincoln confessed that he had always thought a cavalryman should be about six feet four, but "now five feet four seems about right." This credited Sheridan with an inch less than his physical stature, but was a heaping measure of praise from the President, who had learned from his experiences with McClellan, Hooker, Burnside and many others to be wary about praising his generals.

Alexander K. McClure, a Pennsylvania politician and journalist who was very close to the White House, said Lincoln was more certain of Sheridan's personal support than he was of Grant's. The President hesitated to suggest to Grant that some of his soldiers be furloughed home to vote in the coming election, according to McClure, and said, "I have no reason to believe that Grant prefers my election to that of McClellan."

McClure asked, "What about Sheridan?"

Lincoln's face brightened "like the noonday sun emerging from a dark cloud." "Oh, Phil Sheridan, he's all right," the President said with more enthusiasm than the words indicated.[37]

Without any prompting from the White House, Sheridan furloughed home 10,000 Pennsylvania soldiers at electiontime, and that state gave Lincoln a comfortable majority.

As a mark of his gratitude the President sent Assistant Secretary of War Dana to Sheridan's headquarters with the best news of his military career—the commission of major general in the Regular Army. Shortly before midnight, October 23, Dana appeared at Sheridan's camp and was informed that the commanding general had retired. Dana, a quaint little fellow with an egg-shaped head and a growing sense of his own importance, demanded that Sheridan be awakened.

Half asleep, Sheridan stumbled out of his tent to be confronted by Dana and a phalanx of officers standing in the light of an army torch. Unable to resist a few flourishes, Dana read the commission and delivered a midnight oration.

"Sheridan did not say much in reply to my little speech," Dana noted. He seemed more interested in resuming his sleep than exchanging compliments.[38]

The next morning Dana rode with Sheridan through the camps of the Army of the Shenandoah and commented that he had never seen a general so popular with all ranks, not even "Pap" Thomas, the beloved commander of the Army of the Cumberland, or Sherman or Grant. He quoted Sheridan's explanation: "I made up my mind long ago that it is not a good plan to fight battles with paper orders—for the commander to stand on a hill in the rear and send his aide de camps with written orders to the various commanders. My practice has always been to fight in the front rank. . . . The men know when the hard pinch comes I am just as much exposed as any of them."[39]

The Army of the Shenandoah settled down in winter quarters around Kernstown after the battle of Cedar Creek, a semihibernation interrupted only by occasional operations up the Valley to see what Early was doing around Staunton, and by forays against the guerrilla bands whose harassing activities exceeded their efforts of the previous summer. Mrs. Custer and other officers' wives came down from the North and made Winchester a lively and fascinating garrison town. As was the Old Army custom, they brought along their unmarried female relatives in the interests of matchmaking. Sheridan himself seems to have succumbed to a crinolined charmer whose name is lost to history. The rumor reached even the City Point headquarters of the Army of the Potomac that he was engaged to be married; but the attachment came to an end, if it ever existed except in regimental gossip.[40]

Except for the guerrillas and, of course, the young Northern ladies, it would have been a somnolent winter. With Early licking his wounds far up the Valley, never again to take the offensive, Sheridan was able to detach the VI Corps and send it back to Grant and the siege lines of Petersburg. But the guerrillas of Colonel Mosby and his satellites kept him from growing complacent, if there was any risk of that.

Mosby, perhaps the greatest of all American leaders of irregular forces, was an opponent with a skill, determination and daring to match the Federal commander's. He was a very active young man with sharp features, deep-set gray eyes and a bronzed face showing all the wary intelligence of a fox—"his whole expression denoting hard service, energy and love of whiskey," as he was described by an admiring compatriot. There was more than a touch of melodrama to his personality as well as to his exploits: he wore a black cape with a scarlet lining and slept with a pistol under his pillow.[41]

It was Custer who stirred up the hornet's nest early that winter. The cavalry commander, exasperated by the raids on Federal wagon trains, ordered the hanging of six men captured from one of Mosby's forays. Sheridan approved, or at least did not interfere. Colonel Powell hanged another of the guerrilla band in Front Royal a short time later. On November 11 Mosby sent Sheridan a note stating he had hanged seven Union troopers in retaliation but would treat all other captives as prisoners of war if Sheridan would accord Mosby's men the same treatment. This offer only aroused Sheridan's anger, for he refused to consider Mosby's men or any other guerrillas as anything but murderers and thieves. He wrote General Halleck a few days later:

> I will soon commence work on Mosby. Heretofore I have made no attempt to break him up, as I would have employed ten men to his one, and for the reason that I have made a scape-goat of him for the destruction of private rights. [That is, Sheridan represented to the inhabitants of the Valley that the destruction visited upon them was caused by the operations of Mosby and other guerrillas— not the whole truth, of course, but a rudimentary employment of psychological warfare.] Now there is going to be an intense hatred of him in that portion of this Valley which is nearly a desert. I will soon commence on Loudoun County, and let them know there is a God in Israel. Mosby has annoyed me considerably, but the people are beginning to see that he does not injure me a great deal, but causes a loss to them of all that they have spent their lives in accumulating.[42]

If Sheridan needed any encouragement in this policy of scourging the land, a letter from General Sherman, who was about to "make Georgia howl" with his March to the Sea, provided it bountifully. Sherman wrote:

I am satisfied, and have been all the time, that the problem of this war consists in the awful fact that the present class of men who rule the South must be killed outright rather than in the conquest of territory, so that hard, bull-dog fighting, and a great deal of it, yet remains to be done, and it matters little whether it be done close to the borders, where you are, or farther in the interior, where I happen to be; therefore, I shall expect you on any and all occasions to make bloody results.[43]

Accordingly, Sheridan sent Merritt with his cavalry division to show Loudoun County that there was "a God in Israel," as he had promised Halleck. That fertile valley which gave so much aid and comfort to Colonel Mosby was ravaged from one end to the other, its barns burned, its forage and food destroyed or carried off, its livestock driven away. Only the Quakers were spared, on advice from Washington, for they had turned their faces from Mosby and, indeed, all Confederates.

Always the careful steward, the more fearsome shadow of the boy who had kept books in a village store, Sheridan rendered an exact accounting to the War Department (unlike Sherman in Georgia) of the property he seized or destroyed. If only to show his meticulous accuracy in such matters—where a genuine Tartar would not have bothered—this is the list he forwarded to Washington: 3,772 horses; 545 mules; 71 flour mills; one woolen mill; eight sawmills; one powder mill; three saltpeter works; 1,200 barns; seven furnaces; four tanneries; one railroad depot; 435,802 bushels of wheat; 20,000 bushels of oats; 77,176 bushels of corn; 874 barrels of flour; 20,397 tons of hay; 500 tons of fodder; 450 tons of straw; 10,918 beef cattle; 12,000 sheep; 15,000 swine; 250 calves; 12,000 pounds of bacon; 10,000 pounds of tobacco; 947 miles of rail; 2,500 bushels of potatoes; and 1,665 pounds of cotton yarn.[44]

But the biggest prize of all, Mosby, eluded him. Even "Sheridan's Robbers," the scout force organized under Colonel Young, could not reach within revolver shot of him. They did lay a trap for Harry Gilmore, a Marylander whose band was almost as active as Mosby's, after receiving word that Gilmore was going to appear in Moorefield, about 90 miles southwest of Winchester, and recruit members for his band under the guise of a revival meeting. It was learned that Gilmore was living in a farmhouse several miles outside that village in the center of a strong pro-Confederate district. Sheridan himself took charge of planning the capture and sent Colonel Young with a score of his men dressed in Confederate uniforms, followed by 300 cavalrymen. At midnight, February 5, Young reached the farmhouse after telling residents he and his men were being pursued by Union cavalry and needed sanctuary. He found Gilmore sound asleep, with two pistols laid out on a chair next to his bed. Placing a revolver against the guerrilla chieftain's head, Young aroused the sleeper and informed him he was a prisoner of the Federal Government.

The guerrillas' reprisal was just short of devastating—they captured one of Sheridan's leading generals. At three o'clock in the morning of February 21, 1865, they invaded the town of Cumberland, Maryland, and broke into the hotel where General Crook had his headquarters. Like Gilmore, Crook was sound asleep and had to be awakened by his captors. They took him and General Benjamin F. Kelley, who had been sleeping in another room, forced them to mount horses waiting outside, and again eluded Union pickets on the road leading south. There was a touch of mystery and romance to this affair, for one of the members of the band had a sister who married Crook later that year after the war was over. Crook and Kelley were taken to Richmond and exchanged a short time later.[45] It was a season of surprises, professional and personal, for General Crook.

With the coming of spring the armies were stirring themselves out of the Virginia mud for a campaign that must end the war. Sherman had cut a path of destruction across Georgia to the Atlantic and marched north into the Carolinas. Hood's Western army had been torn apart by Thomas at Nashville. Only Lee at Petersburg and Joseph Johnston in the Carolinas were still to be destroyed, but there was still plenty of fight left in these remnants. The war, it was obvious, would end only when Lee was forced to surrender. The trouble, from Sheridan's viewpoint, was that Grant was still obsessed with operations against Lynchburg; afterward, Grant indicated, Sheridan could join Sherman in North Carolina.

With, perhaps, a little twisting by Sheridan's hands events made it impractical for him to go to Sherman, and he did not sorrow over them. He wanted to be in at the kill, not riding around the Carolinas in Sherman's wake. On February 7, 1865, Sheridan set out on an expedition up the Valley with his two cavalry divisions of the Army of the Potomac; the rest of the Army of the Shenandoah was left behind with General Hancock, his successor as commanding general, Middle Military Division. There was a sharp fight with Early at Waynesboro in which Sheridan captured 1,600 officers and men, 11 pieces of artillery and 17 battle flags. It was the end of all effective Confederate resistance in the Shenandoah.

The Confederate garrison at Lynchburg had been reinforced, so Sheridan decided to cross the James to the east. The bridges had been burned, however, and Sheridan had only eight pontoons in his train. Without any great grief he concluded that it would be impossible to join Sherman. His alternate instructions were to return to Winchester, if unable to take Lynchburg, but he decided this too was impractical and that it would be better to wreck the Virginia Central again and the James River canal, then join Grant before Petersburg—as he had urged for months. No one thought to accuse him of insubordination, of course, but it would seem that Sheridan made things work out his own way, without undue deference to Grant's plans.

Sheridan and his two cavalry divisions traversed familiar ground to reach the Army of the Potomac over muddy roads and through drenching spring rains—the South Anna, Ashland, Hanover Junction, White House Landing on the Pamunkey. Grant first learned of these wanderings when he received a message from Sheridan at White House Landing asking for supplies. Sheridan's command was so exhausted by its "mud march" along bottomless roads and through 16 days of incessant rain that it would have to rest for several days before joining the army on the Petersburg front. If Sheridan twisted his orders around a bit to achieve his surprising appearance, General Grant and the nation soon had cause for gratitude that he had not been too literal.

14

A VERY PUNCH OF SOLDIERS

SHERIDAN and his command returned to a very weary, dispirited and almost demoralized Army of the Potomac. For months it had been bogged down in the muddy trenches before Petersburg. The long stalemate, the malaria and swamp fever, the consistent failure of all methods—assault, siege approaches, sapping operations—to drive Lee out of his system of fortifications had reduced the Federal army's morale to its lowest point since Fredericksburg. Not only the miserable troops in the line but their commanders up to and including Grant were disheartened and looked on the coming operations with more dread than enthusiasm.

The unexpected appearance of General Sheridan gave them all a tremendous lift: his victories in the Valley had showed them that the art of maneuver, of marching, fighting and winning, was not yet lost; war was not yet entirely a sport for human moles. The Shenandoah campaign had caught the imagination of soldiers and civilians alike. "Only timid financiers, sutlers and congressional excursionists paid the least attention to the armies on the James," observed George Alfred Townsend, war correspondent for the New York *Herald*. When Sheridan rode along the infantry lines, the men cheered not only for his victories in the Valley but the probability that he would lead them all out of their bondage to bomb shelters, abatis, *cheveaux de frise*, crumbling breastworks, sodden clothing and rations, and all the dreary paraphernalia of siege warfare. He gave them a hope of action, a hope more intuitive than reasoning. He was a symbol of their flickering faith that the war might really end some day, and with a bang rather than a whimper.

"The personality of the man, not less than his renown, affected people," Townsend wrote. "A very Punch of soldiers, a sort of Rip Van Winkle in regimentals, it astonished folks that with so jolly and grotesque a guise, he held within him energies like lightning, the bolts of which had splintered the fairest parts of the border."[1] In the Army of the Potomac he was the man they all talked about; Grant and Meade were colorless by comparison. He had tossed away his old plug hat and now affected a pork-pie "which for various uses from an umbrella to a nightcap has no equal."

They talked about his spectacular profanity when his temper was aroused or he was in the thick of battle. The general belief, Townsend said, was that "the general's tongue is a mint where strange oaths are coined of most unique and awful pattern." Actually, as his staff knew, his reputation for blasphemy was not entirely deserved. A certain amount of judicious swearing was necessary to prove to the troops he was no namby-pamby. In moments of great excitement, in the crisis of a battle, he usually became more soft-spoken, and he disliked officers who lost their heads and began shouting. "Damn you, sir," he growled at one roaring subordinate who galloped up to headquarters with bad news, "don't yell at me!"

The army respected him, too, for carrying out his orders to devastate the Valley "literally but not riotously."[2]

Sheridan found Grant still obsessed with the idea of Sheridan and Sherman meeting in the Carolinas and carrying out joint operations. Sheridan could help Sherman trap Joe Johnston, then both could tackle Lee from the rear. Grant "referred . . . to the tortuous course of my march from Waynesboro," but did not reprimand his subordinate for failure to accomplish the previous plan or its alternative. In fact, he seemed buoyed up by the enthusiasm and energy that Sheridan invariably brought with him, much as Sherman's vibrant intellect had often stimulated him in their Western campaigns. At their City Point conference Grant disclosed his plan for the cavalry's employment in the campaign to force Lee out of Petersburg and into the open country where he could be cut to pieces. Sheridan was to pass around the left flank of the army along the Danville Railroad, then cross the Roanoke River and join Sherman.

Sheridan expressed himself bluntly in opposition. "I showed plainly that I was dissatisfied with it. . . . It would be bad policy to send me down to the Carolinas with a part of the Army of the Potomac, to come back to crush Lee after the destruction of General Johnston's army; such a course would give rise to charges that [Grant's] own forces around Petersburg were not equal to the task. . . ."[3]

According to Grant, however, his underlying motive in ordering the cavalry corps to move out by the left flank was more to damage Lee than to have Sheridan hook up with Sherman against Johnston. "I contemplated capturing Five Forks, driving the enemy from Petersburg and Richmond and terminating the contest," Grant wrote in his *Memoirs*. Like many generals compiling their autobiographies, he was susceptible to writing from hindsight. There is no mention in any of his dispatches or orders of that period to show he intended that Sheridan should capture Five Forks. Grant was intent on persuading Sheridan to link with Sherman, although he wrote, "My hope was that Sheridan would be able to . . . get on the enemy's right flank and rear and force them to weaken their center to protect their right, so that an assault in the center might be successfully made."

"I tell you I'm ready to strike out and smash them up now. Let me go!" Sheridan told the general in chief. He believed that, once he got in Lee's rear, smashed up the railroads supplying the besieged army in Petersburg and forced the Rebels to come out fighting in the open, the Confederacy's doom would be pronounced.

Grant's mind worked slowly on this as on other such occasions, especially since Sherman, his most intimate military collaborator, was urging the combined operations in North Carolina. The conferences were interrupted for a meeting with President Lincoln, who was staying aboard the steamer *River Queen* off City Point. The President had become so anxious over the army's coming campaign he "could not endure the delays in getting the news to Washington," Sheridan said. Lincoln appeared to Sheridan "not very cheerful" and often "dejected," asking worriedly about the coming operations and laying particular stress on the question, "What would be the result when the army moved out to the left, if the enemy should come down and capture City Point?" The query was prompted, Sheridan believed, by the Confederate assault on and capture of Fort Steadman, an important point in the Union siege lines, a few days before. Sheridan's reply was that Grant's blows on the Confederate right would give Lee all he could handle without trying to mount a counterblast.[4]

Next day, March 27, General Sheridan went to Hancock Station, the headquarters of his cavalry corps, to supervise preparations for moving out two days later. His new title, reflecting Grant's determination to put him above an ordinary corps commander and give him increased authority as well as responsibility, was "Commander in Chief of the Army of the Shenandoah, serving with the Army of the Potomac," which almost made him the equal of General Meade.

That afternoon he received a surprising and perturbing telegram from General Grant: "General Sherman will be here this evening to spend a few hours. I should like to have you come down." As he traveled over the rickety military railroad to City Point, Sheridan brooded over the certainty that Sherman had come north to press for the combined-operations scheme. It was almost midnight when he arrived at the shanty which Grant used as his personal quarters. As he feared, Sherman argued for the proposal with all the eloquence and logic at his command. Sheridan replied with considerable heat. "My uneasiness made me somewhat too earnest, I fear," he admitted later, "but General Grant soon mollified me, and smoothed matters over by practically repeating what he had told me . . . at the close of our interview the day before." Sheridan not only believed the plan was bad strategy but, it may be inferred, he had no intention of operating in the shadow of Sherman's slightly greater prestige.

The redheaded and quick-tempered Sherman did not give up easily. "Very early the next morning," as Sheridan recalled, General Sherman invaded his quarters before Sheridan was awake. Sherman briskly awakened his junior and, planking himself down on the edge of the bed, renewed his argument of the night before. He desisted only when he saw that Sheridan could not be swayed.[5]

When Grant gave Sheridan his orders on March 28 for the movement of his cavalry corps, they concluded with instructions either to return to the army or join Sherman after destroying the railroads supplying Lee. Sheridan still feared that the second alternative might be imposed on him. Later Grant told one of his staff officers that there was a deeper motive for this shilly-shallying. "I had a private talk with Sheridan after I gave him his written instructions at City Point. When he read that part of them which directed him, in certain contingencies, to proceed south along the Danville railroad and coöperate with Sherman by operating in Joe Johnston's rear, he looked so unhappy that I said to him, as I followed him out of the tent, that that part of the instructions was put in only as a blind, so that if he did not meet with entire success the people of the North, who were then naturally restless and apt to become discouraged, might not look upon a temporary check as an entire defeat of a definite plan,—and that what I really expected was that he would remain with the armies operating against Lee, and end matters right here. This made him happy, and he has started out perfectly confident of the success of the present movement."[6]

If this was true, and the alternative of Sheridan's joining Sherman was only part of a cover plan, it seems odd that Grant should have gone to the length of deceiving Sherman, too, and having his closest collaborator come all the way to City Point at such a crucial time.

As the forces under Grant began their viselike movement the next day to squeeze Lee out of Petersburg and Richmond, the Union corps were disposed as follows: General Weitzel with part of the Army of the James before Richmond, Parke and Wright in front of Petersburg, Ord extending to the intersection of Hatcher's Run and the Vaughn Road, then Humphreys and Warren on the left wheeling forward to operate with Sheridan as his infantry support.[7] In the cavalry corps there had been several changes of command. Sheridan took advantage of Torbert's absence on leave to replace him as chief of cavalry with Wesley Merritt, the hard-jawed, clean-shaven young man with a consistent record of success as a regimental, brigade and divisional commander. Devin replaced Merritt in charge of the First Division, Custer still led the Third, and George Crook had been given the Second Division, Gregg having resigned shortly before Crook was exchanged as a prisoner of war after being captured. Merritt was put over Devin and Custer, while Crook reported directly to Sheridan.

In effect, Sheridan was a semi-independent army commander, with both Warren's V Corps and Humphreys' II Corps in supporting distance to be called on by him if necessary.

General Lee already had been informed of the Union cavalry's concentration on his right flank. Believing it indicated a forthcoming raid on his communication lines, he decided to attempt to drive a wedge between Sheridan and the infantry. Fitzhugh Lee was ordered to the road complex of Five Forks with his cavalry, and he was followed by two infantry divisions under Pickett, who was to be in charge of the operation. Lee also shifted his infantry to his right to catch Warren and Humphreys with a counterpunch near the intersection of White Oak Road and Boydton Road where the Union trenches ended. The success of the Union turning movement depended on Sheridan's speed and daring in reaching Lee's rear and doing as much damage as possible there while the bulk of the Union forces advanced on the Petersburg defenses.

On the chilly and cloudy morning of March 29 the long columns of cavalry started out at the walking pace which always portended hard fighting up the line. They moved through damp woods and over roads that were soon churned into a muddy froth by the thousands of hoofs. Sheridan had more than 12,000 men in his three divisions and a powerful complement of horse artillery. All his troopers were armed with repeating carbines and offered a fire power vastly superior to anything Lee could throw at them. The cavalry passed over a country crisscrossed by slow-moving streams and covered with great stretches of thicket and stunted trees—malaria country, poorly drained, where only corduroyed roads were serviceable in the wet season.

On the first day's march the cavalry seized and occupied Dinwiddie Court House against slight opposition. It was a crossroads village with a half-dozen houses and a ramshackle tavern, but it was of considerable importance as a point of approach against Lee's rear and the Southside and Danville railroads. "Getting it without cost repaid us for floundering through the mud," Sheridan reported.

Torrential rains had started falling again that afternoon, and soon "whole fields had become beds of quicksand in which horses sank to their bellies, wagons threatened to disappear altogether, and it seemed as if the bottom had dropped out of the roads." Colonel Porter of Grant's staff commented, "It looked as if the saving of that army would require the services, not of a Grant, but of a Noah." Soldiers called out to their officers, "I say, when are the gunboats coming up?"[8]

Sheridan and his staff made themselves fairly comfortable at the Dinwiddie Hotel, gathering around a piano in the parlor and harmonizing with some lovely but bedraggled ladies who had fled from Petersburg and Richmond. The ladies, with charming naïveté, appealed to Sheridan and his officers not to fight a battle in the vicinity, said Lieutenant Colonel Frederic C. Newhall, the adjutant general, and "we gave our knightly words of honor not to bring red war to the doorstep of the Dinwiddie Hotel."[9] Only coffee was available for dinner, the headquarters mess wagon being bogged down far to the rear with the rest of the corps train, but the cavalry officers were in good spirits, and not only because of the feminine influence.

Sheridan was elated because Lee had made no effort to hold Dinwiddie Court House—a "fatal mistake," thought the Union cavalryman. He was further delighted when he got a written order from Grant, who had moved his headquarters to Gravelly Run, to abandon all thoughts of a raid to the Carolinas and concentrate on turning Lee's flank.

Next morning he went to Gravelly Run, where his enthusiasm ran like an electric current through army headquarters. Since the rain was falling again, some generals were advising Grant that the offensive should be postponed until the weather and the state of the roads improved. Colonel Porter said Sheridan became "very animated" as he discussed the prospects of annihilating Lee in the near future. "He warmed up with the subject as he proceeded, threw the whole energy of his nature into the discussion."

A staff officer asked how he would arrange to procure forage if the offensive was continued.

"Forage?" Sheridan snorted. "I'll get all the forage I want. I'll

haul it out if I have to set every man in the command to corduroying roads, and corduroy every mile of them from the railroad to
Dinwiddie. I tell you I'm ready to strike out tomorrow and go to
smashing things!''

Colonel Porter described how Sheridan paced the floor and
"chafed like a hound in the leash." Grant's staff urged him to go
in and transmit some of his enthusiasm to Grant, because "it would
still further confirm him in his judgment to hear such words."
Sheridan finally agreed the commanding general might be in need
of such tonic, if other generals were spreading pessimism about
continuing the movement. After Sheridan talked to him that morning Grant decided to push forward all along the front.[10]

There was not much that even the eager Sheridan could do about
forward movement the rest of that day. Wagon trains and artillery
were bogged down far in the rear. Grant cautioned him in an afternoon dispatch to wait until "it dries up a little, or we get the roads
around our rear repaired." Several British officers paid a visit to
Sheridan's headquarters at Dinwiddie Court House, and one exclaimed, "Blast the country! It isn't worth such a row, you know.
A very good place to be exiled, to be sure, but what can you ever
make of it?"[11] It was a day of fire fights in the dripping woods,
of brief clashes along the sodden roads, as the contending armies
groped toward each other. "The movement of troops was almost
impossible," Sheridan reported. But he managed to send General
Merritt out with Devin's division and one brigade of Crook's on
a reconnaissance along the White Oak Road almost to Five Forks,
and there was "heavy skirmishing throughout the day."[12] Merritt
was able to report that the enemy was massing at Five Forks and
would probably strike at the cavalry corps the next morning. Between Sheridan and Warren's infantry corps to the right of him
there was an inviting gap, and Lee could be depended on to make
the most of it.

The next day, March 31, both Sheridan and Warren were heavily
engaged, Lee being fully aware that he must beat off this wide
turning movement or be forced out of Petersburg and Richmond.
If Sheridan turned north toward Five Forks, as he was evidently
planning, the Southside Railroad would be in considerable jeop-

ardy. The Confederate corps under A. P. Hill struck at Warren, whose march had been forced in the direction of Humphreys' II Corps rather than Sheridan's right flank because of the direction of the roads. Warren's divisions were in column rather than line of battle, and his leading formations were quickly driven in by Hill's attack. A stanch defense line was found behind an overflowing stream. That afternoon Hill was not only stopped in his tracks but was counterattacked with such vigor by both Warren and Humphreys that he had to retire behind field works and was barely able to hold his ground.

Meanwhile, General Pickett caught Sheridan's columns moving out toward Five Forks. The Confederates got between Crook and Merritt and drove on toward Dinwiddie Court House in a "series of irregular advances to puzzle anyone but a cavalryman," as Correspondent Townsend wrote. Sheridan drew in his forces like a covered-wagon train under Indian attack, threw out a line of trenches to cover Dinwiddie, ordered Custer to leave one brigade behind to protect the trains coming up from the rear and bring everything else forward. The horse artillery finally arrived and was placed in line. The enemy, Sheridan reported, was deceived by his withdrawal and "followed it up rapidly, making a left wheel and presenting his rear to my line of battle." Shortly before sundown Pickett charged the entrenched cavalry and was met by "such a shower of lead that nothing could stand up against it." One repulse was enough for that day, and Pickett settled down in the woods behind the plain now littered with hundreds of his slaughtered infantry. With five cavalry brigades Sheridan had managed to hold off Pickett's two infantry divisions and the cavalry commands of Fitzhugh Lee, Rooney Lee and Rosser.[13]

Word came to Dinwiddie of Warren's successful stand against Hill that afternoon, and Sheridan immediately perceived that between the two separate engagements the Confederates had exposed themselves to a devastating counterstroke. Not only had communications between Pickett and Hill been severed, but Warren could now take Pickett in the rear while Sheridan attacked him frontally. Sheridan sent his brother and aide, Captain Michael V. Sheridan, spurring off to Grant and Meade.

The opportunity did not escape Meade, who telegraphed Grant at 9:45 P.M., "Would it not be well for Warren to go down with his whole corps and smash up the force in front of Sheridan?" Half an hour later Grant's reply came: "Let Warren move in any way you propose, and urge him not to stop for anything. . . ."

This admonition to Warren was of great significance, as was to be demonstrated within a few hours. Grant said later, "I was very much afraid that at the last moment he would fail Sheridan," although he believed Warren to be "a man of fine intelligence, great earnestness, quick perception and could make his dispositions as quickly as any other officer." The question, as most officers who had associated with him knew, was whether Warren *would* move quickly. West Point and years in the Regular Army had failed to eradicate a streak of perversity in his character that had been confounding his superiors for years.

General Grant sent Colonel Horace Porter to Sheridan's headquarters with the instruction, "Tell him the contemplated movement is left entirely in his hands, and he must be responsible for its execution."[14] In addition to this oral order Grant telegraphed Sheridan that night, "You will assume command of the whole force sent to operate with you, and use it to the best of your ability to destroy the force which your command has fought so gallantly today."[15] The general in chief evidently was determined that there would be no dispute over who commanded this offensive wing, that Warren would have no basis for claiming he was not under Sheridan's orders.

Colonel Porter found Sheridan enthusiastic over the prospects of cutting off and destroying Pickett but dubious about the value of Warren and the V Corps as his partners in the enterprise. Pickett's force, Sheridan told Porter, "is in more danger than I am—if I am cut off from the Army of the Potomac, it is cut off from Lee's army, and not a man of it should ever be allowed to get back to Lee. We at last have drawn the enemy's infantry out of its fortifications, and this is our chance to attack it." According to Colonel Porter, Sheridan "begged" him to ride to Grant and have Wright's VI Corps sent instead of Warren's because the former "had been under him in the battles in the Valley of Virginia, and knew his way of fighting." Porter, however, pointed out that Wright's corps was far to the right and rear, awaiting the assault on the defenses of Petersburg; since Sheridan intended to attack before dawn, the VI Corps could not possibly reach him in time.[16]

Nor did Warren and the V Corps. Instead of driving his undoubtedly weary divisions toward Pickett's rear, he sent telegram after telegram to army headquarters suggesting changes in the plan, proposing different routes toward Pickett, asking for time to rebuild a bridge—and the night passed with Warren, the perfectionist, polishing away at a battle plan that never came off.

A well-educated Engineer Corps officer, he had served long and valiantly with the Army of the Potomac, and was one of the authentic heroes of Gettysburg, where he had spotted the importance of seizing and holding Little Round Top, without which Meade could not have held the line against Lee, for it would have been enfiladed. But he was also "captious and impatient of control," as General James H. Wilson observed, and had little respect for or confidence in his superiors. Wilson told of hearing Meade ask him to co-operate with Sedgwick during an operation in the Wilderness campaign. The New Yorker's arrogant reply was "General Meade, I'll be Goddamned if I'll cooperate with Sedgwick or anyone else. You are the commander of this army and can give your orders and I'll obey them; or you can put Sedgwick in command and he can give the orders and I will obey them; or you can put me in command and I will give the orders and Sedgwick shall obey them; but I'll be Goddamned if I'll *cooperate* with Sedgwick or anybody else."[17] It would seem that Grant's apprehension over Warren's willingness to subordinate himself to Sheridan, and Sheridan's preference for another corps to co-operate with him against Pickett, were well justified.

As the hours of darkness waned Sheridan became increasingly worried that Warren would not attack in time to trap Pickett before Dinwiddie Court House. At three o'clock in the morning (April 1) he sent a dispatch to the infantry commander: "I understand you have a division at J. Boisseau's; if so, you are in rear of the enemy's line and almost on his flanks. I will hold on here."[18]

Inevitably General Pickett took alarm at his scouts' reports of

Federal infantry massing slowly behind him. He hastily retreated to Five Forks and began improving a line of old trenches which formed a protective crescent facing south and covering the vital road net.

Sheridan was in a tearing rage when he learned that Warren had not moved up fast enough to trap Pickett. If he had made the march according to schedule, the enemy would have been caught between Sheridan's cavalry and Warren's three infantry divisions plus McKenzie's cavalry division attached to V Corps for the operation. A subsequent and costly battle would not have been necessary. "Had General Warren moved according to the expectations of the lieutenant-general [Grant], there would appear to have been but little chance for the escape of the enemy's infantry in front of Dinwiddie Court-House," Sheridan stated in his report.[19] Apologists for General Warren have maintained that it was impossible for him to reach the designated position by midnight—as Grant had informed Sheridan he would—but this hardly excused his arrival much later than midnight.[20]

In the advance on Five Forks the Federal forces almost completed boxing the compass during their long pursuit of the Army of Northern Virginia. For more than three years the direction had been southward, until the fortifications of Petersburg held Grant transfixed during the winter of 1863-1864. With Sheridan's breakout, followed by an advance of the balance of Grant's armies, the direction was westward. Now, with Pickett disposing his divisions to cover the withdrawal of Lee's right wing, Sheridan was driving northward against Five Forks and its surrounding pine forests. Pickett's forces, he was advised, were aligned along the White Oak Road, which ran east and west, roughly parallel to the Southside Railroad.

Colonel Porter observed that Sheridan "became as restive as a racer . . . struggling to make the start. He . . . paced up and down . . . and fretted like a caged tiger. . . . And then another batch of staff-officers were sent out to gallop through the mud and hurry up the columns."

Sheridan wasted no time grieving over the misspent opportunity, but quickly followed Pickett to Five Forks. He pushed Devin and

Custer in pursuit under Merritt's direction and allowed the V Corps to rest at Boisseau's Farm until the time came for it to join in the attack on Pickett. "I felt certain the enemy would fight at Five Forks—he had to," Sheridan said. Devin and Custer were ranged along the Confederate trenches south of the town, with Crook in reserve. Then Warren's corps was moved up to swing north and west, accompanied by McKenzie's cavalry, and drive in Pickett's left flank. Meanwhile, Devin and Custer were expected to demonstrate as noisily as possible to keep Pickett worried about his right.[21] The cavalry demonstration was as gay as it was noisy. Colonel Porter encountered one of its bands the day before, in rehearsal for the battlefield concert, playing "Nellie Bly," he said, "cheerily as if it were furnishing music for a country picnic."[22]

The V Corps was ordered to march to its jump-off position on the Gravelly Church Road, near the junction with White Oak Road, and Warren joined Sheridan for a conference at which the latter explained his battle plan in detail. Grant already had sent Colonel Babcock of his staff with authority for Sheridan to relieve Warren if necessary, but Sheridan did not mention it. A short time later he rode to Gravelly Church, where Warren's divisions were to form for the attack. The V Corps was just arriving, but Warren unconcernedly lolled under a tree making a sketch of the ground. "His manner gave me the impression that he wished the sun to go down before dispositions for the attack could be completed," Sheridan afterward reported.[23]

Sheridan expressed his anxiety over Warren's dilatory movements as follows: "This battle must be fought and won before the sun goes down. All the conditions may be changed in the morning; we have but a few hours of daylight left us. My cavalry are rapidly exhausting their ammunition, and if the attack is delayed much longer they may have none left."[24] This anxiety could not be communicated to General Warren, even though Sheridan pointed out that "Lee's right was less than three miles from my right" and might prevent the attack on Pickett by striking the Federal rear. To all this, Warren replied in an indifferent tone and with a lackadaisical manner that "Bobby Lee was always getting people into trouble."[25]

This so irritated Sheridan that he did not conceal his extreme annoyance with Warren before his staff, as military etiquette required. Colonel Newhall recorded: "We remarked to each other that there would be a deuce of a row if the V Corps was not ready to move out soon. He evidently considered that General Warren was throwing cold water on the proposed assault; and if he arrived at that conclusion, doubtless General Warren helped him to it by something more than an indifferent manner."[26]

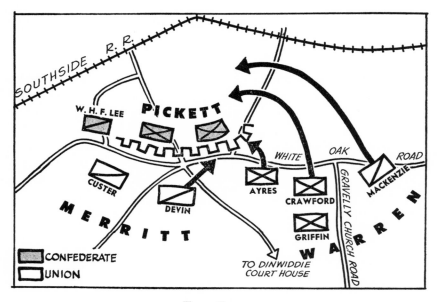

FIVE FORKS

It was four o'clock before Warren attacked. His divisions under Ayres, Griffin and Crawford were to swing obliquely against Pickett's trenches where they were bent back at almost a right angle to the White Oak Road. Ayres's division was to attack the hinge of the enemy trench line covering Five Forks; Crawford, followed by Griffin, was to cut around the Confederate left and take the refused angle of trenches in reverse. Their right flank was to be protected by McKenzie's cavalry. The whole wheeling movement to the left would be like a gigantic door slamming on Pickett and cutting him off from the rest of the Army of Northern Virginia. The trouble was that Crawford at first swung out too far on the right and was followed by Griffin. Ayres, without support on his right, attacked on schedule. The enemy took advantage of his isolation to pour a heavy fire on him from the angle. Sheridan immediately sent word to Warren, who could not be found at the critical moment, then to Griffin, for immediate correction of the attack on the right.

When it looked as though Ayres's infantry might be staved in under Confederate counterattack Sheridan rode into the melee at the angle, accompanied only by Colonel Porter and a few aides. Amid the broken lines he shouted, "Where's my battle flag?" A cavalry sergeant spurred up to him with the swallow-tailed, red-and-white flag of the cavalry corps. Sheridan grabbed it and ordered the line forward again, "dashing from one point of the line to another, waving his flag, shaking his fist, encouraging, threatening, praying, swearing, the very incarnation of battle."

On the right and the left the Union attack finally got under way, and it was irresistible. Sheridan led the decisive charge himself, carrying the headquarters guidon and finally jumping Rienzi over the Confederate breastworks. At the angle alone 1,500 Confederates surrendered—an indication of the crumbling morale of the opposing army.

"Whar do you want us-all to go?" a docile Southerner called to General Sheridan. In high humor Sheridan shouted back, "Go right over there. Drop your guns; you'll never need them any more. You'll be safe over there. Are there any more of you? We want every one of you fellows."

The "forked lightning" that Sheridan was said to carry with him at the height of a pitched battle was crackling furiously that day. The general hurried along a skirmish line advancing on a Confederate force concealed in pine thickets. A skirmisher, struck in the neck by a bullet, staggered and spouted blood. "I'm killed," he cried, and keeled over. "You're not hurt a bit," Sheridan yelled. "Pick up your gun, man, and move right on to the front." These words so galvanized the man that he leaped up and rushed forward a dozen paces before he fell over dead.

Death was all around Sheridan, but it could not overawe him or even depress his spirits at the moment. An aide rode up and informed him that Colonel Forsyth, his chief of staff, had been killed.

"I don't believe a word of it!" Sheridan declared.

Ten minutes later Forsyth showed up without a scratch. It was a tribute more to Sheridan's sanguine temperament, which refused to contemplate disaster until it was upon him, than to his powers of prophecy.

On the right, Crawford and Griffin had thrown a hook around the Confederate left and were taking prisoners by the hundreds. The Federal cavalry, on the left, swarmed through the pine thickets; the troopers in their tight-fitting uniforms and short jackets, carrying their short carbines, looked "as though they had been especially equipped for crawling through knot-holes," Colonel Porter observed. The incessant rattle of their magazine guns "created a racket in those pine woods that sounded as if a couple of army corps had opened fire."[27]

Correspondent Townsend of the New York *Herald* watched the enemy make a desperate last stand in the symbolic afterglow of sunset. "A colonel with a shattered regiment came down upon us in a charge. . . . Twice they halted, and poured in volleys, but came on again like the surge from the fog, depleted, but determined; yet, in the hot faces of the carbineers, they read a purpose as resolute. . . . While they pressed along, swept all the while by scathing volleys, a group of horsemen took them in flank. It was an awful instant; the horses recoiled; the charging column trembled like a single thing. . . ." The Southern remnants formed a hollow square and stood off the Federal cavalry, mounted and dismounted, until their colonel and most of his men had fallen. The survivors broke and fled.[28]

By sundown Pickett's wing, the only force Lee had available for offensive action, was broken and routed. Five Forks was the Waterloo of the Confederacy. Sheridan took 6,000 prisoners, six guns, 13 battle flags. There was nothing left for Lee but to withdraw from Petersburg, abandon Richmond and flee to the southwest in hope of joining with Joe Johnston and making some vaguely considered stand in the mountains—if Phil Sheridan and his cavalry permitted.

Before he could consider pursuit Sheridan paused briefly to deal with General Warren. Without further ceremony or consultation Sheridan relieved him of his command, ordered him to report to General Grant and installed General Griffin as commander of the V Corps.

Removing the Hero of Little Round Top started one of the bitterest and most enduring controversies of the Civil War, which was not really ended even after a Court of Inquiry submitted its findings 17 years later. Like the removal of Fitz John Porter by John Pope, it was debated in army circles for years after its leading characters were dead. One of the principal (if unofficial) charges against Sheridan was that he was prejudiced against Warren on a personal basis, but there is little evidence to support this. Just two days before Five Forks Warren wrote to his wife about Sheridan in friendly terms, and their one previous clash had been over a matter of road priority in the advance to Spotsylvania. Only after he had been relieved did General Warren write his wife that the Western generals had formed a clique against their Eastern colleagues. In a letter on April 2 he said: "Ever since General Grant came here, every chance and favor has been given to the Western generals, and they have shown a spirit that is extremely sectional. Coldness in their ordinary discourse and remarks behind our backs have made this only too apparent."[29]

What is now known as combat fatigue may have caused General Warren to slip so badly and so often that day. Certainly he was not, at Five Forks, the cool and precise commander he had been at Gettysburg.

In his report Warren stated that "we were too far to our right of the enemy's left flank," implying that Sheridan was to blame, but the fault lay in an inaccurate sketch Warren himself drew for the operation—Warren, the brilliant topographical engineer! He had drawn the line of Pickett's trenches too far to the right (the east, that is).[30] And then he had compounded this blunder, when he rode out to correct the line of attack taken by Crawford's and Griffin's divisions, by getting lost in the woods. During the critical hour of Ayres's attack at the hinge of Pickett's defenses and the flanking marches of Griffin and Crawford, Warren lost control of his corps entirely. It was only Sheridan's skillful disposition of the infantry, said War Correspondent Townsend, that saved the V Corps from wandering out of the battle.[31] Had Warren's infantry not been brought to bear on Pickett's left and rear, Sheridan's cavalry would have been in considerable danger from a Confederate counterattack.

According to Colonel Newhall of Sheridan's staff, the removal of Warren was decided on purely military considerations, for Sheridan "sincerely believed that he was not in a proper frame of mind to conduct vigorous operations; that he overestimated the ability and strength of the enemy; that he hesitated to strike boldly, and impaired the efficiency of his corps by his own apathy; that in fine he was a millstone hanging around the necks of 15,000 men, and a clog to their steps toward victory."[32]

In his final report on the battle of Five Forks, Sheridan made four specific charges against Warren: (1) Warren failed to reach him on time early on April 1; (2) he was unskillful in the tactical handling of his corps; (3) he failed to exert himself in bringing the V Corps up to Gravelly Run Church before attacking Pickett's left, and (4) "during the engagement portions of his line gave way when not exposed to a heavy fire, and simply from want of confidence on the part of the troops, which General Warren did not exert himself to inspire."[33]

Battle and pursuit ended, Sheridan lay down beside a roaring fire late on the night of April 1 with a saddle for a pillow. He had been up all the night before, had spent a rigorous day under fire and had taken the hard decision to relieve Warren, but his mind was still active, still shooting off sparks. Without consulting a map he gave orders for the disposition of his various divisions, four of cavalry and three of infantry. With all his preoccupations he found time to "give points now and then" to the New York *World's* representative, whose dispatch on the battle of Five Forks was reprinted in the London press and acclaimed a model of war correspondence.[34] All around him were the inevitable stigmata of battle, even in victory. The lights of burying parties moved in the background. Ambulances came creaking with their burdens from the dark woods where the wounded lay moaning. A comparative silence fell like a shroud on the air still quivering with the blasts of cannon and trumpets, charging hoofs and rumbling caissons, the nervous rattle of carbines, the beat of drums, the silvery cry of bugles. Near by was Gravelly Run Church, now a field hospital. Blood ran down the cracks in the rude planking underfoot. Dripping stretchers brought in from distant fields "new recruits for death and sorrow," soon to lie under the busy knives of the surgeons.[35]

But a commander cannot brood too long over burying parties and field hospitals. Volleys of musketry could be heard far off on the right, with the less frequent but resounding counterpoint of a battery of field guns, and on the left gunboats anchored in the James took up the thunderous theme. Sheridan turned his thoughts to tomorrow and a quick end to the pain and death of this "brothers' war."

The bivouac fires died down, and sleep silenced the men who had dealt the death blow of the Confederacy.

15

"SHERIDAN, THE INEVITABLE"

ON SUNDAY, April 2, the skies over Richmond were appropriately gray and gloomy, promising a squally spring rain. There were urgent conferences at the Confederate White House over the defeat of Pickett at Five Forks the preceding afternoon and the possibility that General Lee would be forced to order a general withdrawal of the Army of Northern Virginia. Nevertheless, President Jefferson Davis, weary and ailing, attended services at St. Paul's Church that morning; perhaps the fiery Reverend Mr. Minnigerode would give him new heart, a revived faith in the eventual victory of the Southern cause.

President Davis had not been sitting long in his pew when a messenger tiptoed down the aisle and passed a message to him. Parishioners whose heads were bent over their prayer books watched out of the corners of their eyes as Davis ripped open a telegram. Paler but expressionless, the President rose and walked firmly out of the church. The telegram had been from Lee—the army was pulling out of Petersburg and abandoning Richmond; there was nothing else for it to do if it was to be preserved from annihilation. In a few hours, under President Davis' directions, government clerks were burning documents in the streets. Before he left that night on a special train for Danville and a hoped-for meeting with General Lee, the Confederate capital was a scene of rioting, pillage and violence, a city rocked by demolition blasts and lighted by burning arsenals and warehouses.

Phil Sheridan was on the loose again, slashing at the Confederate right flank, riding hard to get in the rear and cut off the retreating army. By now the Confederates were becoming accustomed if not reconciled to the specter of Sheridan and his cavalry clawing at their retreating columns. "Sheridan, the inevitable," they called him.[1] The enemy knew him as one Federal general who could not be satisfied with a token or two of victory but who hung on like a terrier—Sherman's phrase—a general with the "killer instinct" who had as little tolerance for half-winning as he had for losing altogether. Southerners considered Grant an inexorable Suvorov, but Sheridan was his sword arm.

It was before dawn, and long before Davis received the fateful telegram from Lee, when Sheridan probed again for the Confederate line of retreat. A fresh infantry division under General Nelson A. Miles (who was to be a famous Indian fighter) came up from army reserve and was directed toward Sutherland's Depot. As they marched up the railroad Miles's soldiers caught sight of Sheridan mounted on his black charger and "greeted the general all along the column with such hearty cheers as had been seldom heard in the army since the old enthusiastic days, when everybody believed that the generals were born to command and that every campaign was to end the rebellion."[2] Miles with his "very fine and spirited division," as Sheridan reported, drove the enemy across Hatcher's Run and was just about to deliver a decisive blow when Meade ordered the division returned to the control of General Humphreys of II Corps. "Wishing to avoid wrangles"—especially since the removal of Warren had aroused a hot and immediate controversy—Sheridan did not protest, but he pointed out that Grant intended him to have the division and that if the attack had been launched, Lee's retreat would have been seriously hampered.[3]

Later that day Lee began withdrawing in good order from Petersburg, as Grant ordered Wright and Parke to drive into the Confederates' outer works, being anxious to have all his commands move against the enemy simultaneously so Lee could not use his interior lines to strike suddenly at Sheridan.[4] General A. P. Hill, one of the last of Lee's Old Guard, was killed during the withdrawal. General Lee then divided his army into two wings, the right under General R. S. Ewell, the left under General James Longstreet, since the retreat was being conducted along both sides of the Appomattox river.

The question in the Federal generals' minds was, Where would Lee bring his wings together for the expected withdrawal into the highlands of western Virginia? Both Grant and Sheridan believed the assembly point would be Amelia Court House, and their prognosis proved correct. To Sheridan fell the responsibility of seeing to it that Lee lost men, equipment and supplies with every mile of his retreat. He pushed the cavalry corps out ahead, followed by the infantry of the V Corps and McKenzie's cavalry, the latter acting as a mobile reserve. On April 3 the Southside Railroad was cut at Ford's Depot, the same day that Weitzel's XXV Corps occupied a burning and disorderly Richmond. The enemy was fleeing on the main road along the Appomattox, leaving behind hundreds of stragglers and deserters. Next day Sheridan ordered Crook to drive ahead for the Danville Railroad between Jetersville and Burkeville, cutting the last rail link between Richmond-Petersburg and the West. Crook moved north toward Jetersville along the Danville road, but not before Sheridan reached there in advance of the V Corps and accompanied only by a squadron of Regular Army cavalry. At Jetersville one of the troopers captured a messenger bearing a dispatch from Lee's chief commissary to the commissaries at Lynchburg and Danville:

The army is at Amelia Court House, short of provisions. Send 300,000 rations quickly to Burkeville Junction.[5]

Sheridan believed Lee's only hope of making good his retreat was to attack the "comparatively small force" at Jetersville and continue to Burkeville Junction to pick up his supplies. The Federal commander therefore hurried Merritt and the V Corps into Jetersville, where they entrenched immediately with orders to hold until the main body of the Army of the Potomac arrived. Crook also was on his way north to Jetersville, which was only seven miles below Amelia Court House. It was not until the next afternoon, April 5, that the II and VI Corps arrived to relieve Sheridan's vanguard.[6]

General Lee, his troops starving and his horses dropping from hunger and exhaustion, stayed at Amelia Court House until the evening of April 5, collecting food and forage in the countryside. But he could delay no longer, he realized, as reports came in that Sheridan was cutting his line of retreat to the south and west. South of Sheridan, Ord's infantry divisions from the Army of the James were marching fast to impose another barricade against Lee's movement toward the western mountains. It would take a night march and possibly a rear-guard action the next day to extricate his army from possible annihilation.

Behind the swallow-tailed guidon of the cavalry corps Sheridan's troopers hurried down the roads to get around and attack the head of Lee's column.

Jubilant Negroes squatted along the roadsides, cheering the passing Federals.

"Where are the Rebs?" Sheridan asked a white-haired old contraband who "was leaning over a fence, doing uncouth homage and flourishing wonderful salaams with a tattered hat."

"Siftin' south, suh, siftin' south," the Negro replied.[7]

The "sifting" process was an urgent matter for Lee, who was forced to send his trains ahead, followed by his infantry, resulting in numerous traffic jams. The Confederates had hardly evacuated Amelia Court House when Meade's infantry moved in and continued on the path of Lee's retreat.

As well as any of the field generals, Sheridan knew how desperate was the state of the Rebel army. He ordered Crook's division to go out ahead. At Paine's Crossroads, Davies' brigade caught up with a column of Confederate artillery and wagons rushing westward, burned almost 200 wagons and captured five guns. The rest of Crook's division was hurried forward. The same dash could not be coaxed out of Meade and his infantry, however.

It was obvious to Sheridan that Lee was trying to escape and save his trains at the same time, so "I was most anxious to attack him when the Second Corps began to arrive, for I felt certain that unless we did so he would succeed in passing by our left flank, and would thus again make our pursuit a stern-chase; but General Meade, whose plan of attack was to advance his right flank on Amelia Court House, objected to assailing before all his troops were up."

Unable to sway Meade toward a more vigorous pursuit, Sheridan informed Grant he would swing all his cavalry except McKenzie's division to his left to give more weight to Crook's spearhead. To lend emphasis to his argument for more vigor in the pursuit he enclosed a captured letter from a Confederate colonel to his mother, which began, "Our army is ruined, I fear. . . ."[8]

Sheridan's attitude toward the fleeing enemy bordered dangerously on contempt. A report came to him that there was an outbreak of firing along the front. He simply told Colonel Newhall of his staff, "Tell General Crook to drive them away," as if the enemy consisted of nothing more than so many flies to be swatted.[9]

It was on the morning of April 6 that Sheridan was granted a chance to strike another blow as crippling as the battle of Five Forks. After a hurried conference with General Grant, who had come to the front at his suggestion, the cavalry commander ordered Crook to seize the crossroads near Deatonsville, post a brigade there and continue moving parallel with the retreating Confederate column. Behind Crook came Devin and Custer under Merritt. At this critical juncture General Meade requested the return of the V Corps to army control, which, Sheridan reported, "I afterward regretted."

The cavalry observed Ewell's Corps moving hastily in the direction of Farmville. Sheridan ordered Crook to interpose himself between Ewell and the other Confederate wing under Longstreet, attack the wagon trains and force Ewell to fight a battle on the banks of Sailor's Creek.[10]

It appeared that the Confederate infantry had become crowded against their trains to the right. Crook slipped in between the infantry and its transport just west of Sailor's Creek and forced a fight. Ewell would have to commit his whole wing if he hoped to extricate Anderson's command, a reinforced division. Anderson threw up fieldworks in a hurry, knowing from his Valley experiences how swiftly Sheridan moved to attack.

This was the terrain west of Sailor's Creek as described by Colonel Newhall with his customary adeptness in such matters: "Stretching far away to the right and left, until lost in counter currents of tableland, is a broad plateau, shelving down gradually from the edge of the woods to Sailor's Creek (which trickles into the Appomattox); a shelf that will hold an army, but, until our arrival, upheld nothing save a barn and a tree or two."[11]

With three Confederate infantry divisions, Lee's whole right wing, cut off from the main body of the enemy, Sheridan was determined to make Sailor's Creek another Winchester, another Five Forks, only more conclusive if possible. The problem was to pin Ewell down and make him fight with his whole corps rather than just Anderson's command, which the Confederate would willingly and rightly have sacrificed to make good his escape with the other two divisions. Custer and Devin were ordered to charge Anderson's fieldworks while Crook circled around them and cut off the only road by which the enemy might retreat. Then Crook was to strike Anderson's rear. Meanwhile, Sheridan requested the immediate advance of Wright's VI Corps on his right to engage the rest of Ewell's Corps while the cavalry worked over Anderson. The quickly formulated battle plan worked to perfection, as such plans rarely do except against an enemy as debilitated as the Confederates.[12]

With Crook on his right flank and rear and Merritt with his dismounted troopers assaulting frontally, Anderson fought "like a tiger at bay," as Sheridan observed, but was soon cut to pieces by superior numbers. Meanwhile, Wheaton's and Seymour's divisions of VI Corps advanced against Ewell to the Federal right, with Getty's division, of valorous memory at Cedar Creek, coming up in support. The whole Confederate wing—raked from flank to flank by Federal artillery, then struck front, right and rear by infantry and cavalry—was broken in a dozen places. The defeat was complete: Ewell and his generals must surrender or needlessly sacrifice the lives of their surviving soldiers. So they surrendered with 7,000 of their troops. Anderson and about 2,000 men fled through the woods to the Appomattox River, but most of them were captured before nightfall by Devin's cavalry and Getty's infantry.[13]

Into Sheridan's hands had fallen Generals Ewell, Kershaw, Barton, Corse, Dubose and Custis Lee (the young son of Robert E. Lee), 16 pieces of light and heavy artillery (several of them from the fallen defenses of Richmond), and 400 wagons. There was a rancorous episode involving General Wright and a rather pointless quarrel over the credit for the victory at Sailor's Creek,[14] but otherwise Sheridan was justified in his satisfaction with the events of April 6 and his belief that "the battle has never been accorded the prominence it deserves" because it was "so overshadowed by the stirring events" of the three succeeding days. If Five Forks was the Army of Northern Virginia's deathblow, Sailor's Creek was its *coup de grâce*. Almost half of Lee's army had been swept from the field in a few days, and he had only Longstreet's wing with which to attempt the march to join Joe Johnston.

To the despondent and broken Richard S. Ewell, once one of Lee's fiercest fighters, it was obvious that the game was up. He and his fellow captives sprawled around Sheridan's campfire that evening, and Colonel Newhall noted: "Ewell is sitting on the ground hugging his knees, with his face bent down between his arms, and if anything could add force to his words, the utter despondency of his air would do it. The others are mostly staid, middle-aged men, tired to death nearly, and in no humor for a chat."[15] The brooding Ewell became more talkative a little later, after Sheridan and his officers shared their supper with the prisoners. General Ewell urged Sheridan to send Lee a flag of truce and "demand his surrender in order to save any further sacrifice."

Sheridan curtly replied that such matters were beyond his province, but he passed along the suggestion to General Grant. The general in chief wrote Lee the next day, "The results of the last week must convince you of the hopelessness of further resistance on the part of the Army of Northern Virginia in this struggle." But Lee, still trying to make good his retreat, replied immediately that he must know the terms Grant was willing to propose before he could consider surrender. Grant insisted, "The men and officers surrendered shall be disqualified for taking up arms against the Government of the United States until properly exchanged." This sounded too much like "unconditional surrender" for the still unbowed Lee. He decided on another attempt to break through the encroaching armies and, most persistent of all, the "inevitable Sheridan."

Meanwhile, not too elated over the immediate prospect of Lee's surrendering without further arguments by force of arms, General

Sheridan began reaching out toward Farmville for Lee's retreating columns. In announcing the capture of six Confederate general officers he had concluded, "If the thing is pressed, I think that Lee will surrender." Grant relayed this confident message back to City Point, where Lincoln waited in melancholy and anxiety for the word that Lee had given up. Lincoln's laconic comment was relayed back to Sheridan: "Let the thing be pressed." It was further proof that the President and the general in chief realized Sheridan was one general who did not need a laborious directive to engage the enemy; it was reminiscent of Grant's two-word order that opened the Valley campaign—"Go in."

Sheridan did indeed press the enemy, never giving Lee a moment to rest, to forage for supplies, even to form a plan for lashing back. The last days of the Army of Northern Virginia were not so much a fight as a foot race. The surviving corps under Longstreet was harried every moment. Ord's infantry was swinging south in a parallel movement while the Federal cavalry nipped at the Rebel's heels, appeared suddenly on his flanks, swarmed all over him the moment he settled down to draw a breath. At Farmville, General Crook overtook the main column and attacked its trains on the north side of the Appomattox. This drew an angry counter-attack which cost Gregg's brigade a number of losses by capture, among them Gregg himself.

On the night of April 7 Sheridan, receiving word of Crook's engagement, realized that Lee had abandoned all hope of reaching Danville to the southwest and would probably try to make for Lynchburg. Accordingly he now planned to throw his cavalry across that path and hold Lee until the infantry could come up from the rear. He ordered his entire command to head for Appomattox Depot that evening and recalled Crook to Prospect Station. Merritt had gone into bivouac on Buffalo Creek, and McKenzie's cavalry division had undertaken a reconnaissance along the Lynchburg Railroad.[16]

On the day's march Sheridan had seen for himself two contrasting Southern attitudes toward the conquerors. With his staff he stopped to lunch under the great oaks of a stately old house near Prince Edward Court House, and afterward the young gentlemen of the military gathered around a piano and sang. A dimpled young lady of the house "informed us that we needn't be in a hurry to go—Yankees were not so very black, after all, as they had been painted. She promised to remember our sins in her orisons, and we went on our wicked way. . . ." The other side of the coin was symbolized later that afternoon by "a stiff old gentleman sitting on his high piazza and scowling severely." Colonel Newhall recalled.

Sheridan, without noticing the scowl, sat on the steps, lighted a cigar and pulled out his maps. "How far is it to Buffalo Creek?" he asked his unwilling host.

"Sir, I don't know," the plantation aristocrat replied haughtily.

The young general gave him a sharp glance. "The devil you don't! How long have you lived here?"

"All my life."

"Very well, sir, it's time you did know where Buffalo Creek is." Sheridan turned to an aide. "Captain! Put this gentleman in charge of a guard, walk him down to Buffalo Creek, and show it to him."[17]

In a very short time the long and sometimes violent dream of such gentry would end not many miles to the West in a shabby little dwelling hardly suited to the tragic grandeur of the moment.

Next day, April 8, Sheridan ordered all his cavalry to advance on Appomattox Depot at once. One of his scouts had brought back word that four long trains loaded with invaluable supplies for Lee's remaining forces were waiting on a siding inadequately guarded. Custer handled the affair with dash and skill. He sent two regiments to the South to break up the tracks and prevent the trains from escaping. Then he charged the depot under the fire of a concealed battery. A brisk fight developed. Custer had run into Lee's advance guard, leading the Southern remnants on the Lynchburg Turnpike. They were only five miles south of Appomattox Court House, which Sheridan had already selected as the point to interpose his cavalry between Lee and the western mountains. Custer drove off the Confederates and captured a hospital train, 25 field guns and a large park of wagons.

Now Lee had lost all his supplies. He had left only his weary veterans, his courage and his hope of fighting his way through. More realistic was Sheridan's estimate of the situation, dispatched to General Grant that evening from his headquarters near Appomattox Depot: "If General Gibbon and the V Corps can get up tonight we will perhaps finish the job in the morning. I do not think Lee intends to surrender until compelled to do so." To other commanders—Ord and Gibbon of the Army of the James, Griffin of the V Corps—he sent advice that, if they pressed on toward Appomattox Court House, by night marches if necessary, there was now no means by which the enemy could escape—Lee had "reached 'the last ditch.' "[18] Custer still pursued the enemy on the roads leading toward Appomattox. General Grant was "serenely smoking on the piazza of the Farmville Hotel while farming out the remnant of the Confederacy to his various partners in the undertaking."[19] He had comparatively little to do in this last stage of the campaign except approve the measures Sheridan was suggesting and taking to surround Lee and demonstrate to him the futility of further resistance.

That night, in a leaden-hearted conference, General Lee told his surviving commanders their only hope was to let General Gordon lead an assault on the Federal forces ringing them and hope they could achieve a break-through.

Sunday, April 9, was the deathday of the Army of Northern Virginia. The Federal cavalry had been up all night, moving in on Appomattox. Ord's corps from the Army of the James came up to support Sheridan. Griffin's V Corps had also moved into the ring of forces around Lee.

In accordance with Lee's orders Gordon's Corps, shrunken to the size of a healthy brigade, attacked Sheridan's cavalry. The Confederate attack was pressed with desperate energy, especially after the first assault troops discovered that they were opposed by dismounted cavalry rather sketchily entrenched. Two new field guns and their teams were captured by the Confederates, and Gordon's hopes of breaking through were soaring.[20]

Disillusionment followed swiftly. The Union cavalry screen parted like the curtain in a theater and disclosed a new actor on the scene—the infantry of Ord's Army of the James and its heavier armament, rank on rank of foot soldiers waiting motionlessly but ready for action.

Gordon's attack had met with "some success," but now it came to a standstill. "In spite of Sheridan's attempts to hold [Lee], our cavalry were falling back in confusion before Lee's infantry. We were barely in time," reported General Ord.[21] By forced marches Ord had brought up two divisions of his XXIV Corps and one of the XXV. It was a moment of happy improvisation by the two army commanders.

To the Confederates it seemed like a theatrical bit of business, allowing them to pierce the cavalry screen only to be confronted by three divisions of infantry. It convinced them, however, that further fighting would be futile, would only lengthen the final casualty lists. Already Lee was boxed in on the west, south and east; retreating to the north, he could be supplied only by the few wagons left to him. "The enemy discontinued his attack as soon as he caught sight of our infantry," Sheridan reported.[22] The Confederates retreated to a ridge fronting Appomattox Court House while General Lee reconciled himself to the inevitable. Sheridan, Ord and Griffin closed in on the remnants of the enemy still able and willing to bear arms.

An aide-de-camp sent by Custer rode up with the news that the North had been waiting four years to hear: "Lee has surrendered— do not charge—the white flag is up." Shortly after sending back this jubilant message Custer received an unexpected dressing-down from General Longstreet, who refused to be awed by the splendor of Custer's appearance.

Custer rode up to "Old Pete" Longstreet and loudly demanded his surrender.

The crusty Longstreet informed Custer that General Lee was in communication with General Grant and that he would not recognize any subordinate.

"Oh, Sheridan and I are independent of Grant today, and we will destroy you if you don't surrender at once," Custer airily replied.

Longstreet then delivered a brief but pungent lecture on military courtesy and concluded, "Now, go and act as you and Sheridan choose and I will teach you a lesson you won't forget! Now go!" Custer rode back to his own lines a noticeably chastened young man.[23]

Meanwhile, Sheridan—accompanied only by a sergeant bearing the headquarters guidon, according to his own account, although Gordon said he had a "mounted escort as large as one of Fitz Lee's regiments"[24]—rode toward the courthouse to confer with the enemy generals Gordon and Wilcox. Gordon recalled that their conversation went as follows:

"We have met before, I believe, at Winchester and Cedar Creek in the Valley," Sheridan began brusquely.

"I was there," Gordon acknowledged.

"I had the pleasure of receiving some artillery from your government, consigned to me through your commander, General Early," Sheridan said.

General Gordon's spirited retort was interrupted by an outbreak of musketry to the right. Sheridan demanded the meaning of the firing while a truce was in effect. It developed that General Geary, a hot-blooded South Carolinian commanding a brigade, had refused to acknowledge the existence of the truce. "I do not care for white flags: South Carolinians never surrender," he growled. He subsided, however, on receiving a direct order from Gordon.[25]

The Confederate corps commander informed Sheridan that "General Lee asks a suspension of hostilities pending the negotiations which he is having with General Grant."

To this Sheridan replied stiffly, "I will entertain no terms except that General Lee shall surrender to General Grant on his arrival here."

A few minutes later Longstreet rode up and repeated the assurance given by Gordon that there was no doubt of Lee's intention to surrender. Sheridan was satisfied with the word of a West Pointer, especially one so universally respected as "Old Pete" Longstreet, and agreed to a cessation of hostilities until Grant and Lee could meet and discuss terms. But, thinking it just possible that the Confederates were using the truce as a method of gaining time while some of their troops slipped away, he took the precaution of writing to Lee and protesting that he had spotted some of the enemy's troops in motion.

It was 1:00 P.M. before Grant and his staff arrived at the crossroads just outside Appomattox Court House and were met by Generals Sheridan and Ord.

"How are you, Sheridan?" Grant inquired casually.

"First rate, thank you," Sheridan replied. He then explained that most of Lee's forces were "down in that valley" and that the Confederate leader was waiting at the McLean house.

"Come, let us go over," Grant said.

It was all as commonplace on the surface as a group of farmers negotiating the sale of some property.

But Lee, resplendent in gold braid and shining sword, elegant, dignified and proud even amid the ruins of his once powerful army, provided an aura of high tragedy in the drab setting of the McLean house. The victors, except for Sheridan, were almost abashed in the presence of the splendid loser. The Federal generals gathered around Lee with all the deference of a group of boy graduates taking leave of a beloved teacher. Grant, in comparison, was suffering from a sick headache and wore a shabby, road-stained uniform with no insignia except a pair of "dingy" shoulder straps (as Sheridan observed).

Sheridan, Ord and other of Grant's lieutenants waited outside the McLean house while Grant and Colonel Babcock of his staff came to an agreement with Lee and Colonel Marshall, his military secretary, on the terms of surrender. Essentially Lee agreed to surrender the 28,231 men remaining in his command, while Grant allowed them to be paroled to their homes and spared the rigors of the Federal military prisons; moreover, he permitted them all, officers and men, to retain their personal baggage, side arms and horses or mules. It may have been Lee's magnificent presence that dominated the McLean house that Sunday afternoon, but Grant's magnanimity cast a longer and warmer beam. When Lee mentioned that his army was without rations, Sheridan having captured the last of the Confederate trains, Grant asked his cavalry commander if he could send food to the surrendered forces. Sheridan responded that he could spare 25,000 rations at once.[26] Nor was this the end of Grant's generosity: he forbade the firing of victory salutes and cheering in the Union lines, for there was sadness as well as joy in watching an honorable foe go down in defeat.

Sheridan was affected least of all by the chivalric atmosphere. To the last he could regard Lee with the respect due him as an able soldier, but without any degree of veneration, no matter how fashionable it was at the moment.

With barely concealed annoyance he watched his fellow generals showing deference to the enemy commander—even Grant, who was often diffident but rarely awed. Grant, noting Lee's bright braid and polished sword, apologetically explained that his own dress regalia was in a baggage wagon far to the rear. He eagerly recalled to Lee their meeting in Mexico during the war of 1846 and remarked that he would have known Lee anywhere. The aloof Virginian could not return the compliment. Lee recalled the occasion of their meeting, but added that he had been unable to remember what Grant looked like. With Seth Williams, Grant's adjutant general, Lee was somewhat more cordial: Williams had been his own adjutant when Lee was superintendent of West Point.

Sheridan waited impatiently for these polite exchanges to end. Then, as Horace Porter recalled, "General Sheridan . . . stepped up to General Lee and said that when he discovered some of the Confederate troops in motion during the morning, which seemed to be a violation of the truce, he had sent him (Lee) a couple of notes protesting against this act, and as he had not had time to copy them he would like to have them long enough to make copies."

The grandeur of the moment was not so inhibiting that Sheridan, always the careful keeper of records, could forget that his files were not complete. Perhaps, too, he was somewhat irritated with his colleagues for the consideration shown a man who, to Sheridan, was, after all, merely the leader of an unsuccessful rebellion.

General Lee did not take offense, but removed the notes from a breast pocket and handed them over with a few words "expressive of regret that the circumstance had occurred, and intimating that it must have been the result of some misunderstanding."[27]

Lee and Colonel Marshall, the only Confederate officers present at the surrender conference, rode off to their shattered army after

Grant and Lee politely lifted their hats to each other in parting.
The fact that the meeting in the McLean house became a part of
the American folk drama, a symbol of the reconciliation of the
North and the South, was due equally to Lee's dignity in defeat,
showing the South that the loser could still hold his head high, and
to Grant's forbearance in victory, showing the North that the
winner could afford to be generous. There were, of course, a great
many incidents in succeeding years which disclosed that the South
could forget its lesson in dignity and the North its example of
magnanimity. A number of them involved General Sheridan, who
could not easily erase from his memory the bloodshed and destruction he had witnessed in the course of the war.

Immediately after the surrender, however, Sheridan was in a
kindly mood. He rode off with Generals Ingalls and Williams to
visit old friends on the Confederate side. The three Northern generals brought back Generals Cadmus M. Wilcox, Longstreet, Heth,
Gordon, Pickett and others for a sort of reunion with Grant. Longstreet and Wilcox had attended Grant's wedding, and Heth had
served with him in Mexico.[28]

Before the Union generals left the McLean house there was a
spirited auction for articles of furniture used in the historic scene.
Sheridan was given first choice. He bought the little pine table on
which the surrender had been signed, paying with two 10-dollar
gold pieces he had carried for more than a year to be used in the
event of his capture. He presented it to General Custer as a gift
to Mrs. Custer, whom he had long admired because her husband
was "the only one of his officers who had not been spoiled by
marriage." Next day he wrote her a cordial little note:

I respectfully present to you the small writing table on which the
conditions for the surrender of the Confederate Army of Northern Virginia were written by Lt. General Grant—and permit me
to say, Madam, that there is scarcely an individual in our service
who has contributed more to bring this about than your very gallant husband.[29]

The morning after the surrender at Appomattox the cavalry
corps began moving back to Petersburg, with most of the troopers

anticipating their discharge within a few weeks. En route, at Nottoway Court House, Sheridan heard that President Lincoln had been assassinated, but he refused to believe it until the report was confirmed the next day by an official telegram. At Petersburg the cavalry was ordered to march on Greensboro, North Carolina, where it was to co-operate with Sherman in persuading Joe Johnston that he, too, had better surrender. By April 24 Sheridan reached South Boston on the Dan River and learned there that Johnston had surrendered.

Sheridan and his staff and leading subordinates then proceeded to Washington under orders. They were, of course, the toast of the capital. For it was the cavalry, supported and reinforced by the infantry, that had sealed off the Valley after three victories in rapid succession; had wrecked Stuart's cavalry so that it never again humiliated Northern generals with daring sweeps into their rear; had broken Lee's right and forced him to come out of the Richmond-Petersburg defenses; and had finally prevented him from making good his retreat. It was the cavalry and its far-ranging guidons that had caught the public imagination, perhaps a little more than it deserved.

Sheridan and his commanders, looking much too youthful to be general officers, gathered at Brady's photographic gallery for group photographs. An even more comradely occasion was a dinner at Willard's Hotel with the champagne foaming and the toasts becoming more fervent with every swallow of wine.

The cavalrymen lifted their glass to:

Merritt, with his boyish face, his quick brain and his knowledge of when to be dashing and when to be cautious;

Custer, who rode into battle like a whirlwind with "his broad sombrero turned up from his hard, bronzed face, the ends of his crimson cravat floating over his shoulders, gold galore spangling his jacket sleeves, a pistol in his boot, jangling spurs on his heels, and a ponderous claymore swinging at his side";

Devin, "of the school of Polonius," a scholar on horseback;

Gibbes, the soft-spoken and hard-riding;

Irvine Gregg, "cool as a clock";

Smith, "steady as a lighthouse";

Crook, easygoing in camp, a firebrand in battle;
Davies, "earnest and dashing";[30]

and to *Sheridan*, whose leadership had never been doubted or questioned by these skeptical, ambitious young men of his command. Without political influence or personal patronage he had risen by his own talents, character and courage to take his place beside Grant, Sherman and Thomas as the greatest of the Union generals. At the age of thirty-four he had known more fame, held more responsibility than any young general before or since in American history.

His first great victory had been over himself, when he lunged at Cadet Sergeant Terrill with a lowered bayonet but conquered his temper in an instant that could have ruined him. From then on he used his aggressive nature as a banner to inspire others in battle rather than an instrument of self-destruction. In that critical moment of self-knowledge and self-control he learned to trust himself and his own judgment and refused to let another's doubts or behavior influence his own course of conduct, whether it was a comrade's or an enemy's.

At Booneville he handled a numerically superior enemy with such confidence that 90 mounted men charging the Confederate rear brought him victory. At Perryville he stood aside from the squabbles and jealousies and alarms of other Union generals, then calmly held off half the Confederate forces with one division. At Stone's River he took such a toll of Bragg's advance in the Round Forest that the Union army was able to regroup and eventually win the battle. At Chickamauga he held his division together while those to the left and right of him dissolved in panic, and thus was able to protect Thomas' withdrawal from Horseshoe Ridge.

Refusing to be awed by Jeb Stuart's reputation, he struck the Confederate cavalry a mortal blow at Yellow Tavern. In the Shenandoah he broke all Confederate resistance in exactly one month and three pitched battles. Pursuing Lee toward Appomattox, he drove boldly ahead in disregard of the cautioning of infantry generals still dazzled by memories of the fearsome Lee counterstroke.

In Sheridan the elements of audacity and caution and an unmatched appreciation of the value of swift maneuver were so well balanced that he never made an important error in generalship, either of commission or omission. The war had ended, but the nation still had many uses for that generalship in the years when the frontier was pushed steadily westward and the army turned from conquest of the South to "pacification" of the Indians.

16

SHERIDAN vs. NAPOLEON, LOUISIANA AND TEXAS

THE combat leader who can adapt himself to civil administration as successfully as he has withstood the dangers and chances of error on the battlefield is extremely rare in American history. Few brilliant soldiers have the ability to deal with social and political problems, particularly those so complex and embittered as exist on the losing side of a civil war. The capacity for quick and bold action in the field seemingly cancels out ability to cope with administering occupied territory.

It is, perhaps, too much to expect of a soldier that he should exhibit a high quality of statecraft after being trained all his life to cut through human problems with a peremptory order and to disdain politics as the sport of fat, conniving civilians. It was especially optimistic to demand statesmanship of an American army officer trained at West Point in the middle of the last century, long before there was any instruction in the art of civil administration, and at a time when a commander of occupied territory was expected to answer resistance with a rolling up of the artillery rather than with conferring, ameliorating and compromising. After the Civil War the victorious Northern generals were faced with ruling, not conquered foreigners, but other Americans in the long-range objective of winning back their wholehearted loyalty. To the immense and ramified problem of soothing as well as keeping order in the South, General Sheridan brought only his brief experience as ruler of the Yamhill Reservation in Oregon—and a surplus of self-confidence.

The day after Sheridan arrived in Washington he was told by

General Grant to hold himself in readiness to take charge of restoring Louisiana and Texas to the Union. The general in chief,
with his fondness for "cover plans," had a deeper motive in sending
his most dependable and aggressive field commander to the border.
In the first letter of instructions Grant concerned himself with out-
lining a procedure against Confederate General E. Kirby Smith
and his debilitated Army of Trans-Mississippi, and with informing
Sheridan that General Canby's army of 25,000 plus the IV and
XXV Corps (the first at Nashville, the latter at City Point) were
to be transferred to his command.

With all his love of action Sheridan was disappointed at receiving
the assignment.

In the Grand Review of the Union soldiers, the Army of the
Potomac was scheduled for May 23, with Sherman's "bummers," to
march the next day, and Sheridan wanted to lead his cavalry corps.
But Grant said it was "absolutely necessary" that Sheridan proceed
to his new command at once. The head of the Federal armies revealed that more important things were stirring in the Southwest
than merely hunting down Kirby Smith's remnants.

Grant believed that the French must be persuaded, by threat
of force if necessary, to leave Mexico. In 1861, while the American government was more concerned with Secession than with
violations of the Monroe Doctrine, French, English and Spanish
warships had entered Mexican ports after President Benito Juarez
announced a two-year moratorium on the republic's debts. Only
Napoleon III of France, who "tried to play the part of the first
Napoleon without the ability to sustain the role," as Grant commented, landed troops in Mexico. In the next year he engineered
the accession of Maximilian and Carlota to the throne of the Mexican "empire."

Knowing that Maximilian was only a Napoleonic puppet, Secretary of State Seward had endeavored throughout the Civil War to
end the French occupation, without an iota of success. There was
no doubt of Napoleon III's determination to maintain French influence over Mexico, for he wrote that, "while creating immense
outlets for our commerce," it would "procure raw material which
is indispensable to our industry." Maximilian had rendered all pos-

sible assistance to the Confederate government. The North particularly resented the traffic in arms and other supplies which operated between the Mexican town of Bagdad and the Confederate commissary by way of Matamoros and Brownsville. Juarez, on the other hand, controlling parts of northern Mexico, had allowed Union forces to cross his territory and attack Confederate forces in Arizona, thereby thwarting a Southern plan to seize southern New Mexico and Arizona and open a Confederate corridor from Texas to the Pacific.

General Grant was determined to restore the Mexican republic, not only because of resentment over Maximilian's aid to the Confederacy, but because his sympathies were entirely with the Juarez government. One of his closest friends was Romero, the Juarez ambassador to Washington. Ever since he fought in the Mexican War he had admired and respected the Mexican people, and he had never lost vague feelings of guilt over the American seizure of their territory.

Despite Grant's great prestige, it was necessary to move carefully in helping Juarez and discouraging the French. Secretary of State Seward was opposed to any active employment of Federal troops on the border that might involve a war with the European powers. So there was need for secrecy. The general's son, Frederick D. Grant, many years later told General Grenville M. Dodge that he found two confidential letters from his father to Sheridan in a private letterbook. One gave Sheridan permission to befriend General Santa Anna, the evil genius of Mexican affairs for many years and commander of the Mexican forces in the war of 1846, providing he was favorable to Benito Juarez.

The second secret letter even more sharply defined Grant's intention of subverting the State Department's plan for solving the Maximilian problem by diplomatic means, and of applying military force instead to hasten the fall of the French puppet and the departure of Marshal Bazaine's French-Austrian army of occupation. It was quoted by Fred Grant, in essence, as suggesting that there were lots of arms left by soldiers on both sides and if they fell into Juarez's hands he [Grant] did not care, and Sheridan could lose them. Some five or six of our batteries and some 40,000 stands of arms could be lost in that way. If any of these fell into the hands of Maximilian, Sheridan would have to account for them. . . .[1] Sheridan entered into Grant's schemes wholeheartedly.

His restoration to good spirits was helped by a tribute from the cavalry corps that was all the more valued because it was spontaneous and came from the hearts of the rank and file. He was sitting in his room at Willard's on Sunday, May 21, the day before his departure and two days before the Grand Review, grumpy over being deprived of the honor of riding at the head of his corps and wondering whether one day would really make so much difference in chasing down poor old Kirby Smith. There was a blare of bands, a steady drumming of hoofs audible over the spring rainstorm. It was the cavalry corps, come to pay its own private homage to the chief who had led it in its most successful campaigns. The corps had been ordered to move to a camp closer to Washington, near Bladensburg, in preparation for the review. "Sheridan's Robbers" decided to march via Willard's Hotel, which was far from the direct route. Sheridan stepped out on the balcony to review his corps—the long files of troopers behind their battle flags and guidons, the dashing horse artillery, the miles-long wagon train that had sustained its marches. Rain soaked their uniforms and turned the street into a frothy mud bath, but the veterans of the Wilderness, the Valley and the drive to Appomattox gave their commander the "eyes right" with snap and precision. It was one of the happiest surprises of Sheridan's life. Tears trickled down with the raindrops on his face. He believed it would be his last glimpse of these regiments.[2]

While Sheridan was traveling south the corps passed in review at the head of the Army of the Potomac. Not unexpectedly General Custer stole the show. Accidentally or on purpose he lost control of his horse and dashed past the reviewing stand at the gallop, golden curls flying—"not in the stately and sedate manner of a warrior chief on his prancing charger, but shooting like the wind," one of his officers noted. "Was this a disappointment or was the sensation agreeable? Who among the spectators or performers at this state occasion will forget 'how Custer's horse ran away with him'?" As one of his biographers said, "That runaway is at once his biography and his epitaph."[3]

Before Sheridan arrived in New Orleans word reached him that Kirby Smith had capitulated. All attention could now be given to the problem of persuading the French to leave Mexico. The irritating aspects of the situation were only increased by the fact that some of Kirby Smith's troops were fleeing across the Rio Grande with their arms and equipment to join the imperial forces. In all, Sheridan concluded, 2,000 Confederate soldiers had taken refuge south of the border. They were followed by Southern bigwigs, civil and military, including Generals John B. Magruder, Jo Shelby, James E. Slaughter and John B. Walker, who had grandiose plans for establishing a Confederate colony.

To offset these possibly menacing developments Sheridan was given cavalry divisions under Custer and Merritt for deployment in Texas. War with France was entirely possible, Sheridan told Custer in New Orleans. From their staging areas on the Red River, Custer was to lead a column from Alexandria to Houston, Merritt from Shreveport to San Antonio. General Frank Herron led an infantry division to occupy Galveston, and General Fred Steele took another to Brazos Santiago to cover Brownsville and the Rio Grande line. Subsequently the IV Corps (in which Sheridan had served as a division commander at Missionary Ridge and in the Knoxville campaign) was directed to Victoria, most of the XXV Corps to Brownsville, Sheridan's intention being to "concentrate at available points in the State an army strong enough to move against the invaders of Mexico if occasion demanded."[4]

Sheridan and his generals, not without provocation from across the border, were keyed up to a militant pitch, ready to cross the Rio Grande with their veteran formations if any overt act warranted a declaration of war. The troops, knowing they could expect more of the hardship and less of the glory than their generals, were approaching a state of disaffection. Custer was impelled to take harsh measures when the 3rd Michigan Cavalry showed its feelings by turning out on parade with uniforms in deliberate disarray, hats turned backward, jackets inside out and sidearms worn on the wrong side. Custer could have laughed it off, and that would probably have been the end of the matter, but he declared the regiment in a state of mutiny and arrested 90 men. A sergeant was singled out, court-martialed and sentenced to die. Custer paraded his whole division on the day of execution, and the sergeant and a deserter also under the death sentence were brought before the firing squad. At the last moment Custer spared the sergeant's life, and only the deserter fell before the firing squad. Discipline was restored, but doubtless Custer had lost the admiration of his men forever.

Without actually sending his troops across the Rio Grande, Sheridan did everything possible to give Maximilian and Napoleon III the idea that armed intervention would result if Benito Juarez was not restored to the presidential palace in Mexico City. He believed that, if Secretary of State Seward had not been "unalterably opposed to any act likely to involve us in war," the "speedy evacuation of the entire country by Maximilian" could have been effected. Sheridan kept shifting his troops along the border as if preparing to attack. He conferred openly with members of the Juarez government—which had very little left to govern. He rode to Fort Duncan, where he had once served as a lieutenant, and ostentatiously inquired about the best military roads across the border. Alarm increased to panic among the imperial forces when Sheridan ordered a pontoon train sent to Brownsville.

There had been provocations from the other side of the Rio Grande, many incidents involving shots fired across the border. An artillery officer stationed at Brownsville reported on November 15, 1865, that the steamer *San Antonio*, flying the French flag, "fired a large number of shots" into his camp.[5] The French complained constantly to Seward of violations of neutrality committed by Sheridan's army, but they could not claim clean hands themselves. Early in 1866 Sheridan prepared for the Adjutant General's office a brief on "Franco-Mexican violations of neutrality" which asserted that: (1) Maximilian permitted large and continuing quantities of arms, ammunition, medicine, boots, uniforms and blankets to be sold in Matamoros to the Confederate States of America; (2) when the Confederates were driven out of Brownsville they crossed the border and sold cannon, caissons, harness and many bales of cotton to the imperial forces; (3) the imperial forces had fired across the border many times at American troops; and (4)

Kirby Smith had crossed into Mexico with 40 wagons loaded with ammunition, English rifles and two pieces of artillery.[6]

From all over Mexico Sheridan's intelligence agents forwarded news of the deterioration of Maximilian's regime. Some were members of his command, the celebrated "Sheridan's Robbers" who had operated against Mosby and the guerrillas of the Shenandoah, still under the direction of Major Young; others were American businessmen and expatriates who had settled around Mexico City since the war of 1846. Through these sources Sheridan was able to keep Washington informed almost daily of developments in the doomed and vainglorious reign of Maximilian and Carlota. His letter books and dispatch files for 1866 and 1867 are filled with accounts of his secret agents and their accurate predictions of a short life for the "empire." Through them can be traced, in brief, the last days of Maximilian and the parallel failure of the Confederate colony at Cordoba, 60 miles west of Vera Cruz, where the Southern gentlemen had been given large landholdings and were expected to form a sort of elite corps for Imperial Mexico.

Early in 1866 Sheridan forwarded information to Washington that his old opponent, Jubal Early, even more disgruntled and misanthropic than during the war, a curmudgeon to the end, had joined the Confederate colony. "I can assure you," he said, "that many more ex-Rebel generals will yet go, and with no good in their hearts for the United States Government."[7] Two weeks later he assigned General Horatio G. Wright, former commander of the VI Corps, to take charge of United States dispositions along the Rio Grande, instructing him to "restore the equilibrium there . . . break up all fillibustering parties and see that the orders which I have given General Weitzel to preserve neutrality are carried out."[8]

That summer Sheridan was able to report to Grant that imperial troops had been withdrawn from northern Mexico. "I strongly advise that President Juarez be urged to come down to Monterey. . . ." He also informed Grant that General Lew Wallace, whom the general in chief had detested ever since his division got lost during the battle of Shiloh, had "arrived off Brazos" with "some other sharks," although "their services are not regarded" and "I doubt if they can do much good."[9] General Wallace was trespassing on Sheridan's territory, being assigned to New Mexico and having no official business on the Texas border.

Sheridan grew increasingly irritated over Seward's "willy-nilly" methods. "It required the patience of Job to abide the slow and poky methods of our State Department, and, in truth, it was often very difficult to restrain officers and men from crossing the Rio Grande with hostile purpose."[10] He believed that, if he was forbidden to exert greater military pressure on Maximilian, the State Department should take measures against migration of any more Southern colonists to Cordoba. Seward failed to take any such action, despite Sheridan's prodding, so with Grant's approval Sheridan published an order forbidding embarkation from any port in Louisiana and Texas of any persons bound for Mexico without permits issued by his headquarters. Such permits were not easy to obtain unless the applicant had a provable record of opposition to the departed Confederacy.

To the Liberal forces of President Juarez, Sheridan sent a steady stream of military assistance and constant advice to take the offensive against the imperial army. During the winter of 1866 and the spring of 1867, 30,000 muskets were supplied to Juarez from the Baton Rouge arsenal alone. In the maze of political intrigue—there were many rivals of Juarez whose only bond with him was the determination to drive out the imperialists—Sheridan did not always fare too well. One of these rivals was General Caravajal, whom Sheridan sized up as an "old wretch" and a braggart when he interviewed him in Matamoros. Sheridan believed Caravajal would lose the city either to Canales or to Cortinas, two other contenders for power in northern Mexico, but he recommended Major Young, who had represented him for so long in "confidential" matters, to act as liaison between Caravajal and Sheridan's headquarters in New Orleans. Several weeks later Young came to New Orleans with the news that Caravajal had induced him to recruit a bodyguard of fifty men and had been given $7,000 to buy their arms and supply them for the journey to Matamoros. Pleading that his honor was at stake, Major Young persuaded the dubious Sheridan to provide him with additional funds and arrange for a schooner to carry the freebooters to Brazos.

By the time Young and his band reached Brownsville they learned Caravajal had been deposed by Canales. The latter refused their services, and Young decided to march up the Rio Grande on the American side, then cross over and offer them to General Escobedo, entering Mexico near the Ringgold Barracks. A band of former Confederates and Mexican renegades attacked the Young party as they attempted to cross the Rio Grande. Young and more than half of his followers were killed, and only a score of them managed to continue the trek and join General Escobedo "in such plight as to be of little use."

The disaster to Young and his party, Sheridan said, practically ended "all open participation of American sympathizers with the Liberal cause, but the moral support afforded by the presence of our forces continued. . . ." To this "moral support" was soon added the weight of arms and ammunition.

During the winter of 1866-1867 it became evident that Maximilian could not long withstand the popular resentment of his regime. Sheridan directed General Sedgwick, at Brazos Santiago, to speed up assistance to Juarez, referring to Maximilian as "the Imperial buccaneer representing the so-called Imperial Government of Mexico."[11] Sheridan passed along the information from one of his agents—whose letters to the New Orleans headquarters were never signed, so their services have remained anonymous—that the Maximilian government was splitting open from inner tensions. "Marshal Bazaine has private ambitions of his own and is not on good terms with Max."[12]

Sheridan knew even before the French generals in Mexico that evacuation of the army of occupation was going to be speeded under American pressure. Somehow he obtained a cable from Napoleon III to General Castelnau, routed from Paris through the French consulate in New Orleans to Mexico City, and had it deciphered by a telegraph operator in his headquarters—a fascinating bit of cloak-and-dagger work which he never described fully. Napoleon's orders to Castelnau read: ". . . Do not compel the Emperor to abdicate, but do not delay the departure of the troops; bring back all those who will not remain there. Most of the fleet has left." Napoleon sent the cable, Sheridan noted, just as Carlota, already broken in mind and spirit, arrived in Paris to beg him for reinforcements for her husband.[13]

Although deserted by the man who had put him on the throne of Mexico, Maximilian demonstrated a moral and physical courage that Sheridan had not believed he possessed. An agent informed Sheridan that "Max keeps a stiff upper lip, said yesterday if they drove him out of Mexico City he would defend Orizaba and if driven thence he would take to San Juan D. Ulloa."[14] Less than two weeks later an agent in Vera Cruz forwarded the information that 22 French war vessels and transports had arrived in the past 12 days. "Nine transports have left, taking away about 10,000 men, inclusive of the Austrian contingent." The evacuation was to be completed by March 15, the informant said, and the French rear guard was already posted to fight off any interference from republican forces.[15]

Sheridan was informed that Maximilian took the field in person "as a last card," with only 2,500 infantry and 1,500 cavalry under his command, opposing 15,000 under Diaz, the ablest of the republican commanders and subsequently to reign long and sternly as the dictator of Mexico.[16] The tragedy of the Mexican "empire" was swiftly running its course. Maximilian and his crumbling little force of Mexicans—most of them loyal for mercenary reasons or because they could expect only the firing squad when Juarez regained power—held out through the spring of 1867. Then came the news that Maximilian's "army" had been annihilated and its commander captured and executed. Sheridan relayed to Grant: "Maximilian was condemned and shot on June 19. Austrian Imperial troops at Vera Cruz are requesting transportation from that point home, badly scared. Juarez refuses to deliver the body of Maximilian. If this is true it is but the end of the rebellion which had its commencement in this country and its tragic termination in Mexico."

Possibly because he respected Maximilian's final brave and quixotic stand against the republicans, Sheridan did his best to save him from the firing squad at Queretaro. He hired a steamer to rush an appeal from Secretary of State Seward across the Gulf of Tampico; it was borne by one of Sheridan's scouts and delivered to General

Escobedo at Queretaro, but the republican commander would not consider clemency for his royal prisoner.

Against the mistaken fear of Secretary Seward that the United States might become involved in a war with France, Sheridan had labored effectively to bluff the imperial forces out of northern Mexico. He had then strengthened the republicans so that Bazaine was forced to evacuate ahead of schedule, leaving Maximilian's native troops to be quickly routed. Sheridan's demonstrations along the Rio Grande were instrumental in persuading Napoleon III to withdraw his support. The French Marshal MacMahon gave the opinion in 1866 that "it might be worth a fight" even against Grant, if he were commanding on the border, but not against Sheridan. Another factor, of course, was the fact that Prussia defeated Austria that year and was causing France much concern for her own borders, a concern justified five years later.

Historians have generally credited Sheridan with a skillful show of bluff and deception along the Mexican border which preserved the Monroe Doctrine's integrity and warned other intruders from the shores of the Western Hemisphere for many years. Sheridan's experiences with the "willy-nilly" State Department, however, had nourished in him a contempt for civilian "interference" in affairs that he regarded as purely military. This attitude was soon to prove his downfall as the proconsul of Louisiana and Texas.

In the spring and summer of 1867 successive Acts of Congress placed in the hands of the military the power and responsibility of ruling over the conquered states of the former Confederacy. Abraham Lincoln had determined on a policy of moderation in restoring the South to the Union. After first inclining toward a Draconian program Andrew Johnson came to agree with the rather vague outline of reconstruction passed down by his predecessor. On the other hand, General Grant, scenting the possibility of political opportunities with the opponents of Lincoln and Johnson, sided with the Radical Republicans, who were determined that the South would never again be a political or economic power in the Federal Union. Dominating Congress, they were united in demanding that the former Confederate states be disfranchised and that the liberated Negroes, however unprepared for immediate assumption of their civil rights, should rule over their former masters. The result, of course, was a self-perpetuating legacy of racial bitterness still very much with us.

George W. Julian, a prominent dialectician of the Radicals, proposed the gallows for Jefferson Davis and Robert E. Lee and confiscation of all large landholdings, which would be divided among the freedmen and "leave not enough to bury the landowner's carcass in." As for Negro suffrage, in Julian's opinion, "When the Government decided that the negro was fit to carry a gun to shoot the rebels down, it thereby pledged itself irrevocably to give him the ballot to vote the rebels down." Even for some Radicals this formula was too violent. An Indianapolis newspaper characterized Julian as having "the temper of a hedgehog, the adhesiveness of a barnacle, the vanity of a peacock, the vindictiveness of a Corsican, and the duplicity of the devil."[17]

Under the so-called Military Bill, Sheridan was placed in charge of the Fifth Military District; the territory under his control, Louisiana and Texas, was the same, but his power was vastly increased. The general of each of the five districts was given the right to dismiss civil officeholders if he believed they were not supporting his program; could substitute military commissions for intransigent judges; could provide for constitutional conventions and establish new boards of registration for voters. Under the new oath of allegiance hardly anyone but Negroes, carpetbaggers and the few Unionists who had remained loyal through the war would be allowed to vote.

Throughout Louisiana, Sheridan was resented by the whites. They were enraged by his handling of the political crisis of the summer of 1866, when a movement was begun to reinstate the constitutional convention of the Banks regime, which had been discredited even by Congress. When the convention was reassembled in New Orleans, Canal Street was lined by hundreds of armed and raging whites. A large Negro delegation marched between their glowering ranks to the city hall, and there a murderous clash ensued. The police joined in attacking the Negroes and driving them away from their convention quarters. Thirty-eight Negroes were killed and 46 were wounded. Only a few white persons suffered injury.

When the riot occurred Sheridan was returning from Texas, and he did not arrive in the city until a day later. In his report to Washington he blamed the police for not stopping it and various local and state officials for inciting it.[18] Liberal whites of Louisiana and moderates of the North, however, believed Sheridan should have forbidden the convention to assemble. A Congressional investigating committee subsequently commended Sheridan's report and declared, "It was the determined purpose of the mayor of the city of New Orleans to break up this convention by armed force."

When the Reconstruction laws were passed by Congress over the President's veto General Sheridan believed that "the plan of reconstruction presented was, beyond question, the policy endorsed by the people of the country." Therefore, in the rigidly obedient manner of a soldier carrying out orders he proceeded to administer his military district of Louisiana and Texas. "I felt certain," he said, "that the President would endeavor to embarrass me by every means in his power, not only on account of his pronounced personal hostility, but also because of his determination not to execute but to obstruct the measures enacted by Congress."[19]

Eight days after the Reconstruction laws went into effect Sheridan proceeded summarily to remove Mayor Monroe of New Orleans, who had threatened to arrest the constitutional convention delegates as disturbers of the peace; Judge Abell, who had declared the convention illegal; and Attorney General Herron. The replacements he selected were men of the Radical persuasion. On June 3, 1867, he further offended unreconstructed Southerners by removing Governor J. Madison Wells from office.

The dispute with Governor Wells involved a $4,000,000 appropriation to repair the levees in flooded districts of Louisiana. Sheridan suspected him of packing the Board of Levee Commissioners with his own appointees and surveying the possibilities of graft. The Louisiana legislature also quarreled with Wells over how the appropriation was to be expended. Sheridan explained to Secretary Stanton that Wells was "a political trickster and a dishonest man" and appointed his own levee board. The governor immediately appealed to President Johnson, enclosing Sheridan's order and pointing out that the board was "purely civil" with no vacancies existing. Wells said he was "compelled to regard [the removal] as an extraordinary exercise of power on the part of General Sheridan."[20]

President Johnson grew much more alarmed over Sheridan's Cromwellian interpretation of the new Reconstruction laws when the general ordered the boards registering voters to exclude all those who could not prove their loyalty to the Union. By July 26 the whites on the voting lists were outnumbered by the Negroes, 41,166 to 78,230. Johnson and his Cabinet debated how to liberalize the voting laws, although Secretary Stanton asserted that under the Reconstruction Acts the various military district commanders "were invested with absolute power."[21] Attorney General Henry Stanbery wrote an opinion on enforcement of the laws as liberal as possible to the Southern citizens, ruling that an applicant for registration must be accepted if he took the prescribed oath of allegiance.

Sheridan fired back to Washington his untactful opinion that the Stanbery interpretation opened "a broad and macadamized road for perjury and fraud to travel." And he was encouraged in this rather arrogant attitude by General Grant, who was now the darling of the Radicals in Congress. Sheridan complained to Grant that "It must be recollected that I have been ordered to execute a law to which the President has been in bitter antagonism." To this Grant soothingly replied: "Enforce your own construction of the military bill until ordered to do otherwise. The opinion of the Attorney-General has not been distributed to the district commanders in language or manner entitling it to the form of an order, nor can I suppose that the President intended it to have such force."[22]

The Northern press, except those newspapers firmly committed to the Radical viewpoint, was not sympathetic to the generals' intransigence. The New York *Times* believed that Sheridan's insubordination had no parallel in recent military history.[23] Horace Greeley in his New York *Tribune* declared that, if Attorney General Stanbery was right, "then Congress is criminally wrong. If right we can no more reconstruct the South under this bill than we could under Mr. Swinburne's last poem."[24]

Sheridan next turned his attention to Texas, where his department commander, General Charles Griffin, reported, "There is scarcely an officer in this state, whose duty it is to arrest crime, that will turn or raise his hand against the scoundrels." Griffin, of course, referred to officers of the state government.[25] And from many Union sympathizers in the state Sheridan heard that ex-Confederates were literally able to get away with murder. The report of a Unionist in Rusk County particularly angered Sheridan. It told how three Federal soldiers were killed in the spring of 1866, and how the authorities refused to take action against the killers although their identity was known to all. Sheridan's informant suggested that a squad of soldiers be sent to make the arrest, since the local law enforcers refused to do so. A detachment was ordered to Rusk County, but the murderers escaped. Sheridan forwarded all the correspondence in the matter to Grant "as a specimen of the manner in which civil officers in the state of Texas ignored the perpetration of crimes upon the persons and property of Union citizens."[26]

Sheridan complained to Governor Throckmorton, who had been a Unionist but had stifled his feelings sufficiently for service in the Confederate Army as a brigadier general, that Unionists in Jack County were being robbed without interference from the civil authorities. But Sheridan refused to take action against drunken Federal soldiers who set fire to a block of business buildings in Brenham, Texas, and caused $130,000 worth of damage. And he ignored the appeal of Texas officials and citizens for troops to protect them from Indian raiders in border counties. Governor Throckmorton appealed to Stanton, who, surprisingly, upheld the governor and ordered Sheridan to send the 4th U. S. Cavalry to the frontier. On July 30 Sheridan removed Throckmorton from office and replaced him with E. M. Pease, who had lost the recent election to Throckmorton by an overwhelming majority.

By the end of July President Johnson was convinced that General Sheridan must be relieved of his command. Cabinet officers warned the President that Sheridan's removal would "strengthen the extreme Radicals, who really wanted the President to take this step in order that they might make successful war against him."

Sheridan, the secretaries believed, had been "spoiled by partisan flattery and the encouragement of the Radical conspirators."[27] In the opinion of Secretary of the Navy Gideon Welles, Sheridan was "really but a secondary personage after all in the business. He would never have pursued the course he has if not prompted and encouraged by others to whom he looked,—from whom he received advice if not orders."[28]

On July 31, one day after Sheridan removed Governor Throckmorton, he was himself replaced by General Winfield Scott Hancock, whose diplomatic manner and moderate views were expected to have an amelioriating effect on the Texans and Louisianans. The protest of General Grant—"General Sheridan has performed his civil duties faithfully and intelligently. His removal will only be regarded as an effort to defeat the laws of Congress"[29]—was unavailing.

His warmest admirer could not claim that Sheridan had made a success as proconsul of Louisiana and Texas. He had failed to appreciate the complexities of civil law and the difficulties of fairly well-disposed officials who were answerable to their own people as well as the military commander. "I was only following orders" is a military excuse as ancient as the profession of arms, but it had considerable validity in this case. At the age of thirty-six, with no previous experience in such matters except administering the affairs of wild Indians in the Northwest, he was expected to govern two great states whose citizenry, bitter and humiliated in defeat, would have resented the subtlest and mildest of interim administrators. So, in his dilemma, he followed the advice of General Grant and Secretary of State Stanton and the dictates of the Reconstruction Acts.

Grant and Stanton were his immediate superiors, and he had the soldier's respect for chain of command. The Reconstruction Acts were his manual of arms. A more worldly commander would not have interpreted them so literally. But it was sheer melodrama to picture Sheridan in dire conspiracy with Republican agents and carpetbag dictators. In peace as in war Sheridan looked only to Grant for orders and advice. As for his personal sympathies and animosities, there was no doubt that he felt little compassion for the conquered South, especially for its aristocracy. He had long viewed with contempt, and perhaps a little involuntary awe, the aspirations of the lords of the plantations; almost from boyhood he had nurtured a strong distaste for their manners, methods and ambitions. Unlike other Federal soldiers, he had no friendly intercourse with such Southern soldiers as Beauregard, Longstreet and Hood, then living in New Orleans. The enemy was still the enemy.

Washington had sent a blunt, hardheaded soldier to perform tasks that would have taxed a Machiavelli. His failure—and it was not the only one in that arena, for the wily political general Ben Butler also had failed there—was honest and inevitable.

President Johnson had only himself to blame for allowing the intransigent Sheridan to remain so long the instrument of his changing policy. Months before they differed on the application of Reconstruction measures, Sheridan made his attitude clear. Rather gloatingly he wrote Johnson that the South was already "Northernized," and that "In two or three years, there will be almost a total transfer of landed property. The North will own every railroad, every steamboat, every large mercantile establishment, and everything which requires capital to carry it on. . . ." As a grace note in closing Sheridan added, "We can afford to be lenient to this last annoyance—impotent ill-feeling."[30] Sheridan's definition of "leniency" simply was not President Johnson's.

17

FRONTIER COMMAND

THE grievous complexities of the Indian problem just after the Civil War ended and the "westward course of empire" began were never stated with more eloquence, simplicity and honesty than by Red Dog, a member of the Sioux delegation who appeared on the platform of Cooper Union early in June 1870—six years before part of the Sioux nation and the 7th Cavalry met on the banks of the Little Big Horn. For their tragic appeal to the good will and understanding of the white man, Red Dog, his chief Red Cloud and their companions cast off their barbaric paint and feathers and dressed in black clothes and tall Lincolnian hats. There was incongruity in their dress but so much dignity and solemnity in their bearing that not a titter came from their audience. Red Dog said:

". . . When the Great Spirit raised us, he raised us with good men for counselors, and he raised you with good men for counselors. But yours are all the time getting bad while ours remain good. These are my young men. I am their chief. Look among them and see if you can find any among them who are rich. They are poor because they are all honest. Whenever I call my young men together in council, they listen to what I say.

"When the Great Father first sent men out to our people, I was poor and thin. Now I am large and stout and fat. It is because so many liars have been sent out there—and I have been stuffed with their lies.

"I know all of you are men of sense and men of respect, and I therefore ask you confidently that when men are sent out to our country, they shall be righteous men and just men, and will not do us harm.

"I don't want any more men sent out there who are so poor that they think only of filling their pockets. We want those who will help to protect us on our reservations, and save us from those who are viciously disposed toward us."

Red Cloud's appeal was briefer but equally moving:

"You have children. So have we. We want to rear our children well and ask you to help us in doing so."[1]*

But their eloquence was wasted on an audience already sympathetic to the Indians and the tragedy of their displacement on the plains and mountains where they had roamed freely for centuries. The rest of the young, vigorous and expanding nation could hear only the call of rich new lands and limitless opportunity.

When Sheridan was ordered to take command of the Department of the Missouri in September 1867, he was somewhat better equipped to deal with Indians than he had been to rule Louisiana and Texas. He had learned something of Indian ways in the Pacific Northwest, although the Chinook tribes were quite different from the hardy Plains nations, and he firmly believed that the Indian "could be made to walk the white man's way," as the border people never tired of saying. His superiors believed him eminently better suited to pacifying Indians than ameliorating Southerners, and so he became one of four department commanders under General William T. Sherman, who commanded the Division of the Missouri.[2]

For many years the Indians of the Plains had been undergoing a gradual compression of their living space. They had been pushed across the Mississippi, then, during the Monroe Administration, had been settled "permanently" on a vast range of reservations west of the Arkansas, Missouri and Iowa borders. Nothing could have been

---

* Quoted from *The Wild Seventies* by Denis Tilden Lynch (copyright, 1941, D. Appleton-Century Co., Inc.). Used by permission of Appleton-Century-Crofts, Inc.

less permanent than that solemn promise of white man to Indian that he would have space in which to roam forever. Gold-rushers followed Mormon columns; ranchers, farmers, miners and railroad-construction gangs followed Mormons. The Indians began to resist these recurring invasions with all the fury of a proud race suddenly hemmed in by the locomotive, the barbed-wire fence, the telegraph line, and the blue-uniformed troops necessary to protect the civilized encroachments.

During the Civil War the Cheyenne and Arapaho were ordered to leave their hunting preserves in Colorado and settle down in the sandy wastes near Fort Lyon. The tribes went on the warpath and forced Coloradans to seek the protection of military posts. Governor John Evans called out the militia, which soon restored a measure of order. In the fall of 1864 two of the dissident chiefs, Black Kettle and White Antelope, surrendered with their 700 tribesmen at Fort Lyon, whose commandant promised they would be protected from the Colorado militia if they settled down along Sand Creek. The two chiefs accepted this pledge and built their lodges along the creek. On November 29, 900 militiamen under Colonel J. M. Chivington suddenly attacked the lodges, killed more than 100 men, women and children, and drove the rest into the mountains. Black Kettle was one of those who escaped the massacre and rejoined the outlaw tribes. To the South, the Comanche and the Kiowa had been harassing the border settlements before, during and after the Civil War, despite Federal attempts to conciliate them.

In 1867 public opinion demanded that the Government make a determined attempt to arrive at a general and peaceful settlement of the Indian problems. Congress appointed a peace commission including N. G. Taylor, the Commissioner of Indian Affairs, and General Sherman, who accepted with reluctance. At Fort Laramie the commissioners arrived at an agreement with Red Cloud and the Sioux, providing that the military would abandon the Powder River road and Forts Philip Kearny and C. F. Smith and that the Sioux, in return, would allow travel across the northern part of their country.

The commissioners then met with the Southern Plains Indians at Medicine Lodge and negotiated a more favorable settlement with the Cheyenne, the Arapaho, the Kiowa and the Comanche. The Federal representatives agreed that whites would not make their homes in most of the country between the Arkansas and Platte rivers; the Indians, that railroads to the Pacific would be built through their lands and that they would retire to reservations in the Indian Territory.

Both these treaties, as it turned out, looked much better on paper than they worked out in actuality. The trouble was, Sheridan observed, that many of the younger Indians were "bitterly opposed to what had been done, and claimed that most of the signatures had been obtained by misrepresentation and through proffers of certain annuities, and promises of arms and ammunition to be issued in the spring of 1868."[3] Not only that: white prospectors and ranchers failed to respect the treaties, even though the Indians had yielded up much in agreeing to them. The white encroachment continued, sometimes through purchase of land at extremely low prices, sometimes through bribery of chiefs, fraud or force.

Sheridan had had sufficient experience in the Northwest to understand how the whites dealt with the Indians. But he was a man of his times, and few but a handful of Eastern humanitarians much cared about the treatment of the Indians. Among military men, Generals Hazen and Howard were rare exceptions in the higher ranks. Sheridan shared the belief of his contemporaries that the Indian was a savage who did not deserve his fertile wilderness and would make no decent use of it. Yet with the years, as will be seen, his attitude became tempered with greater understanding of the Indians and their lost barbaric glory.

Shortly after assuming command of his department—which consisted of the states of Missouri and Kansas, Indian Territory and New Mexico—Sheridan took a long leave of absence. His first in years, it was necessitated by the hard campaigning in the field and three summers in New Orleans when cholera and yellow fever were epidemic. After a brief visit to his home in Somerset he journeyed to New York and indulged his growing enjoyment of that opulent, sometimes almost garish High Society which flourished in the postwar years.

Neither opulent nor garish, but highly cultivated in the antebellum fashion was one of his hosts, George Templeton Strong, eminent at the New York bar and now even more celebrated as the keeper of a pungent diary. Sheridan came to dinner at Strong's home with his aide, Colonel Crosby, "among the handsomest young men I ever saw." The diarist could not say the same for Sheridan:

The general is a stumpy, quadrangular little man, with a forehead of no promise and hair so short that it looks like a coat of black paint. But his eyes and mouth show force, and of all our chieftains he alone has displayed the capacity of handling men in actual shock of battle, turning defeat into victory, rallying a broken, fugitive mob and hurling them back upon the enemy.

Strong feared the dinner "would be a bore," but found Sheridan's conversation "pleasant." After dinner Sheridan, Crosby and two beautiful young guests, the Misses Minnie Vail and Fanny Smythe, gaily trooped off to a performance of *A Midsummer Night's Dream.*[4]

In March 1868 Sheridan returned to duty, journeying first to Fort Larned, then to Fort Dodge, to "find out for myself the actual state of feeling among the savages." The older tribesmen were fairly well satisfied with the Medicine Lodge treaty, which gave the Comanche and the Kiowa a reservation of 3,000,000 acres between the Red and Washita rivers, and the Cheyenne and Arapaho bands a 4,500,000-acre reservation to the north. All the tribes were to be accorded government rations of beef, flour, sugar and coffee. Later on teachers, farmers and blacksmiths, as well as seed for planting and farm implements with which to till the soil were to be supplied to aid them in the comparatively sedentary life to which the treaties committed them. But Ten Bears spoke for many of his tribesmen when he told the commissioners in a voice trembling with anger, "I was born upon the prairie, where the wind blew free and there was nothing to break the light of the sun. I want to die there and not within walls."

As always, Sheridan made up his own mind about the Indian problems. He listened to Indian agents, to the settlers, to officers with long experience on the Plains, and eventually to the Indians themselves. A delegation of Cheyenne and Arapaho followed him from Fort Larned to Fort Dodge, asking to speak to him about their grievances. Sheridan was determined to avoid a formal council with representatives of the various tribes, because he felt he could not interfere with agreements made by the Federal commissioners. Learning that the chief complaint was that the Indians had not received the promised annuities with which to buy food and that they were facing starvation, Sheridan finally received them at Fort Dodge. "I fed them pretty freely," he recalled, in hope that full bellies might keep them off the warpath. For the sake of hundreds of homesteaders entering his department and of the Indians themselves, he felt that he showed "my willingness to temporize a great deal."

Even while conciliating the tribesmen, however, he employed three scouts, William Comstock, Abner S. Grover and Richard Parr, to keep a close watch on them and report to Forts Wallace, Dodge and Larned. Their reports were correlated by Lieutenant F. W. Beecher, who was ordered to give General Sheridan every week a comprehensive summary of the movements and temper of the tribes. Sheridan hoped that the summer would pass peacefully, knowing that the Indians rarely went raiding after the prairies rustled with the first intimations of the north wind.

In July, however, came the first portents of trouble. The Cheyenne broke camp near Fort Dodge and moved off to the north of the Arkansas River instead of heading for their reservations south of it. The Indian War of 1868 flared up when these bands raided a settlement of friendly Kaw near Council Grove, then a white settlement near by. Meanwhile, the Kiowa and Comanche camped near Fort Larned and appealed to Colonel Alfred Sully for the government issue of rifles and ammunition which had been promised them. Sully allowed himself to be persuaded to turn over the guns and bullets, and a few days later they were being expended in the Saline and Solomon valleys, where the Comanche and Kiowa joined the Cheyenne in killing, raping and robbing the whites. "Indian diplomacy had overreached Sully's experience," Sheridan grimly commented.

The whole border was aflame that autumn. The four dissident

tribes could put 6,000 warriors in the field, while Sheridan's command totaled about 2,600. Of these, 1,200 were cavalry and 1,400 were infantry—the 7th and 10th Cavalry, the 3rd and 5th Infantry, and four companies of the 38th Infantry. Nevertheless, he laid down the principle: "Punishment must follow crime."

Obviously the punishment of Indians who preferred raiding to farming could not be carried out by fighting them their way. Until now Federal commanders had sent out punitive columns in hope of catching the miscreants and bringing them to battle, and almost invariably they had met only with humiliation. It was like chasing mosquitoes with a howitzer. Generals like Hancock with glittering reputations from Civil War campaigns were made to look utterly foolish by the "best light cavalry in the world," the Plains Indians.

General Sheridan had no intention of sacrificing his own hard-won reputation in such hopeless pursuits. So he planned a winter campaign. It had never been done before, and first mention of such an innovation brought cries of warning from veteran officers in the border garrisons. One expert, the old mountain man Jim Bridger, came out of his St. Louis retirement to journey to Fort Hays and attempt to dissuade Sheridan in person. But Sheridan reasoned that, "as the soldier was much better fed and clothed than the Indian, I had one great advantage, and that, in short, a successful campaign could be made if the operations of the different columns were energetically conducted."[5]

As always, Sheridan planned carefully and cautiously even for the most audacious movement. The Indian would be like a hibernating bear, lying in his winter camp, but he could be dangerous even in somnolence. The main column, which Sheridan would accompany, would consist of the 7th Cavalry under George A. Custer, an infantry battalion and the 19th Kansas Volunteer Cavalry to be mustered into Federal service under Colonel Samuel J. Crawford, the governor of Kansas. This column would strike for the headwaters of the Red River. Two other columns would march deep into Indian Territory, hopeful of catching the tribesmen when they were debilitated by the disease and hunger of winter.

Sheridan established his forward headquarters at Fort Hays and painstakingly gathered all possible intelligence concerning the winter camps of the hostiles. He authorized Colonel George A. Forsyth, long a member of his staff, to organize a company of 50 scouts (which nearly came to grief on the Arickaree fork of the Republican river).[6] Sheridan also began selecting scouts and guides to accompany the punitive expeditions. As chief scout for the main column he picked Ben Clark, who not only could speak Cheyenne but knew the character and customs of all the Plains tribes. Long after he had moved to Chicago as lieutenant general and to Washington as general of the army, Sheridan continued to telegraph Ben Clark whenever he wanted accurate information on Indian plans, moods and movements. General Hugh L. Scott, who served under Sheridan as a young officer, said Sheridan had a much stronger regard for scouts, guides and frontiersmen than most soldiers. Post commanders, observed Scott, "seldom knew about anything off their parade-ground and took little interest in the Indian."[7]* This was in direct contrast to Sheridan, who always wanted to know everything about the enemy or potential enemy. He even commissioned Clark to compile a dictionary and grammar of the Cheyenne tongue.

Another great favorite of Sheridan's was one William F. Cody, who became better known as Buffalo Bill. Debunkers have claimed Buffalo Bill's fame was largely manufactured by publicity agents, but they disregarded General Sheridan's testimony to his skill and daring, particularly as a dispatch bearer. During the autumn of 1868, when Sheridan recruited him, Cody carried an important dispatch from Fort Larned to Fort Hays, Sheridan's headquarters. Then he volunteered to continue to Fort Dodge immediately, and, after only a few hours rest, embarked on a journey of 160 miles through country abounding in Indians. From Dodge he rode back to Larned, from Larned to Hays again. In 60 hours, Sheridan recorded, Buffalo Bill covered 350 miles. On his second trip from Fort Larned, Cody brought Sheridan the information where the Cheyenne winter camps were located.[8]

---

* From *Some Memories of a Soldier* by Hugh L. Scott (copyright, 1928, The Century Company). This and other passages from the same book used by permission of Appleton-Century-Crofts, Inc.

Many officers on the frontier, unlike his favorite scouts and guides, failed to measure up to Sheridan's standards in activity, curiosity, interest in their duties, aggressiveness and leadership. Some had been spoiled by Civil War fame, some by the boredom of garrison life even on the wild frontier, some by heavy drinking. Men who had led corps against the Confederates—like A. J. Smith, XVI Corps, reduced to colonel commanding the 7th Cavalry—suddenly found themselves leading regiments; brigadiers were reduced to commanding battalions, and more than a few majors and captains who were not West Pointers had to accept noncommissioned rank. Mrs. Custer confided to her diary that many of her dinner partners were wine-addled before they rose, with some difficulty, from the table; and in her husband's letters there were a number of references to officers who had succumbed to delirium tremens even on the march. The officers, like their men, all too often could find surcease from the monotony of life in a prairie fort only at the bottom of a bottle.[9]

Before he began the winter campaign General Sheridan decided he must have Custer at the head of his leading column if the operation was to have the dash and impetus he demanded. Custer had been suspended from duty for one year after a court-martial had found him guilty of deserting his command in 1867 and other charges. On Sheridan's representations Custer was released from suspension and eagerly joined him at Fort Hays.

Although now only a lieutenant colonel of the 7th Cavalry, a disheartening comedown from division commander, Custer was quite unabashed by this and by his suspension. He did not hesitate to assert himself in offering immediate advice to his superior. He pointed out to the indulgent Sheridan that his brevet rank of major general made him superior to Lieutenant Colonel Alfred Sully, a brevet brigadier general, and Sheridan agreed.[10] All too often, through the succeeding years, Sheridan would thus uphold Custer, but it was not merely a matter of favoritism. Custer was one officer Sheridan felt he could rely on for quick and aggressive action, and one, too, it must be admitted, who would not quail at riding into an Indian village populated by women and children, as well as braves, to slaughter and burn and destroy with little regard for the humanities. "Punishment must follow crime" . . . and Custer must follow the marauder, his wife and children, brandishing fire and sword, armored in a furious self-righteousness.

Under leaden skies, on November 15, 1868, Sheridan and the main column left Fort Hays with 11 troops of the 7th Cavalry, five companies of infantry under Major John H. Page and two troops of the 19th Kansas Cavalry acting as Sheridan's escort. Colonel Sully already had established Camp Supply at the confluence of the Beaver and Wolf creeks as an advance base. There the column was to be met by the 19th Kansas, which had set out earlier from To-peka. Almost simultaneously the other columns, under Colonel A. W. Evans and Brigadier Eugene A. Carr, were starting from Forts Bascom and Lyon. The plan was that all three columns, converging in the heart of the Indian Territory, would drive the tribesmen before them and eventually transfix them on a three-headed spear.

The first night out, Sheridan had reason to remember the venerable Jim Bridger's words, "You can't hunt Indians on the Plains in the winter, for blizzards don't respect man or beast." A blizzard struck the column as it bedded down under tents, then a gale blew down the tents and would not permit them to be put up again. Blizzards, Sheridan found, also failed to respect major generals. He spent the night shivering under a wagon.

Sheridan had even studied meteorological records of border posts in gambling for fair weather during the early stages of the campaign—an unusual precaution for a frontier commander. He was beginning to see that war was becoming more of a science and less of an art every day. Still the column ran into another heavy snowstorm before it reached Camp Supply six days later. The Kansas volunteer regiment had not yet arrived but, the tracks of a war party having been noted in the valley of Beaver Creek, leading from the Washita where the dissident villages were believed to be located, immediate action was decided on. Custer was directed to follow the war party's tracks. Three days later Colonel Crawford and the Kansans arrived at Camp Supply.

The Kansans, mostly beardless boy volunteers, noted approvingly that General Sheridan was "quite jovial and does not put on much style." Pomposity, too often the accretion of fame, never afflicted him; he was always simple, often affable and always approachable. He did not set himself above or even aside from his troops, and he never ceased to remark on how necessary it was for an officer to share the hardships as well as the dangers of his men. The Kansans saw that he mingled with them on equal terms, and they thought none the less of him for it. Moreover, he "camped in a tent when the weather was fair or foul, marching at our head in snow and rain, enduring all the hardships of wind and weather."[11]

Custer's command, 700 troopers, followed the tracks of the Cheyenne war party for four days. Just before dawn of November 27 they looked down into the valley of the Washita, where Black Kettle's Cheyenne and some Arapaho had established their winter village in a cottonwood grove. According to DeB. Randolph Keim of the New York *Herald*, who accompanied the Sheridan expedition, Sheridan's instructions to Custer had been brutally simple: "Proceed south in the direction of the Antelope Hills, thence toward the Washita river, the supposed winter seat of the hostile tribes; destroy their villages and ponies; kill or hang all warriors and bring back all women and children."[12]

Custer decided to attack at dawn, with his command split into four columns which were to make concentric attacks on the sleeping village. He made no effort to ascertain whether Black Kettle's village—he was the Black Kettle who had lost many of his tribe in Colonel Chivington's infamous attack at Sand Creek—had been guilty of raiding the Kansas border. What followed was scarcely more creditable than Chivington's slaughter in Colorado. Troopers converged on the village as the regimental band struck up the stirring "Garry Owen." Carbines rattled in the shattered stillness of the winter dawn. Black Kettle was shot to death at the door of his lodge. Braves, squaws, papooses were slaughtered as they attempted to flee. Before the carbines stopped their deadly chatter, 103 warriors and an unreported number of women and children were killed, and 53 women and children were captured.[13] In Custer's command only two officers and nine enlisted men had been killed and 14 wounded in the attack on the village.

But the tragedy—and disgrace—of the "battle" of Washita was not yet ended. Despite the surprise, hundreds of Indians had managed to escape downriver through a gap between two squadrons. Young Major Joel H. Elliott, leading one of Custer's squadrons, saw the Indians in flight, shouted, "Here goes for a brevet or a coffin," and spurred after them with 19 troopers following him. While Elliott rode off to his inglorious destiny, Custer and the rest of his command shot most of the 875 captured Indian ponies, destroyed mounds of Indian property (including such items as 700 pounds of tobacco, more than a thousand furs, various weapons) and conducted an inventory of the booty.

It was growing late. Mounted warriors were gathering on bluffs overlooking the village. Lieutenant E. S. Godfrey, Troop K, rode back from reconnaissance with alarming information. The valley was swarming with Indians! The country downriver was dotted with villages. Also Lieutenant Godfrey had heard firing from the direction in which Major Elliott had gone in pursuit. The gunfire continued for some time, but Colonel Custer made no effort to investigate it or find Elliott. He hurriedly ordered the village burned as surrounding Indian war parties began closing in. In his official report Custer claimed that he sent scouts out looking for the missing Elliott and his troopers. At any rate, he withdrew the regiment, still almost 700 strong, and left Elliott and his men to their fate.[14] Never again, it was said, did Custer have the entire confidence or respect of the 7th Cavalry.

The greatly admired and highly competent Captain Frederick W. Benteen of that regiment wrote a bitter account of the Washita affair for a St. Louis newspaper, which concluded:

But surely some search will be made for our missing comrades. No, they are forgotten. Over them and the poor ponies, the wolves will hold high carnival, and their howlings will be their only requiem. Slowly trudging, we return to our train, some twenty miles away, and with bold exulting hearts learn from one another how many dead Indians have been seen. . . .[15]

For all his regard for Custer, General Sheridan was too much of a soldier to let the Washita affair pass by on Custer's rather insufficient explanation that he had been "forced" to leave the burning village without determining what had happened to Elliott. Writing of it a score of years after, and even then restraining his doubts about his subordinate's conduct out of loyalty to Custer's widow, Sheridan commented:

There was no definite information as to the [Elliott] detachment, and Custer was able to report nothing more than that he had not seen Elliott since just before the fight began. His theory was, however, that Elliott and his men had strayed off on account of having no guide, and would ultimately come in all right to Camp Supply or make their way back to Fort Dodge; a very unsatisfactory view of the matter, but . . . it was . . . altogether too late to make any search for him.[16]

With the whole column, including the 19th Kansas, dismounted because most of its horses had perished on the march from Topeka, Sheridan then moved down the Washita toward the battleground and in the direction of the Wichita Mountains, hoping to catch up with the fleeing Indians. Two miles south of Black Kettle's village he and his officers found the mutilated bodies of Elliott and his troopers lying in a circle where they had fought to the last cartridge: a grisly tableau to be reproduced in greater detail eight years hence with Custer himself re-enacting the tragic and foolish role young Elliott had played. Custer lost forever the wholehearted trust of his commander, although their personal friendship continued, on the December afternoon when Sheridan looked down at the bodies of Elliott and his troopers.

It was a rigorous winter campaign, ending at Fort Cobb, but the aftermath was just as bitter as the winter nights under canvas whipped by winds and snowstorms. The destruction of Black Kettle's village brought an outcry of protest in the East. Sheridan was impelled to assure General Sherman that fears of "anticipated massacre" were groundless. But he aggressively defended his belief that wild Indians should be adequately clothed and fed on reservations, that they should be more than adequately guarded, and that those who spent their summers in war parties must be quickly and sternly punished. To this, Indian Agent Wynkoop, former guardian of the Cheyenne, replied, "A few thousand dollars for subsistence for these starving Indians at the proper time would have saved millions to the treasury, saved many white men's lives, saved the necessity of hunting down and destroying innocent Indians for the faults of the guilty." Yet there was no doubt that Black Kettle's village and that of his neighbors on the Washita harbored many raiders. A white woman and her child were found on the banks of the Washita, murdered after the attack on the village; and in the lodges were found household furnishings and other possessions looted by braves who had raided the Saline and Solomon valleys that summer.[17]

Sheridan's service on the frontier soon assumed a much wider character. While he was preparing for the winter campaign in November 1868, Ulysses S. Grant was elected President of the United States. Long before his inauguration Grant planned to give Sheridan increased rank and authority, and this determination was not altered by protests against the harshness of the Washita campaign. Both Grant and Sheridan saw a parallel between the Indian problem—police action, it would probably be called today—and the Civil War. The quicker resistance ended, they believed, the less bloodshed and suffering there would be.

Generals Meade and Thomas each believed he was entitled to the lieutenant general's rank and command of the Military Division of the Missouri, which would be vacated when Sherman was promoted to Grant's place as General of the Army. Each was grievously disappointed when it was refused him, though it was refused with as much tact as possible. Grant believed that only Sheridan could take care of the Indians and the complexities of the whole advancing frontier with the firmness required.

One night before the inauguration Grant summoned Thomas to his home and asked him how he would like to take over the Military Division of the Pacific. "As for myself," Thomas replied, "I would have no objection to serving there, but on Mrs. Thomas' account I would not want to take her any farther away from her friends in the East."

Mrs. Grant, hoping to ease her husband's embarrassment with a facetious remark, told Thomas, "Your having a wife is one reason you should go there instead of Sheridan, as he ought to stay here, where he can get one."[18] It was to be a half-dozen years, however, before Sheridan pleased his friends—and himself, immensely—by taking a wife.

He was riding in an ambulance just outside Fort Hays when a courier brought the dispatch from Washington announcing that Sherman now commanded the army, he the frontier. That meant, of course, that he would be much farther removed from the scenes of action, anchored behind a desk in Chicago except for inspection trips. He would not again come so close to an Indian fight as he had been to the attack on Black Kettle's village. Lieutenant generals do not lead cavalry charges. But his life would always be active.

Activity in the gay summer of 1869, for Sheridan, was largely social. President Grant and his lively family went to Long Branch, New Jersey, the most fashionable of the nation's watering places. They invited Sheridan to join them, perhaps in furtherance of Mrs. Grant's design to see him well and safely married. Mrs. Custer, whose charm was at least as potent as hers, had not yet brought this about, and Mrs. Grant was to fail just as notably. Bachelorhood suited him, and like most Irishmen, he was expert at evading matchmakers.

Sheridan and the Grants stayed at the Stetson House. The President kept a pair of fast-stepping bays in a near-by stable and delighted in dashing down the country roads and showing off his horsemanship. Grant needed cheering, Sheridan could see, for he had recently been saddened by the death of General Rawlins, who had devoted life and health to him ever since the beginning of the Civil War. Reporters for the New York newspapers who swarmed over the resort noted that there was little to do except drink, play billiards and attend the frequent balls. All three of these pursuits were undertaken energetically by Phil Sheridan. Excellent beaches gleamed white in the sun, but few paid much attention to them. Young ladies liked to dress in elaborate bathing costumes, pose prettily at a safe distance from the water and scream daintily for the protection of strong men when a breaker came plunging toward the shore.

Both Grant and Sheridan were lionized, the latter submitting to flattery and blandishment without the slightest show of resistance.

One night Sheridan, who "cut quite a swath" on the dance floor, according to the society reporter of the New York *World*, inveigled the President onto the floor. The dance about to be played was the Lancers. "Please join us, General," Sheridan said, "out of honor to the cavalry."

"Well, if you put it that way, Sheridan . . ."

But Grant, who could keep the movement of a score of divisions in his head, soon became lost in the convolutions of the intricate dance and was "a sorry figure." He walked off the floor, glowering at the man who had coaxed him into such humiliation and who was whirling about as intrepidly as he had ever appeared on the battlefield.[19]

On the frontier which Sheridan commanded, the situation was comparatively quiet for the next year or two. In the spring of 1870, as he set out on an inspection tour of the military installations in northern Utah and Montana, there were rumors of war in Europe. Prussia, having conquered Austria in 1866, was at the point of collision with France, whose Napoleon III had the grandiose ambition if not the talent of the Prussian Count Bismarck. In Helena, Montana, Sheridan received dispatches indicating war would break out in a matter of days. He cut short his journey and returned to Chicago. At the age of thirty-nine, holding the nation's second highest military post, he was still eager and capable of learning. Prussia and France were the two great military powers of the Continent, and it was possible that observing such a mighty clash would prove educational to a professional soldier. The Prussians, it was known, had learned the importance of a great railway net from their own observers in the American Civil War. It would be interesting to see how they adapted those lessons.

Sheridan immediately obtained Grant's permission to go to Europe as the United States Army observer. The President was again at Long Branch for the summer, and Sheridan stopped off to confer with him. Grant wanted to know to which army Sheridan pre-

ferred to attach himself, and was pleased that his choice was the
Prussian. Sheridan was certain the Prussians would win. Both
hoped to see the defeat of Napoleon III, whom they regarded as
a charlatan and still detested for his intervention in Mexico.[20] Sheridan was accompanied abroad by James W. Forsyth, his former
aide-de-camp and friend of long standing.

The general was in a characteristic hurry to reach the battle lines.
He spent only one day in England, and in Belgium he sent his re-
grets that he would not be able to pay a courtesy call on the queen,
although it had already been arranged by the American minister.
Reports that a great battle was to be fought in the vicinity of
Gravelotte sent him rushing in that direction with the eagerness
of an old fire horse smelling smoke. In their haste he and Forsyth
abandoned all dignity and rode a hay wagon into the Prussian headquarters town of Pont-à-Mousson, the armies of the North German Confederation having already crossed the border.

The evening of his arrival, August 17, 1870, Sheridan presented
himself to William I; Count Bismarck, the chancellor of Prussia;
Albrecht von Roon, the war minister, and General Helmuth von
Moltke, the chief of staff and a very able soldier. It was the eve of
battle, but these punctilious gentlemen gravely debated what it
would be proper for Sheridan to wear as he followed the German
armies. Undress-uniform-minus-sword, it was decided.

Sheridan wrote at length to Grant, to Sherman and in his memoirs of his experiences and observations in the Franco-Prussian War,
but they were quite well summed up in a letter to the President
sent from Rheims on September 13: "I have seen much of great
interest, and especially have been able to observe the difference
between European battles and those of our own country. I have
not found the difference very great, but that difference is to the
credit of our country."[21]

The American observer made a very favorable impression on
the German military and political leaders, particularly Bismarck,
the only one who could speak English. Bismarck often asked Sheridan anxiously which side of the conflict was favored by American
public opinion.[22]

Von Moltke had characterized the American Civil War as a contest between "armed mobs," but Sheridan witnessed a number of blunders on both sides that greatly reduced his respect for Continental generalship. At Gravelotte he saw thousands of German cavalrymen fall in a senseless charge against French infantry posted along a sunken road commanding a ravine. It had all the brave stupidity of Burnside's attacks on Fredericksburg. Hearing German artillery officers boast about the murderous efficiency of their Krupp guns, he went forward several times after a position had been carried to examine the ground and found that the effect of the barrage had been negligible. The German infantry was superbly trained and obediently advanced into terrific fire, but without spirit, almost like automatons.

There was no doubt, however, of the forcefulness of the German leadership. Sheridan saw Bismarck himself cast aside the dignity of the chancellorship, leap out of his carriage with a revolver in hand and clear a village street blocked with baggage wagons. "It is the only way to get through," he explained ruefully. On the Chalons road, when the Uhlans streamed back from their senseless attack on the sunken road, he watched King William, who was in his seventies, "berating a throng of fugitives in German so energetic as to remind me forcibly of the 'Dutch' swearing that I used to hear in my boyhood in Ohio."

In the rarefied atmosphere of the Prussian high command Sheridan, with his fame as a cavalry leader and Indian fighter, got along on comradely terms with Bismarck and Von Moltke. One morning, after they had slept on the floor of a French farmhouse, the Chancellor's nephew scrounged two eggs from a farmer, Sheridan bought four bologna sausages from the German version of a sutler's wagon, and Count Bismarck located coffee and brandy to top off the breakfast.

His opinion of the French, after watching them submit to a hopeless siege at Metz and allow themselves to be outfought and outgeneraled on almost every field, was anything but favorable. The soldier in the ranks fought with courage occasionally, when well led, but was likely to take to his heels if the leadership was poor. And it was mostly poor, especially at the higher levels, where "stupendous errors" were committed. As for Napoleon III, who gave himself up to King William after Bazaine was bottled up at Metz and MacMahon surrendered at Sedan, he behaved with the poltroonery which Sheridan had expected of him.

After watching the German armies close in on Paris for the long siege and inevitable capitulation, Sheridan decided he had had enough of war. With Forsyth at his side—it was probably a pity that Mark Twain was not his companion—he "paid his respects" without undue humility to a number of the crowned heads of Europe. The courts of Belgium, Austria, Italy, Greece and Turkey all were visited and extended their hospitality to the jaunty little American general who had helped to win some vague intramural fight with his countrymen back in the sixties and who—this was of greater interest—was engaged in subduing the wild red Indians in the Western wilderness.

It was Turkey and her exotic customs that aroused Sheridan's greatest curiosity and Constantinople delighted him above other European capitals. The Grand Vizier rode out to the Esplanade with him and they watched the various ladies of the Sultan's harem take their afternoon airing in their carriages. "Every now and then," Sheridan noted, "an occupant, unable or unwilling to repress her natural promptings, would indulge in a mild flirtation, making overtures by casting demure side-glances, throwing us coquettish kisses, or waving strings of amber beads with significant gestures, seeming to say: 'Why don't you follow?' But this we could not do if we would, for the Esplanade throughout its entire length was lined with soldiers, put there to guard the harem. . . ."[23] Sheridan always remembered the Grand Vizier with much gratitude for allowing him—very informally—to review the Sultan's harem. That certainly was something to talk about out west when he lounged around a bivouac fire with his officers and the time came for storytelling!

18

HEADQUARTERS CHICAGO

GENERAL SHERIDAN returned to Chicago from his European tour just in time to preside over the Great Chicago Fire of 1871 with his usual vigor and his congenital disdain for the feelings of politicians. It developed that he could not even assume the role of fire fighter without becoming involved in a rancorous controversy.

At ten o'clock on the night of October 7 a fire broke out on South Clinton Street, just north of Van Buren, and destroyed four blocks of dwellings, mostly two-story lodging houses. The next night, a Sunday, flames again turned the skies over Chicago a livid smoky scarlet. This time the fire raged for days. The second fire, it was generally agreed, started in a cow barn at the rear of the home of Patrick O'Leary on DeKoven street. Whether Mrs. O'Leary's cow really kicked over the lantern and thus deserved to become the most notorious bovine in history has never been established to the satisfaction of serious historians.

By the time General Sheridan went downtown at midnight of October 8 the flames had surrounded his headquarters at Washington and LaSalle and he was forced to set up a temporary command post near the lake front. There he saw for himself how panic infected even the steadiest of men. A friend of his, a prominent physician noted for courage and coolness in an emergency, arrived at Sheridan's new headquarters in a buggy to volunteer his services. The doctor had left his home believing he had saved his most valuable possessions, but all he had carried away was an empty picture frame and a coal scuttle.

A mass meeting on the evening of October 9 passed resolutions begging that regular troops be brought to Chicago to preserve order. Sheridan soon had infantry arriving on trains from Omaha, Leavenworth and Louisville.

One of his patrols encountered a drunken and violent citizen who not only defied them but attempted to assault them. The man was shot and killed. Later an attempt was made to have Sheridan, the mayor and other officials indicted for murder by the Cook County Grand Jury. The indictment was quashed, but Sheridan was exposed later to other evidence that gratitude is a short-lived emotion.[1]

A powerful wind swept the flames to the north and northeast. "Conley's Patch," a brawling Irish slum, went up like a scrap of celluloid. Everything north of Van Buren was turned into a charcoal kiln except for a few brick chimneys and walls left standing. Two editors of the Chicago *Tribune* described how rich and poor alike were seized by panic as the flames chewed their way through the wooden city:

Mobs of men and women rushed wildly from street to street, screaming, gesticulating, and shouting . . . intercepting each other as if just escaped from a madhouse. . . . Elegant ladies, who had hardly supposed themselves able to lift the weight of a pincushion, astonished themselves by dragging trunks through the streets. . . . Barrels of liquor were rolled from saloons, and men and boys staggered about the streets. Hordes of thieves entered the stores. . . .[2]

The heat of the flames was so intense that it was felt at Holland, Michigan, 100 miles across the lake. In 27 hours, 17,450 buildings were destroyed, including most of the railroad stations and public buildings, 1,600 stores, 60 factories, 28 hotels. Among the buildings that went up in smoke was that which harbored the Military Division of the Missouri, Sheridan's headquarters, and all of its files went with it.[3] A third of the population was homeless. Perhaps another third was drunk. Looters seemed to spring out of the sidewalks.

The fire was brought completely under control by October 12, by which time 250 dead were counted and the property loss ran to $200,000,000. The quick assistance of the Army as ordered by General Sheridan and approved by Secretary of War W. W. Bel-

knap aroused a political controversy, the raking up of state rights
and the waving of the "bloody shirt." This partisan conflagration
began roaring almost as soon as the real embers cooled.

While the emergency existed and everyone turned to him for
help and advice, General Sheridan was in his glory. It was like a
flaming big battle—trying tc save Chicago, blowing up blocks of
buildings as one would throw in a counterattack to save a threatened portion of a battle line, watching the fire burn itself out in a
tapering salient near the suburb of Lake View and the Lake Michigan shore. At such an exciting time, engrossed in orders to his
soldiers, the city firemen and the volunteers, Sheridan couldn't always remember to be tactful. When he learned that one of the few
hotel owners whose establishment was undamaged had raised his
rates from $2.50 a day to $6.00, he summarily turned out the
proprietor, installed one of his orderlies as manager and dropped
the rates to their prefire level. His troops patrolled the city with
fixed bayonets, routed gangs of hoodlums, broke up organized looting, restored order as quickly as possible. Out of Army stores he
turned over 7,000 blankets to the Chicago Relief and Aid Society,
set up 800 tents for the homeless and distributed 100,000 rations.

Mayor Mason had requested the Army's aid without having time
to consult the governor of Illinois. The governor, John M. Palmer,
was an old comrade in arms of General Sheridan's, a retired major
general of volunteers who had commanded a division alongside him
at Stone's River and Chickamauga. For all that, the governor was
mortally offended. He alleged that the mayor should have called
on the state militia to preserve order, that Sheridan had violated the
rights of Illinois by ordering his troops into action. Palmer, although elected on the Republican ticket in 1868, had been denounced as a renegade for adopting the Southern view of state
rights. He charged Sheridan also with unconstitutional acts in organizing a "special posse." So here was a great political blaze with
the politically innocent Sheridan at its hot center.[4]

Palmer took the matter to the state supreme court. The citizens
of Chicago, grateful to Sheridan for seeing to their shelter, nourishment and protection, rallied to his support. He received thousands
of letters of thanks and many resolutions of gratitude from vari-

ous civic organizations. Roscoe Conkling, the New York political leader—or misleader, in the opinion of many—offered to defend him "should legal proceedings be set on foot against you." On November 13 Sheridan replied to Conkling, "The attempt made by Governor Palmer to annoy me was criminally malicious and has aroused the indignation of all citizens." He also thanked Secretary of War Belknap for his support and "your kind indorsement of my conduct during and after the fire."[5] But the Illinois supreme court upheld Palmer.

Feuding between former comrades was very common for several decades after the Civil War. Indeed, after every war there are a scramble for laurel, a battle of memoirs, a long guerrilla conflict among various generals over credit for various victories and blame for various defeats. Governor Palmer had his particular grievance against the military hierarchy formed by Grant, Sherman and Sheridan.

Shortly after the capture of Atlanta, Palmer, a corps commander in the Army of the Cumberland, asked for reassignment because Sherman insisted that he take orders from General Schofield, commanding the Army of the Ohio. In Palmer's view, Schofield was junior in rank. Like many volunteer officers, Palmer was convinced that West Pointers had a "trade-union" attitude that worked against civilian soldiers. This long-cherished grudge may have caused his eruption over Sheridan's use of Federal troops during the Chicago fire; it was too intemperate to be grounded merely in a hair-splitting concern over state rights.

Since they had an unhappy effect on the postwar Army in which Sheridan was a leading figure until his death, and since Sheridan was involved in several feuds himself, the internecine disputes of Union generals may be worthy of brief consideration. Mark Twain, who knew General Grant and a number of other Civil War leaders quite well, was amazed at the utter frankness with which they discussed one another.

Grant himself, although he tried to rise above bickering, was distinctly unfriendly toward Joe Hooker, whom he regarded as a fourflusher. He was inclined to deprecate the great talents of George H. Thomas, whom he almost relieved just before the victory at Nashville. And his relations with General Sherman did not have quite that Damon-and-Pythias quality which idolatrous biographers have attributed to them. When Sherman's memoirs were published and Grant heard that they reflected on him, as well as on other generals, he flew into a rage and was not mollified until he read the volumes himself and was satisfied that Sherman had done no material damage to his reputation.

In letters from Sherman to William E. Church, editor of the influential *Army and Navy Journal*, which have just been unsealed, he revealed his strong distrust of the men around Grant and even of Grant personally. In one, written after he had been persuaded to transfer his headquarters from St. Louis to Washington, he told Church he was trying to avoid quarreling with Grant. "My conscience tells me that when we come to balance accounts, he will find himself largely my debtor," Sherman wrote. "I sometimes chafe under a sense of wrong that he may have enticed me to Washington to rid himself of a house in a bad neighborhood at an exorbitant price. . . . My faith in his friendship is shaken, and when again he wants it, it may be less than he supposes."[6] Like many honest men, Sherman was saddened and embittered by the grafters and spoilsmen with whom Grant surrounded himself after he became President. To Church, shortly after Grant's death, he wrote:

. . . General Grant was not a saint, he was *very* human and therefore the more acceptable to the great mass of people—at times he had about him and was influenced by men not of the highest order of ability or virtue, and his faith in "his" boys was something beautiful to contemplate, though it involved his ruin and actually his death.[7]

The main reason for estrangement between Grant and Sherman, it was obvious, was Grant's attachment to some shady characters in his immediate circle. One of the shadier was Secretary of War W. W. Belknap, who was forced to resign when his wife was exposed as a peddler of post-trading franchises in the West. Another was Colonel Orville E. Babcock of Grant's wartime staff, later his secretary and confidential representative, who was indicted as a member of the St. Louis "whisky ring" for "conspiracy to defraud the revenue." Grant used his Presidential influence to have Babcock acquitted and then appointed him inspector of lighthouses. The vice of avarice, reaching into his personal and political families, touched the character of Grant himself. General Richard Taylor, after an interview with Grant in 1872, said the President "knew to the last shilling the various sums voted to the Duke of Wellington" and accepted various gifts without a thought of looking for attached strings.[8] Senator Hoar said of him that "selfish and ambitious men" wangled their way into his favor and "studied Grant as the shoemaker measures the foot of his customer."[9]

Sheridan's bitterest enemies, of course, were General Warren, removed during the Appomattox campaign, and Averell, relieved in the Valley. In 1869, when Sheridan was on his way to Long Branch as the President's guest, he met Averell in a hotel lobby, shook hands and murmured some perfunctory greeting. Next day he received a note from Averell, stiff as an invitation to pistols at dawn, reminding that he had ended Averell's military career by removing him from command of his cavalry division after Fisher's Hill. It read:

Your proffered courtesy at an unexpected meeting today surprised me but it being in a public place . . . I was determined to await some more fitting occasion to make a proper statement of my sentiments. . . . I was the victim of a grievous wrong and cannot permit you to entertain the impression I am willing to resume friendly intercourse with you. . . .[10]

Warren was still demanding a court of inquiry into the justice of his removal as commander of the V Corps, but would have to wait until the Hayes Administration before it was granted.

Crook secretly but heartily had it in for Sheridan, believing he had been slighted when the laurel was distributed for the victories of Winchester and Fisher's Hill. (The fact Crook was caught by surprise at Cedar Creek but not censured by Sheridan, he conveniently ignored).

Sheridan and William B. Hazen were often at odds; they still argued over who captured what guns at the crest of Missionary Ridge, and Hazen, in addition, was a leading advocate of a softer policy toward the Indians.

Sheridan never forgot his treatment by General Curtis during the Pea Ridge campaign, when he was a staff captain and was relieved for preventing some of Curtis' favorites from large-scale horse stealing. ("No authority can compel me to jayhawk or steal," said Sheridan.[11])

With Grant and Sherman his relations were always cordial but never intimate. He was able to speak frankly to his immediate superiors, as he had during the war when he disagreed with them. When General Sherman moved his headquarters to St. Louis—because he preferred that city to the boiling intrigues of the capital—Sheridan lectured him sternly:

You will shake the confidence of the people and the Army in the stability and steadiness which they have always attached to your character. You bring a condition on the Army which will ruin it forever, by establishing a precedent which places its General in Chief in retirement for all time to come. You endanger its very existence by putting its command in the hands of the Secretary of War, whose office lasts for only four years. . . . Are you, as head of the Army, at liberty to break us down because you have been or may be subjected to annoyance in Washington?[12]

A perfect confidence and a close-to-perfect understanding on professional matters existed between Grant and Sheridan. There was never a discernible moment of conflict between them. But Sheridan held himself carefully aloof from the political and economic intrigues of the Grant Administration, which were as malignant as any in American history. No one ever suggested that Sheridan was involved in any of the scandals that tarred Grant's Presidency. His life was so uncomplicated that all of his check stubs and bank deposit books may be found in the Sheridan Papers.

Among the livelier disputes of Union generals still unresolved a half-dozen years after the war was that involving Fitz John Porter, who had been accused by John Pope—now one of Sheridan's department commanders—of being unco-operative at Second Bull Run and had been cashiered.[13] General Hooker detested virtually every general officer in the army, with the exception of Thomas, and had a special hate for Grant, Sherman, McClellan, Burnside, Howard and Slocum, the latter two being corps commanders whom he blamed for the defeat at Chancellorsville. Sherman and John A. Logan, now an Illinois senator who had served as a corps commander under him in the Atlanta campaign, had been unfriendly ever since Sherman gave command of the Army of the Tennessee to Howard, a West Pointer. After publication of his memoirs Sherman also was forced to defend himself against the former officers and partisans of Thomas, McPherson, Schofield and other associates who claimed that he had damaged their idols in burnishing his own reputation. Friends of Thomas and Meade claimed that both men died of broken hearts because they had not been made lieutenant generals along with Sheridan. Actually Thomas suffered a stroke in San Francisco (where he commanded the Military Division of the Pacific) while composing a wrathful answer to a letter in a New York newspaper which asserted that Schofield was the architect of victory at Nashville; Thomas was certain that Schofield had written the letter. Gordon Granger had good reason to hate Grant, who had relegated him to obscure commands in New Mexico, despite the national fame he won by marching to Thomas' aid at Chickamauga. Halleck was cordially detested by almost all the higher-ranking officers who had served under or with him in the Civil War, particularly Grant, Sherman, Pope, Hooker and McClellan. Meade couldn't forgive the vainglorious Sickles for his mistakes at Gettysburg. Ben Butler and Baldy Smith couldn't stand the sight of each other after the thorough botch they made of the Army of the James. James H. Wilson and George A. Custer rarely mentioned each other without a sneer. As late as 1879 General Stanley faced a court-martial on a charge of conduct unbecoming an officer for having accused General Hazen of cowardice during the battle of Stone's River.

All this is only a sampling of personal animosities arising from the Civil War. At lower levels they multiplied in number and virulence. As head of a military division Sheridan had to be as careful in selecting officers for various garrisons and commands as the hostess of a Washington dinner party compiling her guest list. How could he expect efficiency if, for instance, he assigned one of Fitz John Porter's ex-officers to serve under Pope at Fort Leavenworth, or if he put Hazen and Stanley in the same regiment?

During the last years of his lively bachelorhood, however, he did not devote too much time to brooding over such matters. He had become one of the lions of Chicago, out dining and dancing almost every night he was in the city, although he had scant facilities for repaying social obligations. He lived in a "plain though comfortable house" on Michigan Boulevard, with an elderly Negro woman as his housekeeper, until he moved into the Palmer House, which was a sort of headquarters for Army officers going to and from their Western commands. His brother, Captain Michael V. Sheridan, usually lived with him, since he too was a bachelor, was a member of the general's staff (and had been since the Tullahoma campaign) and was congenial with his older brother. Mike, in fact, was the only member of his family with whom General Sheridan was on intimate terms. After his father died, his mother, brothers and sisters stayed on in Somerset. A dozen years younger than Phil, Mike had more of his spirit and venturesome qualities than the rest of the family, and they were virtually inseparable until the day Phil died.

Rich living agreed with Sheridan's temperament but not his figure. A sharp-tongued friend commented that Phil now looked, from a side view, like "a low comedy man." He had become rotund. General Crook commented on "his bloated little carcass." His hair started to gray fast in his early forties. Officers who had not seen him for years could see little resemblance between this Sheridan, who looked like an unsuccessful dry-goods merchant, and the young Sheridan of the Civil War campaigns, gaily reaping the whirlwind, riding toward Cedar Creek and rallying his broken divisions. Longer acquaintance showed them, however, that the essential ramrod inside the man was neither rusted nor bent. He was still tough, flexible and capable of lightning flashes of thought or activity. There simply was no longer much call on the man of action.

Brother Mike said that even a lieutenant general's salary was not sufficient to keep Phil far above the level of solvency. "He could not save—at least he did not—for if he had money in hand he gave it and spent it freely." Any old soldier loitering around his headquarters with a hard-luck story was assured of a handout, even if the general had to borrow from a companion.[14]

When social life of increasing elegance enticed Sheridan soon after he became famous as cavalry commander of the Army of the Potomac, he refused to affect any pomposity or peacock airs. He was still unobtrusive whenever possible. Once he and a party of friends went trout fishing in Wisconsin. An elderly farmer heard that Phil Sheridan was in the party. He asked Sheridan to point out the great cavalryman. Sheridan identified himself, but the farmer protested, "I don't believe it! How could a little man with such a low voice as yourn command a big army?"[15]

His only business venture was undertaken in partnership with General Crook and several other men. They combined to reopen the old Murchie mine in Nevada City, Nevada, which had yielded up to $17 a ton back in the fifties. The partners kept sinking new shafts because of a "tantalizing vein of quartz," but their hopes were never fully realized. The venture was finally abandoned after its last year's profit of $15,000 was used to pay off debts but failed to provide a dividend.[16]

Sheridan always went west with eagerness and quickening enthusiasm, although not always with Spartan simplicity. One summer he took an ultrafashionable hunting party out on the Great Plains, composed of young men of New York's "fastest society set," including James Gordon Bennett, son of the founder of the New York *Herald*. Most of them he had met at Long Branch when a guest of the Grants.[17] The young gentlemen did not suffer too much discomfort in their forays against the buffalo. In their train were 16 wagons to haul tents and supplies, two to carry ice for the wine. Whenever a buffalo was killed the whole party paused to open champagne and toast its slayer. Buffalo Bill Cody came along, dressed in a white buckskin suit and a scarlet shirt, to act as guide and make certain that plenty of buffalo were killed. He also taught Sheridan's society friends—the general was already acquainted with the custom—to take a shot of bourbon before breakfast in the Western manner. "It's better than brushing your teeth," Cody explained.[18]

In the fall of 1871, after he had finished fire fighting and skirmishing with Governor Palmer, Sheridan was asked by General Sherman to take out another hunting party, this one with Grand Duke Alexis of Russia as the guest of honor. The recent American purchase of Alaska had brought Russian-American relations to their most felicitous phase in history, and the United States was eager to show its appreciation of the bargain by entertaining the young duke on a magnificent scale.

Sheridan, planning the hunt with all the care he gave to a military campaign, enlisted the resources of the Military Division of the Missouri to assure the success of the royal hunt. He directed General Pope, the new commander of the Department of Missouri, to locate the Southern bison herd and report its movements daily, as if it were a menacing war party of Indians. Colonel Forsyth was ordered to take charge of mess arrangements and hire the best available chef to provide the kind of menu to which a ducal stomach had become accustomed. He assigned Brigadier General Innis N. Palmer to take charge of the party itself. Colonel Custer and Buffalo Bill were invited to join. Major General E. O. C. Ord was to turn Omaha Barracks into a supply depot. Spotted Tail and his Sioux band were persuaded to come along and provide local color. Sheridan was so preoccupied with all these preparations that he was forced to refuse an invitation to attend a banquet for the Grand Duke on January 8, 1872, at St. Louis.

Alexis was especially pleased by the thought that Spotted Tail would be in the party. But, he asked Sheridan, what would be a suitable gift to Indian royalty? Perhaps he had in mind a handful of jewels or an odd scepter he happened to be carrying in his baggage. Sheridan assured him that four pairs of red blankets would suit Spotted Tail perfectly.[19]

On July 10 Sheridan met the Grand Duke at the North Platte railroad station in Chicago and conducted the entourage westward. At Denver the party paused to await word from Army scouts on the exact location of the buffalo. A formal ball was in progress when Sheridan received a telegram saying the herd had been located in Kit Carson County, Colorado. Forthwith cavalry horses were loaded on the special train. The grand duke's companions bade their dancing partners farewell and set out in the middle of the night. On January 14 Sheridan was able to inform Secretary of War Belknap, "The Grand Duke killed his first buffalo today in a manner which elicited the admiration of the party with me."

Sheridan and Chalkley Beeson, a musician at the Denver ball who had dropped his fiddle and come along, watched the hunt from a ridge near where the train was halted. Beeson told how a wounded calf cut off from the stampeding herd dashed toward them. "Catch the little fellow by the tail and I'll put him out of his misery," Sheridan ordered the musician. Beeson caught the young buffalo and held him until Sheridan came puffing up and shot him with his pistol.

Years later Beeson, who became the leader of a famous cowboy band, met Sheridan at a gathering in Chicago and listened to the general tell of the ducal expedition. "I, too, was on that hunt," Beeson remarked.

Sheridan turned to him, cocking his head. "I don't remember you," he said.

"You should!" Beeson retorted. "I'm the man who held the buffalo by the tail while you killed it."[20]

The night of the successful hunt was made more memorable for the Grand Duke and his friends by an elaborate fete arranged by General Sheridan. Chinese lanterns were hung in near-by trees. The whole crowd, including Spotted Tail and his braves, sat down to a sumptuous dinner. Champagne was served to all. The after-dinner speeches were orotund. Possibly emboldened by the rare wine, Spotted Tail suggested in his address that Sheridan would become an even greater chief if he allowed the Sioux to hunt south of the Platte River until their farms on the reservation were producing a livelihood.

Often when he dealt with Indians, particularly if they had been behaving well of late, Sheridan dispensed blarney with all the skill supposedly imparted by his ancestry. This night he replied to Spotted Tail with the courtly deference he accorded the Grand Duke himself.

"I am very glad to see Spotted Tail here," he said. "I have great respect for him, because he has faithfully fulfilled his treaty obligations. . . . I appreciate the force and justice of his requests. . . . So long as we are at peace with each other I see no objection to his people hunting buffalo south of the river Platte."[21]

Hobnobbing with royalty and the young bucks of New York society was a very rare distraction for Sheridan from the affairs of his vast command. He gave eager audience to any officers, scouts and other informed persons passing through Chicago to or from the West. General Hugh Scott, when a young lieutenant, was flattered by the attention shown him by General Sheridan.

He saw me in an arm-chair against the wall in the lobby, came and sat down by me, tipped his chair back against the wall, and talked to me for an hour about conditions in the Northwest. I had all the Indian gossip of the Plains—what Sitting Bull was thinking about—which the General could get from nobody else except Ben Clark. When he called me "Scott," placing me on a conversational level with himself, I swelled up with pride so that Chicago could scarcely hold me. Both Sheridan and his brother always asked me to dinner whenever I passed through Chicago, and I never appealed to either of them for help in vain. The General left me to go to the barber shop, and a scion of a prominent Philadelphia family, whom I had known when he was in college at Princeton, came up and asked me who had been talking to me. I replied, "General Sheridan." When he asked where he had gone, I said, "To the barber shop," and about an hour afterward I met him again and he told me he had bought the razor with which the General had been shaved.[22]

Sheridan followed the affairs of every post in his command with diligence and interest, even in minor matters seemingly beneath the notice of a lieutenant general. When he heard that Spotted Tail and his Sioux band were going to visit Fort McPherson he cautioned General Ord, commanding the post, that such visits "always give rise to troubles. . . . It leads to trouble with the Indians, Indian

Agents and Traders. . . . The women mix with the soldiers, quarrels and shooting may take place. . . ."[23]

Sheridan clung to his unsentimental approach to the Indian problem, but he began to see that its solution was more complex than a swordlike swish of the pronouncement, "Punishment must follow crime." To General Sherman he wrote:

There is no one more desirous to avoid trouble with the Indians than I am and there is no one who has a deeper sympathy and desire to see their condition bettered by the effects of civilization and Christianity, but . . . we should not forget that in dealing with Indians, we are dealing with a shrewd sharp people, and that if we believe their falsehoods from a desire to maintain friendly relations with them we do not advance the general object which we have in view.

The next day he complained to the general in chief about the legal aspects of administering the frontier command:

We have had so much trouble on the subject of whiskey selling on the frontier as to make every officer timid, even when acting in strict obedience to orders on the subject. We do not fully know what Indian Territory is, except in the case of defined Indian reservations, and there has been no authoritative decision that I am aware of on the subject. The territories occasionally claim civil jurisdiction over all ground not embraced in military or Indian reservations, and occasionally we find ourselves exercising authority in violation of this claim. In fact the whole subject is in a very unsatisfactory condition and needs illuminating by some competent authority.[24]

In a more sardonic mood, while addressing a joint session of the Texas state legislature in 1875, he opposed calling a halt to the slaughter of buffalo on the Southern Plains. Instead, he advocated giving each buffalo hunter a medal with a dead buffalo engraved on one side and a "discouraged-looking Indian" on the other. Referring to the white hunters, he told the legislators:

Those men have done more in the last two years and will do more in the next year to settle the Indian question than the entire regular army has done in the last thirty years. They are destroying the Indians' commissary; and it is a well known fact that an army losing its base of supplies is placed at a great disadvantage. Send them powder and lead if you will, and for the sake of peace let them kill, skin, and sell until they have exterminated the buffalo. Then your prairies will be covered with speckled cattle and the festive cowboy, who follows the hunter as a second forerunner of civilization.[25]

Legend has credited—or discredited—Sheridan with the hard-boiled slogan, "The only good Indian is a dead Indian." This, of course, was an old frontier expression coined long before Sheridan came on the scene, and his brother specifically denied that the general ever uttered it to his knowledge, let alone invented it, no matter how much it sounds like one of Sheridan's blunt interpretations of policy.[26]

Sheridan realized that much of the Indian trouble was stirred up by whites: renegades who ran guns and whisky to the tribes, "squaw men" who tried to become more Indian than the Indians, ultrasoft-headed administrators of the Indian Bureau who protected the unregenerate terrorist as well as the tribesman willing to try peaceful pursuits. He apparently approved the ideas in an editorial of the Omaha *Republican* in answer to a speech by Wendell Phillips, the old Abolitionist, who had asked for a softer policy toward the Indians.

Let good, sound, practical, honest men, without consideration of sectarian prejudices, be deputed to look after [the Indian's] general welfare, protect him from the squaw men and other ruffians . . . but no subsidies, no donatives to appease the wrath of "Young-Man-Afraid-of-His-Mother-in-Law" or "Old Variegated Caudal Appendage," no ponies, no tobacco, no whiskey, no improved breech-loading rifles to shoot down our defenseless women and children.[27]

Sheridan pasted the editorial in his scrapbook.

Along the Texas frontier there was a continual killing and burning out of settlers by Kiowa and Comanche raiders. Sheridan wrote Sherman:

. . . I will agree to put a stop to all murders and thefts in Texas if the Government will give me the necessary authority to use the troops and will sustain me while in the execution of this duty. [This was in regard to the complaint of Indian Agent Lawrie Tatum that his Indians were straying off the reservation and committing various crimes.] I have the interest of the Indian at heart as much as anyone and sympathize with his fading out race but . . . it is not only necessary to put him on Reservations but it is also necessary to exercise some strong authority over him. . . .[28]

The appearance of professional buffalo hunters, who were quickly killing off the Indians' principal food supply, caused the more warlike tribes, the Comanche, the Cheyenne, the Apache, the Arapaho and the Kiowa, to pass the war pipe and attack the Kansas, Colorado and Texas frontiers. Sheridan reiterated to the commanding general his promise that, if given complete military control of the reservations and of the pursuit of Indians who strayed off them, he would "close up all Indian troubles forever" within 18 months. Again the cavalry columns probed into badlands where no white man was safe unless he was accompanied by a number of well-armed comrades, preferably with the support of a few howitzers and Gatling guns.[29]

In converging movements similar to the Washita campaign five years before, Federal columns marched into the country of the north fork of the Red River and the Antelope hills. Fourteen pitched battles were fought, the most important one on the Staked Plains. The Indians were followed night and day, their camps attacked, their food destroyed, their pony herds shot up. By November 1874 Sheridan was able to suggest that the campaign could be slackened; band after band of formerly belligerent Indians had returned to their reservations. Because Indians who had not joined the war parties feared for their lives if the raiders were not punished, he recommended that a military commission be convened at Fort Sill to try leaders of the dissident bands. Seventy-five of them were found guilty and sent to Florida for imprisonment. The power of the Southern Plains Indians was effectively crushed.[30]

Sheridan felt no deep qualms about the passing of the Indians' freedom to roam the plains as they had for centuries. As he saw it, and as millions of his countrymen saw it, a barbaric era was being obliterated—with as much humanity as he considered justified—and an agrarian civilization was taking its place. The howling wilderness was being transformed into a vast and fertile stretch of farmlands and settled by millions on ground which once supported only a few thousand savages; towns and cities thrived where once there were only the wickiups of nomadic hunters and warriors. Never in any of his writings, or in any conversation as far as can be determined, did Sheridan reveal a feeling that the Indians were being treated with undue harshness. His conscience was clear.

Early in 1875, after the Southern Plains tribes had been pacified, the untactful leaders of the Grant Administration decided to send Sheridan back to the scene of an earlier failure—Louisiana and its seething political situation. If there was one man in the North completely ineligible to effect a cooling off of political passions at New Orleans, that man was Phil Sheridan. But he was the choice of President Grant and Secretary of War Belknap, presumably because he could be trusted to deal with the fuming Louisianians in true cavalry style, show the still-unreconstructed that the North was not yet ready to forgive all. There was a great deal of mystery thrown around his mission to New Orleans. He was to communicate in cipher only—before codes were in general use, even on the military telegraph—and only with the Secretary of War.[31] His superior, General Sherman, never in sympathy with extreme measures of governing the South, was not taken into confidence; he had once been superintendent of a Louisiana military academy, and, despite his severe treatment of Georgia during the war, he had a nostalgic memory of that service which was never effaced by the bitter necessities of war.

A confidential order detaching Sheridan for the Louisiana mission specified that it was not to "be recorded unless action is taken under it" and referred vaguely to "the inspection and investigation the Secretary of War has directed you to make." Less vaguely

Sheridan was told: "If . . . you should find it necessary to assume command over the Military Division of the South, the President of the United States hereby authorizes and instructs you to take the command accordingly."[32] Grant and his advisers decided on stern measures after the election of November 2, 1874, showed unexpected strength in the Democratic vote. Both the Democrats and the Radical Republicans claimed a number of seats in the state legislature and various state offices. So Sheridan was to take a firm grip on affairs in Louisiana and see to it that Radical Republican interests were protected, functioning more as a somewhat biased policeman than as an officer of the United States Army. General Sherman, although Sheridan's superior, wrote: "Neither the President nor Secretary of War ever consulted me about Louisiana affairs. Sheridan received his orders direct from the Secretary of War. . . . I have tried to save our army and officers from dirty work imposed upon them . . . and may thereby have incurred the suspicion of the President."[33]

Sheridan arrived in New Orleans, jaunty and undismayed by the absence of its traditional hospitality. Indeed, his mere presence was regarded as an affront. The *Picayune* greeted him with the statement, "If there is one man more responsible than another for the misfortunes of Louisiana, that man is General Phil Sheridan." The *Times* remarked acidly that, "as a soother of political difficulties and corrector of political abuses, he is anything but a success."[34] Representative George F. Hoar, Attorney General in the Johnson Administration and presently chairman of the Congressional committee investigating the Louisiana election, was a guest at the Charles Hotel, where General Sheridan and his party also stayed. "When [Sheridan] came into the crowded breakfast-room," Hoar recalled, "there were loud hisses and groans from nearly the whole assembled company. The morning papers teemed with abusive articles. The guests would take these papers, underscore some specially savage attack, and tell the waiter to take it to General Sheridan. . . ." If, knowing his peppery temper, they expected an invitation to a duel, they were roundly disappointed, for, according to Hoar, "the general would glance at it with an unruffled face, and bow and smile toward the sender."

For all his wider experience of the world since his first appearance in New Orleans, Sheridan was still the bluff soldier. The night before Representative Hoar left for Washington the general called on him to say good-by. Hoar wrote:

I was much amused by the simplicity and naïveté with which he discussed the situation. He said, among other things: "What you want to do, Mr. Hoar, when you get back to Washington, is to suspend the what-do-you-call-it." He meant, of course, the *habeas corpus*. He knew there was some uncomfortable thing which stood in his way of promptly suppressing the crimes in Louisiana, where he said more men had been murdered for their political opinions than were slain in the Mexican War.[35]

Federal troops, bayonets fixed, stamped into the state legislature to seat Radical Republicans forcibly, and the Democrats withdrew to sit in a rump session elsewhere. Sheridan, in a communication to Grant which will never live in history as a glorious example of constitutional government, proposed that the protesting Democrats be outlawed as "banditti." "No further action need be taken except that which would devolve upon me." In the South the reaction to this proposal was bitter enough to cause newspapers to call for an armed uprising. In the North, now swinging away from any continued waving of the "bloody shirt," there were mass meetings denouncing "government by the bayonet." Samuel Bowles in his Springfield *Republican* condemned President Grant for sending soldiers on a "revolutionary, treasonable errand." At a mass meeting in the Cooper Union, New York, William Cullen Bryant shouted that Sheridan should "tear off his epaulets and break his sword and fling the fragments into the Potomac, rather than go upon so impious an errand."[36]

Undeterred by such adverse sentiments even in the North, Sheridan went on to send troops to keep the carpetbag government of Mississippi in power behind a hedgehog of Federal bayonets.

At first, as Senator Hoar observed, Sheridan maintained a smiling composure, no matter how bitter the tirades against him in the press or to his face. "Though constantly followed by a hostile crowd, he walked about as if oblivious of its presence and ate his meals as if deaf." He made a point of eating all his meals in public, although it would have spared him much embarrassment if he had taken them in his rooms. Caricatures of him labeled "the extravagant tele-graphist" appeared in all the shopwindows along Canal Street.[37] An Atlanta paper called for Judge Lynch: "It is just possible that a braggart and dirty tool of an upstart like Sheridan may ornament a lamppost."[38] United States Senator Bayard thundered the question, "Who shall say he [Sheridan] is even fit to breathe the air of a Republican government?" on the floor of Congress. A member of the House of Representatives indignantly read him out of the Celtic race: "He has disgraced the name of Ireland. . . . I believe that all liberty-loving sons of Erin will disown him and brand him traitor to the sacred cause of liberty." The New Orleans *Times* abandoned him with heavy irony: "We presume that any attempt to influence General Sheridan by any rational argument would be as futile as the effort to make a Maori chieftain understand the binomial theorem."[39]

For a time he was sustained by such messages from Grant as that of January 6: "The President and the Cabinet confide in your wisdom and rest in the belief that all acts of yours have been and will be judicious."[40] It was just as well for Sheridan, isolated in hostile New Orleans, that he did not know Grant was somewhat inaccurate in describing the sentiment of his Cabinet and that several members were in decided disagreement with the President.

But Sheridan's poise was disturbed by such incidents as his meeting with an old friend, Colonel Palfrey, who had attended West Point with him. Palfrey had served on General Lee's staff during the war.

Sheridan saw him walking along Canal Street and approached him with a smile and outstretched hand. "Hello, Mouse," Sheridan said, using Palfrey's West Point nickname.

"Mouse" belied his nickname, stared at Sheridan belligerently, then stalked away without a word.[41]

An indication of the tension mounting in Sheridan was observed by his friend Lawrence Barrett, the famous actor, who brought his company to New Orleans for a production of *Richelieu* at the New

Varieties Theater. He invited Sheridan to attend and reserved a box for him.

In Act II, with a bravura flourish, Barrett as Richelieu read the line, "Take away the sword; States can be saved without it!" The house, immediately reading a topical parallel, burst into applause and cheers.

When the curtain fell on Act II, Sheridan hurried backstage and, with "a round oath," demanded of Barrett in his dressing room, "Why did you put that into the play?"

Barrett patiently explained that he had only read the line as it had been written many years before, and no insult had been intended.[42]

In the end all the humiliations, the tensions and the abuse of his mission were in vain. Grant was advised against allowing Sheridan to proceed against those whom he proclaimed "banditti." But Grant had more confidence than ever in Sheridan's ability as a proconsul, civil as well as military, although in the civil sphere it was certainly misplaced. The President told Hoar, when he reported on Louisiana affairs in a meeting at the Capitol:

I believe General Sheridan has no superior as a general, either living or dead, and perhaps not an equal. People think he is only capable of leading an army in battle, or to do a particular thing he is told to do. But I mean all the qualities of a commander which enable him to direct as large a territory as any two nations can cover in a war. He has judgment, prudence, foresight, and power to deal with the dispositions needed in a great war. I entertained this opinion of him before he became generally known in the late war.[43]

Less biased observers than Grant have conceded that widespread violence might have burst forth in Louisiana and possibly Mississippi, had it not been for Sheridan's heavy-handed actions and suggestions. Even so dispassionate a critic of the Grant administrations and the Reconstruction period as Professor William B. Hesseltine has granted that Sheridan's "harsh suggestions" were "perhaps the most efficient means of dealing with the Louisiana troubles." He goes on to say:

So far as Louisiana was concerned, Sheridan's assumption of command served to prevent violence. Louisiana had tested his hard rule in the days of its military government, and Democrats refrained from violence while he remained in the city. Insult and imprecation dogged his footsteps, and political murders continued, but the general kept his temper during the abuse, and no Democrat dared make an effort to overthrow the Kellogg government.[44]

Admittedly Sheridan was ill-suited to diplomatic or political missions, but it must be conceded that his "strong medicine" approach to such problems sometimes had a beneficial effect. A continuation of violence in Louisiana and a possible triumph of Ku Klux Klan methods could not have contributed anything but evil to the history of post-Civil War America.

With all the South and much of the North clamoring against him as he returned to the comparative serenity of division headquarters at Chicago, where he had only wild Indians to deal with, General Sheridan could rejoice in the esteem, not only of his President, but of a young lady who had been a member of his mission to Louisiana. She was Miss Irene Rucker, the youngest daughter of General Daniel H. Rucker, quartermaster general of the Division of the Missouri.

Sheridan and the winsome Miss Rucker had met at an army wedding the preceding spring. She was described as "young, beautiful, bright and accomplished, blonde and vivacious." The moment Sheridan caught sight of her in bridesmaid's white he took decisive action. She was only twenty-two years old, and Sheridan was forty-four, but she was an "army brat," born at old Fort Union in 1853, and the general was confident that marriage would work out splendidly for both of them.

Still, it would do no harm to make the auspices as romantic as possible. When the Administration directed him to proceed to New Orleans he coaxed Miss Rucker to accompany his party in order to "give it the appearance of a pleasure trip." There would be adequate chaperonage, since his brother Mike and his wife, who had been married a short time before, would be going along. Several months after their return from New Orleans a Chicago newspaper told the result with a succinct headline:

GREAT CAVALRY LEADER VANQUISHED BY A BLONDE

It was announced that General Sheridan and Miss Rucker would be married June 3, 1875, at the home of her father.[45]

General Crook, who apparently had expected something more flamboyant of Sheridan, described the wedding and reception as "a rather quiet affair." Only members of the family and a number of Sheridan's closest associates were present—Sherman, Pope, Terry, Ord, Perry, Van Vliet, Augur and Whipple—all except General Sherman subordinates in his military division. The reception was held in the back yard of the Rucker home, and ice cream rather than the flowing bowl was the principal item of refreshment.[46]

Sheridan entered domesticity with as much or more enthusiasm as he had shown for bachelor gaiety. Balls, dinner parties, barrooms and other social gathering places saw little of him from that time forward. A frequent visitor at the Sheridan home said that Mrs. Sheridan, when she first took over as hostess for her husband at necessary receptions, "was surprised at the silly remarks made by some of the women and decided that she would think before she spoke, and if she had nothing to say she would remain silent." For a "vivacious blonde" this was undoubtedly a strenuous course in self-discipline, and a splendid tribute to her loving determination to become the admirable wife of a distinguished man. From all accounts she was a devoted wife and mother. Four children were born to the Sheridans—Mary, the eldest; Irene and Louise, the twins; and Philip Henry Jr. They were described as "bright, intelligent and well-bred."[47]

The attachment between General Sheridan and his young wife was strong and enduring. Through the years, whenever Mrs. Sheridan was off visiting her brothers at Army posts or the general was inspecting his Western garrisons, they telegraphed each other daily, reporting the health and antics of their children and confiding in each other as intimately as possible over the impersonal wires. Sheridan to Mrs. Sheridan, at Fort Leavenworth: "Children all very well. Philip especially all right. It is trying to snow here this morning." . . . "The children all very well. They were down at the music store this morning." . . . "The children very well. They think you have gone to church."[48]

19

LAST STAND OF THE SIOUX

FOR the first time in their lives General Sheridan and Colonel Custer found themselves seriously at odds. Gratuitously, it seemed to Sheridan, Custer had appeared before the Congressional committee that was gathering evidence for the impeachment of Secretary of War W. W. Belknap. Already a ruined man, Belknap was accused of selling post traderships through his beautiful but greedy wife, and his impeachment was rendered unnecessary by his subsequent resignation.

Custer testified that the Fort Lincoln post trader (formerly known as the sutler) was a member of Belknap's ring, that 8,000 sacks of corn had been sold to the Government twice—first to the Indian Bureau, then to the military. The impetuous cavalryman's testimony splattered President Grant and his family as well as his administration, for Custer stated that Grant's brother Orvil was involved in the sale of traderships. Custer's testimony was subsequently proved to be based on hearsay, and most of it was discredited. The damage was done, however, and the enraged President Grant ordered that Custer stay in Washington even though the 7th Cavalry rode out under another commander.

The regiment was about to take the field in General Terry's column from Fort Lincoln. With Crook's column from Fort Fetterman and Gibbon's from Fort Ellis, Terry was to join in the Sheridan-designed attack on the Sioux warring under two of their greatest leaders, Sitting Bull and Crazy Horse. It was the greatest concentration of Indian fighting power ever seen on the Plains.

The Sioux had been outraged by the invasion of gold seekers in their old hunting grounds in the Black Hills. That untrammeled region, which had been ceded to the Sioux under the treaty of 1868, was invaded in the summer of 1874 by a column commanded by Colonel Custer. Geologists attached to his expedition confirmed a widespread belief that the Black Hills were veined with high-grade gold ore. And the rush was on, although the army did its best to keep out the prospectors. Civil courts freed the interlopers as quickly as they were arrested by the army.

Another cause of the Northern Plains Indians' growing desperation was the terrific slaughter of the buffalo herds by white hunters. "Once the buffalo, around whose existence the whole economy of the Indian was based, was killed off the nomads had nothing to do but submit to government control and become Agency Indians, degraded, whiskey-crazed, beaten," wrote one of Custer's troopers.[1]

Sheridan was well aware that white settlers, prospectors, gun runners, whisky sellers and corrupt bureaucrats were preying on the Indians and inviting a violent reaction. His indignation at these injustices—although he believed that the displacement of the wild Indian was just and inevitable—could hardly have been matched by the Eastern humanitarians who believed Sheridan was a sort of Cossack hetman who delighted in hounding and exterminating the tribesmen. According to his brother Mike, the general's attitude was this:

The Indians had been placed on reservations under treaties the significance of which they did not fully comprehend, and, instead of being properly protected, were shamefully robbed by corrupt agents, preyed upon by a sordid class of frontiersman, and often treated as public enemies entitled to scant consideration. No well-defined policy had been laid down by the government for the discipline and control of these savages, and no statutes had been provided for their punishment or protection. . . . Appreciating the necessity of an effective legal code, Sheridan time and time again recommended enactments, not only for the punishment of marauding whites, who were constantly encroaching on Indian lands, but for the restraint of the Indians and the punishment of their criminals, the laws to be executed at the agencies by authorized courts. His efforts in this direction were vain, however, Congress simply voting meager annuities, and leaving the solution of the problem of Indian civilization to time and circumstance.[2]

On the occasion of a later Indian rebellion—the long and almost incredible trek of Chief Joseph and his people 1,500 miles from Idaho to the valley of Snake Creek south of the Canadian border—Sheridan was equally blunt in ascribing most of the blame to maladministration of Indian affairs. "Congressional appropriations, already meager to the starvation point, were so mismanaged and diverted by corrupt agents, in collusion with equally corrupt traders and contracts, that the Indians were driven to fight in very desperation."[3] Partly because of Sheridan's tireless campaign by mail and telegraph, Congress was persuaded to reform its methods of dealing with the Indians, but it would not yield to the Army's suggestion that control of the tribes be vested in the military rather than in the Interior Department.

But reform did not come in time to prevent the Sioux's last stand in the high plains of Montana. For two years, as Sheridan had been informed by his scouts and other frontier sources, the Northern Plains tribes had been gathering their strength for a tremendous counterblow at the infiltration of their most prized roaming places.[4] The expedition under Terry, Crook and Gibbon was designed to prevent such a disaster befalling the border settlements.

Although under orders to stay in Washington, with Grant rejecting all his appeals and refusing to grant him an interview, Colonel Custer in despair proceeded to Chicago. Hadn't Sheridan saved him before? Hadn't Sheridan protected him from official onslaughts almost as great as Grant's wrath? He had not stopped to consider that Grant was Sheridan's greatest benefactor and one of his closest friends.

At Sheridan's headquarters Custer stared across his commander's desk at a man whose hard leathery face bore no heartening traces of their friendship. There is no stenographic account of their conversation, but its general tone was this:

"All I ask," Custer declaimed, "is the chance to take the field with my regiment. I'll show 'em. The 7th can lick any force the

Indians can throw into the field, all the Indians on the Plains, if necessary!"

Sheridan's dark eyes glittered with a cold anger, and his words cut like a saber. "Somebody else will command the 7th Cavalry, Custer. The President has directed that you remain in Washington, although you've seen fit to disobey even that order."

"I want the chance to take the field again," Custer pleaded, abject in his fear that the 7th would ride out under another commander. "You've got to give me the opportunity of squaring myself."

"I don't *have* to do anything. Grant has turned his face from you, Custer. You went too damned far. And there's nothing I can do for you."

The desperate Custer journeyed on to St. Paul, the department headquarters, where General Terry was touched by his pleas and gave favorable endorsement to another appeal from Custer to Grant for reinstatement. Sheridan appended this comment to Custer's message forwarded through military channels to the White House:

The following dispatch from General Terry is respectfully forwarded. I am sorry Lieutenant-Colonel Custer did not manifest as much interest in staying at his post to organize and get ready his regiment and the expedition as he now does to accompany it. On a previous occasion, in 1868, I asked executive clemency to enable him to accompany his regiment against the Indians and I sincerely hope that if granted this time, it may have sufficient effect to prevent him from again attempting to throw discredit upon his profession and his brother officers.

General Sherman added his endorsement, and Grant finally relented. This was the opening act in the military tragedy popularly known as Custer's Last Stand.

In June 1876 the three columns were on the move to crush all resistance from the Sioux, who were to be caught between the millstones formed by Terry and Custer coming from the East, Crook from the South and Gibbon from the North. On June 22 Custer managed to detach himself and his regiment from Terry's command; the 7th Cavalry was to follow the trail of a Sioux band up the Rosebud and over to the Little Big Horn, with orders not to bring on a general engagement until Terry could bring up the balance of the column.[5]

Instead, when he sighted the vast Sioux encampment on the grassy bank of the Little Big Horn on June 25 he decided to attack at once. As at the Washita eight years before, he divided his command. Major Reno was ordered to take three troops and descend on the southern end of the Sioux camp, while he himself led five troops to charge down upon the northern side. Captain Benteen was left to protect the pack train with three troops.

Reno attacked as ordered, was quickly overwhelmed by the swarming Sioux warriors and pulled back to the bluffs, where he was soon joined by Benteen. They managed to hold out until Terry came to their rescue. Up the Little Big Horn death and silence shrouded forever exactly what happened to Custer and the 225 men of his command.[6] The five troops, their commander, a newspaper correspondent taken along contrary to orders, even the horses, except for Captain Keogh's badly wounded charger Comanche, were all slaughtered that afternoon by the circling thousands of Sioux warriors. George Armstrong Custer had pursued glory all his life and now found it in death. The public generally acclaimed him a hero, although military men could not forget how Custer had abandoned young Elliott at the Washita, how he had treated Terry without respect, let alone gratitude, how he had disobeyed his orders and attacked the Sioux without determining how strong they were, unnecessarily causing the destruction of his entire command,[7] and how he had always been willing to sacrifice anything and anyone to the greater splendor of himself. Such is glory—sometimes.

The news of the massacre on the Little Big Horn reached General Sheridan in Philadelphia as he conferred there with General Sherman. It was a confidential dispatch from Terry to the War Department, but a newspaperman obtained a copy of it by pretending to be a messenger.

The nation, unprepared for such a disaster, was appalled. The casualty list was nothing compared to that of a minor engagement

in the Civil War, but the fact that Custer's troops were wiped out
to a man seemed to increase the horror of the battle and encourage
its passage into the realm of legend. Throughout the land there
was an outcry for vengeance. Even unreconstructed Southerners
were eager to join in hunting down Sitting Bull, Crazy Horse and
their followers. The Confederate General Jo Shelby, who had been
bitter enough at the end of the war to join the Confederate colony
in Mexico but had since repatriated himself, wrote the President:
"General Custer has been killed. We once fought him, but now
propose to avenge him. Should you determine to call volunteers,
allow Missouri to raise 1,000."[8] General Sheridan, however, believed it was "premature" to call out volunteers. The Regular
Army could handle the Indians if given adequate financing by
Congress and the authority to use whatever measures necessary to
get the Sioux back on the reservations and keep them there.

To General Sherman, who had returned to Washington, Sheridan wrote:

We are all right; give us a little time. I deeply deplore the loss of
Custer and his men. I feel it was an unnecessary sacrifice, due to
misapprehension and a superabundance of courage—the latter extraordinarily developed in Custer. . . . If Congress will give the
$200,000 which I have asked for for the past two years for the
establishing of posts at Tongue river and the mouth of the Big
Horn, it will be in the interest of economy and will settle the Sioux
question.[9]

Sheridan studied the reports of Terry, Crook and Gibbon and
questioned—by letter and in person—other officers who participated
in the campaign. His conclusion was that the tragedy of the Little
Big Horn had been caused largely by Custer's bravado, his faulty
tactics and his failure to determine just how strong the Sioux and
their allies were before he plunged into their midst. Many times
Sheridan had defended Custer; at least once he had saved his career.
He still had not forgotten the rawboned youth who served him so
valiantly in the Civil War campaigns. He knew that Custer would
not have led the 7th Cavalry at the Little Big Horn if he had not

consistently been Custer's patron and friend. In a sense Custer had been a weapon which Sheridan had not discarded quickly enough, before his usefulness had come to its appointed end. In all conscience, even to defend his previous sponsorship of Custer—and all the responsibility it entailed—Sheridan could not take up the cry of the Custer partisans that Reno and Benteen had deserted their chief, that, although fighting off thousands of Sioux themselves, they had cravenly failed to cut their way through to him and his surrounded battalion.

In his report to Sherman of November 25, 1876, Sheridan wrote:

Had the 7th Cavalry been kept together, it is my belief it would have been able to handle the Indians on the Little Big Horn, and under any circumstances it could have at least defended itself; but, separated as it was into three distinct detachments, the Indians had largely the advantage, in addition to their overwhelming numbers.

The massacre of Custer and his command, and its attendant problems, occupied much of Sheridan's time and thought for the next year. One troublesome echo of the battle was that Major Reno was widely condemned for not having pushed on to succor Custer and his dismissal from the army demanded. Immediately after the remnants of the 7th Cavalry had been rescued by Terry, Reno wrote Sheridan:

Strong as they were I believe the 7th Cavalry would have whipped them, properly handled. . . . If I could stand them off with half the Regiment, should not the whole whip them? I think Custer was deceived as to the number of Indians and that he did not give that consideration to the plan of campaign that the subject demanded. He went in hastily and with his usual hurrahs.[10]

A court of inquiry finally cleared Reno in 1879, but disgrace dogged him to his death several years later.

Conscious of his own domestic happiness, Sheridan's heart was touched by scores of letters from the widows of the men who had died on the Little Big Horn—the most touching, perhaps, from Mrs. Custer, whose love for her husband was certainly as fine an element of his life as any victory he won in warfare. She wrote Mike Sheridan two weeks after learning of the massacre:

Oh how good General Sheridan has been to me in his determination to carry out this plan of sending to the battlefield! How much I would like to thank him! I am afraid to do so for fear I will only be bringing to his mind the sorrowful side of our worldly existence.[11]

The dead had been hurriedly buried in shallow graves on the field where they fell, but Sheridan had promised they would be reinterred, if their families wished, far from the scene of their barbaric death. Black-bordered letters give pitiful directions.

A Maine woman wrote, "To think that his body was never recognized and is not even buried is the worst of torture." One of the slain officers was Lieutenant J. J. Crittenden, the son of Major General Thomas L. Crittenden, who had commanded a corps in the Army of the Cumberland at Perryville, Stone's River and Chickamauga. General Crittenden requested that his son's body be buried "where he fell."[12]

On his western inspection tour of 1877, part of which was undertaken in company with General Sherman, Sheridan superintended the removal of the bodies. Custer's was sent to West Point for burial, and Mrs. Custer thanked the general for seeing to it that "the sacred dust of General Custer will repose in civilized lands."[13] General Sheridan bitterly protested to the publisher of the Chicago *Tribune* a story by its correspondent with the Sheridan party that "the bodies were roughly handled and that remains of General Custer and Colonel Tom Custer were not identified but only guessed at." He asked that "on behalf of the bereaved relatives of these officers you will be kind enough to make such a wholesale denial of these stories as will forever set at rest the imaginations of such of your correspondents as desire to earn a few pennies by telegraphing to you sensational stuff on this subject."[14]

In reconnoitering the valleys of the Big Horn and the Yellowstone, Sheridan recorded that peace had descended on the places where so short a time before thousands of bristling Sioux had erected their lodges and wickiups. "The valley of the Little Horn, at this season, was almost a continuous meadow, with grass nearby high enough to tie the tops from each side across a horse's back. This was the country of the buffalo and the hostile Sioux only last year. There are no signs of either now; but in their places we found prospectors, immigrants and tramps."[15] A zoölogist with the Sherman-Sheridan party found a new species of butterfly flitting through the Big Horn mountains and named it for the man who commanded this wilderness rapidly being made safe for all men as well as butterflies—the Thecla Sheridani. It still flutters high above the Great Plains, the one permanent memorial, perhaps, to the fame of Phil Sheridan.[16]

Sheridan was authorized by the Government to order his officers to take over the Sioux agencies and arrest, disarm or dismount the incoming warriors and their families as they believed best. Sitting Bull and some of his followers escaped over the boundary into Canada,[17] but vigorous campaigning by Crook, Terry, Gibbon and Miles soon destroyed the resistance of most of the Northern Plains tribesmen. Two years after the death of Custer there were warnings of another Indian uprising on the prairies. Sheridan wrote Sherman, "I see enough to satisfy me that it is not the Government which is managing the Indians, it is the contractors, traders and supply interests." These men were responsible, he charged, for moving "Red Cloud and Spotted-Tail back from the Missouri River, [and] organizing the dodge for the Arapahoes to join the Shoshones, which enables them to live in their own country so they could profit from trade with the tribes." Sheridan warned the War Department that "they will all be one again on the Powder River" and "we will have the Sioux War over again."[18] The war did not materialize; the alarm had been based on the sort of faulty intelligence from the Indian territories that Sheridan had mentioned earlier in the year:

I think many of the Indian stories coming in from Upper Missouri are Indian exaggerations to some extent. I do not believe Sitting Bull and his outfit have crossed the line, almost any Indian seen anywhere in that section will be considered Sitting Bull for some time to come.[19]

Sheridan's engagements with the Indian Department were livelier than the frontier fighting that season. Commenting on the fact that thousands of Northern Plains tribesmen had decamped from their reservations, he pointed out that "the Indian Department could not have done better than it has in assisting them to get off by permitting them to encamp sixty or seventy miles from the Reserve and allowing them to go in and draw their annuities and rations; and when well loaded down with plunder, there is no one to prevent them from going off." When Secretary of the Interior Carl Schurz criticized Sheridan's report for 1878 the general shot back: "It might be inferred that the [Schurz] letter . . . was intended to intimidate the officers of the Army. Surely the men who have to guard the agencies . . . should have the right to report the causes of the troubles without the danger of being lectured into silence by the Honorable Secretary of the Interior."[20]

The period from the end of the Civil War to World War I was known to soldiers as the Army's "dog days," with only campaigns against the Indians and against the Spanish, briefly, in Cuba and the native insurrectionists, lengthily, in the Philippine Islands, to save the military establishment from stagnation. General Sheridan deserved considerable credit for helping to keep the Army alert, receptive to new theories and techniques of warfare and in fighting trim between the major conflicts. He would not allow the Army to degenerate into a collection of elderly Indian fighters. Unlike too many military men hypnotized by the glory of past wars, he insisted that his officers look to the future and the inevitable changes.

For this purpose he urged, fought for and carried out the establishment of the officers' training school at Fort Leavenworth, the first postgraduate military institution in American history, now the Command and General Staff school. He saw that West Point's teachings might give an officer a good start in his profession, but they must be supplemented by higher education later in his career. Perhaps there was ironic significance in the fact that Sheridan virtually had to evict General John Pope, head of the Department of Missouri, from his headquarters at Fort Leavenworth so that the great stride in American military affairs could be taken. He wrote Sherman that Pope was protesting against giving up the garrison "probably from force of habit, having occupied the present building so long." He did not mention the fact that the man resisting progress, the morning-glory general of Second Bull Run, was the sort of habit-hardened garrison officer who could hardly be expected to understand the concept of a war college. Having survived the Military Academy, this sort had no inclination to submit themselves to book learning again. Sheridan said, "Military headquarters at posts offer so much comfort and happiness to officers that they do not like to change . . . no odds how much benefit the service may derive from it."[21]

In this period there were other vexations growing out of the past—the $416,000 damage suit brought against him by a Louisiana plantation owner and the Warren Court of Inquiry. The suit against Sheridan had been filed by James A. Whalen, who in 1867 was the owner of the Killona plantation in St. Charles parish. He charged that in August of that year Sheridan illegally ordered the seizure of his property. When the general journeyed to New York to testify before the United States Circuit Court hundreds of ladies stormed the Federal Building and harassed the gatekeeper with demands that Phil Sheridan be pointed out to them. Sheridan testified that the plantation had been seized on information that "lawless and insurrectionary persons" had taken it over as a center of resistance to the Federal Government, and that the military-occupation laws give him the power. On December 20, 1878, the jury retired for one hour and found for Sheridan. It was just as well, for the general probably did not have one tenth the sum for which the Louisianian had sued him. Of greater irony was the fact that the plaintiff was represented by the one man whom Louisianians hated worse than Sheridan—Ben Butler, major general of U. S. Volunteers, the barrel-shaped Massachusetts politician who had commanded the Union occupation forces in New Orleans during the war and was popularly believed to have made off with half the silver plate in the conquered city.[22]

Seventeen years after the battle of Five Forks, and several months after the death of General Warren—from anxiety and bitterness over his long fight for vindication, according to his partisans—a court of inquiry delivered its findings. Warren was cleared of three of the four charges on which Sheridan based his removal as commander of the V Corps. Sheridan believed neither the court nor its findings warranted, that the relief of Warren was strictly a matter of military necessity in the midst of active fighting. Senator John A. Logan, himself a Civil War corps commander under Sherman, pledged his determination to stop "this outrageous practice of organizing unauthorized and illegal pretended 'Courts' for the purpose of plastering up the reputation of some who could not gain an enviable reputation by their own course of conduct during the war."[23] Sheridan engaged one of the nation's foremost trial lawyers, Asa Bird Gardner, to represent him at the inquiry and distributed hundreds of copies of Gardner's "Argument on Behalf of General Sheridan" to veterans' organizations, libraries, historical societies and Congressmen throughout the country.[24] His own view, expressed in a letter to Secretary of War Robert T. Lincoln, son of the late President, was that the findings of the court "were not in accordance with the evidence."

They are more in the nature of apologies than annunciation of the facts as shown in the evidence. The General of the Army clearly sees this in his review, and has raised the case to a higher plain where it properly belongs, than that on which the court works, as shown by the apologies and insignificant technical excuses submitted by the court. It is only fair to me, and it is perfectly proper to embrace General Sherman's review in the promulgation of the proceedings to the Army, especially since the reports industriously circulated in the newspapers as to the cause of the death of General Warren.[25]

General Sherman indeed saw that there were greater implications in Warren's removal than the circumstances of the battle itself. The principal conclusion of his review was:

In the clash of arms at or near Five Forks, his [Warren's] personal activity fell short of the standard fixed by General Sheridan, upon whom alone rested the great responsibility for that and succeeding

days. My conclusion is that General Sheridan was perfectly justified in his action in this case, and he must be fully and entirely sustained if the United States expects great victories by her armies in
the future.[26]

At least three times in his later years Sheridan's name was proposed, rather indistinctly, as a candidate for the Presidency. At
the Republican convention of 1880, which nominated Garfield, a
delegate from Wyoming Territory cast his ballot for Sheridan.
The general, who was sitting on the platform, ignored all parlia-
mentary rules and jumped to his feet—without being recognized
by the chair—to shout, "There is no way I can accept a nomination
from this convention unless I would be permitted to turn it over
to my best friend."[27] He meant, of course, General Grant, who
had already served two terms in the White House but was wistfully
available for another nomination.

Sheridan had even better claims to high honors by the Republicans, in a sense, than Grant. He had been a Whig, the forerunner
of a Republican, and in 1864 he had voted for Lincoln. Unlike
most generals, he took enough interest in politics to become a partisan, if not a participant. But when he was mentioned as a candidate in two succeeding Presidential campaigns he forswore all such
ambitions, bluntly telling an Associated Press reporter, "I don't
want that or any other civil office."

20

COMMANDING GENERAL

IN THE autumn of 1883 General Sherman reached
the retirement age. Despite Congress' offer to pass
a bill to allow him to remain at his post and many appeals that he
stay, Sherman retired as commanding general. It was time to give
younger officers a chance, he said, and accordingly Lieutenant General Sheridan reached the nation's highest military office at the comparatively youthful age of fifty-two.

Even this eminence did not incline Sheridan to any efforts at
swank or elegance. In Washington he usually dressed in civilian
clothes and, according to a New York *World* reporter, was far
from an imposing sight. "He wore upon the back of his round,
bullet head an oldfashioned silk hat about two sizes too small; a
short, light, yellow-gray overcoat which had only two buttons and
they were ready to fly off from the undue strain of Sheridan's
round figure. The trousers were a gray plaid and fitted very snugly
to the General's fat legs. His boots were thick-soled and un-
blacked." While his predecessor took an innocent joy in kissing
every pretty girl in reaching distance, the reporter noted, Sheridan "was not as popular as was General Sherman with the ladies.
He was fonder of staying at home than of going about in society.
He took more pleasure in paying attention to his own home and
family."

The years had not toned down his temper or his peppery disposition. One day soon after he became general in chief Sheridan
accompanied General Montgomery Meigs on an inspection of the
new Pension Building (now the General Accounting Office), whose
construction had been supervised by Meigs. After they had toured

the tremendous pile of red brick Meigs asked Sheridan, "Well, what do you think of it?"

"The only thing wrong with it is the damn thing's fireproof" was Sheridan's unflattering reply.[1]

Generally, however, his subordinates found him an understanding superior who would stretch a regulation to help them, especially if they served on the frontier. For an officer seeking leave because his wife was ill, he would support an appeal with the Adjutant General's Office. He would caution the testy General Pope against being too harsh with a subordinate. When a paymaster who had tampered with regimental funds was arrested in Chicago, he agreed that the man should merely be sent away from the fleshpots and back to his regiment. When the Rio Grande flooded and the five companies of infantry at Fort Brown with their families were menaced by a fever epidemic, he immediately ordered a steamer to evacuate the whole post and remove its personnel to Ship Island until the fever season was over. Old comrades seeking West Point appointments for their sons found him quick to endorse their applications. He did all he could to improve the living conditions of soldiers on the frontier within the limits imposed by Congressional control over expenditures.[2]

For all his sympathy for army officers conducting the last campaigns against hostiles in the West, he could and did deal sternly with even his closest associates and oldest comrades if they failed to carry out his orders. General George Crook, whom he had known since boyhood, learned this in 1886, when he was in command of the Department of Arizona and was putting down the last resistance of the Chiricahua Apache and their fearsome chief Geronimo. The War Department authorized Crook to negotiate for the surrender of the Chiricahua, with the provision that "they at once be sent under suitable guard for confinement at Fort Marion, Florida." Without authorization Crook, in negotiating with Geronimo, added the provision that the Chiricahua would be returned to Arizona at the end of their confinement. Sheridan sharply reminded Crook by telegraph that unconditional surrender was insisted on by the President. Crook warned that Geronimo would not accept such terms.

When Geronimo and his renegades fled into the mountains Sheridan was fuming with rage. He telegraphed Crook: "It seems strange that Geronimo and party could have escaped without the knowledge of the scouts." This especially affronted Crook, who relied as much on his scouts as on the Regular Army units in pursuing the Apache through the villainous terrain of his department, and believed that a successful campaign in that territory could be conducted only by use of the mule pack train and scouts. Sheridan was free with his advice:

I do not see what you can do now except to concentrate your troops at the best points, and give protection to the people. You have in your department 46 companies of infantry and 40 companies of cavalry, and ought to be able to do a great deal with such a force.

Resentful of Sheridan's suggesting how to proceed against the fast-riding renegades and mindful of his well-deserved prestige as the foremost of Indian fighters, Crook replied:

That the operations of the scouts in Mexico have not proved as successful as was hoped is due to the enormous difficulties they have been compelled to encounter from the nature of the Indians they have been hunting, and the character of the country in which they have operated, and of which persons not thoroughly conversant with both can have no conception. I believe that the plan upon which I have conducted operations is the one most likely to prove successful in the end. It may be, however, that I am too much wedded to my own views in the matter. . . .

He closed with a request that he be relieved of his command. Sheridan complied at once, with an alacrity that embittered Crook.[3]

Geronimo's was the last flare-up of major proportions along the frontier during Sheridan's tenure as commanding general. Administrative detail took up more of his time than planning operations against the few hostiles still outside the reservations. Besides establishing schools for the instruction of infantry officers at Fort Leavenworth and for cavalry officers at Fort Riley, Sheridan planned the complete reorganization of the Army's peacetime disposition. He proposed the abandonment of most of the border forts, seeking to avoid the dry rot resulting when officers and men were placed in garrisons where there was no longer call for their presence. The Indians were all but completely pacified. The Army's long guard mount of the frontier was over. So the new general in chief ordered the concentration of his troops in comfortable permanent barracks near railroad centers from which they could be rapidly deployed.

A new taste for reflection, following a life of action, encouraged him to look back and consequently to wonder whether all the fighting, even the glory of it, had been worth while and whether war itself had not become an anachronism. In addressing the Centennial of the Constitution at Philadelphia early in 1887 he said:

There is one thing we should appreciate and that is that the improvement in guns and in material of war, in dynamite and other explosives, is rapidly bringing us to a point where war will eliminate itself—when we can no longer stand up and fight each other in battle, and shall have to resort to something else. Now what will that something else be? It will be arbitration. I mean what I say when I express the belief that if anyone here could live until the next centennial he would find that arbitration rules the world.[4]

If this might indicate that Sheridan foresaw the formation of a League of Nations or some sort of United Nations, he has not yet been borne out in this idea that the multiplying potential of destruction bestowed by modern technology would eliminate warfare. Still, a fair number of years out of his century remains to test his prophecy.

Perhaps it was his new interest in the more peaceful pursuits that impelled Sheridan to campaign so vigorously for the establishment of the Yellowstone National Park, for which future generations could remember him with as much gratitude as for any of his more famous exploits. To induce Congress to "safeguard it from speculators and plunderers," Sheridan escorted a large official party—including President Chester A. Arthur, Secretary of War Robert T. Lincoln and other bigwigs—on a tour of the proposed park. He was at his genial best as guide to the eminent sight-seers, but there was one moment when his constitutional asperity rose to the surface. At Fort Washakie a band of Shoshone showed up to entertain the visitors. All wore beads, feathers and paint; a few proudly raised gaudy umbrellas against the noonday sun. It reminded Sheridan of the official with whom he was in dispute. He growled, "I suppose the Secretary of the Interior furnished those parasols."[5]

The last years of his life Sheridan spent quietly—perhaps with intimations that his heart was no longer sound, medically speaking—in his office at the State-War-Navy Building or in the library of his home. Somewhat late in life he became a rather reflective man, given to much reading and much thinking over what he had read. His books, his family and his job were his only interests.

He kept two cases of Indian relics in his office to remind him of his more active years. Almost daily he arrived at his desk at nine o'clock in the morning. A New York *World* reporter, who wrote an exhaustive account of his daily life, noted that it was arranged so that the light shone on the visitor's face. All the portraits on the office walls—Generals Jackson, Worth, Zachary Taylor, Logan, Blair, Meade, McPherson—evidently had been left there by General Sherman. They were men Sherman had either idolized as historical figures or admired as associates and subordinates.

Sheridan's fondest haunt was the library of his home at Rhode Island Avenue and Seventeenth Street, which had been purchased for $44,000 through a fund raised by friends and admirers when he moved from Chicago to Washington. On its red silk walls were hung photographs and paintings of his own particular heroes and army friends—Grant, Sherman, Thomas, Merritt, Crook, Scott, Granger. Most of the wall space, however, was occupied by shelves reaching to the high ceiling and laden with an excellent collection of books—not only military works but English and American classics.[6]

Mrs. Sheridan received her friends and gathered her family around her in the sitting room, separated from the general's library by a portiere. Every week, as demanded by her husband's position, she held a reception for several hundred persons. Sheridan's appearance at these affairs was little more than perfunctory.

In the summer of 1887 he rented a seaside cottage at Nonquit, Massachusetts, overlooking the islands of Martha's Vineyard and Nantucket and shielded by Cape Cod from the off-sea winds. It was such a peaceful and restful summer—and Sheridan so enjoyed the company of its residents, including Swain Gifford, the artist, and Louisa May Alcott—that he started construction of his own summer cottage there immediately.

But his prospect of tranquillity was short-lived.

Early the next year he suffered a series of heart attacks, the severity of which indicated he would not live long. Congress revived the grade of full general, which had been held by Grant and Sherman, and Sheridan was given his fourth star by President Grover Cleveland. The only order he issued as a four-star general promoted his brother Mike and two other aides-de-camp to colonels in the Regular Army.[7] Hundreds of letters and telegrams came to his sickbed from all over the nation. An old West Point classmate, Walter Forward, sent best wishes, although they had not met since graduation. Hundreds of copies of resolutions for his recovery were received from the Grand Army of the Republic, the Loyal Legion, various army societies and veterans' organizations. From General W. L. Elliott in San Francisco came "sympathy from your first brigade commander." Buffalo Bill Cody, whose fame now exceeded Sheridan's, telegraphed: "Dear General, I pray earnestly for your recovery. I wish I could endure in your place."[8]

His country's recognition and gratitude, the immense outpouring of admiring sympathy from all sides were well deserved. Sheridan had earned them. Sheridan had achieved his success not through luck or dash or any other single quality but by a broad combination of exceptional gifts which made him a commander of singular versatility. Though history had permitted him only three years in his young manhood for the full employment of his abilities, those abilities were part of him throughout his adult life, needing only a theater of operations to display themselves.

Attempts to sum him up frequently emphasize one side of his personality, leaving untouched facets which other estimates make paramount. Take for instance the judgments of Grant, Sherman and Sheridan himself.

General Grant described Sheridan as "restless, full of the combative quality, not politic in language, somewhat reticent, half stubborn and fond of hazard enterprises . . . he was the embodiment of heroism, dash and impulse."

When he presided over the unveiling at West Point of the portraits of himself, Grant and Sheridan, General Sherman said: "No three men ever lived on the earth's surface so diverse in mental and physical attributes as the three men whose portraits you now look upon. Different in every respect save one—we had a guiding star, we had an emblem of nationality in our mind, implanted at West Point, which made us come together for a common purpose as the rays of the sun coming together make them burn."

More specifically, after Sheridan's death, General Sherman commented: "General Sheridan impressed me as a typical Irishman, impulsive, enthusiastic, social, and pleasant. With all of his impulsiveness, however, he was a deep thinker. So much stress has been laid upon his dash as an officer that the public did not give him credit for the mental concentration he was capable of. He was a man of brains as well as heart, of thought as well as action. He did not read much but did his thinking from an original basis, and with excellent results. I tell you Sheridan had a great head, well stored with useful knowledge. He was a methodical man, too, and a great worker. He personally went over all of his accounts and estimates in a systematic manner, trusting nothing to chance. Naturally he was not appreciated at his full worth. He was a great soldier and a noble man, and deserved all of the honors bestowed upon him. General Sheridan's services to his country could scarcely be overestimated. He was a man of quick perception, and as a commander had the faculty of grasping the whole situation on a field of battle intuitively, and history already records the valuable work he did in his country's defense."

In an address to a West Point graduating class, while commanding general of the army, Sheridan told his own version of how success came to him: "Whatever I took up, even if it were the simplest of duties, I tried to do it better than it had ever been done before. . . . In the second place I always looked out for the common soldier. Trust your reputation to the private and he will never let your military fame suffer."

Sheridan's reputation was safe and his military fame in no danger of suffering. But his ill-assorted, almost grotesque body was wearing out and breaking down.

Certain that death was approaching, Sheridan was removed to the new cottage at Nonquit, where he could look out to sea. He enjoyed the panorama, but it was vastly different from the turbulent scenes of his active years—the devastation of war in Tennessee and Virginia, the menacing horizon westward from the Army's posts along the frontier, the riotous streets of New Orleans during the Reconstruction, the crushing of the French armies by the Prussian steam roller of 1871. A photograph taken then shows Sheridan on the porch of his cottage with his wife, his brother Mike and his wife, and the four children. The general is leaning back in his chair, calm, relaxed, half smiling. He waited for death that summer, waited without fear. Once, after a painful attack, he smiled at one of his physicians and said, "I almost got away from you that time."[9]

Early in August his condition seemed greatly improved, and the doctor and nurse in constant attendance were hopeful that he would pull through. He was only fifty-seven, after all. On Sunday, August 5, as usual he watched the tide rolling in outside the large window where he sat most of the day. Suddenly another heart attack seized him, worse than all the rest. Toward evening his breathing was painfully labored. Physicians applied every restorative known, spirits of ammonia, a galvanic battery, finally a hypodermic injection of digitalis direct to the heart. His pulse grew fainter, flickered out. Phil Sheridan joined Grant, Thomas, Meade, Lee, Hood, Johnston, Custer, Pickett, McPherson and the many other Civil War figures who had preceded him in death.[10]

There could be no finer tribute to Sheridan the man than the devotion his family paid his memory. His widow, that attractive and comparatively youthful woman, was asked by a friend why she never remarried. "I would rather be the widow of Phil Sheridan than the wife of any man living," she is said to have replied.[11]

In 1908 she unveiled one of the most famous military statues in the world in Sheridan Circle, Washington. Executed by Gutzon Borglum, it shows Sheridan mounted on Rienzi, riding to the faltering battle line at Cedar Creek and yelling to stragglers, as Borglum was informed, "You will sleep in your tents tonight or you will sleep in hell!"[12] His widow, son and daughters moved to a house at 2551 Massachusetts Avenue to be near "Papa's Circle." Every morning, it was said, the three girls leaned out of their bedroom windows and called toward the statue, "Good morning, Papa!"[13]

Funeral services for General Sheridan were conducted at St. Matthew's Catholic Church. A solemn requiem mass was sung, with the Dominican Fathers of Somerset, Ohio—who almost half a century before had solemnly advised against allowing him to go to West Point—providing the choir, and Cardinal Gibbons delivering the sermon. Kneeling on their *prie-dieu* before the coffin were the widow and brothers Mike and John. Under the high altar blue and yellow flowers formed the shoulder strap of a full general. Sheridan's sash and sword lay on top of the coffin. And the draped flag of the cavalry corps headquarters—the red-and-white guidon whose swallow tail had led the advance of the Union armies to Appomattox—stood just above his head.[14] Through streets lined with silent thousands the cortege moved to the slow beat of muffled drums toward Arlington National Cemetery. He lies there today, in the soil of the Commonwealth of Virginia, the soil which less than 90 years ago shook under the thundering hoofbeats of the Cavalry Corps, Army of the Potomac, Major General Philip H. Sheridan commanding.

NOTES AND INDEX

NOTES ON SOURCES

THE three principal sources used in this work were the *Sheridan Papers*, a collection of the general's correspondence (mostly of a public nature), letter books, dispatches and scrapbooks from 1853 to his death, which were given to the Library of Congress by his widow; *The War of the Rebellion . . . Official Records of the Union and Confederate Armies*, for much of his Civil War career; and his *Personal Memoirs*, a more readable account than most military autobiographies. The author is especially indebted to Dr. David C. Mearns, head of the Manuscript Division of the Library of Congress, where the *Sheridan Papers* are to be found, and his able and courteous staff, as well as the staff of the Huntington Library at San Marino, California, and the tireless Sylvester Vigilante of the New York Public Library's American History department.

CHAPTER ONE

THE BELLS OF SOMERSET

1 Greiner, Henry C., *General Phil Sheridan As I Knew Him*. Chicago: J. S. Hyland and Company, 1908. P. 388. Hereafter cited as *Greiner*.

2 J. W. Miller of the Cincinnati *Commercial*. Quoted in *Greiner*, 232.

3 *Greiner*, 314.

4 Sheridan, Philip H., *Personal Memoirs of P. H. Sheridan*. New York: Charles L. Webster & Company, 1888. Vol. I, p. 1. Hereafter cited as *Memoirs*.

5 Hergesheimer, Joseph, *Sheridan*. Boston and New York: Houghton Mifflin Company, 1931. P. 10.

6 Somerset *Press*, October 19, 1905. A story under a Washington dateline read, "There is no longer any dispute as to General Phil Sheridan's birthplace, says T. D. Binckley of New Lexington, who, as chairman of the Sheridan Monument Association, made a vain effort to persuade President Roosevelt to attend the dedication at Somerset on Nov. 2. 'Now that he is dead and there is no hope of his election to the Presidency,' said Binckley, 'his relatives admit that he was born on the ocean, when his parents were coming from Ireland, but his birth was recorded at Albany, N. Y., where they first settled.' "

7 *Sheridan Papers*, Library of Congress, Manuscript Division, Box "One," covering the years 1853-1871.

8 *Memoirs*, I, 3.

9 *Greiner*, 350.

10 Sherman, William T., *Home Letters of General Sherman*, edited by

M. A. DeWolfe Howe. New York: Charles Scribner's Sons, 1909. P. 314.

[11] *The Ohio Guide*. New York: Oxford University Press, 1940. P. 464.

[12] *Greiner*, 20-21.

[13] *Ibid.*, illustration opposite 126. Mrs. Sheridan died at the age of eighty-seven in June 1888, only a few months before the general. Neither knew of the other's fatal illness.

[14] *Ibid.*, 15-16.

[15] *Ibid.*, 38.

[16] *Memoirs*, I, 3.

[17] *Greiner*, 47.

[18] *Memoirs*, I, 4-5.

[19] Sheridan changed his mind about schooling in his later years; after the Civil War he observed to Henry Greiner, as they gazed down on the schoolhouse from Redmond Hill, "That is what made us superior to the South; the little white schoolhouse of the North gave us a great advantage. Education is invincible." *Greiner*, 353.

[20] *Ibid.*, 26-27.

[21] *The Ohio Guide*, 464.

[22] *Greiner*, 45-47.

[23] *Ibid.*, 158-159.

[24] *Ibid.*, 33.

[25] *Memoirs*, I, 5-6.

[26] *Greiner*, 19. In the years following the Civil War, General Sherman sometimes spoke expansively of knowing Phil Sheridan quite intimately in his boyhood. Sherman, however, had a vivid imagination, especially concerning matters of sentiment. It would seem that Sherman, 11 years the senior of Sheridan, could hardly have been very close to a boy so much younger. But the Sherman and Ewing families—especially the Ewings with their Catholic ties—often visited Somerset and the Dominican Fathers who had established themselves there. When the Sherman family fell on bad times young "Cump" was placed in the care of Congressman Ewing and his family.

[27] *Memoirs*, I, 19. According to Henry Greiner, Ritchie's attention was attracted by an incident in Sheridan's boyhood. One day when Phil was seven or eight years old he received permission from his father to ride a newly broken horse from the roadworkers' camp on the Zanesville-Maysville turnpike. The horse ran away with him, heading for its barn. Phil clung to the runaway's mane and bent low as the horse galloped into the barn and almost dashed its rider against the door. Ritchie, according to Greiner, was much impressed by little Phil's coolness and skill on horseback.

[28] Ewing, Hugh, *Autobiography of a Tramp*, mss. in possession of Mrs. Udell Ewing Gault of Milford Center, Ohio. Quoted in Lloyd Lewis' *Sherman: Fighting Prophet*. New York: Harcourt, Brace, 1932. Pp. 47-48.

[29] *Memoirs*, I, 9.

[30] Hergesheimer, *Sheridan*, 23-25.

[31] General Garnett was killed during the Civil War in the Western Virginia mountain campaign, fighting in the Confederate Army. General Porter, a Union corps commander, was cashiered after Second Bull Run on the charge of his commanding general, John Pope, that he had withheld his full support during the battle. Long after the war Porter was exonerated by a court of inquiry. The Porter controversy is thoroughly aired in Otto Eisenschiml's *The Celebrated Case of Fitz John Porter*. Indianapolis: The Bobbs-Merrill Company, 1950. In testifying to Porter's patriotism, the former Secretary of War Simon Cameron declared before a Congressional investigating committee that General Porter persuaded George H. Thomas, a Virginian, to stay in the Union Army.

[32] *Memoirs*, I, 10-11.

[33] For all his pride in Virginia and being a Virginian, Terrill refused to join the Confederacy and became a brigadier in the Union Army. He was killed at Perryville in 1862, hours after he and Sheridan met, shook hands and called off their ancient feud.

[34] *Memoirs*, I, 11.

[35] *Ibid.*, 12.

[36] *Ibid.*, 13. "Decidedly less of a lion," his brother Mike described him. See *Memoirs*, Revised Edition of 1904, Vol. II, p. 571. Hereafter cited as *Memoirs (Revised)*.

[37] Information furnished by the Public Relations Office of the United States Military Academy.

[38] Gleaned from various chapters of Colonel Ernest Dupuy's *Men of West Point*. New York: William Sloane Associates, 1952.

[39] *Greiner*, 317.

[40] *Ibid.*, 71-72. Sheridan's chances of getting a girl had been reduced by a gang of railroad surveyors, who used Somerset as their headquarters and swept a number of the local girls off their feet.

CHAPTER TWO

Eight Years a Shavetail

[1] *Memoirs*, I, 20. Captain McLean's wife, whom Sheridan found "charming," was the daughter of General William B. Franklin, already distinguished in the Regular Army and a future corps commander of the Army of the Potomac under McClellan and Burnside. Sheridan found Captain McLean's "agreeable manners and upright methods" so impressive that he looked back on his service with Company D, 1st Infantry, as "among those events which I remember with most pleasure."

[2] *Ibid.*, 25-27.

[3] *Ibid.*, 29-30.

[4] *Ibid.*, 32-33.

[5] That, of course, was before Bedloe's Island became the pedestal for the Statue of Liberty. It was then an army depot receiving recruits for assignment to posts throughout the nation.

[6] Crook, George, *General George Crook: His Autobiography*, edited by Martin F. Schmitt. Norman: University of Oklahoma Press, 1946. P. 21.

[7] *Ibid.*, 7.

[8] The newly formed cavalry regiment, a pet project of Secretary of War Jefferson Davis, included Albert Sidney Johnston, Robert E. Lee, George H. Thomas, William J. Hardee, Earl Van Dorn, E. Kirby Smith and other subsequently famous Civil War leaders among its officers.

[9] *Memoirs*, I, 37-43.

[10] Crook, *Autobiography*, 24.

[11] Freeman, Douglas Southall, *Lee's Lieutenants*. New York: Charles Scribner's Sons, 1943. Vol. I, 268-269. Rains, a West Point graduate of 1827, became a brigadier in the Confederate Army. During the opening phases of the Peninsula campaign of 1862, in the retreat from Yorktown, he planted land mines to impede the Federal advance with considerable success. The protests against such devices were almost as loud and bitter from his fellow officers as from the enemy. He argued that they were no more inhumane than naval guns bombarding a fortified port, which he characterized as "reversing the scriptural text that it is better for ninety-nine guilty persons to escape than for one innocent to suffer." He was finally assigned to the river defenses of Richmond, where "torpedoes"—mines, as they are now known—were regarded as "clearly admissible" weapons.

[12] *Memoirs*, I, 54-57.

[13] Crook, *Autobiography*, 19-20. Later, when stationed at Fort Jones, Captain Judah's Company E, 4th Infantry, became known as the "Forty Thieves" because of their plundering tendencies.

[14] *Ibid.*, 26-27.

[15] *Memoirs*, I, 57-58.

[16] *Ibid.*, 68-69. Both Ord's and Rains's charges were pigeonholed by the department commander, General John E. Wool, who had had considerable experience with such uncomradely bickering in the Mexican War. Captain Ord became a prominent Union general.

[17] Abbot, Henry L., "Reminiscences of the Oregon War," *Journal of the Military Service Institution of the United States*, Vol. XVL, No. 162, pp. 436-442.

[18] *Memoirs*, I, 70-84.

[19] War Department Archives, General Order No. 14, November 13, 1857.

[20] *Memoirs*, I, 118-120.

21 *Ibid.*, 121.

22 Freeman, *Lee's Lieutenants*, I, 267. Confederate Brigadier Archer had generally bad luck in his subsequent career. Despite his seniority, he was passed over in favor of Hood for command of the Texas Brigade, and never advanced beyond leading a brigade. He was captured at Gettysburg and died shortly after he was released from a Federal prison in 1865.

23 *Memoirs*, I, 123.

CHAPTER THREE

DESK CAPTAIN TO CAVALRY COLONEL

1 Reid, Whitelaw, *Ohio in the War*. Cincinnati: Moore, Wilstach & Baldwin, 1868. Vol. I, 503.

2 *Ibid.*, 500.

3 *Memoirs*, I, 125.

4 *Greiner*, 77.

5 *Memoirs*, I, 126-127.

6 Reid, *Ohio in the War*, I, 501.

7 Sheridan ordered each regiment to send all but two wagons to the army train. While other colonels wired their governors in protest, Dodge hastened to obey the order and set an example. *Cf.* J. R. Perkins, *Trails, Rails and War*. Indianapolis: The Bobbs-Merrill Company, 1929. P. 83.

8 *The War of the Rebellion . . . Official Records of the Union and Confederate Armies*. Washington: Government Printing Office, 1890-1901. Series One, Vol. VIII, pp. 480-481. Hereafter cited as *O. R.*, and, unless otherwise noted, references will be to Series One. This dispatch was dated January 2, 1862.

9 *Ibid.*, 506.

10 *Memoirs*, I, 128-130.

11 Perkins, *Trails, Rails and War*, 84, for telegraph incidents.

12 *Memoirs*, I, 132-135.

13 *Ibid.*, 140-142.

14 *O. R.*, X, Part 1, 864-865.

15 *Ibid.*, Part 2, 278. Dispatches of Sheridan to Pope, commanding the Army of the Mississippi, and Pope to Halleck.

16 Sheridan's brigade was part of the cavalry division of the Army of the Mississippi. Gordon Granger had become division commander by that time.

17 *Memoirs*, I, 153-154.

18 *Ibid.*, 156.

19 Confederate divisions early in the war were much larger than their enemy's, almost the equivalent of a Union corps.

[20] *O. R.*, XVII, Part 1, 19. Quoted from Sheridan's report submitted several days later to division headquarters.

[21] *Ibid.*, 19-20.

[22] *Memoirs*, I, 160-161.

[23] Robertson, John, *Michigan in the War*. Lansing: W. S. George & Co., 1882. Vol. II, p. 616.

[24] *Memoirs*, I, 162.

[25] *O. R.*, XVII, Part 2, 62.

[26] *Ibid.*, 63.

[27] *Ibid.*, 66. General Halleck himself was summoned to Washington as general in chief shortly thereafter. He arrived in time to share Pope's disgrace at Second Bull Run, but he managed to cling to his post until 1864. Then Grant became general in chief and Halleck was made chief of staff.

[28] *O. R.*, XVII, Part 1, 17-18.

[29] *Ibid.*, 18.

[30] *Memoirs*, I, 177-180.

[31] *Ibid.*, 169-171.

[32] Grant, Ulysses S., *Personal Memoirs of U. S. Grant*. New York: Charles L. Webster & Co., 1885. Vol. I, pp. 396-397.

CHAPTER FOUR

The Jealous Generals

[1] Grant, *Memoirs*, I, 402.

[2] *Memoirs*, I, 181-182.

[3] Beatty, John, *Memoirs of a Volunteer*. Edited by Harvey S. Ford. New York: W. W. Norton, 1946. P. 117.

[4] *Memoirs*, I, 190.

[5] *Battles and Leaders of the Civil War*. New York: The Century Co., 1884-1888. Vol. III, p. 61.

[6] *Ibid.*, 43.

[7] *Ibid.*, 61. The grand jury in Louisville indicted General Davis for manslaughter on October 27, 1862, and he was released on $5,000 bail until the case was finally dropped on May 24, 1864.

[8] *Ibid.*, 47. From General Buell's account of the battle of Perryville.

[9] *Memoirs*, I, 12-13. Terrill's brother Joseph, a Confederate general, was killed at Bethesda Church. They were buried in the same grave under a headstone inscribed, "God alone knows which was right."

[10] *Battles and Leaders*, III, 57.

[11] *O. R.*, XVI, Part 1, 1081-1082.

[12] *Memoirs*, I, 194.

[13] *Ibid.*, 195.

[14] *O. R.*, XVI, Part 1, 1082.

[15] *Ibid.*, 1082.

[16] *Ibid.*, 1036.

[17] *Ibid.*, 599.

[18] Reid, *Ohio in the War*, II, 504.

[19] Beatty, *Memoirs of a Volunteer*, 120.

[20] *O. R.*, XVI, Part 1, 93-95.

[21] *Memoirs*, I, 201.

CHAPTER FIVE

DEATH IN THE ROUND FOREST

[1] Castle, Henry A., *Military Order of the Loyal Legion of the United States, Commandery of the District of Columbia*, War Paper No. 34. P. 5. Hereafter referred to as *Castle*.

[2] General Gilbert was reduced to an infantry captain and disappeared into the obscurity from which he had emerged so briefly and disastrously.

[3] *Memoirs*, I, 203.

[4] *Battles and Leaders*, III, 605.

[5] *Memoirs*, I, 220.

[6] *O. R.*, XX, Part 1, 348. From Sheridan's report submitted January 9, 1863, through the usual channels.

[7] *Ibid.*, 348.

[8] *Castle*, 10.

[9] *O. R.*, XX, Part 1, 348.

[10] *Ibid.*, 348.

[11] *Battles and Leaders*, III, 620. From the account of Lieutenant Colonel G. C. Kniffin, then a member of General Crittenden's staff.

[12] W. S. Furay in the Cincinnati *Gazette*, January 4, 1863.

[13] Yaryan, John L., *Stone River. Military Order of the Loyal Legion of the United States, Indiana Commandery*, War Papers, Vol. I.

[14] *O. R.*, XX, Part 1, 350-351.

[15] *Castle*, 10.

[16] *O. R.*, XX, Part 1, 349.

[17] *Battles and Leaders*, III, 623.

[18] *Ibid.*, 627.

[19] *O. R.*, XX, Part 1, 349-350.

[20] *Battles and Leaders*, III, 627.

[21] Yaryan, *Stone River*. Rosecrans' headquarters were in an old and dilapidated log cabin, concealed by a cedar thicket, about a mile behind the battlefront.

[22] *O. R.*, XX, Part 1, 350.

[23] *Battles and Leaders*, III, 634. From General Crittenden's account of the battle of Stone's River.

[24] *O. R.*, XX, Part 1, 209.

[25] Young, John Russell, *Around the World with General Grant*. New York: The American News Co., 1879. Vol. II, p. 304.

CHAPTER SIX

Into the Valley

[1] *Memoirs*, I, 253-255.

[2] *Ibid.*, 259-260. At that time Sheridan said Rosecrans "seemed to manifest special confidence in me, often discussing his plans with me independent of the occasions on which he formally referred them for my views." Whatever bond there was between them may have been strengthened by the fact that both were Catholics, Rosecrans a most devout convert who had a priest attached to his headquarters and who made a delicate distinction between his cursing when excited and ordinary blasphemy.

[3] Sherman's campaign against Atlanta a year hence greatly resembled Rosecrans' strategy to drive Bragg out of Middle Tennessee.

[4] Reid, *Ohio in the War*, II, 507.

[5] Shanks, William F. G., *Personal Recollections of Distinguished Generals*. New York: Harper & Bros., 1866. P. 161.

[6] Dana, Charles A., *Recollections of the Civil War*. New York: D. Appleton and Company, 1898. P. 107.

[7] Crook, *Autobiography*, 103.

[8] *Greiner*, 232.

[9] *Memoirs*, I, 274-276.

[10] O'Connor, Richard, *Thomas: Rock of Chickamauga*. New York: Prentice-Hall, Inc., 1948. P. 21.

[11] *Battles and Leaders*, III, 669. From the account of Major General Emerson Opdycke.

[12] *Ibid.*, 639. From the description of the battle of Chickamauga by Confederate General D. H. Hill, one of the crispest writers and acutest observers on either side of the battle lines.

[13] *Memoirs*, I, 276.

[14] *O. R.*, XXX, Part 1, 579.

[15] *Ibid.*, 579-580. From General Sheridan's report submitted through channels on September 30, 1863, covering his activities from September 2 to 23.

[16] Dana, *Recollections*, 113.

[17] *Ibid.*, 113.

[18] *O. R.*, XXX, Part 1, 580. From Sheridan's report.

[19] *Ibid.*, 580.

20 *Castle*, 5.

21 *O. R.*, XXX, Part 1, 581. In his *Memoirs*, however, Sheridan stated that he arrived in Rossville "about 5 o'clock."

22 Dana, *Recollections*, 118.

23 *Battles and Leaders*, III, 666-667. From Colonel Fullerton's account of Chickamauga.

24 *Memoirs*, I, 283.

25 Shanks, *Personal Recollections*, 268.

26 *O. R.*, XXX, Part 1, 581.

27 *Battles and Leaders*, III, 665.

28 *O. R.*, LII, Part 1, 81.

29 *Battles and Leaders*, III, 665.

30 By comparative casualty rates Chickamauga was a bloodier battle than Gettysburg. It was the bloodiest battle ever fought on the American continent.

31 Beatty, John, *The Citizen Soldier*. Cincinnati: Wilstach, Baldwin and Co., 1879. P. 345.

32 Another critic, less bold than the others, was General Hazen, a brigade commander at Chickamauga, in whose *Narrative of Military Service* there was at least an implication that Sheridan could have rendered better service than he did that afternoon. General Hazen significantly quoted Colonel Thruston's account of Sheridan's refusal to march directly to Thomas along with Davis, significantly did *not* quote the remarks of other generals and staff officers that such an action would have been difficult or impossible to accomplish at the moment and that Sheridan rendered more valuable service on Thomas' left than he could on the right. Many officers believed that Hazen was jealous of Sheridan, who rose to commanding general of the army while the best Hazen could do was chief of the signal corps, and who quarreled with Hazen on a number of subsequent occasions.

33 Gracie, Archibald, *The Truth About Chickamauga*. Boston: Houghton, Mifflin Co., 1911. Pp. 129-130.

34 *O. R.*, XXX, Part 1, 38.

CHAPTER SEVEN

THE RANKS TAKE COMMAND

1 Dana, *Recollections*, 127.

2 *Ibid.*, 123-124.

3 *Memoirs*, I, 297-298.

4 *Ibid.*, 295-296.

5 Beatty, *Memoirs of a Volunteer*, 258.

6 *Memoirs*, I, 301-302.

[7] *Battles and Leaders*, III, 681. Historian John Fiske pointed out that, "had the Rebellion occurred a few years earlier, before our long lines of railway had been built, suppression by military means would have been physically impossible."

[8] Smith was an ambitious Vermonter whose aspirations and conspiratorial tendencies almost negated his undoubted capacities as an officer. It was "Baldy" Smith, while serving in the East, who revealed that General Mc-Clellan was becoming involved with Democratic politicians and probably helped, thereby, to bring down the wrath of the Radical Republicans on McClellan. Later, as will be told, he became entangled with that human buzzsaw among political generals, Ben Butler, after being transferred to the Army of the James.

[9] *Battles and Leaders*, III, 683. From Grant's account of his operations around Chattanooga, substantially the same as given in his *Personal Memoirs*.

[10] *Ibid.*, 684.

[11] Frontal attacks were always anathema to General Thomas, who preferred to let the enemy attack, pin him in position, catch him off balance and then throw in a series of crushing counterattacks. The only frontal attack he undertook was at Kenesaw Mountain during the Atlanta campaign in the spring of 1864, and then only under protest and in obedience to General Sherman's direct orders. It was a costly failure, as Thomas predicted.

[12] *Battles and Leaders*, III, 720-721. From the vivid account of Brigadier General Joseph S. Fullerton, chief of staff of the IV Corps.

[13] *Memoirs*, I, 304.

[14] *Ibid.*, 307.

[15] O. R., XXXI, Part 2, 189. Sheridan's right flank was secured by Hooker's capture of Lookout Mountain.

[16] *Ibid.*, 189-190.

[17] *Ibid.*, 209.

[18] *Ibid.*, 229.

[19] *Ibid.*, 190.

[20] *Battles and Leaders*, III, 725.

[21] Dana, *Recollections*, 150.

[22] O. R., XXXI, Part 2, 81. There was considerable resentment among officers of the IV Corps over General Grant's statement that "Cannon and musket balls filled the air; but the damage done was in small proportion to the ammunition used." Writing in the April 1886 issue of the *Century Magazine*, Captain Benjamin F. Hegler, second-in-command of the 15th Indiana, which participated in the assault, stated: "The inference might be that the assault, though brilliant, was after all a rather harmless diversion. The 15th Indiana, of Sheridan's division, started up the ridge just to the left of Bragg's headquarters with 337 officers and men, and lost 202 killed and wounded, in just 45 minutes, the time taken to advance from the line of works at the foot

of the ridge and to carry the crest. This report I made officially to General Sheridan near Chickamauga creek the morning after the battle."

23 *Ibid.*, 191.

24 *Ibid.*, 192.

25 *O. R.*, XXXI, Part 2, 191-192.

26 *Memoirs*, I, 315-318.

27 Hazen, William B., *A Narrative of Military Service.* Boston: Ticknor and Company, 1885. Pp. 141-142.

28 *Memoirs*, I, 320.

29 Lewis, *Sherman*, 327.

30 *Memoirs*, I, 325-326.

31 Lewis, *Sherman*, 328.

32 *Memoirs*, I, 329.

33 Wilson, James H., *Under the Old Flag.* New York: D. Appleton and Company, 1912. Vol. I, pp. 305-306.

34 *Sheridan Papers*, Manuscript Division of the Library of Congress, Box "One."

35 Hazen, *Narrative*, 238-239.

36 *Memoirs*, I, 331-332.

37 Hazen, *Narrative*, 239-240.

CHAPTER EIGHT

CAVALRY IN THE WILDERNESS

1 *Memoirs*, I, 340-341.

2 An excellent account of General Buford's efforts to make the cavalry more effective in the Eastern theater may be found in *Eleven Generals* by Fletcher Pratt. New York: William Sloane Associates, 1949. Pp. 99-112.

3 In a rough analogy with the American high command of World War II, Halleck was General Marshall, Grant (although not under Halleck's orders) was Eisenhower, Meade was Bradley.

4 *Battles and Leaders*, III, 707.

5 Shanks, *Personal Recollections*, 131-132. One of the most perceptive short studies of Sheridan, his methods and his character was provided by this New York war correspondent. Comparing Sheridan and the other pre-eminent Union generals, Shanks wrote, "Sheridan may be said to be an Inspiration rather than a General, accomplishing his work as much, not to say more, by the inspiriting force of his courage and example as by the rules of war. He supplies to the army the passion and fire which is smothered in Grant and Thomas, and imperfectly developed in Sherman."

6 Porter, Horace, *Campaigning with Grant.* New York: The Century Co., 1897. P. 24. Colonel Porter had been a member of General Thomas' staff at Chattanooga but was brought east by Grant.

[7] *Memoirs,* I, 346-347.

[8] Porter, *Campaigning with Grant,* 24.

[9] *O. R.,* XXXVI, Part 1, 787. The report was written while Sheridan was commanding the occupation forces in Louisiana and Texas, and was sent to General John A. Rawlins, then the army's chief of staff.

[10] It is noteworthy that in World War II conservative infantry generals irked armored-force officers with the same attitude as Meade had toward concentrating the *horse* cavalry.

[11] *Memoirs,* I, 354-356.

[12] Burnside's IX Corps was not technically attached to the Army of the Potomac, although operating with it, and was directly under the command of General Grant.

[13] Buell, Augustus, *The Cannoneer—Story of a Private Soldier.* Washington: The National Tribune Co., 1890.

[14] *O. R.,* XXXVI, Part 1, 773.

[15] *Ibid.,* 774.

[16] *Ibid.,* 776.

[17] *Memoirs,* I, 366-367.

[18] Meade, George Gordon, *The Life and Letters of George Gordon Meade.* Charles Scribner's Sons, 1913. P. 192. Letter of May 1, 1864, to Mrs. Meade.

[19] Lyman, Theodore, *Meade's Headquarters.* Boston: Atlantic Monthly Press, 1922. Pp. 105-106.

[20] Porter, *Campaigning with Grant,* 84.

[21] *Memoirs,* I, 368-369.

[22] *Ibid.,* 369.

CHAPTER NINE

A Charge at Yellow Tavern

[1] *Memoirs,* I, 370-371.

[2] *O. R.,* XXXVI, Part 1, 789.

[3] Davies, Henry E., *General Sheridan.* New York: D. Appleton and Company, 1889. P. 104.

[4] *O. R.,* XXXVI, Part 1, 776. From Sheridan's report on the operation to General Meade, dated May 13, 1864.

[5] *Ibid.,* 776.

[6] *O. R.,* XXXVI, Part 1, 776-778.

[7] *O. R.,* LI, Part 2, 912.

[8] Davies, *Sheridan,* 109.

[9] The trooper who killed Stuart was John A. Huff, a forty-eight-year-old private in Company E, 5th Michigan Cavalry, according to his commanding

officer, Colonel Russell A. Alger. Huff, who had re-enlisted in the cavalry after serving with Berdan's Sharpshooters earlier in the war, was himself killed only 17 days later. Colonel Alger was the young officer who recommended Sheridan for his first regimental command back with the Army of the Mississippi, and who led the attack on the Confederate rear at the battle of Booneville. *O. R.*, XXXVI, Part 1, 828-829.

[10] Davies, *Sheridan*, 110.

[11] *O. R.*, XXXVI, Part 1, 778.

[12] Wilson, *Under the Old Flag*, I, 414.

[13] Faulkner, Joseph, *The Life of Philip Henry Sheridan*. New York: Hurst and Company, 1888. Pp. 152.

[14] *Memoirs*, I, 380. The pioneer in Confederate experiments with land and water mines was Gabriel J. Rains, a brigadier who had been Sheridan's highly unpopular superior officer in the Far West. Most Confederate generals opposed the use of land mines, believing them barbarous and inhuman.

[15] Van de Water, Frederic F., *Glory-Hunter*. Indianapolis: The Bobbs-Merrill Company, 1934. P. 68.

[16] Davies, *Sheridan*, 111-112.

[17] *Memoirs*, I, 386-387.

CHAPTER TEN

ACTION AT TREVILIAN

[1] *Memoirs*, I, 435.

[2] Wilson, *Under the Old Flag*, I, 362.

[3] *The Custer Story*, edited by Marguerite Merington. New York: The Devin-Adair Company, 1950. P. 97. A collection of letters, mostly exchanged by General Custer and his wife, Elizabeth Bacon Custer—many of them unconsciously revealing. Custer claimed that one of Wilson's regiments, the 1st Vermont Cavalry, asked Custer's brigade if it could have "a pair of Custer's old boots" to command them. There is no substantiation of this in the annals of the 1st Vermont. However, Isaac Gause, a trooper in Company E, 2nd Ohio Cavalry, which served under Wilson and later under Custer, related that his regiment "always hooted as the General [Wilson] passed near them, from the 22nd of June until he left the command" (Gause, Isaac, *Four Years with Five Armies*. New York: The Neale Publishing Company, 1908. P. 321). Much of this resentment in the ranks may have arisen because young Wilson, in the enthusiasm of his first field command, enforced strict discipline—which the cavalry, until then, had seldom experienced.

[4] Wilson, *Under the Old Flag*, I, 412-413.

⁵ *Memoirs*, I, 392.

⁶ Porter, *Campaigning with Grant*, 144.

⁷ *O. R.*, XXXVI, Part 1, 21.

⁸ Fitz Lee was General Robert E. Lee's nephew, W. H. F. "Rooney" Lee his son.

⁹ Van de Water, *Glory-Hunter*, 69.

¹⁰ *O. R.*, XXXVI, Part 1, 783.

¹¹ *Ibid.*, 783.

¹² Lyman, *Meade's Headquarters*, 147. Colonel Lyman was a member of General Meade's staff from the beginning of the Wilderness campaign to the end of the war.

¹³ Porter, *Campaigning with Grant*, 179.

¹⁴ Sheridan's directive from General Grant is quoted in *Memoirs*, I, 415-416. On his way back to the army he was to destroy the Virginia Central between Gordonsville and Hanover Junction. For Grant's report on this operation, see *O. R.*, XXXVI, Part 1, 22-23.

¹⁵ Van de Water, *Glory-Hunter*, 70-71.

¹⁶ *O. R.*, XXXVI, Part 1, 24.

¹⁷ *Ibid.*, 186. Casualties of the Trevilian Station expedition amounted to 150 killed, 738 wounded and 624 missing.

¹⁸ *Memoirs*, I, 427.

¹⁹ *Ibid.*, 428-429.

²⁰ Wilson, *Under the Old Flag*, I, 486.

²¹ *Ibid.*, 528-529.

²² *Ibid.*, 397-398.

²³ Merington, *The Custer Story*, 114.

²⁴ Hancock was in command of the expedition north of the James and won Sheridan's respect for "his quick apprehension, his physical courage and soldierly personality," which had made for him the reputation of being the finest corps commander in the Union armies.

²⁵ The Petersburg mine blew a gaping hole in the Confederate works, a crater more than 200 feet long, 50 feet wide and 25 to 30 feet deep. But the Union assault brigades, one of them composed of Negroes whose conduct was considered praiseworthy in the circumstances, crowded into the crater and were allowed by slack leadership to linger there and be massacred when the Confederates recovered from their shock and surprise and poured a terrific fire into the huddled mass of Union infantry. Two of the commanders charged with leading them into the assault were seen drinking and gossiping in a dugout when they should have been directing their men out of and around the crater. As a result of the fiasco under his supervision General Burnside was soon removed and never restored to command.

CHAPTER ELEVEN

"He Will Worry Early to Death"

[1] *O. R.*, XXXVII, Part 2, 223. Dana to Grant, July 12, 1864. During Grant's Vicksburg and Chattanooga campaigns Dana had acted as the War Department's observer. When Early's invasion touched the outskirts of Washington, however, Dana was sent to the capital as Grant's observer, paying special attention to the intrigues and intramural politics at the War Department.

[2] Hay, John, *Lincoln and the Civil War in the Diaries and Letters of John Hay*, edited by Tyler Dennett. New York: Dodd, Mead and Company, 1939. P. 210. Entry of July 14, 1864.

[3] Badeau, Adam, *Military History of Ulysses S. Grant*. New York: D. Appleton & Co., 1885. P. 452.

[4] *O. R.*, XXXVII, Part 2, 374.

[5] *Ibid.*, 408.

[6] *Ibid.*, 433-434.

[7] Grant's spree, assuming it occurred as Rawlins said it did, could have been caused by his intense sorrow over the death in action of Major General James B. McPherson near Atlanta, where he was commanding Grant's old Army of the Tennessee. General McPherson was one of Grant's closest associates among military men and his favorite protégé. He graduated in the same class as Sheridan and Hood, who was the leader of the enemy army at Atlanta. Carl Sandburg and other historians, however, have attributed Grant's drinking that day to his rage over Halleck's appointment to coordinate the forces operating against Early.

[8] *Memoirs*, I, 462-463.

[9] *Complete Works of Abraham Lincoln*, edited by John G. Nicolay and John Hay. New York: The Century Company, 1905. Vol. X, p. 180.

[10] *Memoirs*, I, 463-464.

[11] *Ibid.*, 500.

[12] *Ibid.*, 464-465.

[13] Crook had been transferred to command of the Army of West Virginia, two infantry divisions and a cavalry division under W. W. Averell, after leading a cavalry brigade at Chickamauga.

[14] Freeman, *Lee's Lieutenants*, III, 577.

[15] *O. R.*, XLIII, Part 1, 61.

[16] *Memoirs*, I, 488.

[17] *Battles and Leaders*, IV, 502. From General Merritt's account of Sheridan's campaign in the Shenandoah.

[18] *Ibid.*, 501.

[19] In regard to press and political criticism of his chief for not attacking Early at once, General Merritt wrote: "In the light of criticisms, then, it is

curious that the world is now inclined to call Sheridan reckless and fool-hardy" (*Battles and Leaders*, IV, 506).

[20] *Sheridan Papers*, Box "One."

[21] She was recommended by General Crook, who met her in Winchester before he fought the battle of Kernstown. *Memoirs*, II, 3-6.

[22] *O. R.*, XLIII, Part 1, 28.

[23] *Memoirs*, II, 6.

[24] Grant, *Memoirs*, 328.

[25] *O. R.*, XLIII, Part 1, 47.

[26] *Battles and Leaders*, IV, 507. Sheridan must have been reminded of the lost chance at Spotsylvania, when Warren's infantry interfered with the movement of two of his cavalry divisions.

[27] *Memoirs*, II, 18-19.

[28] *O. R.*, XLIII, Part 1, 47.

[29] The death of General Russell saddened Sheridan particularly, for "in the early days of army life he was my captain and friend, and I was deeply indebted to him . . ." (*Memoirs*, II, 23).

[30] *O. R.*, XLIII, Part 1, 47.

[31] *Ibid.*, 47.

[32] *Battles and Leaders*, IV, 509-510.

[33] *Ibid.*, 510.

[34] *Memoirs*, II, 28-29.

[35] *O. R.*, XLIII, Part 1, 25.

[36] *Ibid.*, 61.

[37] *Sheridan Papers*, Box "One" (1853-1871).

CHAPTER TWELVE

"FORWARD EVERYTHING!"

[1] Crook, *Autobiography*, 129.

[2] DuPont, Henry A., *The Campaign of 1864 in the Valley of Virginia and the Expedition to Lynchburg*. New York: Baker and Taylor, 1925. P. 134.

[3] Hayes, Rutherford B., *Diary and Letters of Rutherford B. Hayes*. Columbus: Ohio State Archeological and Historical Society, 1922-1926. Vol. V, p. 514.

[4] *Memoirs*, II, 35.

[5] Crook, *Autobiography*, 130.

[6] *Ibid.*, 129.

[7] *Ibid.*, 130.

[8] *Battles and Leaders*, IV, 511.

[9] Irwin, Richard B., *History of the Nineteenth Corps*. New York: G. P. Putnam's Sons, 1892. P. 399.

[10] *Memoirs,* II, 38.

[11] Crook, *Autobiography,* 131-132.

[12] Irwin, *History of the Nineteenth Corps,* 400.

[13] Reid, *Ohio in the War,* I, 526.

[14] *Battles and Leaders,* IV, 511.

[15] DeForest, John W., *A Volunteer's Adventures.* New Haven: The Yale University Press, 1946. P. 196.

[16] *Memoirs,* II, 41-42.

[17] *Ibid.,* 42.

[18] Reid, *Ohio in the War,* I, 526. Lee wrote Early in admonition September 27 that he had failed to use "your concentrated strength." (*O. R.,* XLII, Part 1, 558.)

[19] General Wilson was assigned to Sherman, who sent him to join General Thomas in dealing with Hood's Army of Tennessee. Wilson took command of the cavalry corps of the Army of the Cumberland at Nashville. In mid-December Thomas at Nashville fought the only battle of annihilation of the Civil War; the Union's complete success there was due in large part to Wilson's handling of the cavalry. It seems likely that Wilson took with him the lessons he learned as a division commander under Sheridan, for he was determined that, when the infantry finished its job of breaking Hood's line on the hills outside Nashville, the cavalry would see to it that very little of the only Confederate army in the West escaped. Very little did. Wilson launched a night pursuit that ended days later with most of Hood's army dead, wounded or in Federal prison camps. Later in the war he conducted his cavalry into the heart of Alabama and gave the *coup de grâce* to the greatest of Confederate cavalry leaders, Nathan Bedford Forrest.

[20] DeForest, *A Volunteer's Adventures,* 197; *O. R.,* XLIII, Part 1, 30-31.

[21] DeForest, *A Volunteer's Adventures,* 198.

CHAPTER THIRTEEN

A FORTRESS BECOMES A SLAUGHTER PEN

[1] The Longstreet-Early message was indeed a fraud, as Sheridan suspected. In 1890 General Early admitted this in a letter to General Irwin, a Northern writer and Civil War veteran. He said he had learned that the Union signal corps had succeeded in breaking the Confederate code, but his own signal officers had recently devised a new one. So he wrote out the message in the old code and ordered it sent. Actually, as General Irwin pointed out, the "ruse" boomeranged, for "the effect was to put Union commanders on the alert against what was actually about to happen" (Irwin, *History of the Nineteenth Corps,* 407).

[2] *Memoirs,* II, 66.

[3] The white-columned house in Winchester from which Sheridan set out on his historic ride is still preserved and bears a suitable plaque. It is now occupied by the local Elks' Lodge.

[4] *Battles and Leaders*, IV, 515.

[5] *Ibid.*, 514.

[6] DeForest, *A Volunteer's Adventures*, 207.

[7] Crook, *Autobiography*, 133.

[8] DeForest, *A Volunteer's Adventures*, 202-203. Early, of course, did not have 30,000 men in his whole army. His strength was something under 20,000, probably about 18,000. The exact numbers of Early's command at any battle was subject to much mathematical confusion.

[9] *Memoirs*, II, 68-80.

[10] Howard, S. E., "The Morning Surprise at Cedar Creek," *Civil War Papers . . . Massachusetts Commandery, Military Order of the Loyal Legion of the United States*. Published by the commandery, Boston, 1900. Vol. II, pp. 417-422.

[11] *Battles and Leaders*, IV, 419.

[12] Stevens, Hazard, "The Battle of Cedar Creek," *Civil War Papers . . . Massachusetts Commandery*, M.O.L.L.U.S., II, 417-422.

[13] According to General John B. Gordon, however, it was General Early's hesitancy—rather than his men's looting of the Union camps—which caused the letup. Early believed the victory was complete. Gordon recalled that Early rode up just as he was about to renew the attack on the Federal VI Corps and said, "Well, Gordon, this is glory enough for one day. This is the nineteenth. Precisely one month ago today we were going in the opposite direction." Early cut off Gordon's arguments for an immediate assault by declaring that the whole Union army would retreat without further fighting. "And so it came to pass," Gordon commented, "that the fatal halting in the face of a sullen and orderly retreat of this superb Federal corps lost us the great opportunity."

[14] *Gutzon Borglum Papers*, Manuscript Division, Library of Congress. Letter from William N. Hoskins, 8th Vermont Volunteers, to his parents, dated November 4, 1864. Borglum's interest in the Sheridan ride to Cedar Creek will be seen below.

[15] *Memoirs*, II, 81.

[16] Forsyth, George A., *Thrilling Days in Army Life*. New York: Harper & Brothers, 1900. P. 139.

[17] DeForest, *A Volunteer's Adventures*, 221-222.

[18] *O. R.*, XLIII, Part 1, 53.

[19] DeForest, *A Volunteer's Adventures*, 222.

[20] *Ibid.*, 222-223.

[21] *O. R.*, XLIII, Part 1, 54.

[22] DeForest, *A Volunteer's Adventures*, 223.

[23] *O. R.*, XLIII, Part 1, 53.

24 *Ibid.*, 53.

25 DeForest, *A Volunteer's Adventures*, 227.

26 Gause, *Four Years with Five Armies*, 335.

27 O. R., XLIII, Part 1, 53.

28 DeForest, *A Volunteer's Adventures*, 229.

29 O. R., XLIII, Part 1, 54. During the pursuit the Confederate General Ramseur was mortally wounded and fell into the hands of General Custer's command. He had been a classmate of Custer at West Point, and only a few days before had received word from Richmond that his wife had given birth. At Ramseur's request Custer cut off a lock of his hair to be sent to Mrs. Ramseur, and had the body embalmed and sent to Richmond, also at Ramseur's request (Merington, *The Custer Story*, 126-127).

30 Forsyth, *Thrilling Days in Army Life*, 168.

31 O. R., XLIII, Part 1, 59-60.

32 *Battles and Leaders*, IV, 519.

33 O. R., XLIII, Part 1, 62.

34 Sherman, *Home Letters*, 314.

35 O. R., XLIII, Part 1, 54.

36 Crook, *Autobiography*, 134.

37 McClure, Alexander K., *Abraham Lincoln and Men of War Times*. Philadelphia: The Times Publishing Company, 1892. P. 187.

38 Dana, *Recollections of the Civil War*, 248-249.

39 *Ibid.*, 250.

40 Taylor, Emerson Gifford, *Gouverneur Kemble Warren*. Boston: Houghton Mifflin Company, 1932. P. 210. Letter from General Warren, commanding the V Corps with the Army of the Potomac, to his wife, March 30, 1865. "I did not allude to his [Sheridan's] rumored engagement, but I heard the same rumor as you had."

41 Jones, Virgil Carrington, *Ranger Mosby*. Chapel Hill: The University of North Carolina Press, 1944. P. 225. This is a lively account of Mosby's career as a guerrilla leader in the Shenandoah.

42 O. R., XLIII, Part 2, 671-672.

43 *Ibid.*, 553.

44 *Ibid.*, XLIII, Part 1, 37.

45 *Memoirs*, II, 105-108.

CHAPTER FOURTEEN

A VERY PUNCH OF SOLDIERS

1 Townsend, George Alfred, *Rustics in Rebellion*. Chapel Hill: The University of North Carolina Press, 1950. Pp. 244-245. A collection of a young correspondent's brilliant and perceptive dispatches on some of the eastern campaigns.

[2] Newhall, Frederic C., *With General Sheridan in Lee's Last Campaign.* Philadelphia: J. B. Lippincott and Company, 1866. Pp. 11, 17, 23, 27.

[3] *Memoirs,* II, 128.

[4] *Ibid.,* 130.

[5] *Ibid.,* 131-133.

[6] *Battles and Leaders,* IV, 708-709. From "Five Forks and the Pursuit of Lee" by Horace Porter.

[7] *Ibid.,* 709.

[8] *Ibid.,* 709; *Memoirs,* II, 135-136.

[9] Newhall, *With General Sheridan,* 60-61.

[10] *Battles and Leaders,* IV, 710; *Memoirs,* II, 145. According to Sheridan's account, he found Grant and his chief of staff, General Rawlins, arguing about whether to continue operations. Rawlins was in favor of continuance, Grant leaned toward suspension. When the commanding general said it seemed "necessary" to halt further movements Sheridan "at once begged him not to do so, telling him that my cavalry was already on the move in spite of the difficulties, and that although a suspension of operations would not be fatal, yet it would give rise to the very charge of disaster to which he had referred at City Point, and, moreover, that we would surely be ridiculed, just as General Burnside's army was after the mud march of 1863."

[11] Townsend, *Rustics in Rebellion,* 249. This, of course, was typical of the attitude of many European military observers, who not only believed that the country wasn't worth fighting for, but that the contending armies were merely "armed mobs," in the phraseology of Field Marshal von Moltke.

[12] *O. R.,* XLVI, Part 1, 1102.

[13] *Ibid.,* 1103.

[14] *Battles and Leaders,* IV, 711.

[15] Newhall, *With General Sheridan,* 79.

[16] *Battles and Leaders,* IV, 711.

[17] Wilson, *Under the Old Flag,* I, 396. See also Schaff, Morris, *The Battle of the Wilderness.* Boston: Houghton Mifflin Co., 1910. Pp. 129, 333.

[18] *O. R.,* XLVI, Part 1, 1104.

[19] *Ibid.,* 1103.

[20] Taylor, *Gouverneur Kemble Warren,* 218. "There was no possibility under God's Heaven that Warren could get to Sheridan within the time the commander-in-chief had laid down." Mr. Taylor terms Warren's removal "injustice so rank, . . . selfishness so bottomless. . . ."

[21] Actually Pickett was not worrying too much about anything that day, despite the critical position of the Confederate army. General Rosser had caught a large supply of shad the day before and invited Pickett and another blithe spirit, Fitzhugh Lee, to a shad bake far behind the battle lines where Rosser was supposed to be guarding the Confederate wagon trains. What with the fish and other diversions, none of the three generals was on the field

until well after Sheridan had attacked (Freeman, *Lee's Lieutenants*, IV, 665-669).

[22] *Battles and Leaders*, IV, 711.

[23] *O. R.*, XLVI, Part 1, 1105.

[24] *Battles and Leaders*, IV, 713.

[25] *Memoirs*, II, 161. In contrast to his sluggish behavior at Dinwiddie Court House and Five Forks there was his quick decision and action in seizing Little Round Top. He was never slow in carrying out his own conceptions.

[26] Newhall, *With General Sheridan*, 98-99.

[27] *Battles and Leaders*, IV, 713-714. Incidents of the dead skirmisher and Colonel Forsyth, same citation.

[28] Townsend, *Rustics in Rebellion*, 252-253.

[29] Taylor, *Warren*, 229.

[30] Pratt, *Eleven Generals*, 161.

[31] Townsend, *Rustics in Rebellion*, 253.

[32] Newhall, *With General Sheridan*, 117.

[33] *O. R.*, XLVI, Part 1, 1105. The fourth charge referred to the initial repulse of Ayres's division in the center, which was rallied by Sheridan himself. There was considerable testimony that Ayres was under heavy fire; Warren claimed he absented himself to change the direction of the attacks undertaken by Griffin and Crawford, which sounds logical enough. Warren formally asked Sheridan to reconsider the removal order, but the latter replied, "Reconsider? Hell! I don't reconsider my determinations!" *Record of Warren Court of Inquiry*, p. 1058.

[34] Newhall, *With General Sheridan*, 123.

[35] Townsend, *Rustics in Rebellion*, 259-260.

CHAPTER FIFTEEN

"Sheridan, The Inevitable"

[1] *Battles and Leaders*, IV, 719.

[2] Newhall, *With General Sheridan*, 131.

[3] *O. R.*, XLVI, Part 1, 1106.

[4] *Battles and Leaders*, IV, 715.

[5] *O. R.*, XLVI, Part 1, 1107.

[6] *Ibid.*, 1107.

[7] Newhall, *With General Sheridan*, 138.

[8] *Memoirs*, 177-178. The letter was written by Colonel William B. Taylor from Amelia Court House and was dated April 5. He also told his mother, "My trust is still in the justice of our cause, and that of God."

[9] Newhall, *With General Sheridan*, 141.

[10] Also known as Sayler's and Saylor's Creek in many Confederate ac-

counts. The Northerners, including Sheridan, referred to it as Sailor's Creek.

[11] Newhall, *With General Sheridan*, 169.

[12] *O. R.*, XLVI, Part 1, 1107.

[13] *Ibid.*, 1107-1108.

[14] Wright arbitrarily refused to submit his report to Sheridan, as would have been proper since Sheridan was in command of all Union forces at Sailor's Creek. Instead he reported to Meade directly in such a fashion as to indicate that the battle had been fought almost exclusively by the VI Corps. It was perhaps a reflection of the jealousy that had arisen between the infantry and the cavalry over Sheridan's possibly disproportionate share of the publicity attending the Appomattox campaign. Subsequently General Grant bluntly ordered that Wright's report be submitted through the proper channels, pointing out in a communication to Meade that Sheridan "was authorized to assume command of this [the VI] Corps" and "it is considered a matter of simple justice that its action, while under his command, be reported to him."

[15] Newhall, *With General Sheridan*, 188.

[16] *O. R.*, XLVI, Part 1, 1109.

[17] Newhall, *With General Sheridan*, 192-193.

[18] *O. R.*, XLVI, Part 1, 1109.

[19] Newhall, *With General Sheridan*, 195.

[20] Longstreet, James, *From Manassas to Appomattox*. Philadelphia: J. B. Lippincott Co., 1896. P. 613. See also Gibbon, John, *Personal Recollections of the Civil War*. New York: G. P. Putnam's Sons, 1928. P. 361.

[21] *O. R.*, XLVI, Part 1, 1162. General Ord's after-action report.

[22] *Ibid.*, 1109.

[23] Freeman, *Lee's Lieutenants*, III, 736.

[24] *Memoirs*, II, 195-196; Gordon, *Reminiscences of the Civil War*, 628.

[25] *Memoirs*, II, 197.

[26] Marshall, Charles, *An Aide-de-Camp of Lee*. Edited by Sir Frederick Maurice. Boston: Little Brown & Co., 1927. Pp. 268-274.

[27] *Battles and Leaders*, VI, 742.

[28] *Ibid.*, 743.

[29] Merington, *The Custer Story*, 159.

[30] Newhall, *With General Sheridan*, 228-229.

CHAPTER SIXTEEN

SHERIDAN VS. NAPOLEON, LOUISIANA AND TEXAS

[1] Dodge, Grenville M., *Personal Recollections*, Council Bluffs: The Monarch Printing Co., 1914. P. 95. General Dodge, the renowned railroad builder, was intimately associated during and after the war with Generals Grant, Sherman and Sheridan. These friendships proved most valuable to him in

obtaining army protection for his construction crews and in pushing its lines through Indian territory.

[2] Van de Water, *Glory-Hunter*, 123.

[3] *Ibid.*, 126.

[4] *Memoirs*, II, 211-214.

[5] *Sheridan Papers*, Box "Three." Dispatch from Captain F. M. Follette, Battery D, 4th U. S. Artillery, to District of the Rio Grande headquarters.

[6] *Ibid.*, Box "1866."

[7] *Ibid.*, Box "1866." Sheridan to General Rawlins, then army chief of staff, January 28, 1866.

[8] *Ibid.*, Box "1866." Sheridan to General Wright, then commanding the Department of Texas, with headquarters at Galveston, January 17, 1866.

[9] *Ibid.*, Box "1866." Sheridan to Grant, August 16, 1866.

[10] *Memoirs*, II, 217.

[11] *Sheridan Papers*, Box "1866." Letter of instructions, Sheridan to Sedgwick, October 25, 1866. In turning over supplies to Juarez, the United States commanders followed General Grant's suggestion to Sheridan when the latter left Washington. The supplies were dumped where Juarez's officers, by prearrangement, could easily collect and carry them off.

[12] *Ibid.*, Box "Five." Sheridan to Rawlins, January 4, 1866. Sheridan also passed along precise information on the various imperial and republican commanders opposing each other in the Valley of Mexico.

[13] *Memoirs*, II, 226-227. The cable was sent from Paris on January 10, 1867.

[14] *Sheridan Papers*, Box "One." Unsigned letter dated February 11, 1867. The agent added, "Every foreigner is looking for U.S. intervention," with panic growing in the capital and street fighting anticipated.

[15] *Ibid.*, Box "One." Unsigned letter dated February 24, 1867.

[16] *Ibid.*, Box "One." Unsigned letter dated February 14, 1867, sent from Mexico City.

[17] The Indianapolis *Journal*, an organ favorable to Senator Oliver Morton, the state's wartime governor, by no means a moderate in his views of Southern Reconstruction. Quoted in *The Tragic Era*, by Claude G. Bowers. Cambridge: Houghton Mifflin Co., 1929. P. 17.

[18] Sheridan claimed that President Johnson, in giving his report to the newspapers, omitted a paragraph stating that the New Orleans police had attacked the Negro delegation with "firearms, clubs and knives," and terming it "unnecessary and atrocious" murder (*Memoirs*, II, 236). Sheridan was convinced that the President felt "personal enmity" for him.

[19] *Ibid.*, 253.

[20] *Sheridan Papers*, Box "One." Governor Wells to President Johnson, May 22, 1867. In his *Memoirs* (II, 268) Sheridan said his view of Governor Wells was supported by General James B. Steadman, whom he regarded as the president's observer in his headquarters. He quoted a letter from Stead-

man to Johnson saying there was a "want of respect for Governor Wells personally," but that "I believe Sheridan made the removals to embarrass you, believing the feeling at the North would sustain him."

21 Stryker, Lloyd P., *Andrew Johnson.* New York: The Macmillan Co., 1929. P. 477.

22 Cox, Samuel S., *Three Decades of Federal Legislation.* Providence: J. A. and R. H. Reid Co., 1885. P. 546.

23 New York *Times,* June 24, 1867.

24 New York *Tribune,* June 17, 1867.

25 *Sheridan Papers,* Box "One." Griffin to Sheridan, July 15, 1867.

26 *Ibid.,* Box "One." County Clerk B. F. McFarland of Rusk County, Texas, to General Sheridan, March 3, 1867.

27 Stryker, *Andrew Johnson,* 478.

28 Welles, Gideon, *Diary of Gideon Welles.* Boston: Houghton Mifflin Co., 1911. Vol. III, p. 154.

29 *Memoirs,* II, 276. Grant had reassured Sheridan rather cryptically, "Your head is safe above the shoulders, at least so that it cannot be removed to produce pain" (Hesseltine, William B., *Ulysses Grant, Politician.* New York: Dodd Mead and Co., 1935. P. 84). There were several other interesting statements by Grant in regard to Sheridan's removal. He wrote President Johnson, "Sheridan has had difficulties to contend with no other District Commander has encountered. Almost if not quite from the day he was appointed District Commander to the present time, our press has given out that he was to be removed; that the Administration was dissatisfied with him, etc. This has emboldened the opponents to the laws of Congress within his command to oppose him in every way in their power, and has rendered necessary measures which otherwise might never have been necessary." And to Sheridan, on September 8, Grant wrote consolingly, "I feel that your relief from command of the Fifth District is a heavy blow to Reconstruction. All I can say now is that I have sustained your course publicly, privately, and officially, not from personal feeling or partiality, but because you were right. . . . Present movements in this capital . . . fill me with alarm . . ." (Badeau, Adam, *Grant in Peace.* Hartford: S. S. Scranton & Co., 1887. P. 103).

30 Milton, George Fort, *The Age of Hate.* New York: Coward-McCann, Inc., 1930. P. 244.

CHAPTER SEVENTEEN

FRONTIER COMMAND

1 Lynch, Denis Tilden, *The Wild Seventies.* New York: D. Appleton-Century Co., 1941. Pp. 47-48.

2 Sherman had become lieutenant general and Grant a full general in the postwar reorganization of the Army. The Military Division of the Missouri

consisted of all territory west of the Mississippi River as far as the Rockies and north of Texas.

3 *Memoirs,* II, 284.

4 *The Diary of George Templeton Strong.* Edited by Allan Nevins and Malton Halsey Thomas. New York: The Macmillan Co., 1952. Vol. IV, p. 165.

5 *Memoirs,* II, 307.

6 Forsyth and his command were surrounded on Beecher's Island by at least several hundred Sioux and Cheyenne warriors. It was a desperate battle but probably not so bloody as Forsyth reported to Sheridan. Forsyth claimed that a "large number of the fiends" were killed. But the noted Indian authority George Bird Grinnell said that Indians who participated in the fight claimed only nine were killed. See Grinnell, *The Fighting Cheyennes.* New York: Charles Scribner's Sons, 1915. Pp. 267-269.

7 Scott, Hugh L., *Some Memories of a Soldier.* New York: The Century Co., 1928. P. 176.

8 *Memoirs,* II, 300-301.

9 Merington, *The Custer Story,* 193.

10 On October 28, 1868, just before the campaign began, Custer wrote Sheridan, "If he [Sully] goes I hope he will not break up the 7th into two or more columns" (*Sheridan Papers,* Box "One"). Custer would have done well to remember these words almost eight years later before the battle of the Little Big Horn, when he divided his command with fatal consequences. Sully and Custer had been commissioned lieutenant colonels in the Regular Army on the same day, so the quibble over brevet rank was not entirely creditable to Custer.

11 Spotts, David L., *Campaigning with Custer.* Los Angeles: Wetzel Publishing Co., 1928. Pp. 104, 125.

12 Quoted in Van de Water, *Glory-Hunter,* 188.

13 Grinnell, *The Fighting Cheyennes,* 289.

14 Godfrey, General E. S., "Some Reminiscences of the Battle of the Washita," *Cavalry Journal,* October 1928.

15 St. Louis *Democrat,* February 9, 1869. When Custer read the article he announced to a group of his officers that he would wield a dog whip on the author if he ever caught him. Captain Benteen told his superior, "If there's to be a whipping, General, you can start now. I wrote that letter." There was no whipping. Benteen had sent the letter to a friend in St. Louis without any intention of so seriously affronting Custer—however little regard he felt for his commander—by having it published. One of the finest officers on the frontier, he had led a cavalry brigade in the Western armies during the Civil War.

16 *Memoirs,* II, 320.

17 Rister, Carl Coke, *Border Command.* Norman: The University of Oklahoma Press, 1944. The other columns involved in Sheridan's winter cam-

paign were successful in destroying Indian villages and generally harassing bands believed to be hostile toward white settlement. By spring most of the intransigent tribesmen were willing to try again to "walk the white man's road." In powwows at Fort Cobb, Sheridan warned them that he would not stand for their policy of war in the summer, peace in the winter, charity all the year-round; but "I am not a bad chief; I am not a bad man. If you come in here and do as I say, I will not be a bad chief to you. I will probably be in charge of this country for a long time, and will have much to do with you. I have had charge and have been with Indians before, and have always got along well with them."

[18] O'Connor, *Thomas: Rock of Chickamauga*, 358.

[19] New York *World*, July 19, 20, 23, 24, 28, 1869.

[20] Shortly after Sheridan had decided to observe the Prussian armies in the field, the French, whose permission for similar courtesies had been asked by the United States Ambassador without Sheridan's knowledge, brusquely turned down the request. Since they granted similar privileges later to Generals Burnside and Hazen, it seemed that they objected to Sheridan because of his aggressive conduct along the Mexican border a few years previous.

[21] McCutcheon, B. M., *Washington Commandery Papers*, M.O.L.L.U.S., 1888. P. 58.

[22] Of all people, Bismarck, the ironhanded molder of Imperial Germany, claimed to Sheridan that in his youth he had held republican sympathies but that subsequent political experience had shown him "Germany was not sufficiently advanced" for democratic government. *Memoirs*, II, 306.

[23] *Memoirs*, II, 433-434.

CHAPTER EIGHTEEN

HEADQUARTERS CHICAGO

[1] *Memoirs (Revised)*, II, 470-481.

[2] Sheahan, James W. and Upton, George P., *The Great Conflagration*. Privately printed, Chicago, 1871. P. 91.

[3] Sheridan for a year or two after the fire was forced to write many of his officers and other correspondents for duplicates of letters and dispatches. *Sheridan Papers*, Box "1872."

[4] *Sheridan Papers*, Box "One."

[5] *Ibid.*, Box "One." On October 22, 1871, Mayor R. B. Mason tendered Sheridan the official thanks of the city "for the very efficient aid which you have rendered in protecting the lives and property of the citizens."

[6] *William C. Church Papers*, Manuscript Division, Library of Congress, Vol. I. Sherman to Church, July 18, 1874. Until very recently these papers were kept sealed because Church's family feared that some of the correspondence—being the outspoken thoughts of leading military figures—might

injure the families of persons mentioned. Actually there is nothing particularly damaging in the collection.

7 *Ibid.*, Sherman to Church, August 22, 1885.

8 Stryker, *Andrew Johnson*, 495.

9 *Ibid.*, 494.

10 *Sheridan Papers*, Box "One." Averell to Sheridan, July 3, 1869.

11 *Ibid.*, Box labeled "Undated Miscellany."

12 *Ibid.*, Box "1874." Sheridan to Sherman, May 26, 1874.

13 Porter received a measure of justice in 1886 when he was reinstated—24 years after he had been wrongfully removed.

14 *Memoirs (Revised)*, II, 580.

15 *Ibid.*, 578.

16 Crook, *Autobiography*, 238-240.

17 *Daniel O'Drennan Papers*, Manuscript Division, Library of Congress. Box "One." An unclassified newspaper clipping. O'Drennan was a clerk and orderly at Sheridan's headquarters through most of the postwar years.

18 Monaghan, Jay, *The Great Rascal*. Boston: Little, Brown and Company, 1952. Pp. 11-13. A lively account of the life of Ned Buntline, one of the creators of the Buffalo Bill legend.

19 *Sheridan Papers*, Box "1871."

20 Beeson, Chalkley M., "A Royal Buffalo Hunt," *Transactions of the Kansas State Historical Society*, 1907-1908. Vol. X, p. 578.

21 *Memoirs (Revised)*, II, 490.

22 Scott, *Some Memories of a Soldier*, 108-109.

23 *Sheridan Papers*, Box "1872." Sheridan to Ord, March 21, 1872.

24 *Sheridan Papers*, Box "1872." Sheridan to Sherman, September 25-26, 1872.

25 Wallace, Ernest, and Hoebel, E. Adamson, *The Comanche*. Norman: The University of Oklahoma Press, 1952. P. 66.

26 The belief that General Sheridan coined the expression about "the only good Indian" sprang up in the bitter aftermath of the campaign against the Piegans, a branch of the Blackfeet tribe, in January 1870. Under orders from Sheridan five troops of the 2nd United States Cavalry under Colonel E. M. Baker attacked the Piegans' winter camp in the big bend of the Marias River in Montana. The Piegans were accused by white settlers of murder, cattle thieving and house burning. In the half-light of the winter dawn 53 women and children were shot; how many died was not reported. In the East there was widespread condemnation of the Army, and of Sheridan in particular. At this most inopportune time, according to his brother Mike, "some fool friend in Montana attributed to General Sheridan the expression that 'A dead Indian is the only good Indian,' and though he immediately disavowed the inhuman epigram, his assailants continued to ring the change on it for months." Members of the "Indian Ring" were behind the campaign against Sheridan and the army because the action against the Piegans was "the be-

ginning of a permanent peace in Montana, which would impede if it would not wholly stop their illicit traffic with the Indians" (*Memoirs (Revised)*, II, 463-464).

[27] Omaha *Republican*, October 27, 1875. The phrase "without consideration of sectarian prejudices" referred to President Grant's so-called "Quaker policy," in which he proposed, but did not entirely carry out, a plan to put religious denominations in charge of the various Indian agencies.

[28] *Sheridan Papers*, Box "1872." Sheridan to Sherman, July 11, 1872.

[29] Sheridan superintended preparations for the campaign, but returned to his Chicago headquarters when he satisfied himself that Colonel Nelson A. Miles was entirely capable of directing the operation.

[30] Sheridan was determined to keep the punishment of rebellious Indian leaders in military hands. A few years earlier Texas civil courts had found two Kiowa chiefs, Satanta and Big Tree, guilty of marauding and had sentenced them to be hanged. Their sentence was commuted to life imprisonment; then, after great pressure from Northern advocates of a more lenient Indian policy, they were soon given their release from the Huntsville penitentiary. Sheridan denounced the release of the Kiowa chiefs, whom he believed to be "reeking in blood." Kiowa depredations increased immediately after Satanta and Big Tree were pardoned.

[31] Many of his cipher dispatches to the War Department, for the eyes of Secretary of War Belknap and President Grant, are to be found in the *Sheridan Papers*, Box "1875."

[32] *Sheridan Papers*, Box labeled "Undated Miscellany." From Adjutant General E. D. Townsend, December 14, 1874.

[33] Sherman, *Home Letters*, 342.

[34] Quoted in the New York *World*, December 29, 1874.

[35] Hoar, George F., *Autobiography of Seventy Years*. New York: Charles Scribner's Sons, 1903. P. 208.

[36] New York *World*, January 12, 1875.

[37] Lonn, Ella, *Reconstruction in Louisiana*. New York: G. P. Putnam's Sons, 1918. P. 300.

[38] *Congressional Record*, 43rd Congress, 2nd Session, 450.

[39] Lonn, *Reconstruction in Louisiana*, 301, 333.

[40] *Ibid.*, 299.

[41] *Ibid.*, 300.

[42] Rhodes, James Ford, *History of the United States*. New York: The Macmillan Company, 1920. Vol. VII, p. 189. Barrett described the incident to Rhodes in person.

[43] Hoar, *Autobiography of Seventy Years*, 209. At a subsequent dinner party attended by Hoar, a Navy officer remarked that there was nothing he disliked more than a subordinate who always obeyed orders precisely to the letter. President Grant spoke up in approval: "There is a great deal of truth

in what you say. One of the virtues of General Sheridan was that he knew when to act without orders" (Hoar, 209-210).

44 Hesseltine, *Ulysses Grant, Politician*, 351.

45 From the clipping of an unidentified Chicago newspaper, probably the *Inter-Ocean*, of May 3, 1875. It was pasted in one of the scrapbooks kept by General Sheridan.

46 *Army and Navy Journal*, Vol. XII, No. 44, (June 12, 1875). P. 701.

47 Rister, *Border Command*, 198-200.

48 *Sheridan Papers*, Box "1882."

CHAPTER NINETEEN

LAST STAND OF THE SIOUX

1 Windolph, Charles A., *I Fought with Custer*, as told to Frazier and Robert Hunt. New York: Charles Scribner's Sons, 1947. P. 9.

2 *Memoirs (Revised)*, II, 497-498.

3 Chief Joseph, after his fighting retreat in search of a more peaceful existence for his people, finally surrendered to Generals Miles and Howard.

4 *Sheridan Papers*, Box "1874." Sheridan to Sherman, November 23, 1874, on the giving of arms to Sioux tribesmen at the Red Cloud Agency: "What we want at the agency is more troops instead of more guns for Indians."

5 Custer was itching to free himself from Terry's orders. In St. Paul, just after he was reinstated largely because of Terry's counseling and support, he told Captain William Ludlow that he intended to "cut loose" and operate on his own as soon as the chance presented itself. He had been expressly forbidden by General Sherman to bring along any newspapermen, but he was accompanied by Mark Kellogg, correspondent for the New York *Herald*. See Hughes, Colonel R. P., "The Campaign Against the Sioux in 1876," *Journal of the Military Service Institution of the United States*, January 1879.

6 The last message from Custer was a note by his adjutant, Lieutenant Cook, to Captain Benteen which read: "Benteen, come on—big village—be quick—bring packs."

7 General Hugh L. Scott, when a lieutenant of the 7th Cavalry a year later, examined the site of the Sioux village attacked by Custer and counted 1,800 lodges before he gave up the task. There must have been at least 4,000 warriors under Sitting Bull, Crazy Horse and the other chiefs; estimates of the Sioux strength have ranged up to 8,000. The 7th Cavalry numbered less than 600, including the troopers under Custer, Reno, Benteen and others on detached duties.

8 Chicago *Inter-Ocean*, July 9, 1876.

9 *Sheridan Papers*, Box "1876." Sheridan to Sherman, July 7, 1876.

¹⁰ *Ibid.*, Box labeled "Undated Miscellany." Reno's message was dated July 4, 1876, "Camp on Yellowstone River."

¹¹ *Ibid.*, Box "1876." Mrs. Custer to Colonel Michael V. Sheridan, July 20, 1876.

¹² *Ibid.*, Box "1876." Mrs. E. J. Porter of Portland, Maine, to General Sheridan, undated. General Crittenden to Sheridan, May 10, 1876.

¹³ *Ibid.*, Box "1876." Mrs. Custer to Colonel Michael V. Sheridan, July 18, 1877. "I asked that I might have a handful of clay where he was placed last summer if I could have nothing more," Mrs. Custer reminded Colonel Sheridan.

¹⁴ *Ibid.*, Box "1876." Sheridan to Joseph Medill, publisher of the Chicago *Tribune*, July 30, 1877.

¹⁵ Sheridan, Philip H., and Sherman, William T., *Reports of the Inspection of 1877*. Washington: Government Printing Office, 1878. P. 5.

¹⁶ The species, identified by zoölogist W. H. Edwards, is found at 10,000 feet above sea level.

¹⁷ Sheridan, his intelligence inaccurate, as it rarely was, had underestimated the power of Sitting Bull, believing his authority over the Sioux and other Northern Plains tribes was "insignificant," that he was old and "very much crippled by disease." Sitting Bull finally returned to the United States in 1881 and surrendered at Fort Buford, Dakota Territory.

¹⁸ *Sheridan Papers*, Box "1878." Sheridan to Sherman, October 9, 1878.

¹⁹ *Ibid.*, Box "1878." Sheridan to Sherman, January 28, 1878.

²⁰ *Ibid.*, Box "1878." Sheridan to Sherman, January 28 and November 26, 1878.

²¹ *Ibid.*, Box "1881." Sheridan to Sherman, January 4, 1881. General Pope was finally moved to offices in the remodeled arsenal building at Fort Leavenworth.

²² New York *Times*, December 2 to 20, 1878.

²³ *Sheridan Papers*, Box "1882 Official." Senator Logan to General Sheridan, October 24, 1881.

²⁴ *Ibid.*, Box "1882 Official." He sent a copy of the pamphlet also to Prince Bismarck, Chancellor of Germany.

²⁵ *Ibid.*, Box "1882 Official." Sheridan to Robert T. Lincoln, November 15, 1882.

²⁶ *Ibid.*, Box labeled "Undated Miscellany." General Sherman's review of the findings of the Warren court was issued July 15, 1882.

²⁷ Hoar, *Autobiography of Seventy Years*, 397.

CHAPTER TWENTY

Commanding General

¹ Washington *Evening Star*, September 11, 1949.

² *Sheridan Papers*, Box labeled "Undated Miscellany."

[3] Crook, *Autobiography*, 262-265. Although they had been the closest of friends, at least until the last year or two of Sheridan's life, Crook wrote this of Sheridan shortly after his death: "The adulations heaped on him by a grateful nation for his supposed genius turned his head, which, added to his natural disposition, caused him to bloat his little carcass with debauchery and dissipation" (*Autobiography*, 134). Crook was incensed by his relief as commander of the Department of Arizona and by the belief that Sheridan had not given him enough credit for the battles of Winchester and Fisher's Hill. There is no evidence anywhere that General Sheridan was addicted to either "debauchery" or "dissipation," although in his middle years he was not averse to taking a drink. He was not, by any means, a drunkard. General Nelson Miles succeeded Crook in Arizona and by August 1886, following Sheridan's orders and the policy laid down by the Administration, had rounded up the renegade Apache and sent them into Florida exile.

[4] *Memoirs (Revised)*, II, 554-555.

[5] *Ibid.*, 542.

[6] New York *World*, May 28, 1888.

[7] General Orders No. 37, June 1, 1888. Old Records Division, Adjutant General's Office.

[8] *Sheridan Papers*, Box "1888."

[9] *Memoirs (Revised)*, II, 567.

[10] New York *Times*, August 6, 1888.

[11] Washington *Evening Star*, September 11, 1949.

[12] Casey, Robert J., and Borglum, Mary, *Give the Man Room*. Indianapolis: The Bobbs-Merrill Company, 1952. An excellent biography of Gutzon Borglum, whose study of Sheridan preparatory to executing the statue depicting the ride to Cedar Creek convinced him that Sheridan was one of the greatest and personally the most interesting of American generals. Borglum had to use another horse as model for Rienzi, who had preceded his master in death and was preserved, stuffed and mounted, at Governor's Island, now headquarters of the United States First Army.

[13] Washington *Evening Star*, September 11, 1949. When this book was written the three daughters of General Sheridan were still living at 2540 Massachusetts Avenue, still close to "Papa's Circle." They never married. They have survived their brother Philip, Jr., and grandson Philip III. (Letter from Miss Mary Sheridan.)

[14] Faulkner, *Life of Sheridan*, 45-54.

INDEX

Abolitionists, 53

Alexis, Grand Duke of Russia, 322-323

Alger, Horatio, 15, 40

Alger, Russell A., recommends P. H. S. for regimental command, 62; leads charge at Booneville, 66-67

Anderson, R. H., 159, 195

Antietam, battle of, 72, 108

Appomattox Court House, 270

Archer, James J., 52

Army of the Cumberland, created, 86; moves on Murfreesboro, 88; mentioned, 100, 102-103, 110, 123, 126, 129, 133, 315

Army of the James, 175, 243, 267, 269

Army of the Mississippi, 64

Army of Northern Virginia, 151, 253

Army of the Ohio, description of command, 74-76; mentioned, 142

Army of the Potomac, casualties at Cold Harbor, 179; mentioned, 71, 88, 100, 127, 146, 147, 151, 154, 159, 172, 175, 180, 185, 239

Army of the Shenandoah, 195, 199, 206, 214, 217, 234,

Army of the Tennessee, 58, 72, 127, 129

Arthur, Chester A., 353

Averell, W. W., relieved by P. H. S., 212; mentioned, 180, 195, 317

Baird, Absalom, 134

Baltimore, Maryland, 187, 188

Baltimore & Ohio Railroad, 214-215

Banks, Nathaniel P., 175, 193

Barrett, Lawrence, 331-332

Battery E, 5th Maine Light Artillery Regiment, 202

Beatty, John, 74, 82-83, 120, 126

Beauregard, P. G. T., evacuates Corinth, 63; mentioned, 61, 62, 65, 292

Beaver Dam Station, Virginia, 165-166

Belknap, W. W., 336

Benteen, Frederick W., 304, 340, 342

Benton, Thomas Hart, 27

Bismarck, Chancellor of Prussia, 308-310

Black Kettle, 295, 303, 307

Blair, Montgomery, 187

"Bloody Angle," 175

Booneville, Mississippi, battle of, 65-68; mentioned, 62, 64, 65, 98

Borglum, Gutzon, 357

Bradfort's Island, Oregon, 50

Bragg, Braxton, invades Kentucky, 72; movements before Perryville, 79; at Stone's River, 90-98; in Tullahoma campaign, 104-105; maneuvers against Rosecrans, 106-111; commands at Chickamauga, 108-120; at Missionary Ridge, 131-140; defends Richmond, 167-168, 171; mentioned, 34, 70, 88, 109, 129

Brandy Station, Virginia, 151

Breckinridge, John C., 194

Bridgeport, Union base at, 123

Buell, Don Carlos, "dancing master policy," 74-75; at Perryville, 79-83; relieved of command, 86-87; mentioned, 56, 60, 61, 72

Buford, John, 147

Burnside, Ambrose E., leaves Army of the Ohio, 143; failure at Petersburg, 185; mentioned, 129, 141-142, 149, 155, 177

Butler, Ben, 169, 172, 175, 319

Campbell, Archibald P., gives Rienzi to P. H. S., 68; mentioned, 66